A Liturgical Index to The Hymnal 1982

by Marion J. Hatchett

 CHURCH

Church Publishing Incorporated, New York

10 9 8 7 6 5 4

*Church Publishing
Incorporated
445 Fifth Avenue
New York, NY 10016*

Table of Contents

Introduction   1

The Book of Common Prayer

The Daily Office
    Year One   9
    Year Two   87
    Holy Days   165
    Special Occasions   174

Holy Baptism   175

The Holy Eucharist
    Year A   176
    Year B   213
    Year C   237
    Holy Days   260
    The Common of Saints   275
    Various Occasions   278

Pastoral Offices
    Confirmation   289
    The Celebration and Blessing of a Marriage   289
    A Thanksgiving for the Birth or Adoption
        of a Child   290
    Ministration to the Sick   291
    The Burial of the Dead   291

Episcopal Services
    Ordination   292
    Celebration of a New Ministry   293
    The Dedication and Consecration of a Church   293

The Book of Occasional Services

The Church Year
    Advent Festival of Lessons and Music   297
    Vigil for Christmas Eve *or*
        Christmas Festival of Lessons and Music   299
    Service for New Year's Eve   302
    Vigil for the Eve of the Baptism of Our Lord   303
    Candlemas Procession   304
    The Way of the Cross   305
    Rogation Procession   305
    Vigil for the Eve of All Saints' Day   305
    Service for All Hallow's Eve   306

Pastoral Services
    A Vigil on the Eve of Baptism   307
    Celebration for a Home   308
    Anniversary of a Marriage   309
    A Public Service of Healing   309
    Burial of One Who Does Not Profess the Christian
        Faith   309
    The Founding of a Church: Laying of a Cornerstone   309

Episcopal Services
    Consecration of Chrism   309
    Reaffirmation of Ordination Vows   309
    Recognition and Investiture of a Diocesan Bishop *or*
        Welcoming and Seating of a Bishop in the
        Cathedral   310
    Setting Apart for a Special Vocation   310

Lesser Feasts and Fasts

The Weekdays of Lent   313
The Weekdays of Easter Season   318
The Lesser Feasts   323

Introduction

The primary purpose of this index is to provide help in the selection of suitable hymns for the various rites of the Church and for different days and seasons of the Church Year. It should also be helpful in suggesting suitable organ music, anthems, and solos for organists, choir directors, and cantors.

This index lists hymns for use in the Daily Offices and the Holy Eucharist for every day or occasion for which the Book of Common Prayer provides propers. It also suggests hymns for Holy Baptism, for the Pastoral Offices, and for the Episcopal Services of the Book of Common Prayer; for various rites in the Book of Occasional Services; and for each of the propers of Lesser Feasts and Fasts.

One of the most important parts of the planning and preparation for any service is the choice of hymns. Hymns are one of the most vital elements in the participation of the congregation. Hymns set the mood for the rite. Hymns provide a congregational response to lessons and sermons and other important elements in the rites. Hymns are the people's take home package. Because of the musical association people commit hymns to memory more easily and readily than prayers or psalms or other scriptural passages; therefore, the texts of hymns are more likely to recur to people than other texts. People's theology is probably influenced more by the hymns they sing than by the lessons and sermons they hear or the prayers they pray.

Each of the Daily Offices includes one rubric suggesting the possible use of a hymn (after the prayer for mission in both Morning and Evening Prayer, before the Psalmody in An Order of Service for Noonday, after the Lesson in Compline). The Hymnal 1982 provides several office hymns for each of the Daily Offices. This index suggests suitable hymns for Morning and Evening Prayer, mostly chosen because of a relationship to the Psalms or Lessons of the Daily Office Lectionary, Year One and Year Two. Hymns from among these suggestions also might be used quite suitably at Noonday and at Compline. Even when no hymn is sung, especially when a person is reading the office individually, the suggestions of this index would provide suitable devotional material related to the lectionary.

Hymns are suggested for each point in the Eucharistic Rite at which a hymn is allowed by the rubrics: before the Opening Acclamation (Entrance Hymn), after Lessons (Sequence), while the offering is being received and placed on the altar (Offertory Hymn), during the Communion of priest and people (Communion Hymn), and before or after the Post-communion Prayer (Postcommunion Hymn). It should be noted that the rubric in earlier Prayer Books allowing additional hymns before and after any service or sermon has been quite deliberately deleted. The Book of Common Prayer in no case allows a hymn between Gospel and Sermon. Only three rites allow a hymn after the dismissal: The Celebration and Blessing of a Marriage, The Burial of the Dead, and The Ordination of a Bishop (rites which involve unique situations in relation to the procession out of the church). A rubric peculiar to the 1892 edition of the Prayer Book which allowed a hymn at the presentation of the alms is also missing.

The Entrance Hymn sets the tone for the entire service. It may either cover or follow the entrance of the liturgical ministers. The way in which the hymn is used or the number of persons in an entrance procession will sometimes determine the suitability of a hymn that in other circumstances would be a very good choice for the opening of the rite.

The Sequence traditionally follows the Second Lesson (the First Lesson is normally followed by the Psalm which is known as the Gradual). It may provide a reflection on or a response to the Lesson, Psalm, or Epistle which have preceded, or it may anticipate the Gospel which follows. In the late medieval liturgical books it was normally sung immediately after the proper Alleluia Verse (a verse of Scripture introduced and followed by alleluias which has traditionally preceded the reading of the Gospel). Occasionally, however, the Sequence took the place of the Alleluia Verse or preceded it. Decisions as to whether both are used, and as to which should precede the other, should be made on the basis of the lectionary texts and of the texts and musical forms of the Sequence and of the Alleluia Verse (or of the Psalm known as the Tract which replaces the Alleluia Verse in Lent). [1] Hymns that are very long or that arouse the most vigorous congregational participation can sometimes seem to cause the movement of the Liturgy of the Word to fall apart, or can constitute a premature climax, before the reading of the Gospel

[1] For settings of the Gradual Psalms of the Eucharistic Lectionary of the Book of Common Prayer and of Alleluia Verses and Tracts appropriate to that lectionary, see *Church Hymnal Series VI: Gradual Psalms, Alleluia Verses and Tracts* (New York: Church Hymnal Corporation).

and the sermon. Oftentimes a careful selection of stanzas is better than the use of a whole hymn at this point in the rite.

The hymn at the Offertory is the first hymn after the Gospel and sermon. Ideally it should provide a congregational response to the Liturgy of the Word and serve as preparation for participation in the Great Thanksgiving and the Communion which follow. Care should be exercised lest this hymn be so overpowering that, rather than preparing people for their common participation in the great Thanksgiving, it causes this high point in the rite to come across as an anti-climax.

Historically great Psalms of praise, especially 145, 148, and 150, have been associated with the Communion of priest and people. Joyous music is especially appropriate at this climactic point in the rite. Hymns used at this point should not be confined to those from the Holy Eucharist section of the Hymnal. Great hymns of praise which echo the propers of the day are especially appropriate. Hymns with refrains, which enable people to sing as they move to and from the Communion stations, are especially good for use at this point in the rite when the text is appropriate.

The Postcommunion Hymn is the hymn which people are most likely to take with them from the Church, most likely to hum or whistle around the parish house, in the parking lot, or at other times and in other places. This hymn colors their feeling about the entire service which has preceded. Ideally this should be a very familiar hymn based on propers of the day which sends people out, rejoicing in the power of the Holy Spirit, to love and serve the Lord in the world.

In choosing hymns for a particular occasion consideration needs to be given to a number of factors, including the average age of the congregation, the size of the group and their musical abilities, the available vocal and instrumental leadership, the architectural setting (including the size and acoustics of the building), and the relative importance of the day or occasion. When several hymns are used there should be a balance of the familiar and the not quite so familiar.

The Hymnal suggests alternative tunes for a number of hymns. Even when the tune printed with the text is known by the congregation the alternative suggested might be better at certain points in the rite (for example, Dundee would surely be better as a procession from the Church than St. Agnes, printed with "Shepherd of souls, refresh and bless"). Use of the suggested alternative tunes allows for the use of a greater number of texts. An even fuller use of the texts of the book can be achieved by judicious use of the Metrical Index, pages 1,039-1,044.

This index should also suggest to organists, choir directors, and cantors appropriate organ music, anthems, and solos for the various rites and occasions in one or the other of three ways:

(1) It might bring to mind organ music or anthems or solos related to the readings of the day or to the suggested hymns texts.

(2) A tune not yet learned by the congregation might serve as prelude, offertory, or postlude or as music during the Communion of priest and people.

(3) A hymn not yet learned by the congregation or beyond the musical abilities of the particular congregation might serve as an anthem or solo at any of the places which allow for the use of an anthem (before the Opening Acclamation, after Lessons which precede the Gospel, at the time of the Offering, after the Fraction, or during the Communion of priest and people).

The most effective way of teaching new tunes to a congregation is through repeated exposure to them as organ music or as choir anthems or as solos sung by a cantor. The teaching of new hymns in this manner should be high priority for any organist, choir director, or cantor. For the musicians the music can often be made more interesting and challenging by the use of varied harmonizations and accompaniments, descants, and faux-bourdons. A number of descants and varied harmonizations and some faux-bourdons and varied accompaniments are provided in the Hymnal 1982. Many others are readily available.

In this index the relationship of a hymn to one or more of the propers of the day is indicated after the first line of the hymn:

C — Collect
L — Lesson
P — Psalm
E — Epistle
G — Gospel

Other hymns particularly appropriate to the day, the season, or the occasion are indicated by the use of the letter S:

S — *appropriate to the day, season, or occasion*

In the suggestions for the Holy Eucharist when more than one hymn is listed the order in which they are listed is generally to be preferred. Two cautions, however, should be observed:

(1) Many lections encompass diverse themes or incorporate more than one

pericope, and the choice needs to be made on the basis of which theme will be developed in the sermon. See, for example, the Gospel for Proper 7 in Year C (Luke 9:18-24) and the hymn suggestions, page 249.

(2) If a hymn is not being used at one point in the rite it ought to be considered for use at another point. For example, the first hymn listed for the Offertory is often the hymn which relates best to the Gospel, and if an anthem or instrumental music is used instead this hymn might be the best choice for the Communion or Postcommunion Hymn. Before shifting a hymn to a position in the rite other than the one suggested one ought to read through the entire text of the hymn ("Come with us, O blessed Jesus" is not appropriate until after the people have received Communion; if "Christ is made the sure foundation" is shifted to a late point in the rite the last two verses should be left off).

It is the hope of the author that this index will be helpful in relating the music to the rites of the Book of Common Prayer and that it will encourage a fuller use of the riches of the Hymnal 1982.

The Book
of Common
Prayer

The Daily Office: Year One

Week of 1 Advent

SUN	MP	462	The Lord will come and not be slow	E
		73	The King shall come when morning dawns	E
		600, 601	O day of God, draw nigh	E
	EP	68	Rejoice! rejoice, believers	G
		61, 62	"Sleepers, wake!" A voice astounds us	G
MON	MP	53	Once he came in blessing	L
		63, 64	O heavenly Word, eternal Light	L
		73	The King shall come when morning dawns	E
	EP	271, 272	The great forerunner of the morn	G
		444	Blessed be the God of Israel	G
		70	Herald, sound the note of judgment	G
TUE	MP	596	Judge eternal, throned in splendor	L
		63, 64	O heavenly Word, eternal Light	E
	EP	598	Lord Christ, when first thou cam'st to earth	G
WED	MP	543	O Zion, tune thy voice	L
		597	O day of peace that dimly shines	L
		613	Thy kingdom come, O God	L
		65	Prepare the way, O Zion	S
	EP	591	O God of earth and altar	G
		596	Judge eternal, throned in splendor	G
		573	Father eternal, Ruler of creation	G
THU	MP	454	Jesus came, adored by angels	S
		486	Hosanna to the living Lord	S
		63, 64	O heavenly Word, eternal Light	E
	EP	61, 62	"Sleepers, wake!" A voice astounds us	G
		462	The Lord will come and not be slow	S
FRI	MP	63, 64	O heavenly Word, eternal Light	L
		596	Judge eternal, throned in splendor	L
		11	Awake, my soul, and with the sun	E

	EP	672	O very God of very God	S
		600, 601	O day of God, draw nigh	S
SAT	MP	543	O Zion, tune thy voice	L
		57, 58	Lo! he comes, with clouds descending	E
	EP	454	Jesus came, adored by angels	G
		53	Once he came in blessing	G

Week of 2 Advent

SUN	MP	598	Lord Christ, when first thou cam'st to earth	L
		59	Hark! a thrilling voice is sounding	E
		68	Rejoice! rejoice, believers	E
		53	Once he came in blessing	E
	EP	271, 272	The great forerunner of the morn	G
		76	On Jordan's bank the Baptist's cry	G
		70	Herald, sound the note of judgment	G
MON	MP	68	Rejoice! rejoice, believers	E
		61, 62	"Sleepers, wake!" A voice astounds us	E
	EP	57, 58	Lo! he comes, with clouds descending	G
		454	Jesus came, adored by angels	G
		53	Once he came in blessing	G
TUE	MP	591	O God of earth and altar	L
		59	Hark! a thrilling voice is sounding	E
	EP	63, 64	O heavenly Word, eternal Light	G
		68	Rejoice! rejoice, believers	G
		61, 62	"Sleepers, wake!" A voice astounds us	G
		53	Once he came in blessing	G
WED	MP	63, 64	O heavenly Word, eternal Light	E
		57, 58	Lo! he comes, with clouds descending	E
	EP	489	The great Creator of the worlds	G
THU	MP	486	Hosanna to the living Lord!	S
		53	Once he came in blessing	S
	EP	598	Lord Christ, when first thou cam'st to earth	G
FRI	MP	55	Redeemer of the nations, come	L
		54	Savior of the nations, come!	L
		496, 497	How bright appears the Morning Star	L
		56	O come, O come, Emmanuel	L
	EP	61, 62	"Sleepers, wake!" A voice astounds us	G
		640	Watchman, tell us of the night	S
SAT	MP	11	Awake, my soul, and with the sun	E
		9	Not here for high and holy things (sts. 4-6)	E

	EP	454	Jesus came, adored by angels	S
		672	O very God of very God	S

Week of 3 Advent

SUN	MP	63, 64	O heavenly Word, eternal Light	E
		640	Watchman, tell us of the night	E
	EP	271, 272	The great forerunner of the morn	G
		444	Blessed be the God of Israel	G
MON	MP	59	Hark! a thrilling voice is sounding	E
		63, 64	O heavenly Word, eternal Light	E
		57, 58	Lo! he comes, with clouds descending	E
	EP	57, 58	Lo! he comes, with clouds descending	S
		53	Once he came in blessing	S
TUE	MP	125, 126	The people who in darkness walked	L
		640	Watchman, tell us of the night	L
		6, 7	Christ, whose glory fills the skies	L & E
		672	O very God of very God	E
		73	The King shall come when morning dawns	E
	EP	73	The King shall come when morning dawns	S
		54	Savior of the nations, come!	S
WED	MP	53	Once he came in blessing	E
		63, 64	O heavenly Word, eternal Light	E
		59	Hark! a thrilling voice is sounding	E
	EP	75	There's a voice in the wilderness crying	G
		67	Comfort, comfort ye my people	G
		271, 272	The great forerunner of the morn	G
		69	What is the crying at Jordan?	G
THU	MP	596	Judge eternal, throned in splendor	L
		591	O God of earth and altar	E
		63, 64	O heavenly Word, eternal Light	E
	EP	76	On Jordan's bank the Baptist's cry	G
		70	Herald, sound the note of judgment	G
		75	There's a voice in the wilderness crying	G
		67	Comfort, comfort ye my people	G
		69	What is the crying at Jordan?	G
FRI	MP	591	O God of earth and altar	E
		60	Creator of the stars of night	E
		63, 64	O heavenly Word, eternal Light	E
	EP	271, 272	The great forerunner of the morn	G
		444	Blessed be the God of Israel	G
SAT	MP	57, 58	Lo! he comes, with clouds descending	E
		60	Creator of the stars of night	E

		63, 64	O heavenly Word, eternal Light	E
		53	Once he came in blessing	E
		73	The King shall come when morning dawns	E
	EP	70	Herald, sound the note of judgment	G
		76	On Jordan's bank the Baptist's cry	G
		75	There's a voice in the wilderness crying	G
		67	Comfort, comfort ye my people	G
		69	What is the crying at Jordan?	G

Week of 4 Advent

SUN	MP	436	Lift up your heads, ye mighty gates	Ps 24
		496, 497	How bright appears the Morning Star	L
		56	O come, O come, Emmanuel	L
	EP	489	The great Creator of the worlds	G
		56	O come, O come, Emmanuel	S
		66	Come, thou long-expected Jesus	S
MON	MP	597	O day of peace that dimly shines	L
		534	God is working his purpose out	L
		73	The King shall come when morning dawns	E
		57, 58	Lo! he comes, with clouds descending	E
	EP	444	Blessed be the God of Israel	G
		271, 272	The great forerunner of the morn	G
TUE	MP	582, 583	O holy city, seen of John	E
		54	Savior of the nations, come!	S
	EP	271, 272	The great forerunner of the morn	G
		640	Watchman, tell us of the night	S
WED	MP	616	Hail to the Lord's Anointed	Ps 72
		582, 583	O holy city, seen of John	E
		61, 62	"Sleepers, wake!" A voice astounds us	E
		56	O come, O come, Emmanuel	S
		54	Savior of the nations, come!	S
	EP	265	The angel Gabriel from heaven came	G
		270	Gabriel's message does away	G
		263, 264	The Word whom earth and sea and sky	G
		266	Nova, nova	G
THU	MP	60	Creator of the stars of night	E
		6, 7	Christ, whose glory fills the skies	E
		496, 497	How bright appears the Morning Star	E
		672	O very God of very God	E
	EP	268, 269	Ye who claim the faith of Jesus	G
		437, 438	Tell out, my soul, the greatness of the Lord!	G
		258	Virgin-born, we bow before thee	G
FRI	MP	543	O Zion, tune thy voice	L
		73	The King shall come when morning dawns	E

	66	Come, thou long-expected Jesus	S
	55	Redeemer of the nations, come	S
EP	271, 272	The great forerunner of the morn	G
	56	O come, O come, Emmanuel	S
	55	Redeemer of the nations come	S

December 24

MP	71, 72	Hark! the glad sound! the Savior comes	L
	73	The King shall come when morning dawns	E
	496, 497	How bright appears the Morning Star	E
	6, 7	Christ, whose glory fills the skies	E
	444	Blessed be the God of Israel	G

Christmas Eve

EP	60	Creator of the stars of night	E
	252	Jesus! Name of wondrous love!	E
	439	What wondrous love is this	E

Christmas Day and Following

Christmas Day

MP	82	Of the Father's love begotten	E
	84	Love came down at Christmas	E
	439	What wondrous love is this	E
EP	85, 86	O Savior of our fallen race	G
	87	Hark! the herald angels sing	G

First SUN after Christmas

MP	102	Once in royal David's city	E
	496, 497	How bright appears the Morning Star	E
	489	The great Creator of the worlds	E
	452	Glorious the day when Christ was born	E
EP	496, 497	How bright appears the Morning Star	G
	252	Jesus! Name of wondrous love!	G
	248, 249	To the Name of our salvation	G
	81	Lo, how a Rose e'er blooming	G
	250	Now greet the swiftly changing year	G

December 29

MP	678, 679	Surely it is God who saves me	L

		Of the Father's love begotten	E
	82	Of the Father's love begotten	E
	454	Jesus came, adored by angels	E
EP	443	From God Christ's deity came forth	G
	491	Where is this stupendous stranger?	S
	386, 387	We sing of God, the mighty source	S

December 30

MP	543	O Zion, tune thy voice	L
	476	Can we by searching find out God	S
	439	What wondrous love is this	S
EP	489	The great Creator of the worlds	G
	468	It was poor little Jesus	S
	452	Glorious the day when Christ was born	S

December 31

MP	635	If thou but trust in God to guide thee	L
	543	O Zion, tune thy voice	L
	492	Sing ye faithful, sing with gladness	E
	542	Christ is the world's true Light	G
	6, 7	Christ, whose glory fills the skies	G
	490	I want to walk as a child of the light	G
	496, 497	How bright appears the Morning Star	G

Eve of Holy Name

EP	680	O God, our help in ages past	Ps 90
	597	O day of peace that dimly shines	L
	582, 583	O holy city, seen of John	E
	82	Of the Father's love begotten	E

Holy Name

MP	252	Jesus! Name of wondrous love!	E
	251	O God, whom neither time nor space	S
EP	248, 249	To the Name of our salvation	G
	250	Now greet the swiftly changing year	G

Second SUN after Christmas

MP	538	God of mercy, God of grace	Ps 67
	251	O God, whom neither time nor space	E
EP	335	I am the bread of life	G
	649, 650	O Jesus, joy of loving hearts	G

January 2

MP	709	O God of Bethel, by whose hand	L
	636, 637	How firm a foundation, ye saints of the Lord	E
	634	I call on thee, Lord Jesus Christ	E
	401	The God of Abraham praise	E
EP	335	I am the bread of life	G
	690	Guide me, O thou great Jehovah	G

January 3

MP	709	O God of Bethel, by whose hand	L
	453	As Jacob with travel was weary one day	L
	635	If thou but trust in God to guide thee	E
	401	The God of Abraham praise	E
	623	O what their joy and their glory must be	E
EP	478	Jesus, our mighty Lord	G
	708	Savior, like a shepherd lead us	G

January 4

MP	648	When Israel was in Egypt's land	L
	401	The God of Abraham praise	L
	393	Praise our great and gracious Lord	E
	425	Sing now with joy unto the Lord	E
	363	Ancient of Days, who sittest throned in glory	E
EP	457	Thou art the Way, to thee alone	G
	711	Seek ye first the kingdom of God	G
	478	Jesus, our mighty Lord	G

January 5

MP	393	Praise our great and gracious Lord	L & E
	690	Guide me, O thou great Jehovah	L
	545	Lo! what a cloud of witnesses	E
	546	Awake, my soul, stretch every nerve	E
	392	Come, we that love the Lord	G

Eve of Epiphany

EP	532, 533	How wondrous and great thy works, God of praise	L & E
	381	Thy strong word did cleave the darkness	L & E
	125, 126	The people who in darkness walked	L & E
	472	Hope of the world, thou Christ	E

The Epiphany and Following

Epiphany

MP	640	Watchman, tell us of the night	L
	540	Awake, thou Spirit of the watchmen	L
	539	O Zion, haste, thy mission high fulfilling	L
	119	As with gladness men of old	E
	439	What wondrous love is this	E
	544	Jesus shall reign where'er the sun	E
EP	616	Hail to the Lord's Anointed	G
	491	Where is this stupendous stranger?	S

January 7

MP	117, 118	Brightest and best of the stars of the morning	S
	124	What star is this, with beams so bright	S
	536	God has spoken to his people	E
EP	138	All praise to you, O Lord	G
	131, 132	When Christ's appearing was made known (sts. 4-5)	G
	443	From God Christ's deity came forth	G
	135	Songs of thankfulness and praise	G

January 8

MP	380	From all that dwell below the skies	Ps 117
	491	Where is this stupendous stranger?	S
	536	God has spoken to his people	E
EP	448, 449	O love, how deep, how broad, how high	G
	493	O for a thousand tongues to sing	G
	567	Thine arm, O Lord, in days of old	G

January 9

MP	542	Christ is the world's true Light	S
	532, 533	How wondrous and great thy works, God of praise!	S
	536	God has spoken to his people	E
EP	135	Songs of thankfulness and praise (sts. 1-2)	G
	493	O for a thousand tongues to sing	G
	567	Thine arm, O Lord, in days of old	G

January 10

MP	125, 126	The people who in darkness walked	S

		381	Thy strong word did cleave the darkness	S
		536	God has spoken to his people	E
	EP	448, 449	O love, how deep, how broad, how high	G
		472	Hope of the world, thou Christ	G

January 11

	MP	394, 395	Creating God, your fingers trace	Ps 148
		373	Praise the Lord! ye heavens adore him	Ps 148
		432	O praise ye the Lord! Praise him in the height	Pss 148 & 150
		536	God has spoken to his people	E
	EP	633	Word of God, come down on earth	G
		496, 497	How bright appears the Morning Star	S
		439	What wondrous love is this	S
		125, 126	The people who in darkness walked	S

January 12

	MP	543	O Zion, tune thy voice	L
		536	God has spoken to his people	E
		633	Word of God, come down on earth	G
		6, 7	Christ, whose glory fills the skies	G
		465, 466	Eternal light, shine in my heart	G
		371	Thou, whose almighty Word	G

Eve of 1 Epiphany

	EP	71, 72	Hark! the glad sound! the Savior comes	L
		539	O Zion, haste, thy mission high fulfilling	L
		432	O praise ye the Lord! Praise him in the height (omit st. 3)	E
		381	Thy strong word did cleave the darkness	E
		294	Baptized in water	E
		295	Sing praise to our Creator	E

Week of 1 Epiphany

SUN	MP	75	There's a voice in the wilderness crying	L
		67	Comfort, comfort ye my people	L
		489	The great Creator of the worlds	E
		496, 497	How bright appears the Morning Star	E
	EP	633	Word of God, come down on earth	G
		489	The great Creator of the worlds	G
		82	Of the Father's love begotten	G
		491	Where is this stupendous stranger?	G
		476	Can we by searching find out God	G

		386, 387	We sing of God, the mighty source (omit st. 2)	G
MON	MP	294	Baptized in water	E
		432	O praise ye the Lord! Praise him in the height (omit st. 3)	E
		495	Hail, thou once despisèd Jesus!	E
		686	Come, thou fount of every blessing	E
		685	Rock of ages, cleft for me	E
		706	In your mercy, Lord, you called me	E
	EP	120	The sinless one to Jordan came	G
		121	Christ, when for us you were baptized	G
		139	When Jesus went to Jordan's stream	G
		116	"I come," the great Redeemer cries	G
TUE	MP	435	At the Name of Jesus	E
		477	All praise to thee, for thou, O King divine	E
		495	Hail, thou once despisèd Jesus!	E
		492	Sing ye faithful, sing with gladness	E
		421	All glory be to God on high	E
	EP	549, 550	Jesus calls us; o'er the tumult	G
		661	They cast their nets in Galilee	G
		493	O for a thousand tongues to sing	G
		448, 449	O love, how deep, how broad, how high	G
		567	Thine arm, O Lord, in days of old	G
		421	All glory be to God on high	G
WED	MP	636, 637	How firm a foundation, ye saints of the Lord	L
		432	O praise ye the Lord! Praise him in the height (omit st. 3)	E
		467	Sing, my soul, his wondrous love	E
		671	Amazing grace! how sweet the sound	E
		706	In your mercy, Lord, you called me	E
	EP	567	Thine arm, O Lord, in days of old	G
		493	O for a thousand tongues to sing	G
		371	Thou, whose almighty Word	G
		429	I'll praise my Maker while I've breath	G
THU	MP	518	Christ is made the sure foundation	E
		525	The Church's one foundation	E
		495	Hail, thou once despisèd Jesus!	E
		685	Rock of ages, cleft for me	E
		603, 604	When Christ was lifted from the earth	E
	EP	411	O bless the Lord, my soul	G
		493	O for a thousand tongues to sing	G
		567	Thine arm, O Lord, in days of old	G
		566	From thee all skill and science flow	G
FRI	MP	542	Christ is the world's true Light	E
		532, 533	How wondrous and great thy works, God of praise	E
		531	O Spirit of the living God	E

		539	O Zion, haste, thy mission high fulfilling	E
	EP	281	He sat to watch o'er customs paid	G
		469, 470	There's a wideness in God's mercy	G
		467	Sing, my soul, his wondrous love	G
		706	In your mercy, Lord, you called me	G
SAT	MP	636, 637	How firm a foundation, ye saints of the Lord	L
		448, 449	O love, how deep, how broad, how high	E
		455, 456	O love of God, how strong and true	E
		422	Not far beyond the sea, nor high	E
	EP	380	From all that dwell below the skies	Ps 117
		630	Thanks to God whose Word was spoken (omit sts. 3 & 4)	G
		493	O for a thousand tongues to sing	G
		381	Thy strong word did cleave the darkness	G
		135	Songs of thankfulness and praise (sts. 1-3)	G
		567	Thine arm, O Lord, in days of old	G
		458	My song is love unknown	G

Week of 2 Epiphany

		394, 395	Creating God, your fingers trace	Ps 148
SUN	MP	373	Praise the Lord! ye heavens adore him	Ps 148
		432	O praise ye the Lord! Praise him in the height	Ps 150
		390	Praise to the Lord, the Almighty	Ps 150
		443	From God Christ's deity came forth	E
		460, 461	Alleluia! sing to Jesus (omit sts. 2 & 5)	E
	EP	673	The first one ever, oh, ever to know (st. 2)	G
		540	Awake, thou Spirit of the watchmen (sts. 2-3)	G
		541	Come, labor on	G
MON	MP	511	Holy Spirit, ever living	E
		547	Awake, O sleeper, rise from death	E
		521	Put forth, O God, thy Spirit's might	E
		527	Singing songs of expectation	E
	EP	135	Songs of thankfulness and praise (sts. 1-3)	G
		528	Lord, you give the great commission	G
		540	Awake, thou Spirit of the watchmen	G
		493	O for a thousand tongues to sing	G
		590	O Jesus Christ, may grateful hymns be rising	G
		567	Thine arm, O Lord, in days of old	G
TUE	MP	408	Sing praise to God who reigns above	L
		574, 575	Before thy throne, O God, we kneel	E
		674	Forgive our sins as we forgive	E
		21, 22	O God of truth, O Lord of might	E
		593	Lord, make us servants of your peace	E
		347	Go forth for God; go to the world in peace	E

	EP	381	Thy strong word did cleave the darkness	G
		452	Glorious the day when Christ was born	G
		529	In Christ there is no East or West	G
		603, 604	When Christ was lifted from the earth	G
WED	MP	547	Awake, O sleeper, rise from death	E
		5	O Splendor of God's glory bright	E
		490	I want to walk as a child of the light	E
	EP	588, 589	Almighty God, your word is cast	G
		530	Spread, O spread, thou mighty word	G
		505	O Spirit of Life, O Spirit of God	G
		536	God has spoken to his people	G
		541	Come, labor on	G
THU	MP	525	The Church's one foundation	E
		519, 520	Blessed city, heavenly Salem	E
		524	I love thy kingdom, Lord	E
		426	Songs of praise the angels sang	E
		402, 403	Let all the world in every corner sing	E
	EP	615	"Thy kingdom come!" on bended knee	G
		613	Thy kingdom come, O God	G
		24	The day thou gavest, Lord, is ended	G
		534	God is working his purpose out	G
FRI	MP	375	Give praise and glory unto God	L
		408	Sing praise to God who reigns above	L
		252	Jesus! Name of wondrous love	L
		60	Creator of the stars of night	L
		435	At the Name of Jesus	L
		587	Our Father, by whose Name	E
	EP	669	Commit thou all that grieves thee	G
		414	God, my King, thy might confessing	G
		375	Give praise and glory unto God	G
SAT	MP	548	Soldiers of Christ, arise	E
		561	Stand up, stand up for Jesus	E
		617	Eternal Ruler of the ceaseless round	E
	EP	658	As longs the deer for cooling streams	Ps 42
		567	Thine arm, O Lord, in days of old	G
		652, 653	Dear Lord and Father of mankind (sts. 1, 4 & 5)	G
		493	O for a thousand tongues to sing	G
		429	I'll praise my Maker while I've breath	G
		411	O bless the Lord, my soul	G

Week of 3 Epiphany

SUN	MP	413	New songs of celebration render	Ps 98
		460, 461	Alleluia! sing to Jesus (omit sts. 2 & 5)	E
		53	Once he came in blessing	E
		686	Come, thou fount of every blessing	E

	EP	411	O bless the Lord, my soul	Ps 103 & G
		410	Praise, my soul, the King of heaven	Ps 103 & G
		390	Praise to the Lord, the Almighty	Ps
		493	O for a thousand tongues to sing	G
		567	Thine arm, O Lord, in days of old	G
		135	Songs of thankfulness and praise (sts. 1-3)	G
MON	MP	256	A light from heaven shone around	E
		255	We sing the glorious conquest	E
	EP	493	O for a thousand tongues to sing	G
		567	Thine arm, O Lord, in days of old	G
		590	O Jesus Christ, may grateful hymns be rising	G
		429	I'll praise my Maker while I've breath	G
		566	From thee all skill and science flow	G
TUE	MP	685	Rock of ages, cleft for me	L
		542	Christ is the world's true Light	E
		532, 533	How wondrous and great thy works, God of praise	E
		539	O Zion, haste, thy mission high fulfilling	E
		531	O Spirit of the living God	E
	EP	633	Word of God, come down on earth	G
		540	Awake, thou Spirit of the watchmen	G
		528	Lord, you give the great commission	G
WED	MP	495	Hail, thou once despisèd Jesus! (sts. 1 & 2)	E
		432	O praise ye the Lord! Praise him in the height (omit st. 3)	E
		697	My God, accept my heart this day	E
		691	My faith looks up to thee	E
		381	Thy strong word did cleave the darkness	E
	EP	271, 272	The great forerunner of the morn	G
		444	Blessed be the God of Israel	G
		76	On Jordan's bank the Baptist's cry	G
THU	MP	401	The God of Abraham praise	E
		432	O praise ye the Lord! Praise him in the height (omit st. 3)	E
		270	Gabriel's message does away	E
		60	Creator of the stars of night	E
	EP	478	Jesus, our mighty Lord	G
		708	Savior, like a shepherd lead us	G
		300	Glory, love, and praise, and honor	G
		472	Hope of the world, thou Christ	G
FRI	MP	691	My faith looks up to thee (sts. 1 & 2)	E
		401	The God of Abraham praise	E
		671	Amazing grace! how sweet the sound	E
	EP	669	Commit thou all that grieves thee	G
		636, 637	How firm a foundation, ye saints of the Lord	G
		567	Thine arm, O Lord, in days of old	G

		590	O Jesus Christ, may grateful hymns be rising	G
		414	God, my King, thy might confessing	G
SAT	MP	295	Sing praise to our Creator	E
		432	O praise ye the Lord! Praise him in the height (omit st. 3)	E
		294	Baptized in water	
		529	In Christ there is no East or West	E
		581	Where charity and love prevail	E
	EP	702	Lord, thou hast searched me and dost know	Ps 139
		436	Lift up your heads, ye mighty gates	G
		656	Blest are the pure in heart	G
		382	King of glory, King of peace	G
		556, 557	Rejoice, ye pure in heart	G
		435	At the Name of Jesus (sts. 1-5)	G

Week of 4 Epiphany

SUN	MP	436	Lift up your heads, ye mighty gates	Ps 24
		379	God is love, let heaven adore him	L
		580	God, who stretched the spangled heavens	L
		401	The God of Abraham praise	E
		620	Jerusalem, my happy home	E
		624	Jerusalem the golden	E
		623	O what their joy and their glory must be	E
	EP	517	How lovely is thy dwelling place	Ps 84
		634	I call on thee, Lord Jesus Christ	G
		458	My song is love unknown	G
		443	From God Christ's deity came forth	G
		489	The great Creator of the worlds	G
MON	MP	85, 86	O Savior of our fallen race	E
		489	The great Creator of the worlds	E
		448, 449	O love, how deep, how broad, how high	E
		467	Sing, my soul, his wondrous love	E
	EP	633	Word of God, come down on earth	G
		493	O for a thousand tongues to sing	G
		567	Thine arm, O Lord, in days of old	G
		429	I'll praise my Maker while I've breath	G
		135	Songs of thankfulness and praise (sts. 1-3)	G
		411	O bless the Lord, my soul	G
TUE	MP	539	O Zion, haste, thy mission high fulfilling	L
		540	Awake, thou Spirit of the watchmen	L
		640	Watchman, tell us of the night	L
	EP	300	Glory, love, and praise, and honor	G
		320	Zion, praise thy Savior, singing (sts. 5-6)	G
WED	MP	616	Hail to the Lord's Anointed	Ps 72

		544	Jesus shall reign where'er the sun	Ps 72
		401	The God of Abraham praise	E
	EP	536	God has spoken to his people	G
		633	Word of God, come down on earth	G
		567	Thine arm, O Lord, in days of old	G
		429	I'll praise my Maker while I've breath	G
		493	O for a thousand tongues to sing	G
		448, 449	O love, how deep, how broad, how high	G
THU	MP	678, 679	Surely it is God who saves me	L
		432	O praise ye the Lord!	
			Praise him in the height (omit st. 3)	E
		529	In Christ there is no East or West	E
		610	Lord, whose love through humble service	E
	EP	254	You are the Christ, O Lord	G
		675	Take up your cross, the Savior said	G
		484, 485	Praise the Lord through every nation	G
		572	Weary of all trumpeting	G
FRI	MP	51	We the Lord's people, heart and voice uniting (sts. 1-2)	L
		532, 533	How wondrous and great thy works, God of praise	L
		531	O Spirit of the living God	L
		500	Creator Spirit, by whose aid	E
		21, 22	O God of truth, O Lord of might	E
		513	Like the murmur of the dove's song	E
		697	My God, accept my heart this day	E
	EP	136, 137	O wondrous type! O vision fair	G
		133, 134	O Light of Light, Love given birth	G
		129, 130	Christ upon the mountain peak	G
		135	Songs of thankfulness and praise	G
SAT	MP	610	Lord, whose love through humble service	E
		580	God, who stretched the spangled heavens	E
		570, 571	All who love and serve your city	E
	EP	664	My Shepherd will supply my need	Ps 23
		645, 646	The King of love my shepherd is	Ps 23
		663	The Lord my God my shepherd is	Ps 23
		493	O for a thousand tongues to sing	G
		567	Thine arm, O Lord, in days of old	G
		448, 449	O love, how deep, how broad, how high	G
		566	From thee all skill and science flow	G

Week of 5 Epiphany

SUN	MP	643	My God, how wonderful thou art	L
		545	Lo! what a cloud of witnesses	E
		546	Awake, my soul, stretch every nerve	E
		253	Give us the wings of faith to rise	E

	EP	692	I heard the voice of Jesus say (st. 2)	G
		649, 650	O Jesus, joy of loving hearts	G
		678, 679	Surely it is God who saves me	G
		443	From God Christ's deity came forth	G
MON	MP	145	Now quit your care (sts. 3-5)	L
		474	When I survey the wondrous cross	E
		441, 442	In the cross of Christ I glory	E
		473	Lift high the cross	E
		434	Nature with open volume stands	E
		160	Cross of Jesus, cross of sorrow	E
		471	We sing the praise of him who died	E
	EP	448, 449	O love, how deep, how broad, how high	G
		434	Nature with open volume stands	G
		609	Where cross the crowded ways of life	G
		659, 660	O Master, let me walk with thee	G
TUE	MP	148	Creator of the earth and skies	L
		704	O thou who camest from above	E
		151	From deepest woe I cry to thee	E
	EP	574, 575	Before thy throne, O God, we kneel	G
WED	MP	548	Soldiers of Christ, arise	E
		552, 553	Fight the good fight with all thy might (sts. 1 & 2)	E
		563	Go forward, Christian soldier	E
		561	Stand up, stand up for Jesus	E
		483	The head that once was crowned with thorns	E
	EP	480	When Jesus left his Father's throne	G
		587	Our Father, by whose Name	G
		352	O God, to those who here profess	G
		353	Your love, O God, has called us here	G
THU	MP	429	I'll praise my Maker while I've breath	Ps 146
		543	O Zion, tune thy voice	L
		672	O very God of very God	L
		656	Blest are the pure in heart	E
		610	Lord, make us servants of your peace	E
		707	Take my life, and let it be	E
	EP	655	O Jesus, I have promised	G
		701	Jesus, all my gladness (sts. 1 & 2)	G
		475	God himself is with us	G
		707	Take my life and let it be	G
FRI	MP	71, 72	Hark! the glad sound! the Savior comes	L
		627	Lamp of our feet, whereby we trace	E
		631	Book of books, our people's strength	E
		630	Thanks to God, whose Word was spoken	E
		628	Help us, O Lord, to learn	E
	EP	477	All praise to thee, for thou, O King divine	G
		458	My song is love unknown	G
		474	When I survey the wondrous cross	G

		483	The head that once was crowned with thorns	G
		659, 660	O Master, let me walk with thee	G
SAT	MP	680	O God, our help in ages past	Ps 90
		552, 553	Fight the good fight with all thy might (sts. 1-2)	E
		511	Holy Spirit, ever living	E
		555	Lead on, O King eternal	E
		561	Stand up, stand up for Jesus	E
	EP	389	Let us, with a gladsome mind	Ps 136
		493	O for a thousand tongues to sing	G
		429	I'll praise my Maker while I've breath	G
		567	Thine arm, O Lord, in days of old	G
		371	Thou, whose almighty Word	G
		633	Word of God, come down on earth	G

Week of 6 Epiphany

SUN	MP	538	God of mercy, God of grace	Ps 67
		5	O Splendor of God's glory bright	E
		576, 577	God is love, and where true love is	E
		581	Where charity and love prevail	E
		606	Where true charity and love dwell	E
	EP	409	The spacious firmament on high	Ps 19
		431	The stars declare his glory	Ps 19
		687, 688	A mighty fortress is our God	Ps 46
		496, 497	How bright appears the Morning Star	G
		465, 466	Eternal light, shine in my heart	G
		692	I heard the voice of Jesus say (st. 3)	G
		490	I want to walk as a child of the light	G
		542	Christ is the world's true Light	G
MON	MP	489	The great Creator of the worlds	E
		439	What wondrous love is this	E
		458	My song is love unknown	E
		448, 449	O love, how deep, how broad, how high	E
		472	Hope of the world, thou Christ	E
		423	Immortal, invisible, God only wise	E
	EP	436	Lift up your heads, ye mighty gates	G
		486	Hosanna to the living Lord	G
		65	Prepare the way, O Zion	G
		74	Blest be the King whose coming	G
TUE	MP	363	Ancient of Days, who sittest throned in glory	L
		393	Praise our great and gracious Lord	L
		425	Sing now with joy unto the Lord	L
		368	Holy Father, great Creator	E
	EP	711	Seek ye first the kingdom of God	G
		518	Christ is made the sure foundation	G

		51	We the Lord's people, heart and voice uniting (sts. 1-2)	G
		674	Forgive our sins as we forgive	G
		581	Where charity and love prevail	G
WED	MP	359	God of the prophets, bless the prophets' heirs	E
		511	Holy Spirit, ever living	E
	EP	598	Lord Christ, when first thou cam'st to earth	G
		170	To mock your reign, O dearest Lord	G
		495	Hail, thou once despisèd Jesus!	G
THU	MP	535	Ye servants of God, your Master proclaim	E
		511.	Holy Spirit, ever living	E
	EP	596	Judge eternal, throned in splendor	G
		591	O God of earth and altar	G
		401	The God of Abraham praise	G
		526	Let saints on earth in concert sing	G
FRI	MP	511	Holy Spirit, ever living	E
		359	God of the prophets, bless the prophets' heirs	E
	EP	551	Rise up, ye saints of God	G
		581	Where charity and love prevail	G
		643	My God, how wonderful thou art	G
		704	O thou who camest from above	G
		602	Jesu, Jesu, fill us with your love	G
SAT	MP	552, 553	Fight the good fight with all thy might (sts. 1-2)	E
		701	Jesus, all my gladness	E
		574, 575	Before thy throne, O God, we kneel	E
		582, 583	O holy city, seen of John	E
		488	Be thou my vision, O Lord of my heart	E
	EP	707	Take my life and let it be	G
		475	God himself is with us (sts. 1-2)	G
		705	As those of old their first fruits brought	G
		254	You are the Christ, O Lord	G
		450, 451	All hail the power of Jesus' Name	G

Week of 7 Epiphany

SUN	MP	21, 22	O God of truth, O Lord of might	E
		3, 4	Now that the daylight fills the sky	E
		5	O Splendor of God's glory bright	E
		492	Sing, ye faithful, sing with gladness	E
	EP	414	God, my King, thy might confessing	Ps 145
		404	We will extol you, ever-blessed Lord	Ps 145
		478	Jesus, our mighty Lord	G
		708	Savior, like a shepherd lead us	G
		645, 646	The King of love my shepherd is	G

MON	MP	636, 637	How firm a foundation, ye saints of the Lord	E
		472	Hope of the world, thou Christ	E
	EP	560	Remember your servants, Lord	G
		593	Lord, make us servants of your peace	G
		656	Blest are the pure in heart	G
		437, 438	Tell out, my soul, the greatness of the Lord	G
TUE	MP	668	I to the hills will lift mine eyes	Ps 121
		686	Come, thou fount of every blessing	E
		697	My God, accept my heart this day	E
		294	Baptized in water	E
		432	O praise ye the Lord! Praise him in the height (omit st. 3)	E
	EP	543	O Zion, tune thy voice	G
		381	Thy strong word did cleave the darkness	G
		628	Help us, O Lord, to learn	G
		626	Lord, be thy word my rule	G
WED	MP	659, 660	O Master, let me walk with thee	E
		559	Lead us, heavenly Father, lead us	E
	EP	666	Out of the depths I call	Ps 130
		151	From deepest woe I cry to thee	Ps 130
		674	Forgive our sins as we forgive	G
		593	Lord, make us servants of your peace	G
		603, 604	When Christ was lifted from the earth	G
THU	MP	670	Lord, for ever at thy side	Ps 131
		326	From glory to glory advancing, we praise thee, O Lord	E
		657	Love divine, all loves excelling	E
	EP	641	Lord Jesus, think on me	G
		27, 28	O blest Creator, source of light	G
FRI	MP	496, 497	How bright appears the Morning Star	E
		6, 7	Christ, whose glory fills the skies	E
		465, 466	Eternal light, shine in my heart	E
		5	O Splendor of God's glory bright	E
		381	Thy strong word did cleave the darkness	E
		419	Lord of all being, throned afar	E
	EP	593	Lord, make us servants of your peace	G
		674	Forgive our sins as we forgive	G
		603, 604	When Christ was lifted from the earth	G
		568	Father all loving, who rulest in majesty	G
		394, 395	Creating God, your fingers trace	G
SAT	MP	296	We know that Christ is raised and dies no more	E
		209	We walk by faith and not by sight	E
		623	O what their joy and their glory must be	E
		621, 622	Light's abode, celestial Salem	E

		194, 195	Jesus lives! thy terrors now	E
		620	Jerusalem, my happy home	E
	EP	388	O worship the King, all glorious above	Ps 104
		522, 523	Glorious things of thee are spoken	S

Week of 8 Epiphany

SUN	MP	429	I'll praise my Master while I've breath	Ps 146
		552, 553	Fight the good fight with all thy might (sts. 1-2)	E
		511	Holy Spirit, ever living	E
		555	Lead on, O King eternal	E
		561	Stand up, stand up for Jesus	E
	EP	643	My God, how wonderful thou art	G
		682	I love thee, Lord, but not because	G
		704	O thou who camest from above	G
		642	Jesus, the very thought of thee	G
MON	MP	372	Praise to the living God	L
		431	The stars declare his glory	L
		617	Eternal Ruler of the ceaseless round	E
	EP	698	Eternal Spirit of the living Christ	G
		709	O God of Bethel, by whose hand	G
		674	Forgive our sins as we forgive	G
		400	All creatures of our God and King (omit sts. 2, 3 & 6)	G
TUE	MP	408	Sing praise to God who reigns above	L
		676	There is a balm in Gilead	S
		594, 595	God of grace and God of glory	S
	EP	701	Jesus, all my gladness (sts. 1-2)	G
		475	God himself is with us (sts. 1-2)	G
		488	Be thou my vision, O Lord of my heart	G
WED	MP	408	Sing praise to God who reigns above	L
		659, 660	O Master, let me walk with thee	E
		647	I know not where the road will lead	E
	EP	667	Sometimes a light surprises	G
		635	If thou but trust in God to guide thee	G
		669	Commit thou all that grieves thee	G
		388	O worship the King, all glorious above	G
		711	Seek ye first the kingdom of God	G
		709	O God of Bethel, by whose hand	G
THU	MP	425	Sing now with joy unto the Lord	L
		393	Praise our great and gracious Lord	L
		695, 696	By gracious powers so wonderfully sheltered	E
		677	God moves in a mysterious way	E

		669	Commit thou all that grieves thee	E
		636, 637	How firm a foundation, ye saints of the Lord	E
	EP	626	Lord, be thy word my rule	G
		711	Seek ye first the kingdom of God	G
		518	Christ is made the sure foundation	G
		709	O God of Bethel, by whose hand	G
		698	Eternal Spirit of the living Christ	G
FRI	MP	630	Thanks to God, whose Word was spoken (omit sts. 3 & 4)	L
		372	Praise to the living God	L
		703	Lead us, O Father, in the paths of peace	S
		482	Lord of all hopefulness, Lord of all joy	S
	EP	344	Lord, dismiss us with thy blessing	G
		392	Come, we that love the Lord	G
SAT	MP	295	Sing praise to our Creator	E
		363	Ancient of Days, who sittest throned in glory	E
		365	Come, thou almighty King	E
		368	Holy Father, great Creator	E
	EP	380	From all that dwell below the skies	Ps 117
		626	Lord, be thy word my rule	G
		634	I call on thee, Lord Jesus Christ	G
		636, 637	How firm a foundation, ye saints of the Lord	G
		628	Help us, O Lord, to learn	G

Week of Last Epiphany

SUN	MP	394, 395	Creating God, your fingers trace	Ps 148
		373	Praise the Lord! ye heavens adore him	Ps 148
		432	O praise ye the Lord! Praise him in the height	Ps 150 & E
		390	Praise to the Lord, the Almighty	Ps 150
		643	My God, how wonderful thou art	L
		551	Rise up, ye saints of God	L
		581	Where charity and love prevail	L
		368	Holy Father, great Creator	E
	EP	473	Lift high the cross	G
		603, 604	When Christ was lifted from the earth	G
		434	Nature with open volume stands	G
		448, 449	O love, how deep, how broad, how high	G
		655	O Jesus, I have promised	G
MON	MP	489	The great Creator of the worlds	E
		443	From God Christ's deity came forth	E
		496, 497	How bright appears the Morning Star	E
		495	Hail, thou once despisèd Jesus!	E
		448, 449	O love, how deep, how broad, how high	E
		630	Thanks to God whose Word was spoken (omit sts. 3 & 4)	E

	EP	386, 387	We sing of God, the mighty source	G
		489	The great Creator of the worlds	G
		476	Can we by searching find out God	G
		496, 497	How bright appears the Morning Star	G
		421	All glory be to God on high	G
TUE	MP	425	Sing now with joy unto the Lord	L
		363	Ancient of Days, who sittest throned in glory	L
		448, 449	O love, how deep, how broad, how high	E
		495	Hail, thou once despisèd Jesus!	E
		455, 456	O love of God, how strong and true	E
		443	From God Christ's deity came forth	E
		476	Can we by searching find out God	E
	EP	75	There's a voice in the wilderness crying	G
		67	Comfort, comfort ye my people	G
		444	Blessed be the God of Israel	G
		122, 123	Alleluia! song of gladness	S
		619	Sing Alleluia forth in duteous praise	S

Ash Wednesday

	MP	152	Kind Maker of the World, O hear	E
		142	Lord, who throughout these forty days	E
		574, 575	Before thy throne, O God, we kneel	E
	EP	151	From deepest woe I cry to thee	Ps 130
		666	Out of the depths I call	Ps 130
		140, 141	Wilt thou forgive that sin, where I begun	G
		641	Lord Jesus, think on me	G
THU	MP	669	Commit all that grieves thee	Ps 37
		706	In your mercy, Lord, you called me	L
		140, 141	Wilt thou forgive that sin, where I begun	S
		145	Now quit your care	S
		143	The glory of these forty days	S
	EP	121	Christ, when for us you were baptized	G
		139	When Jesus went to Jordan's stream	G
		120	The sinless one to Jordan came	G
		116	"I come," the great Redeemer cries	G
FRI	MP	148	Creator of the earth and skies	E
		150	Forty days and forty nights	E
		152	Kind Maker of the world, O hear	E
		144	Lord Jesus, Sun of Righteousness	E
		146, 147	Now let us all with one accord	E & L
	EP	439	What wondrous love is this	G
		549, 550	Jesus calls us; o'er the tumult	G
SAT	MP	408	Sing praise to God who reigns above	L

		298	All who believe and are baptized	E
		294	Baptized in water	E
		151	From deepest woe I cry to thee	E
		295	Sing praise to our Creator	E
		432	O praise ye the Lord! Praise him in the height (omit st. 3)	E
	EP	658	As longs the deer for cooling streams	Ps 42
		439	What wondrous love is this	G
		489	The great Creator of the worlds	G

Week of 1 Lent

SUN	MP	393	Praise our great and gracious Lord	L
		690	Guide me, O thou great Jehovah	L
		434	Nature with open volume stands	E
		471	We sing the praise of him who died	E
		165, 166	Sing, my tongue, the glorious battle	E
		474	When I survey the wondrous cross	E
		441, 442	In the cross of Christ I glory	E
	EP	411	O bless the Lord, my soul	Ps 103
		681	Our God, to whom we turn	S
		697	My God, accept my heart this day	S
		145	Now quit your care	S
MON	MP	690	Guide me, O thou great Jehovah	L
		443	From God Christ's deity came forth	E
		150	Forty days and forty nights	E
		142	Lord, who throughout these forty days	E
		559	Lead us, heavenly Father, lead us	E
		143	The glory of these forty days	E
		476	Can we by searching find out God	E
	EP	138	All praise to you, O Lord	G
		443	From God Christ's deity came forth	G
		487	Come, my Way, my Truth, my Life	G
TUE	MP	140, 141	Wilt thou forgive that sin, where I begun	E
		443	From God Christ's deity came forth	E
		150	Forty days and forty nights	E
		142	Lord, who throughout these forty days	E
	EP	598	Lord Christ, when first thou cam'st to earth	G
		149	Eternal Lord of love, behold your church	S
WED	MP	686	Come, thou fount of every blessing	E
		697	My God, accept my heart this day	E
		144	Lord Jesus, Sun of Righteousness	E
	EP	473	Lift high the cross	G
		297	Descend, O Spirit, purging flame	G
		295	Sing praise to our Creator	G
		603, 604	When Christ was lifted from the earth	G

THU	MP	641	Lord Jesus, think on me	E
		634	I call on thee, Lord Jesus Christ	E
		144	Lord Jesus, Sun of Righteousness	S
	EP	489	The great Creator of the worlds	G
		448, 449	O love, how deep, how broad, how high	G
		530	Spread, O spread, thou mighty word	G
		465, 466	Eternal light, shine in my heart	G
FRI	MP	495	Hail, thou once despisèd Jesus!	E
		634	I call on thee, Lord Jesus Christ	E
		443	From God Christ's deity came forth	E
		559	Lead us, heavenly Father, lead us	E
	EP	121	Christ, when for us you were baptized	G
		139	When Jesus went to Jordan's stream	G
		120	The sinless one to Jordan came	G
		116	"I come," the great Redeemer cries	G
SAT	MP	443	From God Christ's deity came forth	E
		495	Hail, thou once despisèd Jesus!	E
		150	Forty days and forty nights	E
		142	Lord, who throughout these forty days	E
		143	The glory of these forty days	E
	EP	702	Lord, thou hast searched me and dost know	Ps 139
		649, 650	O Jesus, joy of loving hearts	G
		700	O love that casts out fear	G
		692	I heard the voice of Jesus say (st. 2)	G
		678, 679	Surely it is God who saves me	G

Week of 2 Lent

SUN	MP	500	Creator Spirit, by whose aid	E
		516	Come down, O Love divine	E
		656	Blest are the pure in heart	E
	EP	517	How lovely is thy dwelling place	Ps 84
		603, 604	When Christ was lifted from the earth	G
		588, 589	Almighty God, your word is cast	G
		505	O Spirit of Life, O Spirit of God	G
MON	MP	145	Now quit your care	S
		554	'Tis the gift to be simple	S
		143	The glory of these forty days	S
	EP	540	Awake, thou Spirit of the watchmen	G
		673	The first one ever, oh, ever to know (st. 2)	G
		530	Spread, O spread, thou mighty word	G
TUE	MP	146, 147	Now let us all with one accord	S
		144	Lord Jesus, Sun of Righteousness	S

	EP	567	Thine arm, O Lord, in days of old	G
		493	O for a thousand tongues to sing	G
		429	I'll praise my Maker while I've breath	G
WED	MP	641	Lord Jesus, think on me	E
		148	Creator of the earth and skies	E & L
		574, 575	Before thy throne, O God, we kneel	E
	EP	493	O for a thousand tongues to sing	G
		411	O bless the Lord, my soul	G
		567	Thine arm, O Lord, in days of old	G
THU	MP	148	Creator of the earth and skies	E
		641	Lord Jesus, think on me	E
		63, 64	O heavenly Word, eternal Light	E
	EP	455, 456	O love of God, how strong and true	G
		626	Lord, be thy word my rule	G
		628	Help us, O Lord, to learn	G
		457	Thou art the Way, to thee alone	G
FRI	MP	151	From deepest woe I cry to thee	E
		689	I sought the Lord, and afterward I knew	S
		671	Amazing grace! how sweet the sound	S
	EP	634	I call on thee, Lord Jesus Christ	G
		633	Word of God, come down on earth	G
		444	Blessed be the God of Israel	G
SAT	MP	151	From deepest woe I cry to thee	E
		148	Creator of the earth and skies	E
		432	O praise ye the Lord! Praise him in the height (omit st. 3)	E
		671	Amazing grace! how sweet the sound	E
		495	Hail, thou once despisèd Jesus!	E
		686	Come, thou fount of every blessing	E
	EP	664	My Shepherd will supply my need	Ps 23
		645, 646	The King of love my shepherd is	Ps 23
		663	The Lord my God my shepherd is	Ps 23

Week of 3 Lent

SUN	MP	516	Come down, O Love divine	E
		500	Creator Spirit, by whose aid	E
		656	Blest are the pure in heart	E
	EP	411	O bless the Lord, my soul	G
		567	Thine arm, O Lord, in days of old	G
		493	O for a thousand tongues to sing	G
		429	I'll praise my Maker while I've breath	G
		652, 653	Dear Lord and Father of mankind (sts. 1, 4 & 5)	G

MON	MP	635	If thou but trust in God to guide thee	E
		151	From deepest woe I cry to thee	E
		691	My faith looks up to thee	E
		401	The God of Abraham praise	E
	EP	634	I call on thee, Lord Jesus Christ	G
		458	My song is love unknown	G
		443	From God Christ's deity came forth	G
		489	The great Creator of the worlds	G
TUE	MP	401	The God of Abraham praise	E
		393	Praise our great and gracious Lord	E
		634	I call on thee, Lord Jesus Christ	E
	EP	692	I heard the voice of Jesus say (st. 2)	G
		443	From God Christ's deity came forth	G
		649, 650	O Jesus, joy of loving hearts	G
WED	MP	676	There is a balm in Gilead	L & E
		439	What wondrous love is this	E
		448, 449	O love, how deep, how broad, how high	E
		489	The great Creator of the worlds	E
		167	There is a green hill far away (omit sts. 3, 4)	E
		458	My song is love unknown	E
		686	Come, thou fount of every blessing	E
	EP	27, 28	O blest Creator, source of light	G
		692	I heard the voice of Jesus say (st. 3)	G
		490	I want to walk as a child of the light	G
		465, 466	Eternal light, shine in my heart	G
		672	O very God of very God	G
THU	MP	703	Lead us, O Father, in the paths of peace	L
		445, 446	Praise to the Holiest in the height	E
		450, 451	All hail the power of Jesus' Name	E
		432	O praise ye the Lord! Praise him in the height (omit st. 3)	E
		530	Spread, O spread, thou mighty word	E
	EP	419	Lord of all being, throned afar	G
		626	Lord, be thy word my rule	G
FRI	MP	298	All who believe and are baptized	E
		176, 177	Over the chaos of the empty waters	E
		294	Baptized in water	E
		295	Sing praise to our Creator	E
		149	Eternal Lord of love, behold your Church	E
	EP	505	O Spirit of Life, O Spirit of God	G
		626	Lord, be thy word my rule	G
		440	Blessed Jesus, at thy word	G
		628	Help us, O Lord, to learn	G
SAT	MP	680	O God, our help in ages past	Ps 95
		495	Hail, thou once despisèd Jesus!	E
		252	Jesus! Name of wondrous love	E

		60	Creator of the stars of night	E
	EP	389	Let us, with a gladsome mind	Ps 136
		401	The God of Abraham praise	G
		439	What wondrous love is this	G
		505	O Spirit of Life, O Spirit of God	G
		626	Lord, be thy word my rule	G
		440	Blessed Jesus, at thy word	G
		628	Help us, O Lord, to learn	G

Week of 4 Lent

SUN	MP	538	God of mercy, God of grace	Ps 67
		463, 464	He is the Way	S
		689	I sought the Lord, and afterward I knew	S
		681	Our God, to whom we turn	S
		431	The stars declare his glory	Ps 19
		687, 688	A mighty fortress is our God	Ps 46
		448, 449	O love, how deep, how broad, how high	G
MON	MP	149	Eternal Lord of love, behold your Church	S
		638, 639	Come, O thou Traveler unknown	S
		146, 147	Now let us all with one accord	S
	EP	448, 449	O love, how deep, how broad, how high	G
		443	From God Christ's deity came forth	G
		320	Zion, praise thy Savior, singing (sts. 5-6)	G
		343	Shepherd of souls, refresh and bless (sts. 1-2)	G
TUE	MP	151	From deepest woe I cry to thee	E
		140, 141	Wilt thou forgive that sin, where I begun	E
		144	Lord Jesus, Sun of Righteousness	E
	EP	649, 650	O Jesus, joy of loving hearts	G
		669	Commit thou all that grieves thee	G
		690	Guide me, O thou great Jehovah	G
WED	MP	148	Creator of the earth and skies	L
		516	Come down, O Love divine	E
		500	Creator Spirit, by whose aid	E
		228	Holy Spirit, font of light	E
		226, 227	Come, thou Holy Spirit bright	E
	MP	335	I am the bread of life	G
		343	Shepherd of souls, refresh and bless (sts. 1-2)	G
		649, 650	O Jesus, joy of loving hearts	G
THU	MP	574, 575	Before thy throne, O God, we kneel	L
		299	Spirt of God, unleashed on earth	E
		295	Sing praise to our Creator	E
		698	Eternal Spirit of the living Christ	E
		513	Like the murmur of the dove's song	E

	EP	302, 303	Father, we thank thee who hast planted (st. 1)	G
		335	I am the bread of life	G
		343	Shepherd of souls, refresh and bless (sts. 1-2)	G
		320	Zion, praise thy Savior, singing (sts. 5-6)	G
FRI	MP	447	The Christ who died but rose again	E
		623	O what their joy and their glory must be	E
		621, 622	Light's abode, celestial Salem	E
		530	Spread, O spread, thou mighty word	E
		677	God moves in a mysterious way	E
	EP	335	I am the bread of life	G
		320	Zion, praise thy Savior, singing (sts. 5-6)	G
		343	Shepherd of souls, refresh and bless (sts. 1-2)	G
		302, 303	Father, we thank thee who hast planted (st. 1)	G
SAT	MP	393	Praise our great and gracious Lord	E
		401	The God of Abraham praise	E
		709	O God of Bethel, by whose hand	E
	EP	633	Word of God, come down on earth	G
		634	I call on thee, Lord Jesus Christ	G
		628	Help us, O Lord, to learn	G
		632	O Christ, the Word Incarnate	G

Week of 5 Lent

SUN	MP	422	Not far beyond the sea, nor high	E
		546	Awake, my soul, stretch every nerve	E
		552, 553	Fight the good fight with all thy might	E
	EP	675	Take up your cross, the Savior said	G
		484, 485	Praise the Lord through every nation	G
		572	Weary of all trumpeting	G
MON	MP	532, 533	How wondrous and great thy works, God of praise!	E
		143	The glory of these forty days	S
		145	Now quit your care	S
	EP	371	Thou, whose almighty Word	G
		692	I heard the voice of Jesus say (st. 3)	G
		633	Word of God, come down on earth (st. 3)	G
		493	O for a thousand tongues to sing	G
TUE	MP	668	I to the hills will lift mine eyes	Ps 121
		252	Jesus! Name of wondrous love	E
		248, 249	To the Name of our salvation	E
		152	Kind Maker of the world, O hear	S
	EP	493	O for a thousand tongues to sing	G
		567	Thine arm, O Lord, in days of old	G
		633	Word of God, come down on earth	G
		371	Thou, whose almighty Word	G

WED	MP	530	Spread, O spread, thou mighty word	E
		540	Awake, thou Spirit of the watchmen	E
		531	O Spirit of the living God	E
		539	O Zion, haste, thy mission high fulfilling	E
		535	Ye servants of God, your Master proclaim	E
	EP	151	From deepest woe I cry to thee	Ps 130
		666	Out of the depths I call	
		478	Jesus, our mighty Lord	G
		708	Savior, like a shepherd lead us	G
THU	MP	670	Lord, for ever at thy side	Ps 131
		532, 533	How wondrous and great thy works, God of praise!	E
		537	Christ for the world we sing!	E
		544	Jesus shall reign where'er the sun	
	EP	478	Jesus, our mighty Lord	G
		664	My shepherd will supply my need	G
		645, 646	The King of love my shepherd is	G
		663	The Lord my God my shepherd is	G
		121	Christ, when for us you were baptized	G
		139	When Jesus went to Jordan's stream	G
FRI	MP	689	I sought the Lord, and afterward I knew	S
		697	My God, accept my heart this day	S
		681	Our God, to whom we turn	S
	EP	455, 456	O Love of God, how strong and true	G*
		335	I am the bread of life	G*
		567	Thine arm, O Lord, in days of old	G*
		642	Jesus, the very thought of thee	G**
		643	My God, how wonderful thou art	G**
		704	O thou who camest from above	G**

*John 11:1-27   ** John 12:1-10

SAT	MP	677	God moves in a mysterious way	E
		681	Our God, to whom we turn	S
		695, 696	By gracious powers so wonderfully sheltered	S
	EP	658	As longs the deer for cooling streams	Ps 42
		493	O for a thousand tongues to sing	G*
		567	Thine arm, O Lord, in days of old	G*
		455, 456	O Love of God, how strong and true	G*
		457	Thou art the Way, to thee alone	G*
		465, 466	Eternal light, shine in my heart	G**
		490	I want to walk as a child of the light	G**
		692	I heard the voice of Jesus say (st. 3)	G**

*John 11:20-44   ** John 12:37-50

Holy Week

Palm Sunday

	MP	436	Lift up your heads, ye mighty gates	Ps 24
		156	Ride on! ride on in majesty!	L
		545	Lo! what a cloud of witnesses	E
		494	Crown him with may crowns	E
	EP	164	Alone thou goest forth, O Lord	G
		458	My song is love unknown	G
		486	Hosanna to the living Lord!	G
MON	MP	545	Lo! what a cloud of witnesses	E
		474	When I survey the wondrous cross	E
		471	We sing the praise of him who died	E
		160	Cross of Jesus, cross of sorrow	S
	EP	458	My song is love unknown	G
		156	Ride on! ride on in majesty!	G
TUE	MP	434	Nature with open volume stands	S
		441, 442	In the cross of Christ I glory	S
		498	Beneath the cross of Jesus	S
	EP	448, 449	O love, how deep, how broad, how high	G
		167	There is a green hill far away (omit sts. 3, 4)	G
		161	The flaming banners of our King	S
		162	The royal banners go forward	S
WED	MP	158	Ah, holy Jesus, how hast thou offended	S
		164	Alone thou goest forth, O Lord	S
	EP	474	When I survey the wondrous cross	G
		434	Nature with open volume stands	G
		170	To mock your reign, O dearest Lord	S

Maundy Thursday

	MP	339	Deck thyself, my soul, with gladness	E
		315	Thou, who at thy first Eucharist didst pray	E
	EP	315	Thou, who at thy first Eucharist didst pray	G
		171	Go to dark Gethsemane	S
		164	Alone thou goest forth, O Lord	S

Good Friday

	MP	162	The royal banners forward go	E
		160	Cross of Jesus, cross of sorrow	S
		172	Were you there when they crucified my Lord?	S
		168, 169	O sacred head, sore wounded	S

EP	173	O sorrow deep!		G
	172	Were you there when they crucified my Lord?		G
	458	My song is love unknown		G
	163	Sunset to sunrise changes now		S
	161	The flaming banners of our King		S
	159	At the cross her vigil keeping		S

Holy Saturday

MP	173	O sorrow deep!		S
	172	Were you there when they crucified my Lord?		S
	458	My song is love unknown		G
EP	173	O sorrow deep!		S
	172	Were you there when they crucified my Lord?		S
	458	My song is love unknown		S

Easter Week

Easter Day

MP	202	The Lamb's high banquet called to share		L
	174	At the Lamb's high feast we sing		L
	179	"Welcome, happy morning!" age to age shall say		S
	175	Hail thee, festival day! (Easter)		S
EP	187	Through the Red Sea brought at last, Alleluia!		L
	199, 200	Come, ye faithful, raise the strain		L
	207	Jesus Christ is risen today, Alleluia!		G
	208	Alleluia, alleluia, alleluia! The strife is o'er		G
	184	Christ the Lord is risen again!		G
	196, 197	Look there! the Christ, our Brother, comes		G

MON MP	205	Good Christians all, rejoice and sing!		E
	208	Alleluia, alleluia, alleluia! The strife is o'er		E
	185, 186	Christ Jesus lay in death's strong bands		E
	184	Christ the Lord is risen again!		E
	492	Sing, ye faithful, sing with gladness		E
EP	194, 195	Jesus lives! thy terrors now		G
	457	Thou art the Way, to thee alone		G
	463, 464	He is the Way		G
	487	Come, my Way, my Truth, my Life		G
	484, 485	Praise the Lord through every nation		G

TUE MP	208	Alleluia, alleluia, alleluia! The strife is o'er		E
	185, 186	Christ Jesus lay in death's strong bands		E
	298	All who believe and are baptized		E
	296	We know that Christ is raised and dies no more		E

	EP	199, 200	Come ye faithful, raise the strain	G
		187	Through the Red Sea brought at last, Alleluia!	S
		178	Alleluia, alleluia! Give thanks to the risen Lord	S
WED	MP	180	He is risen, he is risen!	S
		211	The whole bright world rejoices now	S
		196, 197	Look there! the Christ, our Brother, comes	S
	EP	392	Come, we that love the Lord	G
		198	Thou hallowed chosen morn of praise	G
		513	Like the murmur of the dove's song	G
THU	MP	184	Christ the Lord is risen again!	E
		208	Alleluia, alleluia, alleluia! The strife is o'er	E
		185, 186	Christ Jesus lay in death's strong bands	E
		205	Good Christians all, rejoice and sing!	E
		492	Sing, ye faithful, sing with gladness	E
	EP	458	My song is love unknown	G
		319	You, Lord, we praise in songs of celebration (st. 2)	G
		176, 177	Over the chaos of the empty waters	S
		191	Alleluia, alleluia! Hearts and voices heavenward raise	S
FRI	MP	207	Jesus Christ is risen today, Alleluia!	E
		205	Good Christians all, rejoice and sing!	E
		208	Alleluia, alleluia, alleluia! The strife is o'er	E
	EP	512	Come, gracious Spirit, heavenly Dove	G
		204	Now the green blade riseth from the buried grain	S
		190	Lift your voice rejoicing, Mary	S
SAT	MP	484, 485	Praise the Lord through every nation	E
		511	Holy Spirit, ever living	E
		506, 507	Praise the Spirit in creation	E
		182	Christ is alive! Let Christians sing	S
	EP	698	Eternal Spirit of the living Christ	G
		193	That Easter day with joy was bright	S

Week of 2 Easter

SUN	MP	429	I'll praise my Maker while I've breath	Ps 146
		51	We the Lord's people, heart and voice uniting	E
		49	Come, let us with our Lord arise	S
		181	Awake and sing the song	S
	EP	457	Thou art the Way, to thee alone	G
		194, 195	Jesus lives! thy terrors now	G
		484, 485	Praise the Lord through every nation	G
MON	MP	371	Thou, whose almighty word	E
		542	Christ is the world's true Light	E
		492	Sing, ye faithful, sing with gladness	E
		208	Alleluia, alleluia, alleluia! The strife is o'er	E

		205	Good Christians all, rejoice and sing!	E
	EP	495	Hail, thou once despisèd Jesus!	G
		483	The head that once was crowned with thorns	G
TUE	MP	542	Christ is the world's true Light	E
		371	Thou, whose almighty word	E
		5	O splendor of God's glory bright	E
	EP	419	Lord of all being, throned afar	G
		484, 485	Praise the Lord through every nation	G
WED	MP	488	Be thou my vision, O Lord of my heart	E
		665	All my hope on God is founded	E
		475	God himself is with us	E
	EP	657	Love divine, all loves excelling	G
		447	The Christ who died but rose again	S
		181	Awake and sing the song	S
THU	MP	295	Sing praise to our Creator	E
		294	Baptized in water	E
	EP	76	On Jordan's bank the Baptist's cry	G
		70	Herald, sound the note of judgment	G
		67	Comfort, comfort ye my people	G
		75	There's a voice in the wilderness crying	G
FRI	MP	492	Sing, ye faithful, sing with gladness	E
		295	Sing praise to our Creator	E
		294	Baptized in water	E
		5	O splendor of God's glory bright	E
		3, 4	Now that the daylight fills the sky	E
	EP	121	Christ, when for us you were baptized	G
		139	When Jesus went to Jordan's stream	G
		116	"I come," the great Redeemer cries	G
SAT	MP	610	Lord, whose love through humble service	E
		603, 604	When Christ was lifted from the earth	E
		581	Where charity and love prevail	E
		585	Morning glory, starlit sky	E
	EP	380	From all that dwell below the skies	Ps 117
		120	The sinless one to Jordan came	G
		559	Lead us, heavenly Father, lead us	G
		284	O ye immortal throng	G

Week of 3 Easter

SUN	MP	394, 395	Creating God, your fingers trace	Ps 148
		373	Praise the Lord! ye heavens adore him	Ps 148
		432	O praise ye the Lord! Praise him in the height	Ps 150
		390	Praise to the Lord, the Almighty	Ps 150
		610	Lord, whose love through humble service	E

		366	Holy God, we praise thy Name	E
		364	O God, we praise thee, and confess	E
	EP	47	On this day, the first of days	S
		52	This day at thy creating word	S
		50	This is the day the Lord hath made	S
MON	MP	603, 604	When Christ was lifted from the earth	E
		581	Where charity and love prevail	E
		576, 577	God is love, and where true love is	E
		606	Where true charity and love dwell	E
		704	O thou who camest from above	E
	EP	448, 449	O love, how deep, how broad, how high	G
		71, 72	Hark! the glad sound! the Savior comes	G
TUE	MP	700	O love that casts out fear	E
		610	Lord, whose love through humble service	E
		568	Father all loving, who rulest in majesty	E
		573	Father eternal, Ruler of creation	E
		379	God is love, let heaven adore him	E
	EP	567	Thine arm, O Lord, in days of old	G
		448, 449	O love, how deep, how broad, how high	G
		633	Word of God, come down on earth	G
		371	Thou, whose almighty word	G
WED	MP	298	All who believe and are baptized	E
		489	The great Creator of the worlds	E
	EP	567	Thine arm, O Lord, in days of old	G
		493	O for a thousand tongues to sing	G
		371	Thou, whose almighty word	G
THU	MP	698	Eternal Spirit of the living Christ	E
		711	Seek ye first the kingdom of God	E
		302, 303	Father, we thank thee who hast planted (st. 1)	E
		518	Christ is made the sure foundation	E
	EP	661	They cast their nets in Galilee	G
		530	Spread, O spread, thou mighty word	G
FRI	MP	581	Where charity and love prevail	E
		576, 577	God is love, and where true love is	E
		606	Where true charity and love dwell	E
	EP	411	O bless the Lord, my soul!	G
		493	O for a thousand tongues to sing	G
		429	I'll praise my Maker while I've breath	G
		566	From thee all skill and science flow	G
SAT	MP	476	Can we by searching find out God	E
		491	Where is this stupendous stranger?	E
		181	Awake and sing the song	S
	EP	658	As longs the deer for cooling streams	Ps 42
		281	He sat to watch o'er customs paid	G

467	Sing, my soul, his wondrous love	G
469, 470	There's a wideness in God's mercy	G
706	In your mercy, Lord, you called me	G

Week of 4 Easter

SUN	MP	413	New songs of celebration render	Ps 98
		623	O what their joy and their glory must be	E
		621, 622	Light's abode, celestial Salem	E
		400	All creatures of our God and King	E
	EP	411	O bless the Lord, my soul!	Ps 103
		410	Praise, my soul, the King of heaven	Ps 103
		390	Praise to the Lord, the Almighty	Ps 103
		392	Come, we that love the Lord	G
		344	Lord, dismiss us with thy blessing	G
		636, 637	How firm a foundation, ye saints of the Lord	G
		626	Lord, be thy word my rule	G
		628	Help us, O Lord, to learn	G
MON	MP	432	O praise ye the Lord! Praise him in the height (omit st. 3)	E
		326	From glory to glory advancing, we praise thee, O Lord	E
		392	Come, we that love the Lord	E
		344	Lord, dismiss us with thy blessing	E
	EP	458	My song is love unknown	G
		493	O for a thousand tongues to sing	G
		567	Thine arm, O Lord, in days of old	G
		630	Thanks to God whose Word was spoken (omit sts. 3, 4)	G
TUE	MP	421	All glory be to God on high	E
		492	Sing, ye faithful, sing with gladness	E
		483	The head that once was crowned with thorns	E
		495	Hail, thou once despisèd Jesus! (sts. 1-2)	E
		307	Lord, enthroned in heavenly splendor (omit sts. 2, 3)	E
	EP	560	Remember your servants, Lord	G
		593	Lord, make us servants of your peace	G
		437, 438	Tell out, my soul, the greatness of the Lord	G
WED	MP	422	Not far beyond the sea, nor high	E
		628	Help us, O Lord, to learn	E
		440	Blessèd Jesus, at thy word	E
	EP	593	Lord, make us servants of your peace	G
		674	"Forgive our sins as we forgive"	G
		347	Go forth for God; go to the world in peace	G
		603, 604	When Christ was lifted from the earth	G
		602	Jesu, Jesu, fill us with your love	G
THU	MP	298	All who believe and are baptized	E

		296	We know that Christ is raised and dies no more	E
		294	Baptized in water	E
		432	O praise ye the Lord! Praise him in the height	
			(omit st. 3)	E
	EP	626	Lord, be thy word my rule	G
		628	Help us, O Lord, to learn	G
		344	Lord, dismiss us with thy blessing	G
		392	Come, we that love the Lord	G
		636, 637	How firm a foundation, ye saints of the Lord	G
FRI	MP	574, 575	Before thy throne, O God, we kneel	E
		296	We know that Christ is raised and dies no more	E
		298	All who believe and are baptized	E
		542	Christ is the world's true Light	E
		529	In Christ there is no East or West	E
	EP	567	Thine arm, O Lord, in days of old	G
		493	O for a thousand tongues to sing	G
		371	Thou, whose almighty word	G
		538	God of mercy, God of grace	G
		566	From thee all skill and science flow	G
SAT	MP	674	"Forgive our sins as we forgive"	E
		576, 577	God is love, and where true love is	E
		581	Where charity and love prevail	E
		606	Where true charity and love dwell	E
		426	Songs of praise the angels sang	E
		402, 403	Let all the world in every corner sing	E
	EP	702	Lord, thou hast searched me and dost know	Ps 139
		271, 272	The great forerunner of the morn	G
		444	Blessed be the God of Israel	G
		70	Herald, sound the note of judgment	G

Week of 5 Easter

SUN	MP	436	Lift up your heads, ye mighty gates	Ps 24
		432	O praise ye the Lord! Praise him in the height	E
		295	Sing praise to our Creator	E
		49	Come, let us with our Lord arise	S
		182	Christ is alive! Let Christians sing	S
	EP	517	How lovely is thy dwelling-place	Ps 84
		711	Seek ye first the kingdom of God	G
		698	Eternal Spirit of the living Christ	G
MON	MP	5	O splendor of God's glory bright	E
		564, 565	He who would valiant be	E
		655	O Jesus, I have promised	E
	EP	643	My God, how wonderful thou art	G
		382	King of glory, King of peace	G
		641	Lord Jesus, think on me	G

		469, 470	There's a wideness in God's mercy	G
TUE	MP	425	Sing now with joy unto the Lord	L
		187	Through the Red Sea brought at last, Alleluia!	L
		363	Ancient of Days, who sittest throned in glory	L
		593	Lord, make us servants of your peace	E
		610	Lord, whose love through humble service	E
		707	Take my life, and let it be	E
	EP	588, 589	Almighty God, your word is cast	G
		626	Lord, by thy word my rule	G
		440	Blessèd Jesus, at thy word	G
		505	O Spirit of Life, O Spirit of God	G
		536	God has spoken to his people	G
WED	MP	616	Hail to the Lord's Anointed	Ps 72
		544	Jesus shall reign where'er the sun	Ps 72
		409	The spacious firmament on high	L
		431	The stars declare his glory	L
		547	Awake, O sleeper, rise from death	E
	EP	603, 604	When Christ was lifted from the earth	G
		529	In Christ there is no East or West	G
		669	Commit thou all that grieves thee	G
THU	MP	408	Sing praise to God who reigns above	L
		5	O splendor of God's glory bright	E
		3, 4	Now that the daylight fills the sky	E
		593	Lord, make us servants of your peace	E
		347	Go forth for God; go to the world in peace	E
	EP	493	O for a thousand tongues to sing	G
		429	I'll praise my Maker while I've breath	G
		371	Thou, whose almighty word	G
FRI	MP	581	Where charity and love prevail	E
		576, 577	God is love, and where true love is	E
		606	Where true charity and love dwell	E
	EP	411	O bless the Lord, my soul!	G
		567	Thine arm, O Lord, in days of old	G
		635	If thou but trust in God to guide thee	G
		566	From thee all skill and science flow	G
SAT	MP	187	Through the Red Sea brought at last, Alleluia!	L
		628	Help us, O Lord, to learn	E
		632	O Christ, the Word Incarnate	E
		631	Book of books, our people's strength	E
		603, 604	When Christ was lifted from the earth	E
		472	Hope of the world, thou Christ	E
	EP	664	My Shepherd will supply my need	Ps 23
		645, 646	The King of love my shepherd is	Ps 23
		663	The Lord my God my shepherd is	Ps 23
		528	Lord, you give the great commission	G

| | | 320 | Zion, praise thy Savior, singing (sts. 5-6) | G |
| | | 300 | Glory, love, and praise, and honor | G |

Week of 6 Easter

SUN	MP	409	The spacious firmament on high	L
		431	The stars declare his glory	L
		492	Sing, ye faithful, sing with gladness	E
	EP	290	Come, ye thankful people, come (sts. 2-4)	G
		588, 589	Almighty God, your word is cast	G
		534	God is working his purpose out	G
		600, 601	O day of God, draw nigh	G
		24	The day thou gavest, Lord, is ended	G
MON	MP	393	Praise our great and gracious Lord	L
		687, 688	A mighty fortress is our God	E
		584	God, you have given us power to sound	E
		628	Help us, O Lord, to learn	E
		636, 637	How firm a foundation, ye saints of the Lord	E
	EP	484, 485	Praise the Lord through every nation	G
		675	Take up your cross, the Savior said	G
		254	You are the Christ, O Lord	G
TUE	MP	416	For the beauty of the earth	E
		610	Lord, whose love through humble service	E
		628	Help us, O Lord, to learn	E
		605	What does the Lord require	E
		292	O Jesus, crowned with all renown	E
	EP	698	Eternal Spirit of the living Christ	G
		360, 361	Only-begotten, Word of God eternal	G
		711	Seek ye first the kingdom of God	G
		518	Christ is made the sure foundation	G
WED	MP	667	Sometimes a light surprises	G
		665	All my hope on God is founded	G
		711	Seek ye first the kingdom of God	G

Eve of Ascension

	EP	374	Come, let us join our cheerful songs	E
		417, 418	This is the feast of victory for our God	E
		307	Lord, enthroned in heavenly splendor (omit sts. 2, 3)	E
		495	Hail, thou once despisèd Jesus!	E

Ascension Day

	MP	215	See the Conqueror mounts in triumph	E
		220, 221	O Lord Most High, eternal King	E
		450, 451	All hail the power of Jesus' Name!	E

		483	The head that once was crowned with thorns	E
		214	Hail the day that sees him rise, Alleluia!	S
		216	Hail thee, festival day!	S
	EP	436	Lift up your heads, ye mighty gates	Ps 24
		222	Rejoice, the Lord of life ascends	G
		217, 218	A hymn of glory let us sing	G
FRI	MP	460, 461	Alleluia! sing to Jesus!	E
		495	Hail, thou once despisèd Jesus!	E
		443	From God Christ's deity came forth	E
		219	The Lord ascendeth up on high	E
	EP	129, 130	Christ, upon the mountain peak	G
		136, 137	O wondrous type! O vision fair	G
		133, 134	O Light of Light, Love given birth	G
SAT	MP	680	O God, our help in ages past	Ps 90
		443	From God Christ's deity came forth	E
		495	Hail, thou once despisèd Jesus!	E
		219	The Lord ascendeth up on high	E
		460, 461	Alleluia! sing to Jesus!	E
	EP	389	Let us, with a gladsome mind	Ps 136
		448, 449	O love, how deep, how broad, how high	G
		566	From thee all skill and science flow	G
		371	Thou, whose almighty word	G

Week of 7 Easter

SUN	MP	538	God of mercy, God of grace	Ps 67
		432	O praise ye the Lord! Praise him in the height	E
		481	Rejoice, the Lord is King!	S
		49	Come, let us with our Lord arise	S
		450, 451	All hail the power of Jesus' Name!	S
	EP	409	The spacious firmament on high	Ps 19
		431	The stars declare his glory	Ps 19
		687, 688	A mighty fortress is our God	Ps 46
		492	Sing, ye faithful, sing with gladness	G
		535	Ye servants of God, your Master proclaim	G
		609	Where cross the crowded ways of life	G
MON	MP	443	From God Christ's deity came forth	E
		326	From glory to glory advancing, we praise thee, O Lord	E
		704	O thou who camest from above	E
	EP	458	My song is love unknown	G
		478	Jesus, our mighty Lord	G
		655	O Jesus, I have promised	G
		564, 565	He who would valiant be	G
TUE	MP	443	From God Christ's deity came forth	E
		401	The God of Abraham praise	E

	EP	540	Awake, thou Spirit of the watchmen	G
		541	Come, labor on	G
		528	Lord, you give the great commission	G
		535	Ye servants of God, your Master proclaim	G
WED	MP	228	Holy Spirit, font of light	L
		226, 227	Come, thou Holy Spirit bright	L
		443	From God Christ's deity came forth	E
		460, 461	Alleluia! sing to Jesus!	E
	EP	536	God has spoken to his people	G
		531	O Spirit of the living God	G
THU	MP	495	Hail, thou once despisèd Jesus!	E
		460, 461	Alleluia! sing to Jesus!	E
		443	From God Christ's deity came forth	E
	EP	602	Jesu, Jesu, fill us with your love	G
		603, 604	When Christ was lifted from the earth	G
		610	Lord, whose love through humble service	G
FRI	MP	478	Jesus, our mighty Lord	L
		460, 461	Alleluia! sing to Jesus!	E
		443	From God Christ's deity came forth	E
		447	The Christ who died but rose again	E
	EP	642	Jesus, the very thought of thee	G
		701	Jesus, all my gladness	G
		488	Be thou my vision, O Lord of my heart	G
		382	King of glory, King of peace	G
SAT	MP	460, 461	Alleluia! sing to Jesus!	E
		686	Come, thou fount of every blessing	E
		495	Hail, thou once despisèd Jesus!	E
		574, 575	Before thy throne, O God, we kneel	G
		500	Creator Spirit, by whose aid	G

Eve of Pentecost

	EP	294	Baptized in water	E
		432	O praise ye the Lord! Praise him in the height	E

Day of Pentecost

	MP	226, 227	Come, thou Holy Spirit bright	L
		500	Creator Spirit, by whose aid	L
		501, 502	O Holy Spirit, by whose breath	L
		223, 224	Hail this joyful day's return	S
		225	Hail thee, festival day!	S
		506, 507	Praise the Spirit in creation	S
		513	Like the murmur of the dove's song	S
	EP	230	A mighty sound from heaven	S
		229	Spirit of mercy, truth, and love	S

		506, 507	Praise the Spirit in creation	S

Eve of Trinity Sunday

		388	O worship the King, all glorious above!	Ps 104
		369	How wondrous great, how glorious bright	L
		422	Not far beyond the sea, nor high	E

Trinity Sunday

	MP	363	Ancient of Days, who sittest throned in glory	S
		362	Holy, holy, holy! Lord God Almighty!	S
		370	I bind unto myself today	S
		365	Come, thou almighty King	S
	EP	29, 30	O Trinity of blessèd light	S
		295	Sing praise to our Creator	S
		371	Thou, whose almighty word	S

The Season After Pentecost

Proper 1

MON	MP	393	Praise our great and gracious Lord	L
		425	Sing now with joy unto the Lord	L
		363	Ancient of Days, who sittest throned in glory	L
		704	O thou who camest from above	E
		151	From deepest woe I cry to thee	E
	EP	258	Virgin-born, we bow before thee	G
		500	Creator Spirit, by whose aid	G
		228	Holy Spirit, font of light	G
		5	O splendor of God's glory bright	G
TUE	MP	668	I to the hills will lift mine eyes	Ps 121
		483	The head that once was crowned with thorns	E
		548	Soldiers of Christ, arise	E
		552, 553	Fight the good fight with all thy might	E
		563	Go forward, Christian soldier	E
		561	Stand up, stand up for Jesus	E
	EP	574, 575	Before thy throne, O God, we kneel	G
WED	MP	593	Lord, make us servants of your peace	E
		656	Blest are the pure in heart	E
		707	Take my life, and let it be	E
	EP	666	Out of the depths I call	Ps 130

		151	From deepest woe I cry to thee	Ps 130
		366	Holy God, we praise thy Name	G
		364	O God, we praise thee, and confess	G
		454	Jesus came, adored by angels	G
THU	MP	670	Lord, for ever at thy side	Ps 131
		628	Help us, O Lord, to learn	E
		627	Lamp of our feet, whereby we trace	E
		630	Thanks to God whose Word was spoken	E
		631	Book of books, our people's strength	E
	EP	665	All my hope on God is founded	G
		574, 575	Before thy throne, O God, we kneel	G
		701	Jesus, all my gladness	G
		667	Sometimes a light surprises	G
		709	O God of Bethel, by whose hand	G
		711	Seek ye first the kingdom of God	G
FRI	MP	552, 553	Fight the good fight with all thy might (sts. 1-2)	E
		511	Holy Spirit, ever living	E
		555	Lead on, O King eternal	E
		561	Stand up, stand up for Jesus	E
	EP	68	Rejoice! rejoice, believers	G
		701	Jesus, all my gladness	G
		61, 62	"Sleepers, wake!" A voice astounds us	G
SAT	MP	636, 637	How firm a foundation, ye saints of the Lord	E
		635	If thou but trust in God to guide thee	E
		669	Commit thou all that grieves thee	E
	EP	388	O worship the King, all glorious above!	Ps 104
		596	Judge eternal, throned in splendor	G
		574, 575	Before thy throne, O God, we kneel	G
		661	They cast their nets in Galilee	G

Proper 2

MON	MP	472	Hope of the world, thou Christ	E
		489	The great Creator of the worlds	E
		439	What wondrous love is this	E
		458	My song is love unknown	E
		423	Immortal, invisible, God only wise	E
	EP	392	Come, we that love the Lord	G
		344	Lord, dismiss us with thy blessing	G
		148	Creator of the earth and skies	G
		574, 575	Before thy throne, O God, we kneel	G
TUE	MP	368	Holy Father, great Creator	E
	EP	567	Thine arm, O Lord, in days of old	G
		493	O for a thousand tongues to sing	G
		566	From thee all skill and science flow	G

WED	MP	359	God of the prophets, bless the prophets' heirs!	E
		511	Holy Spirit, ever living	E
	EP	24	The day thou gavest, Lord, is ended	G
		380	From all that dwell below the skies	G
		339	Deck thyself, my soul, with gladness	G
		344	Lord, dismiss us with thy blessing	G
THU	MP	535	Ye servants of God, your Master proclaim	E
		511	Holy Spirit, ever living	E
	EP	148	Creator of the earth and skies	G
		598	Lord Christ, when first thou cam'st to earth	G
		590	O Jesus Christ, may grateful hymns be rising	G
FRI	MP	511	Holy Spirit, ever living	E
		359	God of the prophets, bless the prophets' heirs!	E
	EP	656	Blest are the pure in heart	G
		437, 438	Tell out, my soul, the greatness of the Lord!	G
		670	Lord, for ever at thy side	G
SAT	MP	527	Singing songs of expectation	L
		552, 553	Fight the good fight with all thy might (sts. 1-2)	E
		701	Jesus, all my gladness (sts. 1-2)	E
		574, 575	Before thy throne, O God, we kneel	E
		582, 583	O holy city, seen of John	E
	EP	380	From all that dwell below the skies	G
		339	Deck thyself, my soul, with gladness	G
		202	The Lamb's high banquet called to share	G

Proper 3

SUN	MP	394, 395	Creating God, your fingers trace	Ps 148
		373	Praise the Lord! ye heavens adore him	Ps 148
		432	O praise ye the Lord! Praise him in the height	Ps 150
		390	Praise to the Lord, the Almighty	Ps 150
		686	Come, thou fount of every blessing	E
		624	Jerusalem the golden	E
		619	Sing alleluia forth in duteous praise	E
	EP	344	Lord, dismiss us with thy blessing	G
		392	Come, we that love the Lord	G
		500	Creator Spirit, by whose aid	G
		516	Come down, O Love divine	G
MON	MP	372	Praise to the living God!	L
		431	The stars declare his glory	L
		636, 637	How firm a foundation, ye saints of the Lord	E
		472	Hope of the world, thou Christ	E
	EP	675	Take up your cross, the Savior said	G
		484, 485	Praise the Lord through every nation	G
		654	Day by Day	G

TUE	MP	408	Sing praise to God who reigns above	L
		686	Come, thou fount of every blessing	E
		697	My God, accept my heart this day	E
	EP	645, 646	The King of love my shepherd is	G
		469, 470	There's a wideness in God's mercy	G
		664	My Shepherd will supply my need	G
WED	MP	408	Sing praise to God who reigns above	L
		659, 660	O Master, let me walk with thee	E
		559	Lead us, heavenly Father, lead us	S
	EP	140, 141	Wilt thou forgive that sin, where I begun	G
		641	Lord Jesus, think on me	G
		467	Sing, my soul, his wondrous love	G
		469, 470	There's a wideness in God's mercy	G
		693	Just as I am, without one plea	G
THU	MP	669	Commit thou all that grieves thee	Ps 37
		425	Sing now with joy unto the Lord	L
		393	Praise our great and gracious Lord	L
		326	From glory to glory advancing, we praise thee, O Lord	E
		657	Love divine, all loves excelling	E
		505	O Spirit of Life, O Spirit of God	E
	EP	488	Be thou my vision, O Lord of my heart	G
		402, 403	Let all the world in every corner sing	S
		31, 32	Most Holy God, the Lord of heaven	S
FRI	MP	630	Thanks to God whose Word was spoken (omit sts. 3, 4)	L
		372	Praise to the living God!	L
		6, 7	Christ, whose glory fills the skies	E
		465, 466	Eternal light, shine in my heart	E
		5	O splendor of God's glory bright	E
		419	Lord of all being, throned afar	E
		381	Thy strong word did cleave the darkness	E
	EP	707	Take my life, and let it be	G
		701	Jesus, all my gladness	G
		475	God himself is with us (sts. 1-2)	G
SAT	MP	209	We walk by faith, and not by sight	E
		194, 195	Jesus lives! thy terrors now	E
		623	O what their joy and their glory must be	E
		621, 622	Light's abode, celestial Salem	E
		620	Jerusalem, my happy home	E
	EP	658	As longs the deer for cooling streams	Ps 42
		609	Where cross the crowded ways of life	G
		582, 583	O holy city, seen of John	G
		574, 575	Before thy throne, O God, we kneel	G
		437, 438	Tell out, my soul, the greatness of the Lord!	G

Proper 4

SUN	MP	413	New songs of celebration render	Ps 98
		393	Praise our great and gracious Lord	L
		425	Sing now with joy unto the Lord	L
		363	Ancient of Days, who sittest throned in glory	L
	EP	411	O bless the Lord, my soul!	Ps 103
		410	Praise, my soul, the King of heaven	Ps 103
		390	Praise to the Lord, the Almighty	Ps 103
		615	"Thy kingdom come!" on bended knee	G
		443	From God Christ's deity came forth	G
		489	The great Creator of the worlds	G
		439	What wondrous love is this	G
MON	MP	298	All who believe and are baptized	E
		213	Come away to the skies	E
		176, 177	Over the chaos of the empty waters	E
		296	We know that Christ is raised and dies no more	E
		492	Sing, ye faithful, sing with gladness	E
	EP	541	Come, labor on	G
		655	O Jesus, I have promised	G
TUE	MP	408	Sing praise to God who reigns above	L
		705	As those of old their first fruits brought	L
		559	Lead us, heavenly Father, lead us	E
		656	Blest are the pure in heart	E
		500	Creator Spirit, by whose aid	E
	EP	415	When all thy mercies, O my God	G
		396, 397	Now thank we all our God	G
		567	Thine arm, O Lord, in days of old	G
WED	MP	574, 575	Before thy throne, O God, we kneel	E
		148	Creator of the earth and skies	E
		144	Lord Jesus, Sun of Righteousness	E
		683, 684	O for a closer walk with God	E
	EP	61, 62	"Sleepers, wake!" A voice astounds us	G
		59	Hark! A thrilling voice is sounding	G
		53	Once he came in blessing	G
THU	MP	705	As those of old their first fruits brought	E
		292	O Jesus, crowned with all renown	E
		610	Lord, whose love through humble service	E
		474	When I survey the wondrous cross	E
		707	Take my life, and let it be	E
		477	All praise to thee, for thou, O King divine	E
	EP	698	Eternal Spirit of the living Christ	G
		695, 696	By gracious powers so wonderfully sheltered	G
		709	O God of Bethel, by whose hand	G
		711	Seek ye first the kingdom of God	G
FRI	MP	705	As those of old their first fruits brought	L

		393	Praise our great and gracious Lord	L
		425	Sing now with joy unto the Lord	L
	EP	641	Lord Jesus, think on me	G
		670	Lord, for ever at thy side	G
		140, 141	Wilt thou forgive that sin, where I begun	G
		656	Blest are the pure in heart	G
		437, 438	Tell out, my soul, the greatness of the Lord!	G
SAT	MP	709	O God of Bethel, by whose hand	L
		9	Not here for high and holy things	E
		292	O Jesus, crowned with all renown	E
		610	Lord, whose love through humble service	E
		705	As those of old their first fruits brought	E
	EP	702	Lord, thou hast searched me and dost know	Ps 139
		480	When Jesus left his Father's throne	G
		655	O Jesus, I have promised	G
		701	Jesus, all my gladness	G

Proper 5

SUN	MP	436	Lift up your heads, ye mighty gates	Ps 24
		282, 283	Christ, the fair glory of the holy angels	E
		48	O day of radiant gladness	S
		47	On this day, the first of days	S
	EP	517	How lovely is thy dwelling-place	Ps 84
		567	Thine arm, O Lord, in days of old	G
		493	O for a thousand tongues to sing	G
		300	Glory, love, and praise, and honor	G
		472	Hope of the world, thou Christ	G
MON	MP	617	Eternal Ruler of the ceaseless round	E
		548	Soldiers of Christ, arise	E
	EP	493	O for a thousand tongues to sing	G
		633	Word of God, come down on earth	G
		567	Thine arm, O Lord, in days of old	G
		495	Hail, thou once despisèd Jesus!	G
		458	My song is love unknown	G
TUE	MP	594, 595	God of grace and God of glory	S
		367	Round the Lord in glory seated	S
		11	Awake, my soul, and with the sun	S
	EP	489	The great Creator of the worlds	G
		448, 449	O love, how deep, how broad, how high	G
		469, 470	There's a wideness in God's mercy	G
		382	King of glory, King of peace	G
WED	MP	616	Hail to the Lord's Anointed	Ps 72
		544	Jesus shall reign where'er the sun	Ps 72
		659, 660	O Master, let me walk with thee	E
		647	I know not where the road will lead	E

	EP	592	Teach me, my God and King	G
		482	Lord of all hopefulness, Lord of all joy	G
		611	Christ the worker	G
THU	MP	677	God moves in a mysterious way	E
		669	Commit thou all that grieves thee	E
		695, 696	By gracious powers so wonderfully sheltered	E
		636, 637	How firm a foundation, ye saints of the Lord	E
	EP	458	My song is love unknown	G
		71, 72	Hark! the glad sound! the Savior comes	G
		65	Prepare the way, O Zion	G
		74	Blest be the King whose coming	G
		486	Hosanna to the living Lord!	G
		436	Lift up your heads, ye mighty gates	G
FRI	MP	703	Lead us, O Father, in the paths of peace	S
		482	Lord of all hopefulness, Lord of all joy	S
		551	Rise up, ye saints of God!	S
	EP	590	O Jesus Christ, may grateful hymns be rising	G
		598	Lord Christ, when first thou cam'st to earth	G
		458	My song is love unknown	G
		51	We the Lord's people, heart and voice uniting (sts. 1-2)	G
Sat	MP	295	Sing praise to our Creator	E
		363	Ancient of Days, who sittest throned in glory	E
		365	Come thou almighty King	E
		368	Holy Father, great Creator	E
	EP	664	My Shepherd will supply my need	Ps 23
		645, 646	The King of love my shepherd is	Ps 23
		663	The Lord my God my shepherd is	Ps 23
		271, 272	The great forerunner of the morn	G
		444	Blessed be the God of Israel	G
		70	Herald, sound the note of judgment	G

Proper 6

SUN	MP	532, 533	How wondrous and great thy works, God of praise!	E
		181	Awake, and sing the song	E
	EP	480	When Jesus left his Father's throne	G
		670	Lord, for ever at thy side	G
		574, 575	Before thy throne, O God, we kneel	G
		645, 646	The King of love my shepherd is	G
MON	MP	492	Sing, ye faithful, sing with gladness	E
		483	The head that once was crowned with thorns	E
		484, 485	Praise the Lord through every nation	E
		495	Hail, thou once despisèd Jesus!	E

	EP	598	Lord Christ, when first thou cam'st to earth	G
		170	To mock your reign, O dearest Lord	G
		495	Hail, thou once despisèd Jesus! (sts. 1-2)	G
		483	The head that once was crowned with thorns	G
TUE	MP	437, 438	Tell out, my soul, the greatness of the Lord!	L
		359	God of the prophets, bless the prophets' heirs!	E
		233, 234	The eternal gifts of Christ the King	E
		521	Put forth, O God, thy Spirit's might	E
	EP	591	O God of earth and altar	G
		596	Judge eternal, throned in splendor	G
		665	All my hope on God is founded	G
		573	Father eternal, Ruler of creation	G
WED	MP	230	A mighty sound from heaven	E
		506, 507	Praise the Spirit in creation	E
		531	O Spirit of the living God	E
		514	To thee, O Comforter divine	E
		511	Holy Spirit, ever living	E
	EP	401	The God of Abraham praise	G
		526	Let saints on earth in concert sing	G
THU	MP	483	The head that once was crowned with thorns	E
		492	Sing, ye faithful, sing with gladness	E
		448, 449	O love, how deep, how broad, how high	E
		455, 456	O Love of God, how strong and true	E
	EP	450, 451	All hail the power of Jesus' Name!	G
		254	You are the Christ, O Lord	G
		707	Take my life, and let it be	G
		475	God himself is with us (sts. 1-2)	G
FRI	MP	299	Spirit of God, unleashed on earth	E
		295	Sing praise to our Creator	E
		294	Baptized in water	E
		432	O praise ye the lord! Praise him in the height (omit st. 3)	E
		296	We know that Christ is raised and dies no more	E
	EP	454	Jesus came, adored by angels	G
		53	Once he came in blessing	G
		598	Lord Christ, when first thou cam'st to earth	G
		655	O Jesus, I have promised	G
		564, 565	He who would valiant be	G
SAT	MP	680	O God, our help in ages past	Ps 90
		707	Take my life, and let it be	E
		701	Jesus, all my gladness	E
		475	God himself is with us	E
	EP	389	Let us, with a gladsome mind	Ps 136
		73	The King shall come when morning dawns	G
		57, 58	Lo! he comes, with clouds descending	G

		454	Jesus came, adored by angels	G
		53	Once he came in blessing	G

Proper 7

SUN	MP	538	God of mercy, God of grace	Ps 67
		636, 637	How firm a foundation, ye saints of the Lord	E
		584	God, you have given us power to sound	E
		655	O Jesus, I have promised	E
		561	Stand up, stand up for Jesus	E
	EP	409	The spacious firmament on high	Ps 19
		431	The stars declare his glory	Ps 19
		678, 688	A mighty fortress is our God	Ps 46
		655	O Jesus, I have promised	G
		564, 565	He who would valiant be	G
		707	Take my life, and let it be	G
MON	MP	182	Christ is alive! Let Christians sing	S
		614	Christ is the King! O friends upraise	S
		647	I know not where the road will lead	S
		452	Glorious the day when Christ was born	S
	EP	61, 62	"Sleepers, wake!" A voice astounds us	G
		68	Rejoice! rejoice, believers	G
		53	Once he came in blessing	G
TUE	MP	483	The head that once was crowned with thorns	E
		495	Hail, thou once despisèd Jesus!	E
		366	Holy God, we praise thy Name	E
		364	O God, we praise thee, and confess	E
		421	All glory be to God on high	E
	EP	598	Lord Christ, when first thou cam'st to earth	G
		448, 449	O love, how deep, how broad, how high	G
		458	My song is love unknown	G
WED	MP	243	When Stephen, full of power and grace	E
	EP	320	Zion, praise thy Savior, singing	G
		322	When Jesus died to save us	G
		329, 331	Now, my tongue, the mystery telling (sts. 1-4)	G
THU	MP	401	The God of Abraham praise	E
		709	O God of Bethel, by whose hand	E
	EP	483	The head that once was crowned with thorns	G
		43	All praise to thee, my God, this night	G
		659, 660	O Master, let me walk with thee	G
FRI	MP	401	The God of Abraham praise	E
		365	Come, thou almighty King	S
		396, 397	Now thank we all our God	S

	EP	495	Hail, thou once despisèd Jesus! (sts. 1-2)	G
		434	Nature with open volume stands	G
		448, 449	O love, how deep, how broad, how high	G
SAT	MP	425	Sing now with joy unto the Lord	E
		527	Singing songs of expectation	S
		555	Lead on, O King eternal	S
	EP	171	Go to dark Gethsemane	G
		158	Ah, holy Jesus, how hast thou offended	G
		164	Alone thou goest forth, O Lord	G
		284	O ye immortal throng	G

Proper 8

SUN	MP	401	The God of Abraham praise	E
		393	Praise our great and gracious Lord	E
		634	I call on thee, Lord Jesus Christ	E
	EP	414	God, my King, thy might confessing	Ps 145
		404	We will extol you, ever-blessèd Lord	Ps 145
		641	Lord Jesus, think on me	G
		574, 575	Before thy throne, O God, we kneel	G
		444	Blessed be the God of Israel	G
		271, 272	The great forerunner of the morn	G
MON	MP	243	When Stephen, full of power and grace	E
		240, 241	Hearken to the anthem glorious	E
		236	King of the martyrs' noble band	E
		237	Let us now our voices raise	E
	EP	171	Go to dark Gethsemane	G
		158	Ah, holy Jesus, how hast thou offended	G
		164	Alone thou goest forth, O Lord	G
TUE	MP	668	I to the hills will lift mine eyes	Ps 121
		298	All who believe and are baptized	E
		176, 177	Over the chaos of the empty waters	E
		299	Spirit of God, unleashed on earth	E
		295	Sing praise to our Creator	E
		296	We know that Christ is raised and dies no more	E
	EP	171	Go to dark Gethsemane	G
		483	The head that once was crowned with thorns	G
		495	Hail, thou once despisèd Jesus! (sts. 1-2)	G
WED	MP	574, 575	Before thy throne, O God, we kneel	E
		656	Blest are the pure in heart	E
		299	Spirit of God, unleashed on earth	E
		432	O praise ye the Lord! Praise him in the height (omit st. 3)	E
	EP	666	Out of the depths I call	Ps 130
		151	From deepest woe I cry to thee	Ps 130

		171	Go to dark Gethsemane	G
		170	To mock your reign, O dearest Lord	G
		168, 169	O sacred head, sore wounded	G
		483	The head that once was crowned with thorns	G
		598	Lord Christ, when first thou cam'st to earth	G
THU	MP	670	Lord, for ever at thy side	Ps 131
		297	Descend, O Spirit, purging flame	E
		294	Baptized in water	E
		176, 177	Over the chaos of the empty waters	E
		298	All who believe and are baptized	E
		296	We know that Christ is raised and dies no more	E
	EP	458	My song is love unknown	G
		171	Go to dark Gethsemane	G
		158	Ah, holy Jesus, how hast thou offended	G
FRI	MP	256	A light from heaven shown around	E
		255	We sing the glorious conquest	E
	EP	598	Lord Christ, when first thou cam'st to earth	G
		164	Alone thou goest forth, O Lord	G
SAT	MP	255	We sing the glorious conquest	E
		256	A light from heaven shown around	E
	EP	388	O worship the King, all glorious above!	Ps 104
		167	There is a green hill far away (omit sts. 3, 4)	G
		165, 166	Sing, my tongue, the glorious battle	G
		172	Were you there when they crucified my Lord?	G
		168, 169	O sacred head, sore wounded	G
		161	The flaming banners of our King	G
		162	The royal banners forward go	G

Proper 9

SUN	MP	429	I'll praise my Maker while I've breath	Ps 146
		686	Come, thou fount of every blessing	E
		167	There is a green hill far away (omit sts. 3, 4)	E
		458	My song is love unknown	E
		455, 456	O Love of God, how strong and true	E
	EP	339	Deck thyself, my soul, with gladness	G
		202	The Lamb's high banquet called to share	G
MON	MP	255	We sing the glorious conquest	E
		256	A light from heaven shone around	E
	EP	160	Cross of Jesus, cross of sorrow	G
		163	Sunset to sunrise changes now	G
		474	When I survey the wondrous cross	G
		168, 169	O sacred head, sore wounded	G
		458	My song is love unknown	G
TUE	MP	528	Lord, you give the great commission	E

		521	Put forth, O God, thy Spirit's might	E
		538	God of mercy, God of grace	E
	EP	492	Sing, ye faithful, sing with gladness	G
		455, 456	O Love of God, how strong and true	G
		448, 449	O love, how deep, how broad, how high	G
		468	It was poor little Jesus	G
		284	O ye immortal throng	G
WED	MP	603, 604	When Christ was lifted from the earth	E
		532, 533	How wondrous and great thy works, God of praise!	E
		529	In Christ there is no East or West	E
		537	Christ for the world we sing!	E
		539	O Zion, haste, thy mission high fulfilling	E
	EP	343	Shepherd of souls, refresh and bless	G
		208	Alleluia, alleluia, alleluia! The strife is o'er	G
		305, 306	Come, risen Lord, and deign to be our guest	G
		184	Christ the Lord is risen again!	G
THU	MP	532, 533	How wondrous and great thy works, God of praise!	E
		537	Christ for the world we sing!	E
		529	In Christ there is no East or West	E
		603, 604	When Christ was lifted from the earth	E
		539	O Zion, haste, thy mission high fulfilling	E
	EP	208	Alleluia, alleluia, alleluia! The strife is o'er (omit st. 3)	G
		182	Christ is alive! Let Christians sing	G
		184	Christ the Lord is risen again!	G
		193	That Easter day with joy was bright (sts. 1-3)	G
FRI	MP	530	Spread, O spread, thou mighty word	E
		492	Sing ye faithful, sing with gladness	E
		448, 449	O love, how deep, how broad, how high	E
		297	Descend, O Spirit, purging flame	E
		366	Holy God, we praise thy Name	E
		364	O God, we praise thee, and confess	E
	EP	120	The sinless one to Jordan came	G
		121	Christ, when for us you were baptized	G
		139	When Jesus went to Jordan's stream	G
		116	"I come," the great Redeemer cries	G
SAT	MP	532, 533	How wondrous and great thy works, God of praise!	E
		529	In Christ there is no East or West	E
		603, 604	When Christ was lifted from the earth	E
	EP	380	From all that dwell below the skies	Ps 117
		661	They cast their nets in Galilee	G
		549, 550	Jesus calls us; o'er the tumult	G
		567	Thine arm, O Lord, in days of old	G
		448, 449	O love, how deep, how broad, how high	G
		421	All glory be to God on high	G

Proper 10

SUN	MP	530	Spread, O spread, thou mighty word	E
		531	O Spirit of the living God	E
		535	Ye servants of God, your Master proclaim	E
		539	O Zion, haste, thy mission high fulfilling	E
		248, 249	To the Name of our salvation	E
		252	Jesus! Name of wondrous love!	E
	EP	598	Lord Christ, when first thou cam'st to earth	G
		590	O Jesus Christ, may grateful hymns be rising	G
MON	MP	705	As those of old their first fruits brought	E
		701	Jesus, all my gladness (sts. 1-2)	E
	EP	567	Thine arm, O Lord, in days of old	G
		493	O for a thousand tongues to sing	G
		371	Thou, whose almighty word	G
		429	I'll praise my Maker while I've breath	G
TUE	MP	544	Jesus shall reign where'er the sun	E
		429	I'll praise my Maker while I've breath	E
	EP	411	O bless the Lord, my soul!	G
		566	From thee all skill and science flow	G
		567	Thine arm, O Lord, in days of old	G
		493	O for a thousand tongues to sing	G
WED	MP	531	O Spirit of the living God	E
		614	Christ is the King! O friends upraise	S
		182	Christ is alive! Let Christians sing	S
		1, 2	Father, we praise thee, now the night is over	S
	EP	281	He sat to watch o'er customs paid	G
		469, 470	There's a wideness in God's mercy	G
		467	Sing, my soul, his wondrous love	G
		706	In your mercy, Lord, you called me	G
THU	MP	669	Commit thou all that grieves thee	Ps 37
		528	Lord, you give the great commission	E
		532, 533	How wondrous and great thy works, God of praise!	E
		531	O Spirit of the living God	E
		537	Christ for the world we sing!	E
	EP	630	Thanks to God whose Word was spoken (omit sts. 3, 4)	G
		493	O for a thousand tongues to sing	G
		381	Thy strong word did cleave the darkness	G
		458	My song is love unknown	G
		567	Thine arm, O Lord, in days of old	G
FRI	MP	439	What wondrous love is this	E
		489	The great Creator of the worlds	E
		476	Can we by searching find out God	E
		443	From God Christ's deity came forth	E

	EP	528	Lord, you give the great commission	G
		540	Awake, thou Spirit of the watchmen	G
		493	O for a thousand tongues to sing	G
		590	O Jesus Christ, may grateful hymns be rising	G
		567	Thine arm, O Lord, in days of old	G
SAT	MP	448, 449	O love, how deep, how broad, how high	E
		455, 456	O Love of God, how strong and true	E
		478	Jesus, our mighty Lord	E
	EP	658	As longs the deer for cooling streams	Ps 42
		452	Glorious the day when Christ was born	G
		529	In Christ there is no East or West	G
		603, 604	When Christ was lifted from the earth	G
		500	Creator Spirit, by whose aid	G
		516	Come down, O Love divine	G

Proper 11

SUN	MP	413	New songs of celebration render	Ps 98
		677	God moves in a mysterious way	E
		610	Lord, whose love through humble service	E
		707	Take my life, and let it be	E
	EP	411	O bless the Lord, my soul!	Ps 103
		410	Praise, my soul, the King of heaven	Ps 103
		390	Praise to the Lord, the Almighty	Ps 103
		551	Rise up, ye saints of God!	G
		541	Come, labor on	G
		326	From glory to glory advancing, we praise thee, O Lord	G
MON	MP	515	Holy Ghost, dispel our sadness	E
		499	Lord God, you now have set your servant free	E
		532, 533	How wondrous and great thy works, God of praise!	E
		529	In Christ there is no East or West	E
	EP	588, 589	Almighty God, your word is cast	G
		536	God has spoken to his people	G
		541	Come, labor on	G
		505	O Spirit of Life, O Spirit of God	G
		530	Spread, O spread, thou mighty word	G
TUE	MP	389	Let us, with a gladsome mind	E
		398	I sing the almighty power of God	E
		388	O worship the King, all glorious above!	E
		423	Immortal, invisible, God only wise	E
	EP	588, 589	Almighty God, your word is cast	G
		536	God has spoken to his people	G
		290	Come, ye thankful people, come (sts. 2-4)	G
		24	The day thou gavest, Lord, is ended	G
		534	God is working his purpose out	G

WED	MP	532, 533	How wondrous and great thy works, God of praise!	E
		529	In Christ there is no East or West	E
		531	O Spirit of the living God	E
		537	Christ for the world we sing!	E
		539	O Zion, haste, thy mission high fulfilling	E
	EP	669	Commit thou all that grieves thee	G
		414	God, my King, thy might confessing	G
		375	Give praise and glory unto God	G
THU	MP	603, 604	When Christ was lifted from the earth	E
		394, 395	Creating God, your fingers trace	E
		532, 533	How wondrous and great thy works, God of praise!	E
		529	In Christ there is no East or West	E
		537	Christ for the world we sing!	E
	EP	538	God of mercy, God of grace	Ps 67
		567	Thine arm, O Lord, in days of old	G
		652, 653	Dear Lord and Father of mankind (sts. 1, 4 & 5)	G
		493	O for a thousand tongues to sing	G
		429	I'll praise my Maker while I've breath	G
FRI	MP	539	O Zion, haste, thy mission high fulfilling	E
		532, 533	How wondrous and great thy works, God of praise!	E
		529	In Christ there is no East or West	E
		531	O Spirit of the living God	E
	EP	567	Thine arm, O Lord, in days of old	G
		493	O for a thousand tongues to sing	G
		590	O Jesus Christ, may grateful hymns be rising	G
		566	From thee all skill and science flow	G
SAT	MP	531	O Spirit of the living God	E
		532, 533	How wondrous and great thy works, God of praise!	E
		537	Christ for the world we sing!	E
		529	In Christ there is no East or West	E
		511	Holy Spirit, ever living	E
	EP	702	Lord, thou hast searched me and dost know	Ps 139
		633	Word of God, come down on earth	G
		540	Awake, thou Spirit of the watchmen	G
		528	Lord, you give the great commission	G

Proper 12

SUN	MP	436	Lift up your heads, ye mighty gates	Ps 24
		610	Lord, whose love through humble service	E
		593	Lord, make us servants of your peace	E
		347	Go forth for God; go to the world in peace	E
	EP	517	How lovely is thy dwelling-place	Ps 84
		610	Lord, whose love through humble service	G
		609	Where cross the crowded ways of life	G
		481	Rejoice, the Lord is King!	G

		602	Jesu, Jesu, fill us with your love	G
MON	MP	394, 395	Creating God, your fingers trace	E
		532, 533	How wondrous and great thy works, God of praise!	E
		531	O Spirit of the living God	E
		539	O Zion, haste, thy mission high fulfilling	E
	EP	444	Blessed be the God of Israel	G
		271, 272	The great forerunner of the morn	G
		76	On Jordan's bank the Baptist's cry	G
TUE	MP	531	O Spirit of the living God	E
		537	Christ for the world we sing	E
		539	O Zion, haste, thy mission high fulfilling	E
		394, 395	Creating God, your fingers trace	E
		532, 533	How wondrous and great thy works, God of praise!	E
	EP	472	Hope of the world, thou Christ	G
		708	Savior, like a shepherd lead us	G
		478	Jesus, our mighty Lord	G
		300	Glory, love, and praise, and honor	G
WED	MP	616	Hail to the Lord's Anointed	Ps 72
		544	Jesus shall reign where'er the sun	Ps 72
		11	Awake, my soul, and with the sun	S
		3, 4	Now, that the daylight fills the sky	S
	EP	636, 637	How firm a foundation, ye saints of the Lord	G
		669	Commit thou all that grieves thee	G
		590	O Jesus Christ, may grateful hymns be rising	G
		567	Thine arm, O Lord, in days of old	G
		414	God, my King, thy might confessing	G
THU	MP	295	Sing praise to our Creator	E
		296	We know that Christ is raised and dies no more	E
		298	All who believe and are baptized	E
		294	Baptized in water	E
		432	O praise ye the Lord! Praise him in the height (omit st. 3)	E
	EP	436	Lift up your heads, ye mighty gates	G
		656	Blest are the pure in heart	G
		382	King of glory, King of peace	G
		556, 557	Rejoice, ye pure in heart!	G
		435	At the Name of Jesus (sts. 1-5)	G
FRI	MP	506, 507	Praise the Spirit in creation	E
		492	Sing, ye faithful, sing with gladness	E
		455, 456	O Love of God, how strong and true	E
		448, 449	O love, how deep, how broad, how high	E
	EP	633	Word of God, come down on earth	G
		493	O for a thousand tongues to sing	G
		567	Thine arm, O Lord, in days of old	G
		411	O bless the Lord, my soul!	G
		429	I'll praise my Maker while I've breath	G

SAT	MP	422	Not far beyond the sea, nor high	E
		408	Sing praise to God who reigns above	E
		148	Creator of the earth and skies	E
		455, 456	O Love of God, how strong and true	E
	EP	664	My Shepherd will supply my need	Ps 23
		645, 646	The King of love my shepherd is	Ps 23
		663	The Lord my God my shepherd is	Ps 23
		300	Glory, love, and praise, and honor	G
		320	Zion, praise thy Savior, singing (st. 5-6)	G

Proper 13

SUN	MP	494	Crown him with many crowns	E
		478	Jesus, our mighty Lord	E
		252	Jesus! Name of wondrous love!	E
		60	Creator of the stars of night	E
	EP	477	All praise to thee, for thou, O King divine	G
		489	The great Creator of the worlds	G
		439	What wondrous love is this	G
MON	MP	298	All who believe and are baptized	E
		176, 177	Over the chaos of the empty waters	E
		294	Baptized in water	E
		296	We know that Christ is raised and dies no more	E
		295	Sing praise to our Creator	E
	EP	536	God has spoken to his people	G
		448, 449	O love, how deep, how broad, how high	G
TUE	MP	632	O Christ, the Word Incarnate	E
		630	Thanks to God whose Word was spoken	E
		633	Word to God, come down on earth	E
	EP	633	Word of God, come down on earth	G
		493	O for a thousand tongues to sing	G
		567	Thine arm, O Lord, in days of old	G
		254	You are the Christ, O Lord	G
WED	MP	299	Spirit of God, unleashed on earth	E
		294	Baptized in water	E
		295	Sing praise to our Creator	E
		176, 177	Over the chaos of the empty waters	E
		298	All who believe and are baptized	E
	EP	675	Take up your cross, the Savior said	G
		484, 485	Praise the Lord through every nation	G
THU	MP	532, 533	How wondrous and great thy works, God of praise!	E
		531	O Spirit of the living God	E
		539	O Zion, haste, thy mission high fulfilling	E
	EP	133, 134	O Light of Light, Love given birth	G
		129, 130	Christ upon the mountain peak	G

		136, 137	O wondrous type! O vision fair	G
FRI	MP	408	Sing praise to God who reigns above	E
		683, 684	O for a closer walk with God	E
	EP	567	Thine arm, O Lord, in days of old	G
		493	O for a thousand tongues to sing	G
		448, 449	O love, how deep, how broad, how high	G
		566	From thee all skill and science flow	G
SAT	MP	680	O God, our help in ages past	Ps 90
		360, 361	Only-begotten, Word of God eternal	E
		509	Spirit divine, attend our prayers	S
	EP	389	Let us, with a gladsome mind	Ps 136
		448, 449	O love, how deep, how broad, how high	G
		434	Nature with open volume stands	G
		609	Where cross the crowded ways of life	G
		659, 660	O Master, let me walk with thee	G

Proper 14

SUN	MP	630	Thanks to God whose Word was spoken	E
		628	Help us, O Lord, to learn	E
		632	O Christ, the Word Incarnate	E
		603, 604	When Christ was lifted from the earth	E
		472	Hope of the world, thou Christ	E
	EP	409	The spacious firmament on high	Ps 19
		431	The stars declare his glory	Ps 19
		687, 688	A mighty fortress is our God	Ps 46
		121	Christ, when for us you were baptized	G
		139	When Jesus went to Jordan's stream	G
		116	"I come," the great Redeemer cries	G
		120	The sinless one to Jordan came	G
MON	MP	525	The Church's one foundation	E
		524	I love thy kingdom, Lord	E
		511	Holy Spirit, ever living	E
	EP	574, 575	Before thy throne, O God, we kneel	G
TUE	MP	564, 565	He who would valiant be	E
		552, 553	Fight the good fight with all thy might	E
		563	Go forward, Christian soldier	E
		555	Lead on, O King eternal	E
	EP	587	Our Father, by whose Name	G
		480	When Jesus left his Father's throne	G
		352	O God, to those who here profess	G
		350	O God of love, to thee we bow	G
		353	Your love, O God, has called us here	G
WED	MP	529	In Christ there is no East or West	E
		603, 604	When Christ was lifted from the earth	E

		537	Christ for the world we sing!	E
	EP	655	O Jesus, I have promised	G
		475	God himself is with us	G
		701	Jesus, all my gladness	G
		707	Take my life, and let it be	G
THU	MP	559, 560	O Master, let me walk with thee	E
		647	I know not where the road will lead	
		556, 557	Rejoice, ye pure in heart!	E
		24	The day thou gavest, Lord, is ended (omit st. 1)	E
	EP	659, 660	O Master, let me walk with thee	G
		483	The head that once was crowned with thorns	G
		458	My song is love unknown	G
		477	All praise to thee, for thou, O King divine	G
		474	When I survey the wondrous cross	G
FRI	MP	256	A light from heaven shone around	E
		255	We sing the glorious conquest	E
	EP	633	Word of God, come down on earth	G
		493	O for a thousand tongues to sing	G
		567	Thine arm, O Lord, in days of old	G
		429	I'll praise my Maker while I've breath	G
		371	Thou, whose almighty word	G
SAT	MP	364	O God, we praise thee, and confess	S
		366	Holy God, we praise thy Name	S
		676	There is a balm in Gilead	S
	EP	458	My song is love unknown	G
		71, 72	Hark! the glad sound! the Savior comes	G
		486	Hosanna to the living Lord!	G
		65	Prepare the way, O Zion	G
		74	Blest be the King whose coming	G
		436	Lift up your heads, ye mighty gates	G

Proper 15

		270	Gabriel's message does away	E
SUN	MP	270	Gabriel's message does away	E
		60	Creator of the stars of night	E
		401	The God of Abraham praise	E
		432	O praise ye the Lord! Praise him in the height (omit st. 3)	E
	EP	414	God, my King, thy might confessing	Ps 145
		404	We will extol you, ever-blessèd Lord	Ps 145
		633	Word of God, come down on earth	G
		444	Blessed be the God of Israel	G
		634	I call on thee, Lord Jesus Christ	G
		50	This is the day the Lord hath made	G
MON	MP	530	Spread, O spread, thou mighty word	E
		647	I know not where the road will lead	E

		532, 533	How wondrous and great thy works, God of praise!	E
	EP	486	Hosanna to the living Lord!	G
		51	We the Lord's people, heart and voice uniting (sts. 1-2)	G
		711	Seek ye first the kingdom of God	G
		518	Christ is made the sure foundation	G
		674	"Forgive our sins as we forgive"	G
TUE	MP	668	I to the hills will lift mine eyes	Ps 121
		647	I know not where the road will lead	E
		559	Lead us, heavenly Father, lead us	E
		555	Lead on, O King eternal	E
		563	Go forward, Christian soldier	E
	EP	598	Lord Christ, when first thou cam'st to earth	G
		170	To mock your reign, O dearest Lord	G
		495	Hail, thou once despisèd Jesus!	G
WED	MP	647	I know not where the road will lead	E
		559	Lead us, heavenly Father, lead us	E
		563	Go forward, Christian soldier	E
		555	Lead on, O King eternal	E
		655	O Jesus, I have promised	E
		564, 565	He who would valiant be	E
	EP	666	Out of the depths I call	Ps 130
		151	From deepest woe I cry to thee	Ps 130
		596	Judge eternal, throned in splendor	G
		591	O God of earth and altar	G
		401	The God of Abraham praise	G
		526	Let saints on earth in concert sing	G
THU	MP	670	Lord, for ever at thy side	Ps 131
		455, 456	O Love of God, how strong and true	E
		468	It was poor little Jesus	E
		364	O God, we praise thee, and confess	E
		366	Holy God, we praise thy Name	E
	EP	551	Rise up, ye saints of God!	G
		581	Where charity and love prevail	G
		643	My God, how wonderful thou art	G
		682	I love thee, Lord, but not because	G
		704	O thou who camest from above	G
FRI	MP	564, 565	He who would valiant be	E
		655	O Jesus, I have promised	E
		647	I know not where the road will lead	E
		555	Lead on, O King eternal	E
		563	Go forward, Christian soldier	E
	EP	450, 451	All hail the power of Jesus' Name!	G
		254	You are the Christ, O Lord	G
		707	Take my life, and let it be	G
		705	As those of old their first fruits brought	G

		475	God himself is with us (sts. 1-2)	G
SAT	MP	468	It was poor little Jesus	E
		455, 456	O Love of God, how strong and true	E
		559	Lead us, heavenly Father, lead us	E
		647	I know not where the road will lead	E
	EP	388	O worship the King, all glorious above!	Ps 104
		598	Lord Christ, when first thou cam'st to earth	G
		655	O Jesus, I have promised	G
		53	Once he came in blessing	G
		564, 565	He who would valiant be	G

Proper 16

		429	I'll praise my Maker while I've breath	Ps 146
SUN	MP	429	I'll praise my Maker while I've breath	Ps 146
		294	Baptized in water	E
		295	Sing praise to our Creator	E
		529	In Christ there is no East or West	E
		581	Where charity and love prevail	E
	EP	692	I heard the voice of Jesus say (st. 3)	G
		542	Christ is the world's true Light	G
		490	I want to walk as a child of the light	G
		465, 466	Eternal light, shine in my heart	G
		496, 497	How bright appears the Morning Star	G
MON	MP	255	We sing the glorious conquest	E
		256	A light from heaven shone around	E
	EP	57, 58	Lo! he comes, with clouds descending	G
		454	Jesus came, adored by angels	G
		53	Once he came in blessing	G
TUE	MP	564, 565	He who would valiant be	E
		655	O Jesus, I have promised	E
		647	I know not where the road will lead	E
		555	Lead on, O King eternal	E
		563	Go forward, Christian soldier	E
	EP	68	Rejoice! rejoice, believers	G
		61, 62	"Sleepers, wake!" A voice astounds us	G
WED	MP	635	If thou but trust in God to guide thee	E
		669	Commit thou all that grieves thee	E
		677	God moves in a mysterious way	E
	EP	458	My song is love unknown	G
		643	My God, how wonderful thou art	G
		682	I love thee, Lord, but not because	G
		642	Jesus, the very thought of thee	G
		704	O thou who camest from above	G
THU	MP	608	Eternal Father, strong to save	E
		641	Lord Jesus, think on me	E
		398	I sing the almighty power of God	E

	EP	320	Zion, praise thy Savior, singing	G
		322	When Jesus died to save us	G
		329, 331	Now, my tongue, the mystery telling (sts. 1-4)	G
FRI	MP	566	From thee all skill and science flow	E
		429	I'll praise my Maker while I've breath	E
		411	O bless the Lord, my soul!	E
	EP	171	Go to dark Gethsemane	G
		164	Alone thou goest forth, O Lord	G
		284	O ye immortal throng	G
SAT	MP	536	God has spoken to his people	E
		530	Spread, O spread, thou mighty word	E
		532, 533	How wondrous and great thy works, God of praise!	E
		531	O Spirit of the living God	E
		539	O Zion, haste, thy mission high fulfilling	E
	EP	380	From all that dwell below the skies	Ps 117
		158	Ah, holy Jesus, how hast thou offended	G
		164	Alone thou goest forth, O Lord	G

Proper 17

SUN	MP	394, 395	Creating God, your fingers trace	Ps 148
		373	Praise the Lord! ye heavens adore him	Ps 148
		432	O praise ye the Lord! Praise him in the height (omit st. 3)	Ps 150
		390	Praise to the Lord, the Almighty	Ps 150
		511	Holy Spirit, ever living	E
		359	God of the prophets, bless the prophets' heirs!	E
	EP	401	The God of Abraham praise	G
		439	What wondrous love is this	G
		536	God has spoken to his people	G
		505	O Spirit of Life, O Spirit of God	G
		626	Lord, be thy word my rule	G
MON	MP	603, 604	When Christ was lifted from the earth	E
		568	Father all loving, who rulest in majesty	E
		602	Jesu, Jesu, fill us with your love	E
		529	In Christ there is no East or West	E
	EP	171	Go to dark Gethsemane	G
		164	Alone thou goest forth, O Lord	G
		158	Ah, holy Jesus, how hast thou offended	G
		448, 449	O love, how deep, how broad, how high	G
		495	Hail, thou once despisèd Jesus! (sts. 1-2)	G
TUE	MP	610	Lord, whose love through humble service	E
		628	Help us, O Lord, to learn	E
		704	O thou who camest from above	E

	EP	158	Ah, holy Jesus, how hast thou offended	G
		164	Alone thou goest forth, O Lord	G
WED	MP	574, 575	Before thy throne, O God, we kneel	E
		11	Awake, my soul, and with the sun	E
		3, 4	Now that the daylight fills the sky	E
		694	God be in my head	E
	EP	158	Ah, holy Jesus, how hast thou offended	G
		458	My song is love unknown	G
		495	Hail, thou once despisèd Jesus! (sts. 1-2)	G
		448, 449	O love, how deep, how broad, how high	G
THU	MP	669	Commit thou all that grieves thee	Ps 37
		656	Blest are the pure in heart	E
		574, 575	Before thy throne, O God, we kneel	E
		670	Lord, for ever at thy side	E
		437, 438	Tell out, my soul, the greatness of the Lord!	E
	EP	170	To mock your reign, O dearest Lord	G
		458	My song is love unknown	G
		168, 169	O sacred head, sore wounded	G
		598	Lord Christ, when first thou cam'st to earth	G
		171	Go to dark Gethsemane	G
FRI	MP	574, 575	Before thy throne, O God, we kneel	E
		582, 583	O holy city, seen of John	E
		605	What does the Lord require	E
	EP	167	There is a green hill far away (omit sts. 3, 4)	G
		172	Were you there when they crucified my Lord?	G
		165, 166	Sing, my tongue, the glorious battle	G
		161	The flaming banners of our King	G
		162	The royal banners forward go	G
SAT	MP	462	The Lord will come and not be slow	E
		63, 64	O heavenly Word, eternal Light	E
		615	"Thy kingdom come!" on bended knee	E
	EP	658	As longs the deer for cooling streams	Ps 42
		168, 169	O sacred head, sore wounded	G
		163	Sunset to sunrise changes now	G
		160	Cross of Jesus, cross of sorrow	G

Proper 18

SUN	MP	506, 507	Praise the Spirit in creation	E
		511	Holy Spirit, ever living	E
		484, 485	Praise the Lord through every nation	E
	EP	411	O bless the Lord, my soul!	Ps 103
		410	Praise, my soul, the King of heaven	Ps 103
		390	Praise to the Lord, the Almighty	Ps 103
		121	Christ, when for us you were baptized	G

		139	When Jesus went to Jordan's stream	G
		116	"I come," the great Redeemer cries	G
MON	MP	704	O thou who camest from above	E
		392	Come, we that love the Lord	E
		344	Lord, dismiss us with thy blessing	E
	EP	458	My song is love unknown	G
		172	Were you there when they crucified my Lord?	G
		173	O sorrow deep!	G
		471	We sing the praise of him who died	G
TUE	MP	527	Singing songs of expectation	E
		617	Eternal Ruler of the ceaseless round	E
		694	God be in my head	E
	EP	492	Sing, ye faithful, sing with gladness	G
		455, 456	O Love of God, how strong and true	G
		284	O ye immortal throng	G
		448, 449	O love, how deep, how broad, how high	G
		468	It was poor little Jesus	G
WED	MP	435	At the Name of Jesus	E
		477	All praise to thee, for thou, O King divine	E
		450, 451	All hail the power of Jesus' Name!	E
		483	The head that once was crowned with thorns	E
		252	Jesus! Name of wondrous love!	E
	EP	117, 118	Brightest and best of the stars of the morning	G
		119	As with gladness men of old	G
		491	Where is this stupendous stranger?	G
		496, 497	How bright appears the Morning Star	G
THU	MP	546	Awake, my soul, stretch every nerve	E
		490	I want to walk as a child of the light	E
		465, 466	Eternal light, shine in my heart	E
		6, 7	Christ, whose glory fills the skies	E
		347	Go forth for God; go to the world in peace	E
	EP	246	In Bethlehem a newborn boy	G
		247	Lully, lullay, thou little tiny child	G
FRI	MP	545	Lo! what a cloud of witnesses	E
		546	Awake, my soul, stretch every nerve	E
		422	Not far beyond the sea, nor high	E
		471	We sing the praise of him who died	E
		474	When I survey the wondrous cross	E
		701	Jesus, all my gladness	E
	EP	70	Herald, sound the note of judgment	G
		76	On Jordan's bank the Baptist's cry	G
		75	There's a voice in the wilderness crying	G
		67	Comfort, comfort ye my people	G
SAT	MP	621, 622	Light's abode, celestial Salem	E
		481	Rejoice, the Lord is King!	E

		556, 557	Rejoice, ye pure in heart!	E
		515	Holy Ghost, dispel our sadness	E
		345	Savior, again to thy dear Name we raise	E
	EP	702	Lord, thou hast searched me and dost know	Ps 139
		139	When Jesus went to Jordan's stream	G
		121	Christ, when for us you were baptized	G
		116	"I come," the great Redeemer cries	G
		120	The sinless one to Jordan came	G

Proper 19

SUN	MP	436	Lift up your heads, ye mighty gates	Ps 24
		506, 507	Praise the Spirit in creation	L
		652, 653	Dear Lord and Father of mankind (sts. 1, 4 & 5)	L
		483	The head that once was crowned with thorns	E
		495	Hail, thou once despisèd Jesus!	E
		536	God has spoken to his people	E
		530	Spread, O spread, thou mighty word	E
	EP	517	How lovely is thy dwelling-place	Ps 84
		598	Lord Christ, when first thou cam'st to earth	G
		458	My song is love unknown	G
MON	MP	581	Where charity and love prevail	E
		576, 577	God is love, and where true love is	E
		606	Where true charity and love dwell	E
	EP	120	The sinless one to Jordan came	G
		448, 449	O love, how deep, how broad, how high	G
		284	O ye immortal throng	G
		559	Lead us, heavenly Father, lead us	G
TUE	MP	434	Nature with open volume stands	E
		471	We sing the praise of him who died	E
		165, 166	Sing, my tongue, the glorious battle	E
		474	When I survey the wondrous cross	E
		441, 442	In the cross of Christ I glory	E
		160	Cross of Jesus, cross of sorrow	E
	EP	125, 126	The people who in darkness walked	G
		381	Thy strong word did cleave the darkness	G
		542	Christ is the world's true Light	G
		499	Lord God, you now have set your servant free	G
WED	MP	616	Hail to the Lord's Anointed	Ps 72
		544	Jesus shall reign where'er the sun	Ps 72
		488	Be thou my vision, O Lord of my heart	E
		629	We limit not the truth of God	E
		694	God be in my head	E
	EP	661	They cast their nets in Galilee	G
		549, 550	Jesus calls us; o'er the tumult	G
		567	Thine arm, O Lord, in days of old	G

		493	O for a thousand tongues to sing	G
		448, 449	O love, how deep, how broad, how high	G
THU	MP	518	Christ is made the sure foundation	E
		525	The Church's one foundation	E
		636, 637	How firm a foundation, ye saints of the Lord	E
	EP	560	Remember your servants, Lord	G
		656	Blest are the pure in heart	G
		593	Lord, make us servants of your peace	G
		437, 438	Tell out, my soul, the greatness of the Lord!	G
FRI	MP	500	Creator Spirit, by whose aid	E
		576	Come down, O Love divine	E
		656	Blest are the pure in heart	E
	EP	560	Remember your servants, Lord	G
		543	O Zion, tune thy voice	G
		381	Thy strong word did cleave the darkness	G
		628	Help us, O Lord, to learn	G
SAT	MP	359	God of the prophets, bless the prophets' heirs	L
		535	Ye servants of God, your Master proclaim	E
	EP	663	The Lord my God my shepherd is	Ps 23
		645, 646	The King of love my shepherd is	Ps 23
		664	My Shepherd will supply my need	Ps 23
		628	Help us, O Lord, to learn	G
		626	Lord, be thy word my rule	G

Proper 20

		256	A light from heaven shone around	E
SUN	MP	256	A light from heaven shone around	E
		255	We sing the glorious conquest	E
	EP	70	Herald, sound the note of judgment	G
		76	On Jordan's bank the Baptist's cry	G
MON	MP	593	Lord, make us servants of your peace	E
		347	Go forth for God; go to the world in peace	E
		659, 660	O Master, let me walk with thee	E
	EP	674	"Forgive our sins as we forgive"	G
		593	Lord, make us servants of your peace	G
		603, 604	When Christ was lifted from the earth	G
TUE	MP	202	The Lamb's high banquet called to share	E
		307	Lord, enthroned in heavenly splendor	
			(omit sts. 2, 3)	E
		185, 186	Christ Jesus lay in death's strong bands	E
		174	At the Lamb's high feast we sing	E
	EP	641	Lord Jesus, think on me	G
		27, 28	O blest Creator, source of light	G
WED	MP	581	Where charity and love prevail	E
		606	Where true charity and love dwell	E

		576, 577	God is love, and where true love is	E
	EP	603, 604	When Christ was lifted from the earth	G
		568	Father all loving, who rulest in majesty	G
		394, 395	Creating God, your fingers trace	G
THU	MP	516	Come down, O Love divine	E
		500	Creator Spirit, by whose aid	E
	EP	33, 34, 35	Christ, mighty Savior, Light of all creation	S
		31, 32	Most Holy God, the Lord of heaven	S
		29, 30	O Trinity of blessèd light	S
FRI	MP	350	O God of love, to thee we bow	E
		352	O God, to those who here profess	E
		353	Your love, O God, has called us here	E
		3, 4	Now that the daylight fills the sky	E
		21, 22	O God of truth, O Lord of might	E
	EP	674	"Forgive our sins as we forgive"	G
		581	Where charity and love prevail	G
		400	All creatures of our God and King	
			(omit sts. 2, 3 & 6)	G
		709	O God of Bethel, by whose hand	G
SAT	MP	680	O God, our help in ages past	Ps 90
		5	O splendor of God's glory bright	S
		703	Lead us, O Father, in the paths of peace	S
	EP	389	Let us, with a gladsome mind	Ps 136
		701	Jesus, all my gladness	G
		488	Be thou my vision, O Lord of my heart	G
		475	God himself is with us (sts. 1-2)	G

Proper 21

SUN	MP	538	God of mercy, God of grace	Ps 67
		521	Put forth, O God, thy Spirit's might	E
		528	Lord, you give the great commission	E
	EP	409	The spacious firmament on high	Ps 19
		431	The stars declare his glory	Ps 19
		687, 688	A mighty fortress is our God	Ps 46
		661	They cast their nets in Galilee	G
		530	Spread, O spread, thou mighty word	G
MON	MP	488	Be thou my vision, O Lord of my heart	E
		701	Jesus, all my gladness (sts. 1-2)	E
	EP	709	O God of Bethel, by whose hand	G
		667	Sometimes a light surprises	G
		711	Seek ye first the kingdom of God	G
		635	If thou but trust in God to guide thee	G
		388	O worship the King, all glorious above!	G
		669	Commit thou all that grieves thee	G

TUE	MP	488	Be thou my vision, O Lord of my heart	E
		701	Jesus, all my gladness (sts. 1-2)	E
	EP	711	Seek ye first the kingdom of God	G
		698	Eternal Spirit of the living Christ	G
		709	O God of Bethel, by whose hand	G
WED	MP	703	Lead us, O Father, in the paths of peace	E
		3, 4	Now that the daylight fills the sky	S
		9	Not here for high and holy things	S
	EP	392	Come, we that love the Lord	G
		344	Lord, dismiss us with thy blessing	G
THU	MP	5	O splendor of God's glory bright	S
		8	Morning has broken	S
		11	Awake, my soul, and with the sun	S
	EP	636, 637	How firm a foundation, ye saints of the Lord	G
		522, 523	Glorious things of thee are spoken	G
		628	Help us, O Lord, to learn	G
		626	Lord, be thy word my rule	G
		634	I call on thee, Lord Jesus Christ	G
FRI	MP	546	Awake, my soul, stretch every nerve	E
		552, 553	Fight the good fight with all thy might (sts. 1-2)	E
		422	Not far beyond the sea, nor high	E
	EP	567	Thine arm, O Lord, in days of old	G
		493	O for a thousand tongues to sing	G
		371	Thou, whose almighty word	G
		566	From thee all skill and science flow	G
		410	Praise, my soul, the King of heaven	G
SAT	MP	307	Lord, enthroned in heavenly splendor (omit sts. 2, 3)	E
		522, 523	Glorious things of thee are spoken	E
		690	Guide me, O thou great Jehovah	E
		685	Rock of ages, cleft for me	E
	EP	458	My song is love unknown	G
		478	Jesus, our mighty Lord	G
		564, 565	He who would valiant be	G
		669	Commit thou all that grieves thee	G

Proper 22

SUN	MP	544	Jesus shall reign where'er the sun	E
		429	I'll praise my Maker while I've breath	E
		52	This day at thy creating word	S
		50	This is the day the Lord hath made	S
	EP	414	God, my King, thy might confessing	Ps 145
		404	We will extol you, ever-blessèd Lord	Ps 145
		493	O for a thousand tongues to sing	G

		567	Thine arm, O Lord, in days of old	G
		566	From thee all skill and science flow	G
MON	MP	525	The Church's one foundation	E
		626	Lord, be thy word my rule	E
		408	Sing praise to God who reigns above	E
		683, 684	O for a closer walk with God	E
	EP	429	I'll praise my Maker while I've breath	G
		411	O bless the Lord, my soul!	G
		493	O for a thousand tongues to sing	G
		567	Thine arm, O Lord, in days of old	G
TUE	MP	668	I to the hills will lift mine eyes	Ps 121
		581	Where charity and love prevail	E
		606	Where true charity and love dwell	E
		576, 577	God is Love, and where true love is	E
	EP	567	Thine arm, O Lord, in days of old	G
		493	O for a thousand tongues to sing	G
		410	Praise, my soul, the King of heaven	G
		411	O bless the Lord, my soul!	G
		566	From thee all skill and science flow	G
WED	MP	322	When Jesus died to save us	E
		320	Zion, praise thy Savior, singing	E
		329, 331	Now, my tongue, the mystery telling (sts. 1-4)	E
		339	Deck thyself, my soul, with gladness	E
	EP	666	Out of the depths I call	Ps 130
		151	From deepest woe I cry to thee	Ps 130
		281	He sat to watch o'er customs paid	G
		706	In your mercy, Lord, you called me	G
		469, 470	There's a wideness in God's mercy	G
		467	Sing, my soul, his wondrous love	G
THU	MP	670	Lord, for ever at thy side	Ps 131
		506, 507	Praise the Spirit in creation	E
		501, 502	O Holy Spirit, by whose breath	E
		228	Holy Spirit, font of light	E
		505	O Spirit of Life, O Spirit of God	E
	EP	590	O Jesus Christ, may grateful hymns be rising	G
		493	O for a thousand tongues to sing	G
		567	Thine arm, O Lord, in days of old	G
		429	I'll praise my Maker while I've breath	G
		566	From thee all skill and science flow	G
FRI	MP	513	Like the murmur of the dove's song	E
		295	Sing praise to our Creator	E
		576, 577	God is Love, and where true love is	E
		581	Where charity and love prevail	E
		606	Where true charity and love dwell	E
	EP	633	Word of God, come down on earth	G

		493	O for a thousand tongues to sing	G
		567	Thine arm, O Lord, in days of old	G
		371	Thou, whose almighty word	G
		429	I'll praise my Maker while I've breath	G
SAT	MP	521	Put forth, O God, thy Spirit's might	E
		295	Sing praise to our Creator	E
		576, 577	God is Love, and where true love is	E
		581	Where charity and love prevail	E
		606	Where true charity and love dwell	E
	EP	388	O worship the King, all glorious above!	Ps 104
		472	Hope of the world, thou Christ	G
		541	Come, labor on	G
		540	Awake, thou Spirit of the watchmen	G
		478	Jesus, our mighty Lord	G

Proper 23

SUN	MP	429	I'll praise my Maker while I've breath	Ps 146
		398	I sing the almighty power of God	E
		423	Immortal, invisible, God only wise	E
		389	Let us, with a gladsome mind	E
	EP	643	My God, how wonderful thou art	G
		641	Lord Jesus, think on me	G
		382	King of glory, King of peace	G
		469, 470	There's a wideness in God's mercy	G
MON	MP	612	Gracious Spirit, Holy Ghost	E
		602	Jesu, Jesu, fill us with your love	E
		585	Morning glory, starlit sky	E
	EP	528	Lord, you give the great commission	G
		540	Awake, thou Spirit of the watchmen (sts. 2-3)	G
		541	Come, labor on	G
		535	Ye servants of God, your Master proclaim	G
TUE	MP	513	Like the murmur of the dove's song	E
		531	O Spirit of the living God	E
		501, 502	O Holy Spirit, by whose breath	E
	EP	655	O Jesus, I have promised	G
		563	Go forward, Christian soldier	G
		530	Spread, O spread, thou mighty word	G
WED	MP	531	O Spirit of the living God	E
		513	Like the murmur of the dove's song	E
		505	O Spirit of Life, O Spirit of God	E
		521	Put forth, O God, thy Spirit's might	E
		694	God be in my head	E
	EP	563	Go forward, Christian soldier	G
		564, 565	He who would valiant be	G
		535	Ye servants of God, your Master proclaim	G

THU	MP	521	Put forth, O God, thy Spirit's might	E
		513	Like the murmur of the dove's song	E
		531	O Spirit of the living God	E
		505	O Spirit of Life, O Spirit of God	E
		694	God be in my head	E
	EP	675	Take up your cross, the Savior said	G
		484, 485	Praise the Lord through every nation	G
		609	Where cross the crowded ways of life	G
		661	They cast their nets in Galilee	G
		572	Weary of all trumpeting	G
FRI	MP	455, 456	O Love of God, how strong and true	E
		492	Sing, ye faithful, sing with gladness	E
		452	Glorious the day when Christ was born	E
		686	Come, thou fount of every blessing	E
		671	Amazing grace! how sweet the sound	E
	EP	458	My song is love unknown	G
		493	O for a thousand tongues to sing	G
		371	Thou, whose almighty Word	G
		429	I'll praise my Maker while I've breath	G
SAT	MP	492	Sing, ye faithful, sing with gladness	E
		445, 446	Praise to the Holiest in the height	E
		191	Alleluia, alleluia! Hearts and voices heavenward raise	E
		455, 456	O Love of God, how strong and true	E
		204	Now the green blade riseth from the buried grain	E
	EP	380	From all that dwell below the skies	Ps 117
		271, 272	The great forerunner of the morn	G
		444	Blessed be the God of Israel	G
		67	Comfort, comfort ye my people	G
		76	On Jordan's bank the Baptist's cry	G
		70	Herald, sound the note of judgment	G
		536	God has spoken to his people	G

Proper 24

SUN	MP	394, 395	Creating God, your fingers trace	Ps 148 & E
		531	O Spirit of the living God	E
		532, 533	How wondrous and great thy works, God of praise!	E
		537	Christ for the world we sing!	E
		539	O Zion, haste, thy mission high fulfilling	E
	EP	540	Awake, thou Spirit of the watchmen (sts. 2-3)	G
		541	Come, labor on	G
		528	Lord, you give the great commission	G
		535	Ye servants of God, your Master proclaim	G
		531	O Spirit of the living God	G
MON	MP	621, 622	Light's abode, celestial Salem	E
		204	Now the green blade riseth from the buried grain	E

		194, 195	Jesus lives! thy terrors now	E
	EP	596	Judge eternal, throned in splendor	G
		598	Lord Christ, when first thou cam'st to earth	G
TUE	MP	458	My song is love unknown	L
		164	Alone thou goest forth, O Lord	L
		621, 622	Light's abode, celestial Salem	E
		194, 195	Jesus lives! thy terrors now	E
		188, 189	Love's redeeming work is done	E
	EP	692	I heard the voice of Jesus say (st. 1)	G
		74	Blest be the King whose coming	G
		457	Thou art the Way, to thee alone	G
		476	Can we by searching find out God	G
WED	MP	188, 189	Love's redeeming work is done	E
		621, 622	Light's abode, celestial Salem	E
		194, 195	Jesus lives! thy terrors now	E
		366	Holy God, we praise thy Name	E
		364	O God, we praise thee, and confess	E
	EP	458	My song is love unknown	G
		567	Thine arm, O Lord, in days of old	G
		493	O for a thousand tongues to sing	G
THU	MP	669	Commit thou all that grieves thee	Ps 37
		705	As those of old their first fruits brought	E
		9	Not here for high and holy things	E
		292	O Jesus, crowned with all renown	E
	EP	538	God of mercy, God of grace	G
		537	Christ for the world we sing!	G
		371	Thou, whose almighty word	G
FRI	MP	617	Eternal Ruler of the ceaseless round	E
		552, 553	Fight the good fight with all thy might (sts. 1-2)	E
		614	Christ is the King! O friends upraise	E
	EP	516	Come down, O Love divine	G
		500	Creator Spirit, by whose aid	G
SAT	MP	603, 604	When Christ was lifted from the earth	E
		576, 577	God is Love, and where true love is	E
		581	Where charity and love prevail	E
		606	Where true charity and love dwell	E
	EP	658	As longs the deer for cooling streams	Ps 42
		392	Come, we that love the Lord	G
		344	Lord, dismiss us with thy blessing	G

Proper 25

SUN	MP	294	Baptized in water	E
		295	Sing praise to our Creator	E

		176, 177	Over the chaos of the empty waters	E
		298	All who believe and are baptized	E
		296	We know that Christ is raised and dies no more	E
	EP	551	Rise up, ye saints of God!	G
		581	Where charity and love prevail	G
		610	Lord, whose love through humble service	G
		602	Jesu, Jesu, fill us with your love	G
MON	MP	307	Lord, enthroned in heavenly splendor (omit sts. 2, 3)	E
		194, 195	Jesus lives! thy terrors now	E
		57, 58	Lo! he comes, with clouds descending	E
		454	Jesus came, adored by angels	E
	EP	500	Creator Spirit, by whose aid	G
		516	Come down, O Love divine	G
		529	In Christ there is no East or West	G
		603, 604	When Christ was lifted from the earth	G
TUE	MP	367	Round the Lord in glory seated	E
		362	Holy, holy, holy! Lord God Almighty!	E
		401	The God of Abraham praise	E
		643	My God, how wonderful thou art	E
		657	Love divine, all loves excelling	E
	EP	588, 589	Almighty God, your word is cast	G
		536	God has spoken to his people	G
		541	Come, labor on	G
WED	MP	374	Come, let us join our cheerful songs	E
		417, 418	This is the feast of victory for our God	E
		439	What wondrous love is this	E
	EP	588, 589	Almighty God, your word is cast	G
		505	O Spirit of Life, O Spirit of God	G
		536	God has spoken to his people	G
THU	MP	417, 418	This is the feast of victory for our God	E
		374	Come, let us join our cheerful songs	E
		439	What wondrous love is this	E
		495	Hail, thou once despisèd Jesus!	E
		434	Nature with open volume stands	E
	EP	588, 589	Almighty God, your word is cast	G
		505	O Spirit of Life, O Spirit of God	G
FRI	MP	686	Come, thou fount of every blessing	E
		473	Lift high the cross	E
		697	My God, accept my heart this day	E
	EP	588, 589	Almighty God, your word is cast	G
		290	Come, ye thankful people, come (sts. 2-4)	G
SAT	MP	286	Who are these like stars appearing	E
		275	Hark! the sound of holy voices	E
		535	Ye servants of God, your Master proclaim	E
		624	Jerusalem the golden	E

EP	702	Lord, thou hast searched me and dost know	Ps 139
	588, 589	Almighty God, your word is cast	G
	24	The day thou gavest, Lord, is ended	G
	615	"Thy kingdom come!" on bended knee	G

Proper 26

SUN	MP	436	Lift up your heads, ye mighty gates	Ps 24
		49	Come, let us with our Lord arise	E
		48	O day of radiant gladness	E
		51	We the Lord's people, heart and voice uniting	E
	EP	517	How lovely is thy dwelling-place	Ps 84
		709	O God of Bethel, by whose hand	G
		711	Seek ye first the kingdom of God	G
		667	Sometimes a light surprises	G
		635	If thou but trust in God to guide thee	G
MON	MP	63, 64	O heavenly Word, eternal Light	E
		53	Once he came in blessing	E
		454	Jesus came, adored by angels	E
	EP	588, 589	Almighty God, your word is cast	G
		536	God has spoken to his people	G
		290	Come, ye thankful people, come (sts. 2-4)	G
		392	Come, we that love the Lord	G
		505	O Spirit of Life, O Spirit of God	G
TUE	MP	402, 403	Let all the world in every corner sing	L
		392	Come, we that love the Lord	L
		420	When in our music God is glorified	L
		494	Crown him with many crowns	E
		481	Rejoice, the Lord is King!	E
	EP	573	Father eternal, Ruler of creation	G
		24	The day thou gavest, Lord, is ended	G
		462	The Lord will come and not be slow	G
		600, 601	O day of God, draw nigh	G
		615	"Thy kingdom come!" on bended knee	G
WED	MP	616	Hail to the Lord's Anointed	Ps 72
		544	Jesus shall reign where'er the sun	Ps 72
		282, 283	Christ, the fair glory of the holy angels	E
		5	O splendor of God's glory bright	S
	EP	489	The great Creator of the worlds	G
		439	What wondrous love is this	G
		443	From God Christ's deity came forth	G
THU	MP	439	What wondrous love is this	E
		287	For all the saints, who from their labors rest (sts. 1-3)	E
		434	Nature with open volume stands	E
		181	Awake and sing the song	E

		253	Give us the wings of faith to rise	E
	EP	444	Blessed be the God of Israel	G
		271, 272	The great forerunner of the morn	G
		76	On Jordan's bank the Baptist's cry	G
		70	Herald, sound the note of judgment	G
FRI	MP	181	Awake and sing the song	E
		532, 533	How wondrous and great thy works, God of praise!	E
	EP	320	Zion, praise thy Savior, singing (sts. 5-6)	G
		690	Guide me, O thou great Jehovah	G
		300	Glory, love, and praise, and honor	G
SAT	MP	596	Judge eternal, throned in splendor	E
		483	The head that once was crowned with thorns	E
		494	Crown him with many crowns	E
		481	Rejoice, the Lord is King!	E
	EP	664	My Shepherd will supply my need	Ps 23
		645, 646	The King of love my shepherd is	Ps 23
		663	The Lord my God my shepherd is	Ps 23
		669	Commit thou all that grieves thee	G
		636, 637	How firm a foundation, ye saints of the Lord	G
		689	I sought the Lord, and afterward I knew	G
		375	Give praise and glory unto God	G

Proper 27

SUN	MP	49	Come, let us with our Lord arise	E
		48	O day of radiant gladness	E
		47	On this day, the first of days	E
		52	This day at thy creating word	E
		50	This is the day the Lord hath made	E
	EP	202	The Lamb's high banquet called to share	G
		339	Deck thyself, my soul, with gladness	G
MON	MP	425	Sing now with joy unto the Lord	L
		393	Praise our great and gracious Lord	L
		690	Guide me, O thou great Jehovah	L
		363	Ancient of Days, who sittest throned in glory	L
		522, 523	Glorious things of thee are spoken	L
		574, 575	Before thy throne, O God, we kneel	E
	EP	656	Blest are the pure in heart	G
		382	King of glory, King of peace	G
		436	Lift up your heads, ye mighty gates	G
		556, 557	Rejoice, ye pure in heart!	G
		435	At the Name of Jesus (sts. 1-5)	G
TUE	MP	709	O God of Bethel, by whose hand	L
		596	Judge eternal, throned in splendor	E
		591	O God of earth and altar	E
		573	Father eternal, Ruler of creation	E

	EP	544	Jesus shall reign where'er the sun	G
		537	Christ for the world we sing!	G
		469, 470	There's a wideness in God's mercy	G
WED	MP	631	Book of books, our people's strength	L
		630	Thanks to God whose Word was spoken	L
		627	Lamp of our feet, whereby we trace	L
		591	O God of earth and altar	E
		573	Father eternal, Ruler of creation	E
		596	Judge eternal, throned in splendor	E
	EP	472	Hope of the world, thou Christ	G
		567	Thine arm, O Lord, in days of old	G
		320	Zion, praise thy Savior, singing (sts. 5-6)	G
		300	Glory, love, and praise, and honor	G
		411	O bless the Lord, my soul!	G
THU	MP	439	What wondrous love is this	E
		202	The Lamb's high banquet called to share	E
		434	Nature with open volume stands	E
		619	Sing alleluia forth in duteous praise	E
	EP	536	God has spoken to his people	G
		448, 449	O love, how deep, how broad, how high	G
FRI	MP	596	Judge eternal, throned in splendor	E
		483	The head that once was crowned with thorns	E
		494	Crown him with many crowns	E
	EP	254	You are the Christ, O Lord	G
		443	From God Christ's deity came forth	G
		525	The Church's one foundation	G
SAT	MP	680	O God, our help in ages past	Ps 90
		286	Who are these like stars appearing	E
		279	For thy dear saints, O Lord	E
	EP	389	Let us, with a gladsome mind	Ps 136
		675	Take up your cross, the Savior said	G
		484, 485	Praise the Lord through every nation	G
		572	Weary of all trumpeting	G

Proper 28

SUN	MP	538	God of mercy, God of grace	Ps 67 & E
		532, 533	How wondrous and great thy works, God of praise!	E
		531	O Spirit of the living God	E
		530	Spread, O spread, thou mighty word	E
		539	O Zion, haste, thy mission high fulfilling	E
	EP	409	The spacious firmament on high	Ps 19
		431	The stars declare his glory	Ps 19
		687, 688	A mighty fortress is our God	Ps 46
		488	Be thou my vision, O Lord of my heart	G
		701	Jesus, all my gladness	G

		475	God himself is with us (sts. 1-2)	G
MON	MP	63, 64	O heavenly Word, eternal Light	E
		53	Once he came in blessing	E
		454	Jesus came, adored by angels	E
	EP	129, 130	Christ upon the mountain peak	G
		133, 134	O Light of Light, Love given birth	G
		136, 137	O wondrous type! O vision fair	G
TUE	MP	582, 583	O holy city, seen of John	E
		623	O what their joy and their glory must be	E
		620	Jerusalem, my happy home	E
		624	Jerusalem the golden	E
		621, 622	Light's abode, celestial Salem	E
	EP	567	Thine arm, O Lord, in days of old	G
		566	From thee all skill and science flow	G
		371	Thou, whose almighty word	G
WED	MP	582, 583	O holy city, seen of John	E
		621, 622	Light's abode, celestial Salem	E
		624	Jerusalem the golden	E
		519, 520	Blessèd city, heavenly Salem	E
		620	Jerusalem, my happy home	E
	EP	434	Nature with open volume stands	G
		455, 456	O Love of God, how strong and true	G
		448, 449	O love, how deep, how broad, how high	G
THU	MP	624	Jerusalem the golden	E
		620	Jerusalem, my happy home	E
		623	O what their joy and their glory must be	E
		621, 622	Light's abode, celestial Salem	E
	EP	480	When Jesus left his Father's throne	G
		670	Lord, for ever at thy side	G
		574, 575	Before thy throne, O God, we kneel	G
FRI	MP	462	The Lord will come and not be slow	E
		73	The King shall come when morning dawns	E
		63, 64	O heavenly Word, eternal Light	E
		454	Jesus came, adored by angels	E
	EP	480	When Jesus left his Father's throne	G
		645, 646	The King of love my shepherd is	G
		469, 470	There's a wideness in God's mercy	G
		593	Lord, make us servants of your peace	G
		581	Where charity and love prevail	G
		576, 577	God is Love, and where true love is	G
SAT	MP	597	O day of peace that dimly shines	L
		6, 7	Christ, whose glory fills the skies	E
		542	Christ is the world's true Light	E
		496, 497	How bright appears the Morning Star	E
		613	Thy kingdom come, O God!	E

		73	The King shall come when morning dawns	E
	EP	674	"Forgive our sins as we forgive"	G
		581	Where charity and love prevail	G
		593	Lord, make us servants of your peace	G
		400	All creatures of our God and King (omit sts. 2, 3 & 6)	G
		406, 407	Most High, omnipotent, good Lord	G

Proper 29

SUN	MP	472	Hope of the world, thou Christ	E
		603, 604	When Christ was lifted from the earth	E
		380	From all that dwell below the skies	E
		532, 533	How wondrous and great thy works, God of praise!	E
		531	O Spirit of the living God	E
	EP	414	God, my King, thy might confessing	Ps 145
		404	We will extol you, ever-blessèd Lord	Ps 145
		481	Rejoice, the Lord is King!	G
MON	MP	472	Hope of the world, thou Christ	E
		298	All who believe and are baptized	E
		296	We know that Christ is raised and dies no more	E
		294	Baptized in water	E
	EP	350	O God of love, to thee we bow	G
		352	O God, to those who here profess	G
		353	Your love, O God, has called us here	G
TUE	MP	668	I to the hills will lift mine eyes	Ps 121
		432	O praise ye the Lord! Praise him in the height (omit st. 3)	E
		298	All who believe and are baptized	E
		296	We know that Christ is raised and dies no more	E
		176, 177	Over the chaos of the empty waters	E
	EP	480	When Jesus left his Father's throne	G
		701	Jesus, all my gladness	G
		475	God himself is with us (sts. 1-2)	G
		707	Take my life, and let it be	G
WED	MP	518	Christ is made the sure foundation	E
		525	The Church's one foundation	E
		51	We the Lord's people, heart and voice uniting (st. 1)	E
		432	O praise ye the Lord! Praise him in the height (omit st. 3)	E
		294	Baptized in water	E
	EP	666	Out of the depths I call	Ps 130
		151	From deepest woe I cry to thee	Ps 130
		655	O Jesus, I have promised	G

		564, 565	He who would valiant be	G
		707	Take my life, and let it be	G
THU	MP	670	Lord, for ever at thy side	Ps 131
		478	Jesus, our mighty Lord	E
		708	Savior, like a shepherd lead us	E
		645, 646	The King of love my shepherd is	E
	EP	541	Come, labor on	G
		551	Rise up, ye saints of God!	G
FRI	MP	455, 456	O Love of God, how strong and true	E
		298	All who believe and are baptized	E
		296	We know that Christ is raised and dies no more	E
		294	Baptized in water	E
		432	O praise ye the Lord! Praise him in the height (omit st. 3)	E
	EP	477	All praise to thee, for thou, O King divine	G
		474	When I survey the wondrous cross	G
		458	My song is love unknown	G
		495	Hail, thou once despisèd Jesus!	G
		483	The head that once was crowned with thorns	G
SAT	MP	483	The head that once was crowned with thorns	E
		484, 485	Praise the Lord through every nation	E
		548	Soldiers of Christ, arise	E
	EP	388	O worship the King, all glorious above!	Ps 104
		633	Word of God, come down on earth	G
		567	Thine arm, O Lord, in days of old	G
		493	O for a thousand tongues to sing	G
		371	Thou, whose almighty word	G
		429	I'll praise my Maker while I've breath	G

The Daily Office: Year Two

Week of 1 Advent

SUN	MP	598	Lord Christ, when first thou cam'st to earth	G
		53	Once he came in blessing	G
		600, 601	O day of God, draw nigh	S
		462	The Lord will come and not be slow	S
	EP	59	Hark! a thrilling voice is sounding	E
		68	Rejoice! rejoice, believers	E
		61, 62	"Sleepers, wake!" A voice astounds us	E
MON	MP	65	Prepare the way, O Zion	G
		486	Hosanna to the living Lord!	G

		74	Blest be the King whose coming	G
		71, 72	Hark! the glad sound! the Savior comes	G
	EP	59	Hark! a thrilling voice is sounding	E
		53	Once he came in blessing	E
		63, 64	O heavenly Word, eternal Light	E
		57, 58	Lo! he comes, with clouds descending	E
TUE	MP	454	Jesus came, adored by angels	G
		486	Hosanna to the living Lord!	G
	EP	60	Creator of the stars of night	E
		672	O very God of very God	E
		73	The King shall come when morning dawns	E
		542	Christ is the world's true Light	E
		40, 41	O Christ, you are both light and day	E
WED	MP	596	Judge eternal, throned in splendor	L
		63, 64	O heavenly Word, eternal Light	G
		444	Blessed be the God of Israel	G
		271, 272	The great forerunner of the morn	G
	EP	462	The Lord will come and not be slow	E
		68	Rejoice! rejoice, believers	E
		61, 62	"Sleepers, wake!" A voice astounds us	E
THU	MP	598	Lord Christ, when first thou cam'st to earth	G
	EP	63, 64	O heavenly Word, eternal Light	E
		53	Once he came in blessing	E
		59	Hark! a thrilling voice is sounding	E
FRI	MP	63, 64	O heavenly Word, eternal Light	G
		53	Once he came in blessing	G
	EP	53	Once he came in blessing	E
		63, 64	O heavenly Word, eternal Light	E
		591	O God of earth and altar	E
		59	Hark! a thrilling voice is sounding	E
SAT	MP	591	O God of earth and altar	G
		596	Judge eternal, throned in splendor	G
		573	Father eternal, Ruler of creation	G
	EP	57, 58	Lo! he comes, with clouds descending	E
		60	Creator of the stars of night	E
		63, 64	O heavenly Word, eternal Light	E
		53	Once he came in blessing	E
		73	The King shall come when morning dawns	E

Week of 2 Advent

SUN	MP	271, 272	The great forerunner of the morn	G
		444	Blessed be the God of Israel	G
	EP	63, 64	O heavenly Word, eternal Light	E

		57, 58	Lo! he comes, with clouds descending	E
MON	MP	61, 62	"Sleepers, wake!" A voice astounds us	S
		672	O very God of very God	S
	EP	57, 58	Lo! he comes, with clouds descending	E
		73	The King shall come when morning dawns	E
		454	Jesus came, adored by angels	E
TUE	MP	672	O very God of very God	S
		640	Watchman, tell us of the night	S
	EP	67	Comfort, comfort ye my people	S
		75	There's a voice in the wilderness crying	S
WED	MP	70	Herald, sound the note of judgment	S
		69	What is the crying at Jordan?	S
	EP	59	Hark! a thrilling voice is sounding	E
THU	MP	76	On Jordan's bank the Baptist's cry	S
		640	Watchman, tell us of the night	S
	EP	53	Once he came in blessing	E
		591	O God of earth and altar	E
FRI	MP	598	Lord Christ, when first thou cam'st to earth	G
		75	There's a voice in the wilderness crying	S
	EP	53	Once he came in blessing	E
		591	O God of earth and altar	E
SAT	MP	56	O come, O come, Emmanuel	L
		53	Once he came in blessing	G
		598	Lord Christ, when first thou cam'st to earth	G
	EP	61, 62	"Sleepers, wake!" A voice astounds us	E
		68	Rejoice! rejoice, believers	E
		547	Awake, O sleeper, rise from death	E

Week of 3 Advent

SUN	MP	543	O Zion, tune thy voice	L
		640	Watchman, tell us of the night	G
		444	Blessed be the God of Israel	G
		65	Prepare the way, O Zion	G
	EP	73	The King shall come when morning dawns	E
		54	Savior of the nations, come!	S
		55	Redeemer of the nations, come	S
MON	MP	67	Comfort, comfort ye my people	L
		57, 58	Lo! he comes, with clouds descending	G
		454	Jesus came, adored by angels	G
		53	Once he came in blessing	G
	EP	53	Once he came in blessing	E

		462	The Lord will come and not be slow	S
TUE	MP	678, 679	Surely it is God who saves me	L
		543	O Zion, tune thy voice	L
		61, 62	"Sleepers, wake!" A voice astounds us	G
	EP	436	Lift up your heads, ye mighty gates	E
		70	Herald, sound the note of judgment	S
		69	What is the crying at Jordan?	S
WED	MP	53	Once he came in blessing	G
		640	Watchman, tell us of the night	S
	EP	69	What is the crying at Jordan?	S
		56	O come, O come, Emmanuel	S
THU	MP	68	Rejoice! rejoice, believers	G
		61, 62	"Sleepers, wake!" A voice astounds us	G
	EP	486	Hosanna to the living Lord!	S
		66	Come, thou long-expected Jesus	S
FRI	MP	543	O Zion, tune thy voice	L
		53	Once he came in blessing	G
		63, 64	O heavenly Word, eternal Light	G
	EP	74	Blest be the King whose coming	S
		55	Redeemer of the nations, come	S
SAT	MP	63, 64	O heavenly Word, eternal Light	G
		53	Once he came in blessing	G
	EP	56	O come, O come, Emmanuel	S
		66	Come, thou long-expected Jesus	S

Week of 4 Advent

		436	Lift up your heads, ye mighty gates	Ps 24
SUN	MP	270	Gabriel's message does away	L
		60	Creator of the stars of night	L
		489	The great Creator of the worlds	G
	EP	74	Blest be the King whose coming	S
		56	O come, O come, Emmanuel	S
		66	Come, thou long-expected Jesus	S
MON	MP	71, 72	Hark! the glad sound! the Savior comes	L
		543	O Zion, tune thy voice	L
		271, 272	The great forerunner of the morn	G
	EP	496, 497	How bright appears the Morning Star	S
		672	O very God of very God	S
		54	Savior of the nations, come!	S
TUE	MP	437, 438	Tell out, my soul, the greatness of the Lord!	L
		265	The angel Gabriel from heaven came	G

		263, 264	The Word whom earth and sea and sky	G
		266	Nova, nova	G
	EP	71, 72	Hark! the glad sound! the Savior comes	S
		672	O very God of very God	S
		55	Redeemer of the nations, come	S
WED	MP	616	Hail to the Lord's Anointed	Ps 72
		268, 269	Ye who claim the faith of Jesus	G
		437, 438	Tell out, my soul, the greatness of the Lord!	G
		258	Virgin-born, we bow before thee	G
	EP	66	Come, thou long-expected Jesus	S
		74	Blest be the King whose coming	S
THU	MP	271, 272	The great forerunner of the morn	G
		640	Watchman, tell us of the night	S
	EP	60	Creator of the stars of night	E
		270	Gabriel's message does away	E
		66	Come, thou long-expected Jesus	S
FRI	MP	543	O Zion, tune thy voice	L
		54	Savior of the nations, come!	L
		55	Redeemer of the nations, come	L
		444	Blessed be the God of Israel	G
	EP	55	Redeemer of the nations, come	S
		54	Savior of the nations, come!	S
		56	O come, O come, Emmanuel	S

December 24

	MP	543	O Zion, tune thy voice	L
		65	Prepare the way, O Zion	L
		56	O come, O come, Emmanuel	G
		496, 497	How bright appears the Morning Star	G
		55	Redeemer of the nations, come	G
		54	Savior of the nations, come!	G

Christmas Eve

	EP	60	Creator of the stars of night	E
		252	Jesus! Name of wondrous love!	E
		439	What wondrous love is this	E

Christmas Day and Following

Christmas Day

MP	78, 79	O little town of Bethlehem	L
	85, 86	O Savior of our fallen race	G
	87	Hark! the herald angels sing	G
EP	82	Of the Father's love begotten	E
	84	Love came down at Christmas	E

First SUN after Christmas

MP	259	Hail to the Lord who comes	G
	257	O Zion, open wide thy gates	G
	499	Lord God, you now have set your servant free	G
EP	97	Dost thou in a manger lie	E
	87	Hark! the herald angels sing	E
	77	From East to West, from shore to shore	E
	492	Sing, ye faithful, sing with gladness	E
	467	Sing, my soul, his wondrous love	E

December 29

MP	138	All praise to you, O Lord	G
	131, 132	When Christ's appearing was made known (sts. 4-5)	G
	443	From God Christ's deity came forth	G
EP	84	Love came down at Christmas	E
	85, 86	O Savior of our fallen race	E
	125, 126	The people who in darkness walked	S
	452	Glorious the day when Christ was born	S

December 30

MP	448, 449	O love, how deep, how broad, how high	G
	493	O for a thousand tongues to sing	G
	567	Thine arm, O Lord, in days of old	G
EP	476	Can we by searching find out God	E
	491	Where is this stupendous stranger?	E
	386, 387	We sing of God, the mighty source	S
	468	It was poor little Jesus	S

December 31

MP	584	God, you have given us power to sound	L
	251	O God, whom neither time nor space	E
	493	O for a thousand tongues to sing	G

| | | 567 | Thine arm, O Lord, in days of old | G |

		567	Thine arm, O Lord, in days of old	G

Eve of Holy Name

	EP	680	O God, our help in ages past	Ps 90
		597	O day of peace that dimly shines	L
		582, 583	O holy city, seen of John	E

Holy Name

	MP	450, 451	All hail the power of Jesus' Name!	L
		543	O Zion, tune thy voice	L
		252	Jesus! Name of wondrous love!	G
		248, 249	To the Name of our salvation	G
		250	Now greet the swiftly changing year	G
	EP	596	Judge eternal, throned in splendor	E
		251	O God, whom neither time nor space	S

Second SUN after Christmas

	MP	538	God of mercy, God of grace	Ps 67
		584	God, you have given us power to sound	L
		335	I am the bread of life	G
		472	Hope of the world, thou Christ	G
	EP	426	Songs of praise the angels sang	E
		593	Lord, make us servants of your peace	E
		592	Teach me, my God and King	E

January 2

	MP	709	O God of Bethel, by whose hand	L
		448, 449	O love, how deep, how broad, how high	G
	EP	547	Awake, O sleeper, rise from death	E
		511	Holy Spirit, ever living	E
		521	Put forth, O God, thy Spirit's might	E
		527	Singing songs of expectation	E

January 3

	MP	652, 653	Dear Lord and Father of mankind (sts. 1, 4 & 5)	L
		496, 497	How bright appears the Morning Star	S
		439	What wondrous love is this	S
	EP	616	Hail to the Lord's Anointed	Ps 72
		574, 575	Before thy throne, O God, we kneel	E
		593	Lord, make us servants of your peace	E
		347	Go forth for God; go to the world in peace	E

January 4

MP	393	Praise our great and gracious Lord	L
	690	Guide me, O thou great Jehovah	L
	6, 7	Christ, whose glory fills the skies	G
	465, 466	Eternal light, shine in my heart	G
EP	547	Awake, O sleeper, rise from death	E
	490	I want to walk as a child of the light	E
	426	Songs of praise the angels sang	E
	402, 403	Let all the world in every corner sing	E
	420	When in our music God is glorified	E

January 5

MP	408	Sing praise to God who reigns above	L
	548	Soldiers of Christ, arise	E
	617	Eternal Ruler of the ceaseless round	E
	455, 456	O Love of God, how strong and true	G
	335	I am the bread of life (sts. 4-5)	G

Eve of the Epiphany

EP	532, 533	How wondrous and great thy works, God of praise!	L & E
	381	Thy strong word did cleave the darkness	L & E
	125, 126	The people who in darkness walked	L & E
	472	Hope of the world, thou Christ	E

The Epiphany and Following

Epiphany

MP	496, 497	How bright appears the Morning Star	L
	532, 533	How wondrous and great thy works, God of praise!	L
	616	Hail to the Lord's Anointed	G
EP	119	As with gladness men of old	E
	439	What wondrous love is this	E
	544	Jesus shall reign where'er the sun	E
	491	Where is this stupendous stranger?	S

January 7

MP	343	Shepherd of souls, refresh and bless (sts. 1-2)	L & G
	335	I am the bread of life	G

		O Jesus, joy of loving hearts	G
	649, 650		
EP	381	Thy strong word did cleave the darkness	E
	432	O praise ye the Lord! Praise him in the height (omit st. 3)	E
	326	From glory to glory advancing, we praise thee, O Lord	E

January 8

MP	380	From all that dwell below the skies	Ps 117
	685	Rock of ages, cleft for me	L
	443	From God Christ's deity came forth	G
	692	I heard the voice of Jesus say (st. 2)	G
EP	496, 497	How bright appears the Morning Star	E
	492	Sing, ye faithful, sing with gladness	E
	421	All glory be to God on high	E
	467	Sing, my soul, his wondrous love	E

January 9

MP	6, 7	Christ, whose glory fills the skies	G
	496, 497	How bright appears the Morning Star	G
	692	I heard the voice of Jesus say (st. 3)	G
	490	I want to walk as a child of the light	G
	542	Christ is the world's true Light	G
EP	381	Thy strong word did cleave the darkness	E
	422	Not far beyond the sea, nor high	E
	386, 387	We sing of God, the mighty source	S

January 10

MP	478	Jesus, our mighty Lord	L & G
	708	Savior, like a shepherd lead us	L & G
	645, 646	The King of love my shepherd is	G
EP	294	Baptized in water	E
	298	All who believe and are baptized	E
	432	O praise ye the Lord! Praise him in the height	E

January 11

MP	457	Thou art the Way, to thee alone	G
	487	Come, my Way, my Truth, my Life	G
	463, 464	He is the Way	G
EP	298	All who believe and are baptized	E

		296	We know that Christ is raised and dies no more	E
		574, 575	Before thy throne, O God, we kneel	E
		542	Christ is the world's true Light	E
		426	Songs of praise the angels sang	E

January 12

	MP	413	New songs of celebration render	Ps 98
		655	O Jesus, I have promised	E
		392	Come, we that love the Lord	G
		344	Lord, dismiss us with thy blessing	G

Eve of 1 Epiphany

	EP	71, 72	Hark! the glad sound! the Savior comes	L
		539	O Zion, haste, thy mission high fulfilling	L
		294	Baptized in water	E
		295	Sing praise to our Creator	E
		432	O praise ye the Lord! Praise him in the height	E
		381	Thy strong word did cleave the darkness	E

Week of 1 Epiphany

SUN	MP	409	The spacious firmament on high	L
		398	I sing the almighty power of God	L
		121	Christ, when for us you were baptized	G
		120	The sinless one to Jordan came	G
		139	When Jesus went to Jordan's stream	G
	EP	686	Come, thou fount of every blessing	E
		294	Baptized in water	E
		706	In your mercy, Lord, you called me	E
		432	O praise ye the Lord! Praise him in the height (omit st. 3)	E
MON	MP	386, 387	We sing of God, the mighty source	L & G
		491	Where is this stupendous stranger?	G
		496, 497	How bright appears the Morning Star	G
		421	All glory be to God on high	G
		476	Can we by searching find out God	G
		489	The great Creator of the worlds	G
	EP	489	The great Creator of the worlds	E
		443	From God Christ's deity came forth	E
		496, 497	How bright appears the Morning Star	E
TUE	MP	445, 446	Praise to the Holiest in the height	L
		295	Sing praise to our Creator	L
		70	Herald, sound the note of judgment	G
		67	Comfort, comfort ye my people	G
		75	There's a voice in the wilderness crying	G

		444	Blessed be the God of Israel	G
	EP	448, 449	O love, how deep, how broad, how high	E
		452	Glorious the day when Christ was born	E
		495	Hail, thou once despisèd Jesus!	E
		450, 451	All hail the power of Jesus' Name!	E
		483	The head that once was crowned with thorns	E
WED	MP	131, 132	When Christ's appearing was made known (sts. 3 & 5)	G
		121	Christ, when for us you were baptized	G
		139	When Jesus went to Jordan's stream	G
		120	The sinless one to Jordan came	G
		439	What wondrous love is this	G
	EP	450, 451	All hail the power of Jesus' Name!	E
		443	From God Christ's deity came forth	E
		476	Can we by searching find out God	E
		559	Lead us, heavenly Father, lead us	E
THU	MP	477	All praise to thee, for thou, O King divine	G
		439	What wondrous love is this	G
		489	The great Creator of the worlds	G
	EP	443	From God Christ's deity came forth	E
		460, 461	Alleluia! sing to Jesus! (omit sts. 2, 5)	E
FRI	MP	131, 132	When Christ's appearing was made known (sts. 4-5)	G
		138	All praise to you, O Lord	G
		135	Songs of thankfulness and praise (sts. 1-2)	G
		443	From God Christ's deity came forth	G
	EP	686	Come, thou fount of every blessing	E
		697	My God, accept my heart this day	E
SAT	MP	598	Lord Christ, when first thou cam'st to earth	G
	EP	380	From all that dwell below the skies	Ps 117
		634	I call on thee, Lord Jesus Christ	E
		641	Lord Jesus, think on me	E

Week of 2 Epiphany

SUN	MP	394, 395	Creating God, your fingers trace	Ps 148
		373	Praise the Lord! ye heavens adore him	Ps 148
		390	Praise to the Lord, the Almighty	Ps 150
		432	O praise ye the Lord! Praise him in the height	Ps 150
		135	Songs of thankfulness and praise (sts. 1-3)	G
		493	O for a thousand tongues to sing	G
	EP	547	Awake, O sleeper, rise from death	E
		521	Put forth, O God, thy Spirit's might	E
		511	Holy Spirit, ever living	E

MON	MP	473	Lift high the cross	G
		297	Descend, O Spirit, purging flame	G
		295	Sing praise to our Creator	G
	EP	219	The Lord ascendeth up on high	E
		495	Hail, thou once despisèd Jesus!	E
		460, 461	Alleluia! sing to Jesus! (sts. 1 & 4)	E
TUE	MP	489	The great Creator of the worlds	G
		448, 449	O love, how deep, how broad, how high	G
		465, 466	Eternal light, shine in my heart	G
		6, 7	Christ, whose glory fills the skies	G
		381	Thy strong word did cleave the darkness	G
	EP	443	From God Christ's deity came forth	E
		455, 456	O Love of God, how strong and true	E
		495	Hail, thou once despisèd Jesus!	E
WED	MP	121	Christ, when for us you were baptized	G
		139	When Jesus went to Jordan's stream	G
		116	"I come," the great Redeemer cries	G
		120	The sinless one to Jordan came	G
	EP	443	From God Christ's deity came forth	E
		326	From glory to glory advancing, we praise thee, O Lord	E
		704	O thou who camest from above	E
THU	MP	573	Father eternal, Ruler of creation	L
		692	I heard the voice of Jesus say (st. 2)	G
		649, 650	O Jesus, joy of loving hearts	G
		700	O love that casts out fear	G
		678, 679	Surely it is God who saves me	G
		658	As longs the deer for cooling streams	G
	EP	443	From God Christ's deity came forth	E
		401	The God of Abraham praise	E
FRI	MP	440	Blessèd Jesus, at thy word	G
		489	The great Creator of the worlds	G
		439	What wondrous love is this	G
	EP	443	From God Christ's deity came forth	E
		460, 461	Alleluia! sing to Jesus! (sts. 1 & 4)	E
SAT	MP	540	Awake, thou Spirit of the watchmen	G
		673	The first one ever, oh, ever to know (st. 2)	G
		530	Spread, O spread, thou mighty word	G
		535	Ye servants of God, your Master proclaim	G
		541	Come, labor on	G
	EP	658	As longs the deer for cooling streams	Ps 42
		495	Hail, thou once despisèd Jesus!	E
		443	From God Christ's deity came forth	E
		219	The Lord ascendeth up on high	E
		460, 461	Alleluia! sing to Jesus! (omit sts. 2, 5)	E

Week of 3 Epiphany

SUN	**MP**	413	New songs of celebration render	Ps 98
		633	Word of God, come down on earth	G
		493	O for a thousand tongues to sing	G
		567	Thine arm, O Lord, in days of old	G
		135	Songs of thankfulness and praise (sts. 1-3)	G
		429	I'll praise my Maker while I've breath	G
	EP	411	O bless the Lord, my soul!	Ps 103
		410	Praise, my soul, the King of heaven	Ps 103
		390	Praise to the Lord, the Almighty	Ps 103
		529	In Christ there is no East or West	E
		603, 604	When Christ was lifted from the earth	E
		542	Christ is the world's true Light	E
MON	**MP**	567	Thine arm, O Lord, in days of old	G
		135	Songs of thankfulness and praise (sts. 1-3)	G
		493	O for a thousand tongues to sing	G
	EP	460, 461	Alleluia! sing to Jesus! (omit sts. 2, 5)	E
		443	From God Christ's deity came forth	E
		447	The Christ who died but rose again	E
TUE	**MP**	493	O for a thousand tongues to sing	G
		567	Thine arm, O Lord, in days of old	G
		429	I'll praise my Maker while I've breath	G
	EP	460, 461	Alleluia! sing to Jesus! (omit sts. 2, 5)	E
		686	Come, thou fount of every blessing	E
		495	Hail, thou once despisèd Jesus!	E
		160	Cross of Jesus, cross of sorrow	E
WED	**MP**	455, 456	O Love of God, how strong and true	G
		457	Thou art the Way, to thee alone	G
		628	Help us, O Lord, to learn	G
		626	Lord, be thy word my rule	G
	EP	495	Hail, thou once despisèd Jesus!	E
		307	Lord, enthroned in heavenly splendor (omit sts. 2, 3)	E
		160	Cross of Jesus, cross of sorrow	E
		219	The Lord ascendeth up on high	E
		368	Holy Father, great Creator	E
		460, 461	Alleluia! sing to Jesus! (omit sts. 2, 5)	E
THU	**MP**	634	I call on thee, Lord Jesus Christ	G
		633	Word of God, come down on earth	G
		444	Blessed be the God of Israel	G
	EP	116	"I come," the Redeemer cries	E
		307	Lord, enthroned in heavenly splendor (omit sts. 2, 3)	E
FRI	**MP**	448, 449	O love, how deep, how broad, how high	G
		443	From God Christ's deity came forth	G
		320	Zion, praise thy Savior, singing (sts. 5-6)	G

		343	Shepherd of souls, refresh and bless (sts. 1-2)	G
	EP	495	Hail, thou once despisèd Jesus!	E
		219	The Lord ascendeth up on high	E
		686	Come, thou fount of every blessing	E
		460, 461	Alleluia! sing to Jesus! (omit sts. 2, 5)	E
		443	From God Christ's deity came forth	E
SAT	MP	649, 650	O Jesus, joy of loving hearts	G
		669	Commit thou all that grieves thee	G
		690	Guide me, O thou great Jehovah	G
	EP	702	Lord, thou hast searched me and dost know	Ps 139
		53	Once he came in blessing	E
		63, 64	O heavenly Word, eternal Light	E
		655	O Jesus, I have promised	E
		623	O what their joy and their glory must be	E

Week of 4 Epiphany

SUN	MP	436	Lift up your heads, ye mighty gates	Ps 24
		493	O for a thousand tongues to sing	G
		567	Thine arm, O Lord, in days of old	G
		633	Word of God, come down on earth	G
		254	You are the Christ, O Lord	G
	EP	517	How lovely is thy dwelling-place	Ps 84
		593	Lord, make us servants of your peace	E
		610	Lord, whose love through humble service	E
		500	Creator Spirit, by whose aid	E
MON	MP	335	I am the bread of life	G
		343	Shepherd of souls, refresh and bless (sts. 1-2)	G
		649, 650	O Jesus, joy of loving hearts	G
	EP	401	The God of Abraham praise	E
		634	I call on thee, Lord Jesus Christ	E
		636, 637	How firm a foundation, ye saints of the Lord	E
TUE	MP	302, 303	Father, we thank thee who hast planted (st. 1)	G
		335	I am the bread of life	G
		343	Shepherd of souls, refresh and bless (sts. 1-2)	G
		320	Zion, praise thy Savior, singing (sts. 5-6)	G
	EP	372	Praise to the living God!	E
		401	The God of Abraham praise	E
		623	O what their joy and their glory must be	E
		624	Jerusalem the golden	E
WED	MP	616	Hail to the Lord's Anointed	Ps 72
		544	Jesus shall reign where'er the sun	Ps 72
		335	I am the bread of life	G
		320	Zion, praise thy Savior, singing (sts. 5-6)	G
		343	Shepherd of souls, refresh and bless (sts. 1-2)	G
		302, 303	Father, we thank thee who hast planted (st. 1)	G

	EP	425	Sing now with joy unto the Lord	E
		363	Ancient of Days, who sittest throned in glory	E
		187	Through the Red Sea brought at last, Alleluia!	E
		393	Praise our great and gracious Lord	E
THU	MP	626	Lord, be thy word my rule	G
		633	Word of God, come down on earth	G
		632	O Christ, the Word Incarnate	G
		381	Thy strong word did cleave the darkness	G
		630	Thanks to God whose Word was spoken (omit sts. 3, 4)	G
	EP	545	Lo! what a cloud of witnesses	E
		546	Awake, my soul, stretch every nerve	E
		253	Give us the wings of faith to rise	E
		558	Faith of our fathers! living still	E
FRI	MP	427	When morning gilds the skies	G
		472	Hope of the world, thou Christ	G
		590	O Jesus Christ, may grateful hymns be rising	G
		402, 403	Let all the world in every corner sing	G
	EP	636, 637	How firm a foundation, ye saints of the Lord	E
		545	Lo! what a cloud of witnesses	E
		574, 575	Before thy throne, O God, we kneel	E
SAT	MP	634	I call on thee, Lord Jesus Christ	G
		458	My song is love unknown	G
		443	From God Christ's deity came forth	G
		489	The great Creator of the worlds	G
	EP	664	My Shepherd will supply my need	Ps 23
		663	The Lord my God my shepherd is	Ps 23
		645, 646	The King of love my shepherd is	Ps 23
		368	Holy Father, great Creator	E
		512	Come, gracious Spirit, heavenly Dove	E
		623	O what their joy and their glory must be	E
		624	Jerusalem the golden	E

Week of 5 Epiphany

SUN	MP	480	When Jesus left his Father's throne	G
		707	Take my life, and let it be	G
		701	Jesus, all my gladness	G
		475	God himself is with us (sts. 1-2)	G
		488	Be thou my vision, O Lord of my heart	G
	EP	707	Take my life, and let it be	E
		656	Blest are the pure in heart	E
		593	Lord, make us servants of your peace	E
MON	MP	443	From God Christ's deity came forth	G
		692	I heard the voice of Jesus say (st. 2)	G
		649, 650	O Jesus, joy of loving hearts	G

		427	When morning gilds the skies	G
	EP	167	There is a green hill far away (omit sts. 3, 4)	E
		614	Christ is the King! O friends upraise	E
		610	Lord, whose love through humble service	E
		219	The Lord ascendeth up on high	E
		665	All my hope on God is founded	E
TUE	MP	489	The great Creator of the worlds	G
		469, 470	There's a wideness in God's mercy	G
		467	Sing, my soul, his wondrous love	G
	EP	478	Jesus, our mighty Lord	E
		708	Savior, like a shepherd lead us	E
WED	MP	6, 7	Christ, whose glory fills the skies	G
		692	I heard the voice of Jesus say (st. 3)	G
		490	I want to walk as a child of the light	G
		465, 466	Eternal light, shine in my heart	G
		496, 497	How bright appears the Morning Star	G
	EP	610	Lord, whose love through humble service	E
		707	Take my life, and let it be	E
THU	MP	419	Lord of all being, throned afar	G
		626	Lord, be thy word my rule	G
	EP	347	Go forth for God; go to the world in peace	E
		593	Lord, make us servants of your peace	E
		610	Lord, whose love through humble service	E
FRI	MP	453	As Jacob with travel was weary one day	L
		709	O God of Bethel, by whose hand	L
		505	O Spirit of Life, O Spirit of God	G
		628	Help us, O Lord, to learn	G
		626	Lord, be thy word my rule	G
	EP	547	Awake, O sleeper, rise from death	E
		59	Hark! a thrilling voice is sounding	E
		400	All creatures of our God and King (omit sts. 2, 3, 6)	E
		406, 407	Most High, omnipotent, good Lord	E
SAT	MP	680	O God, our help in ages past	Ps 90
		401	The God of Abraham praise	G
		439	What wondrous love is this	G
		505	O Spirit of Life, O Spirit of God	G
		440	Blessèd Jesus, at thy word	G
		628	Help us, O Lord, to learn	G
		626	Lord, be thy word my rule	G
	EP	389	Let us, with a gladsome mind	Ps 136
		347	Go forth for God; go to the world in peace	E
		674	"Forgive our sins as we forgive"	E
		593	Lord, make us servants of your peace	E
		406, 407	Most High, omnipotent, good Lord	E
		400	All creatures of our God and King (omit sts. 2, 3, 6)	E

Week of 6 Epiphany

SUN	**MP**	538	God of mercy, God of grace	Ps 67
		655	O Jesus, I have promised	G
		701	Jesus, all my gladness	G
		475	God himself is with us	G
		707	Take my life, and let it be	G
	EP	409	The spacious firmament on high	Ps 19
		431	The stars declare his glory	Ps 19
		687, 688	A mighty fortress is our God	Ps 46
		535	Ye servants of God, your Master proclaim	E
		511	Holy Spirit, ever living	E
MON	**MP**	371	Thou, whose almighty Word	G
		692	I heard the voice of Jesus say (st. 3)	G
		633	Word of God, come down on earth (st. 3)	G
		493	O for a thousand tongues to sing	G
		6, 7	Christ, whose glory fills the skies	G
	EP	371	Thou, whose almighty word	E
		496, 497	How bright appears the Morning Star	E
		542	Christ is the world's true Light	E
		490	I want to walk as a child of the light	E
TUE	**MP**	567	Thine arm, O Lord, in days of old	G
		493	O for a thousand tongues to sing	G
		633	Word of God, come down on earth (st. 3)	G
		371	Thou, whose almighty word	G
	EP	542	Christ is the world's true Light	E
		27, 28	O blest Creator, source of light	E
		371	Thou, whose almighty word	E
WED	**MP**	401	The God of Abraham praise	L
		478	Jesus, our mighty Lord	G
		708	Savior, like a shepherd lead us	G
		663	The Lord my God my shepherd is	G
	EP	488	Be thou my vision, O Lord of my heart	E
		665	All my hope on God is founded	E
		475	God himself is with us	E
THU	**MP**	708	Savior, like a shepherd lead us	G
		478	Jesus, our mighty Lord	G
		645, 646	The King of love my shepherd is	G
		664	My Shepherd will supply my need	G
	EP	295	Sing praise to our Creator	E
		294	Baptized in water	E
FRI	**MP**	638, 639	Come, O thou Traveler unknown	L
		121	Christ, when for us you were baptized	G
		139	When Jesus went to Jordan's stream	G
		116	"I come," the great Redeemer cries	G

	EP	295	Sing praise to our Creator	E
		294	Baptized in water	E
SAT	MP	709	O God of Bethel, by whose hand	L
		455, 456	O Love of God, how strong and true	G
	EP	610	Lord, whose love through humble service	E
		603, 604	When Christ was lifted from the earth	E
		573	Father eternal, Ruler of creation	E
		581	Where charity and love prevail	E
		585	Morning glory, starlit sky	E

Week of 7 Epiphany

	MP	584	God, you have given us power to sound	L
SUN		629	We limit not the truth of God	L
		659, 660	O Master, let me walk with thee	G
		458	My song is love unknown	G
		483	The head that once was crowned with thorns	G
		477	All praise to thee, for thou, O King divine	G
	EP	414	God, my King, thy might confessing	Ps 145
		404	We will extol you, ever-blessèd Lord	Ps 145
		298	All who believe and are baptized	E
		213	Come away to the skies	E
		296	We know that Christ is raised and dies no more	E
		176, 177	Over the chaos of the empty waters	E
MON	MP	584	God, you have given us power to sound	L
		335	I am the bread of life (sts. 4-5)	G
		457	Thou art the Way, to thee alone	G
		455, 456	O Love of God, how strong and true	G
		567	Thine arm, O Lord, in days of old	G
	EP	610	Lord, whose love through humble service	E
		603, 604	When Christ was lifted from the earth	E
		704	O thou who camest from above	E
		581	Where charity and love prevail	E
		576, 577	God is Love, and where true love is	E
		606	Where true charity and love dwell	E
TUE	MP	668	I to the hills will lift mine eyes	Ps 121
		584	God, you have given us power to sound	L
		455, 456	O Love of God, how strong and true	G
		457	Thou art the Way, to thee alone	G
		493	O for a thousand tongues to sing	G
		567	Thine arm, O Lord, in days of old	G
	EP	700	O love that casts out fear	E
		610	Lord, whose love through humble service	E
		379	God is Love, let heaven adore him	E
		471	We sing the praise of him who died	E
		439	What wondrous love is this	E

WED	MP	11	Awake, my soul, and with the sun	L
		598	Lord Christ, when first thou cam'st to earth	G
		457	Thou art the Way, to thee alone	G
		458	My song is love unknown	G
	EP	666	Out of the depths I call	Ps 130
		151	From deepest woe I cry to thee	Ps 130
		139	When Jesus went to Jordan's stream	E
		298	All who believe and are baptized	E
		489	The great Creator of the worlds	E
THU	MP	670	Lord, for ever at thy side	Ps 131
		643	My God, how wonderful thou art	G
		642	Jesus, the very thought of thee	G
		704	O thou who camest from above	G
	EP	698	Eternal Spirit of the living Christ	E
		711	Seek ye first the kingdom of God	E
		302, 303	Father, we thank thee who hast planted (st. 1)	E
		518	Christ is made the sure foundation	E
FRI	MP	458	My song is love unknown	G
		486	Hosanna to the living Lord!	G
		65	Prepare the way, O Zion	G
		74	Blest be the King whose coming	G
		156	Ride on! ride on in majesty	G
		436	Lift up your heads, ye mighty gates	G
	EP	603, 604	When Christ was lifted from the earth	E
		576, 577	God is Love, and where true love is	E
		581	Where charity and love prevail	E
		606	Where true charity and love dwell	E
SAT	MP	584	God, you have given us power to sound	L
		681	Our God, to whom we turn	L
		379	God is love, let heaven adore him	L
		655	O Jesus, I have promised	G
		473	Lift high the cross	G
	EP	388	O worship the King, all glorious above!	Ps 104
		704	O thou who camest from above	E
		151	From deepest woe I cry to thee	E

Week of 8 Epiphany

SUN	MP	429	I'll praise my Maker while I've breath	Ps 146 & G
		633	Word of God, come down on earth	G
		493	O for a thousand tongues to sing	G
		567	Thine arm, O Lord, in days of old	G
		371	Thou, whose almighty word	G
	EP	705	As those of old their first fruits brought	E
		292	O Jesus, crowned with all renown	E
		610	Lord, whose love through humble service	E

MON	MP	473	Lift high the cross	G
		603, 604	When Christ was lifted from the earth	G
		434	Nature with open volume stands	G
		474	When I survey the wondrous cross	G
		490	I want to walk as a child of the light	G
	EP	548	Soldiers of Christ, arise	E
		561	Stand up, stand up, for Jesus	E
		483	The head that once was crowned with thorns	E
		562	Onward, Christian soldiers	E
		563	Go forward, Christian soldier	E
		552, 553	Fight the good fight with all thy might	E
TUE	MP	6, 7	Christ, whose glory fills the skies	G
		672	O very God of very God	G
		692	I heard the voice of Jesus say (st. 3)	G
		465, 466	Eternal light, shine in my heart	G
		496, 497	How bright appears the Morning Star	G
		490	I want to walk as a child of the light	G
	EP	656	Blest are the pure in heart	E
		707	Take my life, and let it be	E
		593	Lord, make us servants of your peace	E
WED	MP	602	Jesu, Jesu, fill us with your love	G
		659, 660	O Master, let me walk with thee	G
	EP	628	Help us, O Lord, to learn	E
		627	Lamp of our feet, whereby we trace	E
		631	Book of books, our people's strength	E
		630	Thanks to God whose Word was spoken	E
THU	MP	158	Ah, holy Jesus, how hast thou offended	G
	EP	552, 553	Fight the good fight with all thy might (sts. 1-2)	E
		555	Lead on, O King eternal	E
		561	Stand up, stand up, for Jesus	E
		511	Holy Spirit, ever living	E
FRI	MP	602	Jesu, Jesu, fill us with your love	G
		610	Lord, whose love through humble service	G
		593	Lord, make us servants of your peace	G
		581	Where charity and love prevail	G
		576, 577	God is Love, and where true love is	G
		606	Where true charity and love dwell	G
	EP	636, 637	How firm a foundation, ye saints of the Lord	E
		635	If thou but trust in God to guide thee	E
		669	Commit thou all that grieves thee	E
SAT	MP	458	My song is love unknown	G
		448, 449	O love, how deep, how broad, how high	G
		572	Weary of all trumpeting	G
	EP	380	From all that dwell below the skies	Ps 117
		392	Come, we that love the Lord	E

| | | 344 | Lord, dismiss us with thy blessing | E |
| | | 704 | O thou who camest from above | E |

Week of Last Epiphany

SUN	MP	254	You are the Christ, O Lord	G
		675	Take up your cross, the Savior said	G
		484, 485	Praise the Lord through every nation	G
		572	Weary of all trumpeting	G
	EP	133, 134	O Light of Light, Love given birth	E
		136, 137	O wondrous type! O vision fair	E
		326	From glory to glory advancing, we praise thee, O Lord	E
		657	Love divine, all loves excelling	E
MON	MP	158	Ah, holy Jesus, how hast thou offended	G
		164	Alone thou goest forth, O Lord	G
	EP	477	All praise to thee, for thou, O King divine	E
		435	At the Name of Jesus	E
		252	Jesus! Name of wondrous love	E
TUE	MP	458	My song is love unknown	G
		495	Hail, thou once despisèd Jesus!	G
		171	Go to dark Gethsemane	G
		598	Lord Christ, when first thou cam'st to earth	G
		170	To mock your reign, O dearest Lord	G
		483	The head that once was crowned with thorns	G
	EP	701	Jesus, all my gladness	E
		488	Be thou my vision, O Lord of my heart	E
		475	God himself is with us (sts. 1-2)	E
		122, 123	Alleluia! song of gladness	S
		554	'Tis the gift to be simple	S

Ash Wednesday

	MP	145	Now quit your care	L
		148	Creator of the earth and skies	G
		144	Lord Jesus, Sun of Righteousness	G
	EP	151	From deepest woe I cry to thee	Ps 130
		666	Out of the depths I call	Ps 130
		152	Kind Maker of the world, O hear	E
		142	Lord, who throughout these forty days	E
		574, 575	Before thy throne, O God, we kneel	E
		146, 147	Now let us all with one accord	E
THU	MP	669	Commit thou all that grieves thee	Ps 37
		667	Sometimes a light surprises	L
		495	Hail, thou once despisèd Jesus	G

		483	The head that once was crowned with thorns	G
	EP	27, 28	O blest Creator, source of light	E
		545	Lo! what a cloud of witnesses	E
		546	Awake, my soul, stretch every nerve	E
		422	Not far beyond the sea, nor high	E
		148	Creator of the earth and skies	E
FRI	MP	140, 141	Wilt thou forgive that sin, where I begun	L
		152	Kind Maker of the world, O hear	L
		419	Lord of all being, throned afar	G
		484, 485	Praise the Lord through every nation	G
	EP	515	Holy Ghost, dispel our sadness	E
		701	Jesus, all my gladness	E
		345	Savior, again to thy dear Name we raise	E
		554	'Tis the gift to be simple	S
SAT	MP	657	Love divine, all loves excelling	G
		143	The glory of these forty days	S
		145	Now quit your care	S
	EP	658	As longs the deer for cooling streams	Ps 42
		635	If thou but trust in God to guide thee	E
		669	Commit thou all that grieves thee	E
		665	All my hope on God is founded	E
		636, 637	How firm a foundation, ye saints of the Lord	E

Week of 1 Lent

SUN	MP	146, 147	Now let us all with one accord	L
		143	The glory of these forty days	L
		144	Lord Jesus, Sun of Righteousness	G
		490	I want to walk as a child of the light	G
	EP	411	O bless the Lord, my soul!	Ps 103
		150	Forty days and forty nights	E
		142	Lord, who throughout these forty days	E
		143	The glory of these forty days	E
		443	From God Christ's deity came forth	E
MON	MP	150	Forty days and forty nights	G
		142	Lord, who throughout these forty days	G
		146, 147	Now let us all with one accord	G
		143	The glory of these forty days	G
		120	The sinless one to Jordan came	G
	EP	434	Nature with open volume stands	E
		471	We sing the praise of him who died	E
		165, 166	Sing, my tongue, the glorious battle	E
		576, 577	God is love, and where true love is	E
		581	Where charity and love prevail	E
		606	Where true charity and love dwell	E

TUE	MP	661	They cast their nets in Galilee	G
		549, 550	Jesus calls us; o'er the tumult	G
		567	Thine arm, O Lord, in days of old	G
		448, 449	O love, how deep, how broad, how high	G
	EP	474	When I survey the wondrous cross	E
		434	Nature with open volume stands	E
		471	We sing the praise of him who died	E
		441, 442	In the cross of Christ I glory	E
		160	Cross of Jesus, cross of sorrow	E
WED	MP	567	Thine arm, O Lord, in days of old	G
		493	O for a thousand tongues to sing	G
		371	Thou, whose almighty Word	G
		429	I'll praise my Maker while I've breath	G
	EP	488	Be thou my vision, O Lord of my heart	E
		629	We limit not the truth of God	E
		443	From God Christ's deity came forth	E
		694	God be in my head	E
THU	MP	567	Thine arm, O Lord, in days of old	G
		411	O bless the Lord, my soul	G
		493	O for a thousand tongues to sing	G
		566	From thee all skill and science flow	G
	EP	636, 637	How firm a foundation, ye saints of the Lord	E
		518	Christ is made the sure foundation	E
		525	The Church's one foundation	E
FRI	MP	281	He sat to watch o'er customs paid	G
		706	In your mercy, Lord, you called me	G
		469, 470	There's a wideness in God's mercy	G
		467	Sing, my soul, his wondrous love	G
	EP	500	Creator Spirit, by whose aid	E
		516	Come down, O Love divine	E
		656	Blest are the pure in heart	E
SAT	MP	1, 2	Father, we praise thee, now the night is over	G
		493	O for a thousand tongues to sing	G
		630	Thanks to God whose Word was spoken (omit sts. 3, 4)	G
		458	My song is love unknown	G
		567	Thine arm, O Lord, in days of old	G
	EP	702	Lord, thou hast searched me and dost know	Ps 139
		535	Ye servants of God, your Master proclaim	E
		681	Our God, to whom we turn	S
		463, 464	He is the Way	S

SUN	MP	626	Lord, be thy word my rule	G
		628	Help us, O Lord, to learn	G
	EP	517	How lovely is thy dwelling-place	Ps 84
		298	All who believe and are baptized	E
		294	Baptized in water	E
		697	My God, accept my heart this day	E
		295	Sing praise to our Creator	E
MON	MP	590	O Jesus Christ, may grateful hymns be rising	G
		567	Thine arm, O Lord, in days of old	G
		528	Lord, you give the great commission	G
		493	O for a thousand tongues to sing	G
		540	Awake, thou Spirit of the watchmen	G
	EP	593	Lord, make us servants of your peace	E
		695, 696	By gracious powers so wonderfully sheltered	S
TUE	MP	500	Creator Spirit, by whose aid	G
		516	Come down, O Love divine	G
		529	In Christ there is no East or West	G
		603, 604	When Christ was lifted from the earth	G
	EP	202	The Lamb's high banquet called to share (sts. 1-4)	E
		638, 639	Come, O thou Traveler unknown	S
		143	The glory of these forty days	S
WED	MP	588, 589	Almighty God, your word is cast	G
		541	Come, labor on	G
		530	Spread, O spread, thou mighty word	G
		505	O Spirit of Life, O Spirit of God	G
	EP	606	Where true charity and love dwell	E
		581	Where charity and love prevail	E
		576, 577	God is Love, and where true love is	E
THU	MP	588, 589	Almighty God, your word is cast	G
		24	The day thou gavest, Lord, is ended (omit st. 1)	G
		534	God is working his purpose out	G
		615	"Thy kingdom come!" on bended knee	G
	EP	516	Come down, O Love divine	E
		500	Creator Spirit, by whose aid	E
		656	Blest are the pure in heart	E
FRI	MP	669	Commit thou all that grieves thee	G
		414	God, my King, thy might confessing	G
		375	Give praise and glory unto God	G
	EP	350	O God of love, to thee we bow	E
		487	Come, my Way, my Truth, my Life	S

		149	Eternal Lord of love, behold your Church	S
SAT	MP	493	O for a thousand tongues to sing	G
		567	Thine arm, O Lord, in days of old	G
		652, 653	Dear Lord and Father of mankind (sts. 1, 4 & 5)	G
		429	I'll praise my Maker while I've breath	G
		411	O bless the Lord, my soul	G
	EP	664	My Shepherd will supply my need	Ps 23
		663	The Lord my God my shepherd is	Ps 23
		645, 646	The King of love my shepherd is	Ps 23

Week of 3 Lent

SUN	MP	457	Thou art the Way, to thee alone	G
		455, 456	O love of God, how strong and true	G
	EP	516	Come down, O Love divine	E
		500	Creator Spirit, by whose aid	E
		512	Come, gracious Spirit, heavenly Dove	E
		228	Holy Spirit, font of light	E
		226, 227	Come, thou Holy Spirit bright	E
MON	MP	590	O Jesus Christ, may grateful hymns be rising	G
		493	O for a thousand tongues to sing	G
		567	Thine arm, O Lord, in days of old	G
		566	From thee all skill and science flow	G
		429	I'll praise my Maker while I've breath	G
	EP	701	Jesus, all my gladness (sts. 1-2)	E
		488	Be thou my vision, O Lord of my heart	E
		146, 147	Now let us all with one accord	S
TUE	MP	677	God moves in a mysterious way	L
		633	Word of God, come down on earth	G
		528	Lord, you give the great commission	G
		540	Awake, thou Spirit of the watchmen	G
	EP	488	Be thou my vision, O Lord of my heart	E
		701	Jesus, all my gladness (sts. 1-2)	E
		487	Come, my Way, my Truth, my Life	S
WED	MP	444	Blessed be the God of Israel	G
		76	On Jordan's bank the Baptist's cry	G
		271, 272	The great forerunner of the morn	G
	EP	689	I sought the Lord, and afterward I knew	S
		463, 464	He is the Way	S
		695, 696	By gracious powers so wonderfully sheltered	S
THU	MP	472	Hope of the world, thou Christ	G
		478	Jesus, our mighty Lord	G
		708	Savior, like a shepherd lead us	G
		300	Glory, love, and praise, and honor	G

	EP	638, 639	Come, O thou Traveler unknown	S
		152	Kind Maker of the world, O hear	S
		145	Now quit your care	S
FRI	MP	590	O Jesus Christ, may grateful hymns be rising	G
		567	Thine arm, O Lord, in days of old	G
		669	Commit thou all that grieves thee	G
		636, 637	How firm a foundation, ye saints of the Lord	G
		414	God, my King, thy might confessing	G
	EP	27, 28	O blest Creator, source of light	E
		422	Not far beyond the sea, nor high	E
		546	Awake, my soul, stretch every nerve	E
		552, 553	Fight the good fight with all thy might	E
SAT	MP	680	O God, our help in ages past	Ps 90
		656	Blest are the pure in heart	G
		382	King of glory, King of peace	G
		435	At the Name of Jesus (sts. 1-5)	G
		436	Lift up your heads, ye mighty gates	G
	EP	142	Lord, who throughout these forty days	E
		150	Forty days and forty nights	E
		149	Eternal Lord of love, behold your Church	E
		690	Guide me, O thou great Jehovah	E
		685	Rock of ages, cleft for me	E

Week of 4 Lent

SUN	MP	538	God of mercy, God of grace	Ps 67
		335	I am the bread of life	G
		302, 303	Father, we thank thee who hast planted (st. 1)	G
		649, 650	O Jesus, joy of loving hearts	G
		343	Shepherd of souls, refresh and bless (sts. 1-2)	G
	EP	431	The stars declare his glory	Ps 19
		687, 688	A mighty fortress is our God	Ps 46
		623	O what their joy and their glory must be	E
		621, 622	Light's abode, celestial Salem	E
MON	MP	633	Word of God, come down on earth	G
		493	O for a thousand tongues to sing	G
		567	Thine arm, O Lord, in days of old	G
		411	O bless the Lord, my soul!	G
		429	I'll praise my Maker while I've breath	G
	EP	626	Lord, be thy word my rule	E
		408	Sing praise to God who reigns above	E
		683, 684	O for a closer walk with God	E
	MP	472	Hope of the world, thou Christ	G
		300	Glory, love, and praise, and honor	G
		320	Zion, praise thy Savior, singing (sts. 5-6)	G

	EP	322	When Jesus died to save us	E
		320	Zion, praise thy Savior, singing	E
		339	Deck thyself, my soul, with gladness	E
		581	Where charity and love prevail	E
		576, 577	God is Love, and where true love is	E
		606	Where true charity and love dwell	E
WED	MP	633	Word of God, come down on earth	G
		493	O for a thousand tongues to sing	G
		567	Thine arm, O Lord, in days of old	G
		429	I'll praise my Maker while I've breath	G
		536	God has spoken to his people	G
	EP	501, 502	O Holy Spirit, by whose breath	E
		505	O Spirit of Life, O Spirit of God	E
		228	Holy Spirit, font of light	E
THU	MP	254	You are the Christ, O Lord	G
		675	Take up your cross, the Savior said	G
		10	New every morning is the love	G
		572	Weary of all trumpeting	G
	EP	513	Like the murmur of the dove's song	E
		295	Sing praise to our Creator	E
		299	Spirit of God, unleashed on earth	E
FRI	MP	133, 134	O Light of Light, Love given birth	G
		136, 137	O wondrous type! O vision fair	G
	EP	576, 577	God is Love, and where true love is	E
		581	Where charity and love prevail	E
		606	Where true charity and love dwell	E
		521	Put forth, O God, thy Spirit's might	E
		511	Holy Spirit, ever living	E
		295	Sing praise to our Creator	E
SAT	MP	401	The God of Abraham praise	L
		386, 387	We sing of God, the mighty source	L
		439	What wondrous love is this	L
		567	Thine arm, O Lord, in days of old	G
		493	O for a thousand tongues to sing	G
	EP	612	Gracious Spirit, Holy Ghost	E
		602	Jesu, Jesu, fill us with your love	E
		585	Morning glory, starlit sky	E

Week of 5 Lent

SUN	MP	401	The God of Abraham praise	G
		439	What wondrous love is this	G
		536	God has spoken to his people	G
		505	O Spirit of Life, O Spirit of God	G
	EP	414	God, my King, thy might confessing	Ps 145
		404	We will extol you, ever-blessèd Lord	Ps 145

		707	Take my life, and let it be	E
		593	Lord, make us servants of your peace	E
		610	Lord, whose love through humble service	E
		347	Go forth for God; go to the world in peace	E
MON	MP	648	When Israel was in Egypt's land	L
		609	Where cross the crowded ways of life	G
		659, 660	O Master, let me walk with thee	G
		434	Nature with open volume stands	G
		448, 449	O love, how deep, how broad, how high	G
	EP	531	O Spirit of the living God	E
		513	Like the murmur of the dove's song	E
		694	God be in my head	E
		505	O Spirit of Life, O Spirit of God	E
TUE	MP	668	I to the hills will lift mine eyes	Ps 121
		648	When Israel was in Egypt's land	L
		574, 575	Before thy throne, O God, we kneel	G
		146, 147	Now let us all with one accord	S
	EP	521	Put forth, O God, thy Spirit's might	E
		505	O Spirit of Life, O Spirit of God	E
		694	God be in my head	E
WED	MP	648	When Israel was in Egypt's land	L
		480	When Jesus left his Father's throne	G
		350	O God of love, to thee we bow	G
		352	O God, to those who here profess	G
		353	Your love, O God, has called us here	G
	EP	151	From deepest woe I cry to thee	Ps 130
		666	Out of the depths I call	Ps 130
		152	Kind Maker of the world, O hear	S
		689	I sought the Lord, and afterward I knew	S
THU	MP	670	Lord, for ever at thy side	Ps 131
		648	When Israel was in Egypt's land	L
		655	O Jesus, I have promised	G
		701	Jesus, all my gladness	G
		707	Take my life, and let it be	G
		475	God himself is with us	G
	EP	657	Love divine, all loves excelling	E
		326	From glory to glory advancing, we praise thee, O Lord	E
		683, 684	O for a closer walk with God	E
FRI	MP	648	When Israel was in Egypt's land	L
		495	Hail, thou once despisèd Jesus (sts. 1-2)	G
		483	The head that once was crowned with thorns	G
		458	My song is love unknown	G
		474	When I survey the wondrous cross	G
		659, 660	O Master, let me walk with thee	G

	EP	465, 466	Eternal light, shine in my heart	E
		419	Lord of all being, throned afar	E
		547	Awake, O sleeper, rise from death	E
		27, 28	O blest Creator, source of light	E
SAT	MP	633	Word of God, come down on earth	G
		493	O for a thousand tongues to sing	G
		567	Thine arm, O Lord, in days of old	G
		371	Thou, whose almighty word	G
		429	I'll praise my Maker while I've breath	G
	EP	658	As longs the deer for cooling streams	Ps 42
		623	O what their joy and their glory must be	E
		621, 622	Light's abode, celestial Salem	E

Holy Week

Palm Sunday

	MP	436	Lift up your heads, ye mighty gates	Ps 24
		156	Ride on! ride on in majesty!	L
		494	Crown him with many crowns	E
		545	Lo! what a cloud of witnesses	E
	EP	598	Lord Christ, when first thou cam'st to earth	G
		164	Alone thou goest forth, O Lord	G
		458	My song is love unknown	G
MON	MP	164	Alone thou goest forth, O Lord	L
		458	My song is love unknown	L
		161	The flaming banners of our King	S
		162	The royal banners forward go	S
	EP	167	There is a green hill far away (omit sts. 3, 4)	S
		498	Beneath the cross of Jesus	S
		160	Cross of Jesus, cross of sorrow	S
TUE	MP	170	To mock your reign, O dearest Lord	G
		434	Nature with open volume stands	S
		441, 442	In the cross of Christ I glory	S
	EP	471	We sing the praise of him who died	S
		479	Glory be to Jesus	S
WED	MP	158	Ah, holy Jesus, how hast thou offended	G
		167	There is a green hill far away (omit sts. 3, 4)	S
	EP	170	To mock your reign, O dearest Lord	S
		474	When I survey the wondrous cross	S

Maundy Thursday

MP	322	When Jesus died to save us	G
	320	Zion, praise thy Savior, singing	G
	329, 330, 331	Now, my tongue, the mystery telling (sts. 1-4)	G
EP	339	Deck thyself, my soul, with gladness	E
	315	Thou, who at thy first Eucharist didst pray	E
	171	Go to dark Gethsemane	S

Good Friday

MP	172	Were you there when they crucified my Lord?	G
	160	Cross of Jesus, cross of sorrow	G
	168, 169	O sacred head, sore wounded	G
EP	163	Sunset to sunrise changes now	E
	161	The flaming banners of our King	E
	162	The royal banners forward go	E
	172	Were you there when they crucified my Lord?	G
	458	My song is love unknown	G
	173	O sorrow deep!	G
	159	At the cross her vigil keeping	S

Holy Saturday

MP	173	O sorrow deep!	S
	172	Were you there when they crucified my Lord?	S
	458	My song is love unknown	S
EP	173	O sorrow deep!	S
	172	Were you there when they crucified my Lord?	S
	458	My song is love unknown	S

Easter Week

Easter Day

MP	202	The Lamb's high banquet called to share	L
	174	At the Lamb's high feast we sing	L
	175	Hail thee, festival day! *Easter*	S
	179	"Welcome, happy morning!" age to age shall say	S
EP	187	Through the Red Sea brought at last, Alleluia!	L
	199, 200	Come, ye faithful, raise the strain	L

		208	The strife is o'er, the battle done	G
		184	Christ the Lord is risen again!	G
		196, 197	Look there! the Christ, our Brother, comes	G
MON	MP	202	The Lamb's high banquet called to share	L
		174	At the Lamb's high feast we sing	L
		183	Christians, to the Paschal victim	G
		203	O sons and daughters, let us sing (sts. 1-3) *Easter*	G
	EP	204	Now the green blade riseth from the buried grain	E
		452	Glorious the day when Christ was born	E
		455, 456	O love of God, how strong and true	E
		492	Sing, ye faithful, sing with gladness	E
		184	Christ the Lord is risen again!	E
TUE	MP	196, 197	Look there! the Christ, our Brother, comes	G
		180	He is risen, he is risen!	G
		178	Alleluia, alleluia! Give thanks to the risen Lord	S
	EP	192	This joyful Eastertide	E
		204	Now the green blade riseth from the buried grain	E
		191	Alleluia, alleluia! Hearts and voices heavenward raise	E
		492	Sing, ye faithful, sing with gladness	E
WED	MP	183	Christians, to the Paschal victim	G
		203	O sons and daughters, let us sing (sts. 1-3) *Easter*	G
		190	Lift your voice rejoicing, Mary	G
	EP	204	Now the green blade riseth from the buried grain	E
		621, 622	Light's abode, celestial Salem	E
		194, 195	Jesus lives! thy terrors now	S
THU	MP	210	The day of resurrection!	L
		176, 177	Over the chaos of the empty waters	G
		182	Christ is alive! Let Christians sing	G
	EP	205	Good Christians all, rejoice and sing!	S
		213	Come away to the skies	S
		204	Now the green blade riseth from the buried grain	E
		621, 622	Light's abode, celestial Salem	E
FRI	MP	207	Jesus Christ is risen today, Alleluia!	G
		180	He is risen, he is risen!	G
		184	Christ the Lord is risen again!	G
	EP	188, 189	Love's redeeming work is done	E
		208	The strife is o'er, the battle done	E
		192	This joyful Eastertide	E
		194, 195	Jesus lives! thy terrors now	E
SAT	MP	187	Through the Red Sea brought at last, Alleluia!	L
		211	The whole bright world rejoices now	S
		212	Awake, arise, lift up your voice	S
	EP	623	O what their joy and their glory must be	E

		621, 622	Light's abode, celestial Salem	E
		209	We walk by faith, and not by sight	E

Week of 2 Easter

SUN	MP	187	Through the Red Sea brought at last, Alleluia!	L
		199, 200	Come, ye faithful, raise the strain	L
		457	Thou art the Way, to thee alone	G
	EP	209	We walk by faith, and not by sight	E
		206	O sons and daughters, let us sing	
			Second Sunday of Easter	S
		193	That Easter day with joy was bright	S
		212	Awake, arise, lift up your voice	S
MON	MP	187	Through the Red Sea brought at last, Alleluia!	L
		199, 200	Come, ye faithful, raise the strain	L
		457	Thou art the Way, to thee alone	G
		194, 195	Jesus lives! thy terrors now	G
		484, 485	Praise the Lord through every nation	G
		487	Come, my Way, my Truth, my Life	G
		463, 464	He is the Way	G
	EP	298	All who believe and are baptized	E
		296	We know that Christ is raised and dies no more	E
		294	Baptized in water	E
		472	Hope of the world, thou Christ	E
TUE	MP	425	Sing now with joy unto the Lord	L
		199, 200	Come, ye faithful, raise the strain	L & G
		226, 227	Come, thou Holy Spirit bright	G
		228	Holy Spirit, font of light	G
		500	Creator Spirit, by whose aid	G
		514	To thee, O Comforter divine	G
	EP	204	Now the green blade riseth from the buried grain	E
		298	All who believe and are baptized	E
		176, 177	Over the chaos of the empty waters	E
		296	We know that Christ is raised and dies no more	E
		432	O praise ye the Lord! Praise him in the height (omit st. 3)	E
WED	MP	198	Thou hallowed chosen morn of praise	G
		513	Like the murmur of the dove's song	G
		392	Come, we that love the Lord	G
		344	Lord, dismiss us with thy blessing	G
	EP	518	Christ is made the sure foundation	E
		51	We the Lord's people, heart and voice uniting (st. 1)	E
		432	O praise ye the Lord! Praise him in the height (omit st. 3)	E
		294	Baptized in water	E

THU	MP	690	Guide me, O thou great Jehovah	L
		458	My song is love unknown	G
		706	In your mercy, Lord, you called me	G
		514	To thee, O Comforter divine	G
		603, 604	When Christ was lifted from the earth	G
		585	Morning glory, starlit sky	G
	EP	478	Jesus, our mighty Lord	E
		708	Savior, like a shepherd lead us	E
		208	The strife is o'er, the battle done	E
		492	Sing, ye faithful, sing with gladness	E
FRI	MP	686	Come, thou fount of every blessing	L
		512	Come, gracious Spirit, heavenly Dove	G
	EP	455, 456	O love of God, how strong and true	E
		298	All who believe and are baptized	E
		296	We know that Christ is raised and dies no more	E
		294	Baptized in water	E
		432	O praise ye the Lord! Praise him in the height (omit st. 3)	E
SAT	MP	698	Eternal Spirit of the living Christ	G
		711	Seek ye first the kingdom of God	G
	EP	380	From all that dwell below the skies	Ps 117
		483	The head that once was crowned with thorns	E
		484, 485	Praise the Lord through every nation	E

Week of 3 Easter

SUN	MP	296	We know that Christ is raised and dies no more	G
		176, 177	Over the chaos of the empty waters	G
		298	All who believe and are baptized	G
		673	The first one ever, oh, ever to know (st. 3)	G
	EP	465, 466	Eternal light, shine in my heart	E
		542	Christ is the world's true Light	E
		27, 28	O blest Creator, source of light	E
MON	MP	75	There's a voice in the wilderness crying	G
		67	Comfort, comfort ye my people	G
		76	On Jordan's bank the Baptist's cry	G
		70	Herald, sound the note of judgment	G
	EP	400	All creatures of our God and King	E
		478	Jesus, our mighty Lord	E
		635	If thou but trust in God to guide thee	E
		527	Singing songs of expectation	E
TUE	MP	76	On Jordan's bank the Baptist's cry	G
		70	Herald, sound the note of judgment	G
		69	What is the crying at Jordan?	G

	EP	326	From glory to glory advancing, we praise thee, O Lord	E
		392	Come, we that love the Lord	E
		344	Lord, dismiss us with thy blessing	E
		432	O praise ye the Lord! Praise him in the height (omit st. 3)	E
WED	MP	116	"I come," the great Redeemer cries	G
		121	Christ, when for us you were baptized	G
		139	When Jesus went to Jordan's stream	G
	EP	421	All glory be to God on high	E
		495	Hail, thou once despisèd Jesus! (sts. 1-2)	E
		492	Sing, ye faithful, sing with gladness	E
		483	The head that once was crowned with thorns	E
THU	MP	443	From God Christ's deity came forth	G
		120	The sinless one to Jordan came	G
		448, 449	O love, how deep, how broad, how high	G
		284	O ye immortal throng	G
		559	Lead us, heavenly Father, lead us	G
	EP	422	Not far beyond the sea, nor high	E
		628	Help us, O Lord, to learn	E
		440	Blessèd Jesus, at thy word	E
FRI	MP	125, 126	The people who in darkness walked	G
		499	Lord God, you now have set your servant free	G
		542	Christ is the world's true Light	G
		381	Thy strong word did cleave the darkness	G
	EP	294	Baptized in water	E
		298	All who believe and are baptized	E
		296	We know that Christ is raised and dies no more	E
		432	O praise ye the Lord! Praise him in the height (omit st. 3)	E
SAT	MP	661	They cast their nets in Galilee	G
		549, 550	Jesus calls us; o'er the tumult	G
		448, 449	O love, how deep, how broad, how high	G
		567	Thine arm, O Lord, in days of old	G
	EP	298	All who believe and are baptized	E
		674	"Forgive our sins as we forgive"	E
		426	Songs of praise the angels sang	E
		420	When in our music God is glorified	E
		402, 403	Let all the world in every corner sing	E

Week of 4 Easter

SUN	MP	413	New songs of celebration render	Ps 98
		690	Guide me, O thou great Jehovah	G
		472	Hope of the world, thou Christ	G
		320	Zion, praise thy Savior, singing (sts. 5-6)	G

		708	Savior, like a shepherd lead us	G
		300	Glory, love, and praise, and honor	G
	EP	410	Praise, my soul, the King of heaven	Ps 103
		390	Praise to the Lord, the Almighty	Ps 103
		411	O bless the Lord, my soul!	Ps 103
		295	Sing praise to our Creator	E
		294	Baptized in water	E
MON	MP	372	Praise to the living God!	L
		560	Remember your servants, Lord	G
		656	Blest are the pure in heart	G
		593	Lord, make us servants of your peace	G
		437, 438	Tell out, my soul, the greatness of the Lord!	G
	EP	564, 565	He who would valiant be	E
		655	O Jesus, I have promised	E
TUE	MP	543	O Zion, tune thy voice	G
		381	Thy strong word did cleave the darkness	G
		628	Help us, O Lord, to learn	G
	EP	408	Sing praise to God who reigns above	E
		478	Jesus, our mighty Lord	E
		689	I sought the Lord, and afterward I knew	E
		706	In your mercy, Lord, you called me	E
		505	O Spirit of Life, O Spirit of God	E
WED	MP	393	Praise our great and gracious Lord	L
		628	Help us, O Lord, to learn	G
		626	Lord, be thy word my rule	G
	EP	614	Christ is the King! O friends upraise	E
		447	The Christ who died but rose again	S
		181	Awake and sing the song	S
THU	MP	372	Praise to the living God	L
		408	Sing praise to God who reigns above	L
		674	"Forgive our sins as we forgive"	G
		593	Lord, make us servants of your peace	G
		603, 604	When Christ was lifted from the earth	G
	EP	632	O Christ, the Word incarnate	E
		627	Lamp of our feet, whereby we trace	E
		633	Word of God, come down on earth	E
FRI	MP	372	Praise to the living God	L
		3, 4	Now that the daylight fills the sky	G
		641	Lord Jesus, think on me	G
	EP	657	Love divine, all loves excelling	E
		326	From glory to glory advancing, we praise thee, O Lord	E
SAT	MP	603, 604	When Christ was lifted from the earth	G
		568	Father all loving, who rulest in majesty	G

		394, 395	Creating God, your fingers trace	G
	EP	702	Lord, thou hast searched me and dost know	Ps 139
		31, 32	Most Holy God, the Lord of heaven	E
		27, 28	O blest Creator, source of light	E

Week of 5 Easter

SUN	MP	436	Lift up your heads, ye mighty gates	Ps 24
		448, 449	O love, how deep, how broad, how high	G
		71, 72	Hark! the glad sound! the Savior comes	G
		447	The Christ who died but rose again	S
	EP	517	How lovely is thy dwelling-place	Ps 84
		636, 637	How firm a foundation, ye saints of the Lord	E
		545	Lo! what a cloud of witnesses	E
		253	Give us the wings of faith to rise	E
		546	Awake, my soul, stretch every nerve	E
MON	MP	182	Christ is alive! Let Christians sing	S
		614	Christ is the King! O friends upraise	S
		472	Hope of the world, thou Christ	S
	EP	194, 195	Jesus lives! thy terrors now	E
		192	This joyful Eastertide	E
		620	Jerusalem, my happy home	E
		621, 622	Light's abode, celestial Salem	E
		623	O what their joy and their glory must be	E
		624	Jerusalem the golden	E
TUE	MP	674	"Forgive our sins as we forgive"	G
		581	Where charity and love prevail	G
		709	O God of Bethel, by whose hand	G
		400	All creatures of our God and King	
			(omit sts. 2, 3 & 6)	G
		406, 407	Most High, omnipotent, good Lord	G
	EP	547	Awake, O sleeper, rise from death	E
		548	Soldiers of Christ, arise	E
WED	MP	544	Jesus shall reign where'er the sun	Ps 72
		616	Hail to the Lord's Anointed	Ps 72
		610	Lord, whose love through humble service	L
		701	Jesus, all my gladness	G
		475	God himself is with us (sts. 1-2)	G
		488	Be thou my vision, O Lord of my heart	G
	EP	347	Go forth for God; go to the world in peace	E
		182	Christ is alive! Let Christians sing	S
		181	Awake and sing the song	S
THU	MP	709	O God of Bethel, by whose hand	G
		388	O worship the King, all glorious above!	G
		667	Sometimes a light surprises	G
		635	If thou but trust in God to guide thee	G

		711	Seek ye first the kingdom of God	G
		669	Commit thou all that grieves thee	G
	EP	704	O thou who camest from above	E
		634	I call on thee, Lord Jesus Christ	E
FRI	MP	705	As those of old their first fruits brought	L
		711	Seek ye first the kingdom of God	G
		698	Eternal Spirit of the living Christ	G
		709	O God of Bethel, by whose hand	G
	EP	295	Sing praise to our Creator	E
		432	O praise ye the Lord! Praise him in the height (omit st. 3)	E
		447	The Christ who died but rose again	S
		204	Now the green blade riseth from the buried grain	S
SAT	MP	392	Come, we that love the Lord	G
		344	Lord, dismiss us with thy blessing	G
	EP	663	The Lord my God my shepherd is	Ps 23
		664	My Shepherd will supply my need	Ps 23
		645, 646	The King of love my shepherd is	Ps 23
		586	Jesus, thou divine companion	E
		592	Teach me, my God and King	E
		611	Christ the worker	E
		482	Lord of all hopefulness, Lord of all joy	E

Week of 6 Easter

SUN	MP	701	Jesus, all my gladness (sts. 1-2)	G
		536	God has spoken to his people	G
		505	O Spirit of Life, O Spirit of God	G
	EP	416	For the beauty of the earth	E
		584	God, you have given us power to sound	E
		628	Help us, O Lord, to learn	E
		398	I sing the almighty power of God	E
MON	MP	588, 589	Almighty God, your word is cast	G
		536	God has spoken to his people	G
		505	O Spirit of Life, O Spirit of God	G
	EP	495	Hail, thou once despisèd Jesus!	E
		392	Come, we that love the Lord	E
		326	From glory to glory advancing, we praise thee, O Lord	E
		344	Lord, dismiss us with thy blessing	E
TUE	MP	588, 589	Almighty God, your word is cast	G
		505	O Spirit of Life, O Spirit of God	G
	EP	368	Holy Father, great Creator	E
WED	MP	709	O God of Bethel, by whose hand	L

		495	Hail, thou once despisèd Jesus! (sts. 1-2)	E
		686	Come, thou fount of every blessing	E
		450, 451	All hail the power of Jesus' Name!	G
		254	You are the Christ, O Lord	G

Eve of the Ascension

	EP	374	Come, let us join our cheerful songs	E
		417, 418	This is the feast of victory for our God	E
		307	Lord, enthroned in heavenly splendor (omit sts. 2, 3)	E
		495	Hail, thou once despisèd Jesus!	E

Ascension Day

	MP	460, 461	Alleluia! sing to Jesus!	G
		481	Rejoice, the Lord is King	G
		214	Hail the day that sees him rise, Alleluia!	G
		217, 218	A hymn of glory let us sing	G
		216	Hail thee, festival day! *Ascension*	G
	EP	436	Lift up your heads, ye mighty gates	Ps 24
		220, 221	O Lord Most High, eternal King	E
		215	See the Conqueror mounts in triumph	E
		219	The Lord ascendeth up on high	E
		450, 451	All hail the power of Jesus' Name!	E
		483	The head that once was crowned with thorns	E
FRI	MP	437, 438	Tell out, my soul, the greatness of the Lord!	L
		636, 637	How firm a foundation, ye saints of the Lord	G
		628	Help us, Lord, to learn	G
		626	Lord, be thy word my rule	G
	EP	432	O praise ye the Lord! Praise him in the height (omit st. 3)	E
		686	Come, thou fount of every blessing	E
		467	Sing, my soul, his wondrous love	E
SAT	MP	680	O God, our help in ages past	Ps 90
		567	Thine arm, O Lord, in days of old	G
		493	O for a thousand tongues to sing	G
		371	Thou, whose almighty word	G
	EP	389	Let us, with a gladsome mind	Ps 136
		518	Christ is made the sure foundation	E
		525	The Church's one foundation	E
		495	Hail, thou once despisèd Jesus!	E

Week of 7 Easter

SUN	MP	538	God of mercy, God of grace	Ps 67
		535	Ye servants of God, your Master proclaim	G
		544	Jesus shall reign where'er the sun	G

		536	God has spoken to his people	G
	EP	409	The spacious firmament on high	Ps 19
		431	The stars declare his glory	Ps 19
		687, 688	A mighty fortress is our God	Ps 46
		368	Holy Father, great Creator	E
		512	Come, gracious Spirit, heavenly Dove	E
		624	Jerusalem the golden	E
MON	MP	567	Thine arm, O Lord, in days of old	G
		493	O for a thousand tongues to sing	G
		566	From thee all skill and science flow	G
		410	Praise, my soul, the King of heaven	G
	EP	483	The head that once was crowned with thorns	E
		460, 461	Alleluia! sing to Jesus!	E
		432	O praise ye the Lord! Praise him in the height (omit st. 3)	E
TUE	MP	458	My song is love unknown	G
		478	Jesus, our mighty Lord	G
		564, 565	He who would valiant be	G
		669	Commit thou all that grieves thee	G
	EP	422	Not far beyond the sea, nor high	E
		448, 449	O love, how deep, how broad, how high	E
		455, 456	O love of God, how strong and true	E
WED	MP	522, 523	Glorious things of thee are spoken	L
		393	Praise our great and gracious Lord	L
		567	Thine arm, O Lord, in days of old	G
		493	O for a thousand tongues to sing	G
		429	I'll praise my Maker while I've breath	G
	EP	220, 221	O Lord Most High, eternal King	E
		492	Sing, ye faithful, sing with gladness	E
		521	Put forth, O God, thy Spirit's might	E
		547	Awake, O sleeper, rise from death	E
		511	Holy Spirit, ever living	E
THU	MP	410	Praise, my soul, the King of heaven	G
		566	From thee all skill and science flow	G
		567	Thine arm, O Lord, in days of old	G
		493	O for a thousand tongues to sing	G
	EP	574, 575	Before thy throne, O God, we kneel	E
		347	Go forth for God; go to the world in peace	E
		593	Lord, make us servants of your peace	E
FRI	MP	281	He sat to watch o'er customs paid	G
		706	In your mercy, Lord, you called me	G
		469, 470	There's a wideness in God's mercy	G
		467	Sing, my soul, his wondrous love	G
	EP	547	Awake, O sleeper, rise from death	E
		490	I want to walk as a child of the light	E

		426	Songs of praise the angels sang	E
		402, 403	Let all the world in every corner sing	E
		430	Come, O come, our voices raise	E
SAT	MP	584	God, you have given us power to sound (sts. 1-3)	L
		656	Blest are the pure in heart	L
		548	Soldiers of Christ, arise	E
		561	Stand up, stand up for Jesus	E
		493	O for a thousand tongues to sing	G
		567	Thine arm, O Lord, in days of old	G
		590	O Jesus Christ, may grateful hymns be rising	G

Eve of Pentecost

EP	51	We the Lord's people, heart and voice uniting (st. 1)	E
	294	Baptized in water	E
	432	O praise ye the Lord! Praise him in the height (omit st. 3)	E

Day of Pentecost

MP	223, 224	Hail this joyful day's return	S
	225	Hail thee, festival day! *Pentecost*	S
	506, 507	Praise the Spirit in creation	S
	513	Like the murmur of the dove's song	S
EP	230	A mighty sound from heaven	E
	229	Spirit of mercy, truth, and love	E
	506, 507	Praise the Spirit in creation	E

Eve of Trinity Sunday

EP	388	O worship the King, all glorious above!	Ps 104
	369	How wondrous great, how glorious bright	L
	422	Not far beyond the sea, nor high	E

Trinity Sunday

MP	421	All glory be to God on high	G
	363	Ancient of Days, who sittest throned in glory	S
	370	I bind unto myself today	S
	365	Come, thou almighty King	S
	362	Holy, holy, holy! Lord God Almighty!	S
EP	29, 30	O Trinity of blessèd light	S
	295	Sing praise to our Creator	S
	371	Thou, whose almighty Word	S
	367	Round the Lord in glory seated	S

Proper 1

MON	MP	567	Thine arm, O Lord, in days of old	G
		493	O for a thousand tongues to sing	G
		371	Thou, whose almighty Word	G
		429	I'll praise my Maker while I've breath	G
	EP	490	I want to walk as a child of the light	E
		699	Jesus, Lover of my soul	E
		371	Thou, whose almighty Word	E
		542	Christ is the world's true Light	E
		496, 497	How bright appears the Morning Star	E
TUE	MP	668	I to the hills will lift mine eyes	Ps 121
		540	Awake, thou Spirit of the watchmen	G
		541	Come, labor on	G
		478	Jesus, our mighty Lord	G
	EP	542	Christ is the world's true Light	E
		371	Thou, whose almighty Word	E
		496, 497	How bright appears the Morning Star	E
		27, 28	O blest Creator, source of light	E
WED	MP	478	Jesus, our mighty Lord	L
		528	Lord, you give the great commission	G
		540	Awake, thou Spirit of the watchmen (sts. 2-3)	G
		541	Come, labor on	G
	EP	666	Out of the depths I call	Ps 130
		151	From deepest woe I cry to thee	Ps 130
		665	All my hope on God is founded	E
		475	God himself is with us	E
		488	Be thou my vision, O Lord of my heart	E
THU	MP	670	Lord, for ever at thy side	Ps 131
		709	O God of Bethel, by whose hand	L
		655	O Jesus, I have promised	G
		530	Spread, O spread, thou mighty word	G
		563	Go forward, Christian soldier	G
	EP	295	Sing praise to our Creator	E
		294	Baptized in water	E
FRI	MP	563	Go forward, Christian soldier	G
		564, 565	He who would valiant be	G
		535	Ye servants of God, your Master proclaim	G
	EP	492	Sing, ye faithful, sing with gladness	E
		295	Sing praise to our Creator	E
		294	Baptized in water	E
SAT	MP	675	Take up your cross, the Savior said	G
		484, 485	Praise the Lord through every nation	G
		609	Where cross the crowded ways of life	G
		661	They cast their nets in Galilee	G
		572	Weary of all trumpeting	G

	EP	388	O worship the King, all glorious above!	Ps 104
		610	Lord, whose love through humble service	E
		573	Father eternal, Ruler of creation	E
		603, 604	When Christ was lifted from the earth	E
		581	Where charity and love prevail	E

Proper 2

MON	MP	458	My song is love unknown	G
		493	O for a thousand tongues to sing	G
		371	Thou, whose almighty Word	G
		429	I'll praise my Maker while I've breath	G
	EP	610	Lord, whose love through humble service	E
		603, 604	When Christ was lifted from the earth	E
		704	O thou who camest from above	E
		581	Where charity and love prevail	E
TUE	MP	584	God, you have given us power to sound	L
		574, 575	Before thy throne, O God, we kneel	L
		656	Blest are the pure in heart	L
		271, 272	The great forerunner of the morn	G
		536	God has spoken to his people	G
		444	Blessed be the God of Israel	G
	EP	379	God is love, let heaven adore him	E
		471	We sing the praise of him who died	E
		700	O love that casts out fear	E
		610	Lord, whose love through humble service	E
		568	Father all loving, who rulest in majesty	E
WED	MP	593	Lord, make us servants of your peace	G
		596	Judge eternal, throned in splendor	G
		598	Lord Christ, when first thou cam'st to earth	G
	EP	298	All who believe and are baptized	E
		489	The great Creator of the worlds	E
THU	MP	692	I heard the voice of Jesus say (st. 1)	G
		74	Blest be the King whose coming	G
		644	How sweet the Name of Jesus sounds	G
		457	Thou art the Way, to thee alone	G
		476	Can we by searching find out God	G
	EP	518	Christ is made the sure foundation	E
		711	Seek ye first the kingdom of God	E
		698	Eternal Spirit of the living Christ	E
		302, 303	Father, we thank thee who hast planted (st. 1)	E
FRI	MP	584	God, you have given us power to sound	L
		458	My song is love unknown	G
		567	Thine arm, O Lord, in days of old	G
		1, 2	Father, we praise thee, now the night is over	G
		493	O for a thousand tongues to sing	G

	EP	581	Where charity and love prevail	E
		576, 577	God is love, and where true love is	E
		606	Where true charity and love dwell	E
SAT	MP	681	Our God, to whom we turn	L
		379	God is love, let heaven adore him	L
		538	God of mercy, God of grace	G
		537	Christ for the world we sing!	G
		371	Thou, whose almighty word	G
	EP	380	From all that dwell below the skies	Ps 117
		703	Lead us, O Father, in the paths of peace	E
		419	Lord of all being, throned afar	E

Proper 3

SUN	MP	581	Where charity and love prevail	G
		551	Rise up, ye saints of God!	G
		704	O thou who camest from above	G
		610	Lord, whose love through humble service	G
		603, 604	When Christ was lifted from the earth	G
	EP	574, 575	Before thy throne, O God, we kneel	E
		656	Blest are the pure in heart	E
		299	Spirit of God, unleashed on earth	E
		432	O praise ye the Lord! Praise him in the height (omit st. 3)	E
MON	MP	516	Come down, O Love divine	G
		500	Creator Spirit, by whose aid	G
		493	O for a thousand tongues to sing	G
		633	Word of God, come down on earth	G
	EP	472	Hope of the world, thou Christ	E
		423	Immortal, invisible, God only wise	E
		489	The great Creator of the worlds	E
		439	What wondrous love is this	E
		448, 449	O love, how deep, how broad, how high	E
TUE	MP	392	Come, we that love the Lord	G
		344	Lord, dismiss us with thy blessing	G
	EP	368	Holy Father, great Creator	E
WED	MP	516	Come down, O Love divine	G
		500	Creator Spirit, by whose aid	G
		529	In Christ there is no East or West	G
		603, 604	When Christ was lifted from the earth	G
	EP	359	God of the prophets, bless the prophets' heirs	E
		511	Holy Spirit, ever living	E
THU	MP	669	Commit thou all that grieves thee	Ps 37
		588, 589	Almighty God, your word is cast	G
		290	Come, ye thankful people, come (sts. 2-4)	G

	EP	535	Ye servants of God, your Master proclaim	E
		511	Holy Spirit, ever living	E
FRI	MP	24	The day thou gavest, Lord, is ended (omit st. 1)	G
		615	"Thy kindom come!" on bended knee	G
		462	The Lord will come and not be slow	G
		534	God is working his purpose out	G
	EP	511	Holy Spirit, ever living	E
		359	God of the prophets, bless the prophets' heirs	E
SAT	MP	588, 589	Almighty God, your word is cast	G
		290	Come, ye thankful people, come (sts. 2-4)	G
		536	God has spoken to his people	G
		392	Come, we that love the Lord	G
		505	O Spirit of Life, O Spirit of God	G
	EP	574, 575	Before thy throne, O God, we kneel	E
		582, 583	O holy city, seen of John	E
		701	Jesus, all my gladness (sts. 1-2)	E
		552, 553	Fight the good fight with all thy might (sts. 1-2)	E
		423	Immortal, invisible, God only wise	E

Proper 4

SUN	MP	413	New songs of celebration render	Ps 98
		698	Eternal Spirit of the living Christ	G
		709	O God of Bethel, by whose hand	G
		711	Seek ye first the kingdom of God	G
		518	Christ is made the sure foundation	G
		360, 361	Only-begotten, Word of God eternal	G
	EP	297	Descend, O Spirit, purging flame	E
		294	Baptized in water	E
		176, 177	Over the chaos of the empty waters	E
		296	We know that Christ is raised and dies no more	E
		298	All who believe and are baptized	E
MON	MP	615	"Thy kingdom come!" on bended knee	G
		573	Father eternal, Ruler of creation	G
		600, 601	O day of God, draw nigh	G
		462	The Lord will come and not be slow	G
	EP	256	A light from heaven shone around	E
		255	We sing the glorious conquest	E
TUE	MP	489	The great Creator of the worlds	G
		439	What wondrous love is this	G
		443	From God Christ's deity came forth	G
	EP	542	Christ is the world's true Light	E
		532, 533	How wondrous and great thy works, God of praise	E
		539	O Zion, haste, thy mission high fulfilling	E
		531	O Spirit of the living God	E

WED	MP	444	Blessed be the God of Israel	G
		271, 272	The great forerunner of the morn	G
		76	On Jordan's bank the Baptist's cry	G
		70	Herald, sound the note of judgment	G
	EP	697	My God, accept my heart this day	E
		495	Hail, thou once despisèd Jesus!	E
		432	O praise ye the Lord! Praise him in the height (omit st. 3)	E
		691	My faith looks up to thee	E
		381	Thy strong word did cleave the darkness	E
THU	MP	320	Zion, praise thy Savior, singing (sts. 5-6)	G
		690	Guide me, O thou great Jehovah	G
		300	Glory, love, and praise, and honor	G
	EP	270	Gabriel's message does away	E
		60	Creator of the stars of night	E
		401	The God of Abraham praise	E
		432	O praise ye the Lord! Praise him in the height (omit st. 3)	E
FRI	MP	689	I sought the Lord, and afterward I knew	G
		590	O Jesus Christ, may grateful hymns be rising	G
		567	Thine arm, O Lord, in days of old	G
		669	Commit thou all that grieves thee	G
		636, 637	How firm a foundation, ye saints of the Lord	G
	EP	691	My faith looks up to thee (sts. 1-2)	E
SAT	MP	656	Blest are the pure in heart	G
		382	King of glory, King of peace	G
		436	Lift up your heads, ye mighty gates	G
		435	At the Name of Jesus (sts. 1-5)	G
		556, 557	Rejoice, ye pure in heart!	G
	EP	702	Lord, thou hast searched me and dost know	Ps 139
		294	Baptized in water	E
		295	Sing praise to our Creator	E
		529	In Christ there is no East or West	E
		581	Where charity and love prevail	E

Proper 5

SUN	MP	436	Lift up your heads, ye mighty gates	Ps 24
		701	Jesus, all my gladness	G
		68	Rejoice! rejoice, believers	G
		61, 62	"Sleepers, wake!" A voice astounds us	G
	EP	517	How lovely is thy dwelling-place	Ps 84
		603, 604	When Christ was lifted from the earth	E
		529	In Christ there is no East or West	E
		537	Christ for the world we sing!	E

MON	MP	544	Jesus shall reign where'er the sun	G
		537	Christ for the world we sing!	G
		469, 470	There's a wideness in God's mercy	G
	EP	614	Christ is the King! O friends upraise	S
		573	Father eternal, Ruler of creation	S
		594, 595	God of grace and God of glory	S
TUE	MP	567	Thine arm, O Lord, in days of old	G
		472	Hope of the world, thou Christ	G
		320	Zion, praise thy Savior, singing (sts. 5-6)	G
		300	Glory, love, and praise, and honor	G
	EP	522, 523	Glorious things of thee are spoken	E
		620	Jerusalem, my happy home	E
		624	Jerusalem the golden	E
		623	O what their joy and their glory must be	E
WED	MP	616	Hail to the Lord's Anointed	Ps 72
		544	Jesus shall reign where'er the sun	Ps 72
		536	God has spoken to his people	G
		448, 449	O love, how deep, how broad, how high	G
	EP	432	O praise ye the Lord! Praise him in the height (omit st. 3)	E
		529	In Christ there is no East or West	E
		610	Lord, whose love through humble service	E
THU	MP	254	You are the Christ, O Lord	G
		525	The Church's one foundation	G
		443	From God Christ's deity came forth	G
		427	When morning gilds the skies	G
	EP	513	Like the murmur of the dove's song	E
		697	My God, accept my heart this day	E
		500	Creator Spirit, by whose aid	E
		21, 22	O God of truth, O Lord of might	E
FRI	MP	675	Take up your cross, the Savior said	G
		484, 485	Praise the Lord through every nation	G
		10	New every morning is the love	G
		572	Weary of all trumpeting	G
	EP	610	Lord, whose love through humble service	E
		551	Rise up, ye saints of God	E
SAT	MP	129, 130	Christ upon the mountain peak	G
		133, 134	O Light of Light, Love given birth	G
		136, 137	O wondrous type! O vision fair	G
	EP	664	My Shepherd will supply my need	Ps 23
		645, 646	The King of love my shepherd is	Ps 23
		663	The Lord my God my shepherd is	Ps 23
		474	When I survey the wondrous cross	E
		434	Nature with open volume stands	E
		471	We sing the praise of him who died	E

		441, 442	In the cross of Christ I glory	E

Proper 6

SUN	MP	344	Lord, dismiss us with thy blessing	L
		11	Awake, my soul, and with the sun	G
		53	Once he came in blessing	G
	EP	532, 533	How wondrous and great thy works, God of praise	E
		537	Christ for the world we sing!	E
		528	Lord, you give the great commission	E
		531	O Spirit of the living God	E
MON	MP	522, 523	Glorious things of thee are spoken	L
		393	Praise our great and gracious Lord	L
		363	Ancient of Days, who sittest throned in glory	L
		567	Thine arm, O Lord, in days of old	G
		566	From thee all skill and science flow	G
	EP	365	Come, thou almighty King	E
		366	Holy God, we praise thy Name	E
		364	O God, we praise thee, and confess	E
TUE	MP	434	Nature with open volume stands	G
		455, 456	O love of God, how strong and true	G
		448, 449	O love, how deep, how broad, how high	G
	EP	408	Sing praise to God who reigns above	E
		369	How wondrous great, how glorious bright	E
		423	Immortal, invisible, God only wise	E
		31, 32	Most Holy God, the Lord of heaven	E
WED	MP	480	When Jesus left his Father's throne	G
		670	Lord, for ever at thy side	G
		574, 75	Before thy throne, O God, we kneel	G
	EP	641	Lord Jesus, think of me	E
		148	Creator of the earth and skies	E
		574, 575	Before thy throne, O God, we kneel	E
THU	MP	593	Lord, make us servants of your peace	G
		3, 4	Now that the daylight fills the sky	G
		581	Where charity and love prevail	G
		576, 577	God is love, and where true love is	G
		645, 646	The King of love my shepherd is	G
		469, 470	There's a wideness in God's mercy	G
	EP	148	Creator of the earth and skies	E
		641	Lord Jesus, think on me	E
		63, 64	O heavenly Word, eternal Light	E
FRI	MP	674	"Forgive our sins as we forgive"	G
		581	Where charity and love prevail	G
		593	Lord, make us servants of your peace	G

		5	O splendor of God's glory bright	G
	EP	151	From deepest woe I cry to thee	E
		148	Creator of the earth and skies	E
SAT	MP	680	O God, our help in ages past	Ps 90
		350	O God of love, to thee we bow	G
		352	O God, to those who here profess	G
		353	Your love, O God, has called us here	G
	EP	389	Let us, with a gladsome mind	Ps 136
		151	From deepest woe I cry to thee	E
		148	Creator of the earth and skies	E

Proper 7

SUN	MP	538	God of mercy, God of grace	Ps 67
		661	They cast their nets in Galilee	G
		596	Judge eternal, throned in splendor	G
		574, 575	Before thy throne, O God, we kneel	G
	EP	603, 604	When Christ was lifted from the earth	E
		529	In Christ there is no East or West	E
		537	Christ for the world we sing!	E
		532, 533	How wondrous and great thy works, God of praise	E
MON	MP	480	When Jesus left his Father's throne	G
		701	Jesus, all my gladness	G
		475	God himself is with us (sts. 1-2)	G
		707	Take my life, and let it be	G
	EP	686	Come, thou fount of every blessing	E
		151	From deepest woe I cry to thee	E
		495	Hail, thou once despisèd Jesus!	E
		671	Amazing grace! how sweet the sound	E
		432	O praise ye the Lord! Praise him in the height (omit st. 3)	E
TUE	MP	655	O Jesus, I have promised	G
		564, 565	He who would valiant be	G
		707	Take my life, and let it be	G
	EP	634	I call on thee, Lord Jesus Christ	E
		401	The God of Abraham praise	E
		151	From deepest woe I cry to thee	E
		691	My faith looks up to thee	E
		381	Thy strong word did cleave the darkness	E
WED	MP	9	Not here for high and holy things	G
		541	Come, labor on	G
		551	Rise up, ye saints of God!	G
	EP	401	The God of Abraham praise	E

		634	I call on thee, Lord Jesus Christ	E
		393	Praise our great and gracious Lord	E
THU	MP	477	All praise to thee, for thou, O king divine	G
		474	When I survey the wondrous cross	G
		458	My song is love unknown	G
		495	Hail, thou once despisèd Jesus!	G
		483	The head that once was crowned with thorns	G
	EP	686	Come, thou fount of every blessing	E
		167	There is a green hill far away (omit sts. 3, 4)	E
		439	What wondrous love is this	E
		489	The great Creator of the worlds	E
		448, 449	O love, how deep, how broad, how high	E
		691	My faith looks up to thee (sts. 1-2)	E
		685	Rock of ages, cleft for me	E
FRI	MP	690	Guide me, O thou great Jehovah	L
		522, 523	Glorious things of thee are spoken	L
		307	Lord, enthroned in heavenly splendor (omit sts. 2, 3)	L
		685	Rock of ages, cleft for me	L
		633	Word of God, come down on earth	G
		493	O for a thousand tongues to sing	G
		567	Thine arm, O Lord, in days of old	G
	EP	270	Gabriel's message does away	E
		445, 446	Praise to the Holiest in the height	E
		295	Sing praise to our Creator	E
		176, 177	Over the chaos of the empty waters	E
		671	Amazing grace! how sweet the sound	E
SAT	MP	486	Hosanna to the living Lord	G
		65	Prepare the way, O Zion	G
		71, 72	Hark! the glad sound! the Savior comes	G
		74	Blest be the King whose coming	G
	EP	298	All who believe and are baptized	E
		294	Baptized in water	E
		296	We know that Christ is raised and dies no more	E
		697	My God, accept my heart this day	E

Proper 8

SUN	MP	567	Thine arm, O Lord, in days of old	G
		566	From thee all skill and science flow	G
		493	O for a thousand tongues to sing	G
		49	Come, let us with our Lord arise	S
	EP	414	God, my King, thy might confessing	Ps 145
		404	We will extol you, ever-blessèd Lord	Ps 145
		422	Not far beyond the sea, nor high	E
		408	Sing praise to God who reigns above	E
		148	Creator of the earth and skies	E

		455, 456	O love of God, how strong and true	E
MON	MP	458	My song is love unknown	G
		486	Hosanna to the living Lord!	G
		51	We the Lord's people, heart and voice uniting (sts. 1-2)	G
	EP	252	Jesus! Name of wondrous love!	E
		60	Creator of the stars of night	E
		270	Gabriel's message does away	E
		495	Hail, thou once despisèd Jesus!	E
TUE	MP	668	I to the hills will lift mine eyes	Ps 121
		641	Lord Jesus, think on me	G
		574, 575	Before thy throne, O God, we kneel	G
		444	Blessed be the God of Israel	G
		271, 272	The great forerunner of the morn	G
	EP	392	Come, we that love the Lord	E
		344	Lord, dismiss us with thy blessing	E
		703	Lead us, O Father, in the paths of peace	E
WED	MP	483	The head that once was crowned with thorns	G
		598	Lord Christ, when first thou cam'st to earth	G
		495	Hail, thou once despisèd Jesus! (sts. 1-2)	G
	EP	666	Out of the depths I call	Ps 130
		151	From deepest woe I cry to thee	Ps 130 & E
THU	MP	670	Lord, for ever at thy side	Ps 131
		339	Deck thyself, my soul, with gladness	G
		202	The Lamb's high banquet called to share	G
	EP	500	Creator Spirit, by whose aid	E
		516	Come down, O Love divine	E
		512	Come, gracious Spirit, heavenly Dove	E
		228	Holy Spirit, font of light	E
		226, 227	Come, thou Holy Spirit bright	E
FRI	MP	591	O God of earth and altar	G
		596	Judge eternal, throned in splendor	G
		665	All my hope on God is founded	G
		573	Father eternal, Ruler of creation	G
	EP	495	Hail, thou once despisèd Jesus!	E
		299	Spirit of God, unleashed on earth	E
		295	Sing praise to our Creator	E
SAT	MP	401	The God of Abraham praise	G
		526	Let saints on earth in concert sing	G
		551	Rise up, ye saints of God!	G
		581	Where charity and love prevail	G
		610	Lord, whose love through humble service	G
	EP	388	O worship the King, all glorious above!	Ps 104
		623	O what their joy and their glory must be	E

		621, 622	Light's abode, celestial Salem	E
		666	Out of the depths I call	E
		530	Spread, O spread, thou mighty word	E

Proper 9

SUN	MP	429	I'll praise my Maker while I've breath	Ps 146
		359	God of the prophets, bless the prophets' heirs	L
		661	They cast their nets in Galilee	G
		549, 550	Jesus calls us; o'er the tumult	G
	EP	532, 533	How wondrous and great thy works, God of praise	E
		531	O Spirit of the living God	E
		539	O Zion, haste, thy mission high fulfilling	E
MON	MP	656	Blest are the pure in heart	G
		670	Lord, for ever at thy side	G
		437, 438	Tell out, my soul, the greatness of the Lord!	G
		665	All my hope on God is founded	G
	EP	698	Eternal Spirit of the living Christ	E
		635	If thou but trust in God to guide thee	E
		375	Give praise and glory unto God	E
		677	God moves in a mysterious way	E
TUE	MP	605	What does the Lord require	G
		610	Lord, whose love through humble service	G
		656	Blest are the pure in heart	G
	EP	447	The Christ who died but rose again	E
		530	Spread, O spread, thou mighty word	E
		460, 461	Alleluia! sing to Jesus! (sts. 1 & 3)	E
		194, 195	Jesus lives! thy terrors now	E
WED	MP	590	O Jesus Christ, may grateful hymns be rising	G
		598	Lord Christ, when first thou cam'st to earth	G
	EP	393	Praise our great and gracious Lord	E
		401	The God of Abraham praise	E
		709	O God of Bethel, by whose hand	E
THU	MP	598	Lord Christ, when first thou cam'st to earth	G
		53	Once he came in blessing	G
		655	O Jesus, I have promised	G
		564, 565	He who would valiant be	G
	EP	532, 533	How wondrous and great thy works, God of praise	E
		536	God has spoken to his people	E
FRI	MP	408	Sing praise to God who reigns above	L
		375	Give praise and glory unto God	L
		454	Jesus came, adored by angels	G
		57, 58	Lo! he comes, with clouds descending	G
		53	Once he came in blessing	G

	EP	248, 249	To the Name of our salvation	E
		252	Jesus! Name of wondrous love!	E
		435	At the Name of Jesus	E
SAT	MP	53	Once he came in blessing	G
		68	Rejoice! rejoice, believers	G
		61, 62	"Sleepers, wake!" A voice astounds us	G
	EP	380	From all that dwell below the skies	Ps 117
		530	Spread, O spread, thou mighty word	E
		540	Awake, thou Spirit of the watchmen	E
		531	O Spirit of the living God	E
		539	O Zion, haste, thy mission high fulfilling	E
		535	Ye servants of God, your Master proclaim	E

Proper 10

SUN	MP	390	Praise to the Lord, the Almighty	Ps 150 & G
		567	Thine arm, O Lord, in days of old	G
		493	O for a thousand tongues to sing	G
		566	From thee all skill and science flow	G
		448, 449	O love, how deep, how broad, how high	G
	EP	564, 565	He who would valiant be	E
		552, 553	Fight the good fight with all your might	E
		563	Go forward, Christian soldier	E
		555	Lead on, O King eternal	E
MON	MP	61, 62	"Sleepers, wake!" A voice astounds us	G
		68	Rejoice! rejoice, believers	G
	EP	532, 533	How wondrous and great thy works, God of praise	E
		537	Christ for the world we sing	E
		536	God has spoken to his people	E
		544	Jesus shall reign where'er the sun	E
TUE	MP	9	Not here for high and holy things	G
		551	Rise up, ye saints of God!	G
		541	Come, labor on	G
		326	From glory to glory advancing, we praise thee, O Lord	G
	EP	513	Like the murmur of the dove's song	S
		452	Glorious the day when Christ was born	S
		629	We limit not the truth of God	S
		31, 32	Most Holy God, the Lord of heaven	S
WED	MP	610	Lord, whose love through humble service	G
		609	Where cross the crowded ways of life	G
		481	Rejoice, the Lord is King	G
		602	Jesu, Jesu, fill us with your love	G
	EP	677	God moves in a mysterious way	E

		46	The duteous day now closeth	E
		33, 34, 35	Christ, mighty Savior, Light of all creation	E
THU	MP	690	Guide me, O thou great Jehovah	L
		458	My song is love unknown	G
		643	My God, how wonderful thou art	G
		682	I love thee, Lord, but not because	G
		704	O thou who camest from above	G
		642	Jesus, the very thought of thee	G
	EP	610	Lord, whose love through humble service	E
		513	Like the murmur of the dove's song	E
		707	Take my life, and let it be	E
		576, 577	God is love, and where true love is	E
		581	Where charity and love prevail	E
		606	Where true charity and love dwell	E
FRI	MP	393	Praise our great and gracious Lord	L
		448, 449	O love, how deep, how broad, how high	G
	EP	610	Lord, whose love through humble service	E
		347	Go forth for God; go to the world in peace	E
		593	Lord, make us servants of your peace	E
SAT	MP	322	When Jesus died to save us	G
		320	Zion, praise thy Savior, singing	G
		329, 330,		
		331	Now, my tongue, the mystery telling (sts. 1-4)	G
	EP	658	As longs the deer for cooling streams	Ps 42
		24	The day thou gavest, Lord, is ended	S
		29, 30	O Trinity of blessèd light	S
		33, 34, 35	Christ, mighty Savior, Light of all creation	S

Proper 11

SUN	MP	413	New songs of celebration render	Ps 98
		567	Thine arm, O Lord, in days of old	G
		493	O for a thousand tongues to sing	G
		1, 2	Father, we praise thee, now the night is over	G
		566	From thee all skill and science flow	G
	EP	410	Praise, my soul, the King of heaven	Ps 103
		390	Praise to the Lord, the Almighty	Ps 103
		411	O bless the Lord, my soul!	Ps 103
		532, 533	How wondrous and great thy works, God of praise	E
MON	MP	171	Go to dark Gethsemane	G
		164	Alone thou goest forth, O Lord	G
		445, 446	Praise to the Holiest in the height	G
		284	O ye immortal throng	G
	EP	547	Awake, O sleeper, rise from death	E

		400	All creatures of our God and King (omit sts. 2, 3 & 6)	E
		406, 407	Most High, omnipotent, good Lord	E
TUE	MP	164	Alone thou goest forth, O Lord	G
		158	Ah, holy Jesus, how hast thou offended	G
	EP	252	Jesus! Name of wondrous love!	E
		60	Creator of the stars of night	E
		478	Jesus, our mighty Lord	E
		593	Lord, make us servants of your peace	E
		347	Go forth for God; go to the world in peace	E
WED	MP	631	Book of books, our people's strength	L
		627	Lamp of our feet, whereby we trace	L
		171	Go to dark Gethsemane	G
		158	Ah, holy Jesus, how hast thou offended	G
		495	Hail, thou once despisèd Jesus! (sts. 1-2)	G
		483	The head that once was crowned with thorns	G
	EP	581	Where charity and love prevail	E
		576, 577	God is love, and where true love is	E
		606	Where true charity and love dwell	E
THU	MP	158	Ah, holy Jesus, how hast thou offended	G
		164	Alone thou goest forth, O Lord	G
	EP	628	Help us, O Lord, to learn	E
		632	O Christ, the Word Incarnate	E
		630	Thanks to God whose Word was spoken	E
		603, 604	When Christ was lifted from the earth	E
		472	Hope of the world, thou Christ	E
FRI	MP	171	Go to dark Gethsemane	G
		448, 449	O love, how deep, how broad, how high	G
		458	My song is love unknown	G
	EP	529	In Christ there is no East or West	E
		603, 604	When Christ was lifted from the earth	E
		532, 533	How wondrous and great thy works, God of praise	E
SAT	MP	458	My song is love unknown	G
		171	Go to dark Gethsemane	G
		158	Ah, holy Jesus, how hast thou offended	G
	EP	702	Lord, thou hast searched me and dost know	Ps 139
		532, 533	How wondrous and great thy works, God of praise	E
		603, 604	When Christ was lifted from the earth	E
		529	In Christ there is no East or West	E

Proper 12

| SUN | MP | 436 | Lift up your heads, ye mighty gates | Ps 24 |

		690	Guide me, O thou great Jehovah	L
		363	Ancient of Days, who sittest throned in glory	L
		393	Praise our great and gracious Lord	L
		381	Thy strong word did cleave the darkness	G
		630	Thanks to God whose Word was spoken (omit sts. 3, 4)	G
	EP	517	How lovely is thy dwelling-place	Ps 84
		532, 533	How wondrous and great thy works, God of praise	E
		531	O Spirit of the living God	E
		539	O Zion, haste, thy mission high fulfilling	E
MON	MP	170	To mock your reign, O dearest Lord	G
		168, 169	O sacred head, sore wounded	G
		598	Lord Christ, when first thou cam'st to earth	G
		483	The head that once was crowned with thorns	G
		495	Hail, thou once despisèd Jesus!	G
	EP	612	Gracious Spirit, Holy Ghost	S
		580	God, who stretched the spangled heavens	S
		570, 571	All who love and serve your city	S
		27, 28	O blest Creator, source of light	S
TUE	MP	167	There is a green hill far away (omit sts. 3, 4)	G
		172	Were you there when they crucified my Lord?	G
		165, 166	Sing, my tongue, the glorious battle	G
		161	The flaming banners of our King	G
		162	The royal banners forward go	G
	EP	527	Singing songs of expectation	S
		524	I love thy kingdom, Lord	S
		532, 533	How wondrous and great thy works, God of praise	S
WED	MP	544	Jesus shall reign where'er the sun	Ps 72
		616	Hail to the Lord's Anointed	Ps 72
		163	Sunset to sunrise changes now	G
		160	Cross of Jesus, cross of sorrow	G
		168, 169	O sacred head, sore wounded	G
		474	When I survey the wondrous cross	G
	EP	492	Sing, ye faithful, sing with gladness	E
		483	The head that once was crowned with thorns	E
		484, 485	Praise the Lord through every nation	E
		495	Hail, thou once despisèd Jesus!	E
THU	MP	458	My song is love unknown	G
		172	Were you there when they crucified my Lord?	G
		173	O sorrow deep!	G
		471	We sing the praise of him who died	G
	EP	521	Put forth, O God, thy Spirit's might	E
		233, 234	The eternal gifts of Christ the King	E
		359	God of the prophets, bless the prophets' heirs	E

FRI	MP	284	O ye immortal throng	G
		492	Sing, ye faithful, sing with gladness	G
		455, 456	O love of God, how strong and true	G
		448, 449	O love, how deep, how broad, how high	G
		468	It was poor little Jesus	G
	EP	230	A mighty sound from heaven	E
		506, 507	Praise the Spirit in creation	E
		531	O Spirit of the living God	E
		514	To thee, O Comforter divine	E
		511	Holy Spirit, ever living	E
SAT	MP	222	Rejoice, the Lord of life ascends	G
		182	Christ is alive! Let Christians sing	G
		460, 461	Alleluia! sing to Jesus! (sts. 1-2)	G
		284	O ye immortal throng	G
	EP	663	The Lord my God my shepherd is	Ps 23
		664	My Shepherd will supply my need	Ps 23
		645, 646	The King of love my shepherd is	Ps 23
		483	The head that once was crowned with thorns	E
		492	Sing, ye faithful, sing with gladness	E
		455, 456	O love of God, how strong and true	E
		448, 449	O love, how deep, how broad, how high	E

Proper 13

SUN	MP	452	Glorious the day when Christ was born	G
		500	Creator Spirit, by whose aid	G
		516	Come down, O Love divine	G
	EP	705	As those of old their first fruits brought	E
		292	O Jesus, crowned with all renown	E
MON	MP	489	The great Creator of the worlds	G
		421	All glory be to God on high	G
		386, 387	We sing of God, the mighty source	G
		476	Can we by searching find out God	G
		496, 497	How bright appears the Morning Star	G
	EP	432	O praise ye the Lord! Praise him in the height (omit st. 3)	E
		296	We know that Christ is raised and dies no more	E
		294	Baptized in water	E
		299	Spirit of God, unleashed on earth	E
		295	Sing praise to our Creator	E
TUE	MP	75	There's a voice in the wilderness crying	G
		67	Comfort, comfort ye my people	G
		444	Blessed be the God of Israel	G
	EP	23	The fleeting day is nearly gone	E
		528	Lord, you give the great commission	E
		521	Put forth, O God, thy Spirit's might	E

WED	MP	139	When Jesus went to Jordan's stream	G
		121	Christ when for us you were baptized	G
		116	"I come," the great Redeemer cries	G
		439	What wondrous love is this	G
		421	All glory be to God on high	G
	EP	492	Sing, ye faithful, sing with gladness	E
		448, 449	O love, how deep, how broad, how high	E
THU	MP	477	All praise to thee, for thou, O King divine	G
		489	The great Creator of the worlds	G
		439	What wondrous love is this	G
	EP	252	Jesus! Name of wondrous love!	E
		248, 249	To the Name of our salvation	E
		435	At the Name of Jesus	E
		518	Christ is made the sure foundation	E
		492	Sing, ye faithful, sing with gladness	E
FRI	MP	138	All praise to you, O Lord	G
		443	From God Christ's deity came forth	G
		487	Come, my Way, my Truth, my Life	G
	EP	506, 507	Praise the Spirit in creation	E
		511	Holy Spirit, ever living	E
		484, 485	Praise the Lord through every nation	E
SAT	MP	680	O God, our help in ages past	Ps 90
		598	Lord Christ, when first thou cam'st to earth	G
	EP	389	Let us, with a gladsome mind	Ps 136
		707	Take my life, and let it be	E
		701	Jesus, all my gladness	E
		475	God himself is with us (sts. 1-2)	E

Proper 14

SUN	MP	538	God of mercy, God of grace	Ps 67
		669	Commit thou all that grieves thee	G
		375	Give praise and glory unto God	G
		414	God, my King, thy might confessing	G
	EP	409	The spacious firmament on high	Ps 19
		431	The stars declare his glory	Ps 19
		687, 688	A mighty fortress is our God	Ps 46
		617	Eternal Ruler of the ceaseless round	S
		594, 595	God of grace and God of glory	S
MON	MP	473	Lift high the cross	G
		297	Descend, O Spirit, purging flame	G
		295	Sing praise to our Creator	G
		489	The great Creator of the worlds	G
	EP	182	Christ is alive! Let Christians sing	S
		614	Christ is the King! O friends uprise	S

		452	Glorious the day when Christ was born	S
TUE	MP	121	Christ, when for us you were baptized	G
		139	When Jesus went to Jordan's stream	G
		120	The sinless one to Jordan came	G
		116	"I come," the great Redeemer cries	G
	EP	483	The head that once was crowned with thorns	E
		495	Hail, thou once despisèd Jesus!	E
WED	MP	692	I heard the voice of Jesus say (st. 2)	G
		649, 650	O Jesus, joy of loving hearts	G
		678, 679	Surely it is God who saves me	G
		658	As longs the deer for cooling streams	G
		440	Blessèd Jesus, at thy word	G
	EP	243	When Stephen, full of power and grace	E
THU	MP	540	Awake, thou Spirit of the watchmen	G
		673	The first one ever, oh, ever to know (st. 2)	G
		530	Spread, O spread, thou mighty word	G
		535	Ye servants of God, your Master proclaim	G
	EP	401	The God of Abraham praise	E
		709	O God of Bethel, by whose hand	E
FRI	MP	567	Thine arm, O Lord, in days of old	G
		493	O for a thousand tongues to sing	G
		429	I'll praise my Maker while I've breath	G
		1, 2	Father, we praise thee, now the night is over	G
	EP	401	The God of Abraham praise	E
		33, 34, 35	Christ, mighty Savior, Light of all creation	S
		31, 32	Most Holy God, the Lord of heaven	S
SAT	MP	493	O for a thousand tongues to sing	G
		567	Thine arm, O Lord, in days of old	G
		371	Thou, whose almighty Word	G
		1, 2	Father, we praise thee, now the night is over	G
		429	I'll praise my Maker while I've breath	G
	EP	401	The God of Abraham praise	E
		425	Sing now with joy unto the Lord	E
		648	When Israel was in Egypt's land	E
		363	Ancient of Days, who sittest throned in glory	E

Proper 15

SUN	MP	493	O for a thousand tongues to sing	G
		590	O Jesus Christ, may grateful hymns be rising	G
		567	Thine arm, O Lord, in days of old	G
		1, 2	Father, we praise thee, now the night is over	G
		566	From thee all skill and science flow	G
	EP	414	God, my King, thy might confessing	Ps 145

		404	We will extol you, ever-blessèd Lord	Ps 145
		593	Lord, make us servants of your peace	E
		347	Go forth for God; go to the world in peace	E
MON	MP	455, 456	O Love of God, how strong and true	G
		457	Thou art the Way, to thee alone	G
		628	Help us, O Lord, to learn	G
		626	Lord, be thy word my rule	G
	EP	243	When Stephen, full of power and grace	E
		240, 241	Hearken to the anthem glorious	E
		237	Let us now our voices raise	E
TUE	MP	668	I to the hills will lift mine eyes	Ps 121
		634	I call on thee, Lord Jesus Christ	G
		633	Word of God, come down on earth	G
		444	Blessed be the God of Israel	G
	EP	298	All who believe and are baptized	E
		296	We know that Christ is raised and dies no more	E
		295	Sing praise to our Creator	E
		176, 177	Over the chaos of the empty waters	E
		299	Spirit of God, unleashed on earth	E
		432	O praise ye the Lord! Praise him in the height (omit st. 3)	E
WED	MP	448, 449	O love, how deep, how broad, how high	G
		443	From God Christ's deity came forth	G
		320	Zion, praise thy Savior, singing (sts. 5-6)	G
		343	Shepherd of souls, refresh and bless	G
	EP	666	Out of the depths I call	Ps 130
		151	From deepest woe I cry to thee	Ps 130
		574, 575	Before thy throne, O God, we kneel	E
		656	Blest are the pure in heart	E
		299	Spirit of God, unleashed on earth	E
		432	O praise ye the Lord! Praise him in the height (omit st. 3)	E
THU	MP	670	Lord, for ever at thy side	Ps 131
		649, 650	O Jesus, joy of loving hearts	G
		669	Commit thou all that grieves thee	G
		690	Guide me, O thou great Jehovah	G
	EP	297	Descend, O Spirit, purging flame	E
		294	Baptized in water	E
		432	O praise ye the Lord! Praise him in the height (omit st. 3)	E
		176, 177	Over the chaos of the empty waters	E
		298	All who believe and are baptized	E
		296	We know that Christ is raised and dies no more	E
FRI	MP	335	I am the bread of life	G
		343	Shepherd of souls, refresh and bless (sts. 1-2)	G
		649, 650	O Jesus, joy of loving hearts	G

	EP	256	A light from heaven shone around	E
		255	We sing the glorious conquest	E
SAT	MP	302, 303	Father, we thank thee who hast planted (st. 1)	G
		335	I am the bread of life	G
		343	Shepherd of souls, refresh and bless (sts. 1-2)	G
		320	Zion, praise thy Savior, singing (sts. 5-6)	G
	EP	388	O worship the King, all glorious above!	Ps 104
		255	We sing the glorious conquest	E
		256	A light from heaven shone around	E

Proper 16

SUN	MP	429	I'll praise my Maker while I've breath	Ps 146 & G
		443	From God Christ's deity came forth	G
		489	The great Creator of the worlds	G
		439	What wondrous love is this	G
	EP	275	Hark! the sound of holy voices	E
		657	Love divine, all loves excelling	E
		495	Hail, thou once despisèd Jesus!	E
MON	MP	591	O God of earth and altar	L
		335	I am the bread of life	G
		320	Zion, praise thy Savior, singing (sts. 5-6)	G
		343	Shepherd of souls, refresh and bless (sts. 1-2)	G
		302, 303	Father, we thank thee, who hast planted (st. 1)	G
	EP	255	We sing the glorious conquest	E
		256	A light from heaven shone around	E
TUE	MP	633	Word of God, come down on earth	G
		626	Lord, be thy word my rule	G
		440	Blessèd Jesus, at thy word	G
		634	I call on thee, Lord Jesus Christ	G
		630	Thanks to God, whose Word was spoken (omit sts. 3, 4)	G
	EP	528	Lord, you give the great commission	E
		521	Put forth, O God, thy Spirit's might	E
		538	God of mercy, God of grace	E
WED	MP	364	O God, we praise thee, and confess	G
		366	Holy God, we praise thy Name	G
		476	Can we by searching find out God	G
	EP	603, 604	When Christ was lifted from the earth	E
		529	In Christ there is no East or West	E
		532, 533	How wondrous and great thy works, God of praise!	E
		539	O Zion, haste, thy mission high fulfilling	E
		542	Christ is the world's true Light	E
THU	MP	634	I call on thee, Lord Jesus Christ	G

		458	My song is love unknown	G
		443	From God Christ's deity came forth	G
		489	The great Creator of the worlds	G
	EP	532, 533	How wondrous and great thy works, God of praise!	E
		537	Christ for the world we sing!	E
		529	In Christ there is no East or West	E
		603, 604	When Christ was lifted from the earth	E
		539	O Zion, haste, thy mission high fulfilling	E
FRI	MP	443	From God Christ's deity came forth	G
		692	I heard the voice of Jesus say (st. 2)	G
		427	When morning gilds the skies	G
		649, 650	O Jesus, joy of loving hearts	G
	EP	530	Spread, O spread, thou mighty word	E
		492	Sing, ye faithful, sing with gladness	E
		448, 449	O love, how deep, how broad, how high	E
		297	Descend, O Spirit, purging flame	E
SAT	MP	6, 7	Christ, whose glory fills the skies	G
		692	I heard the voice of Jesus say (st. 3)	G
		490	I want to walk as a child of the light	G
		542	Christ is the world's true Light	G
		465, 466	Eternal light, shine in my heart	G
	EP	380	From all that dwell below the skies	Ps 117 & E
		532, 533	How wondrous and great thy works, God of praise!	E
		529	In Christ there is no East or West	E
		603, 604	When Christ was lifted from the earth	E

Proper 17

SUN	MP	476	Can we by searching find out God	L
		560	Remember your servants, Lord	G
		656	Blest are the pure in heart	G
		593	Lord, make us servants of your peace	G
	EP	374	Come, let us join our cheerful songs	E
		417, 418	This is the feast of victory for our God	E
		439	What wondrous love is this	E
		307	Lord, enthroned in heavenly splendor (omit sts. 2, 3)	E
		495	Hail, thou once despisèd Jesus!	E
MON	MP	419	Lord of all being, throned afar	G
		386, 387	We sing of God, the mighty source	G
		476	Can we by searching find out God	G
	EP	705	As those of old their first fruits brought	E
		701	Jesus, all my gladness (sts. 1-2)	E
TUE	MP	505	O Spirit of Life, O Spirit of God	G

		440	Blessèd Jesus, at thy word	G
		626	Lord, be thy word my rule	G
		628	Help us, O Lord, to learn	G
	EP	544	Jesus shall reign where'er the sun	E
		429	I'll praise my Maker while I've breath	E
WED	MP	401	The God of Abraham praise	G
		439	What wondrous love is this	G
		505	O Spirit of Life, O Spirit of God	G
		626	Lord, be thy word my rule	G
		440	Blessèd Jesus, at thy word	G
		628	Help us, O Lord, to learn	G
	EP	531	O Spirit of the living God	S
		182	Christ is alive! Let Christians sing	S
		614	Christ is the King! O friends upraise	S
THU	MP	669	Commit thou all that grieves thee	Ps 37
		633	Word of God, come down on earth	G
		692	I heard the voice of Jesus say (st. 3)	G
		371	Thou, whose almighty Word	G
		6, 7	Christ, whose glory fills the skies	G
	EP	532, 533	How wondrous and great thy works, God of praise!	E
		537	Christ for the world we sing!	E
		528	Lord, you give the great commission	E
		531	O Spirit of the living God	E
FRI	MP	194, 195	Jesus lives! thy terrors now	L
		188, 189	Love's redeeming work is done	L
		633	Word of God, come down on earth	G
		371	Thou, whose almighty Word	G
		493	O for a thousand tongues to sing	G
		567	Thine arm, O Lord, in days of old	G
	EP	439	What wondrous love is this	E
		489	The great Creator of the worlds	E
		476	Can we by searching find out God	E
		443	From God Christ's deity came forth	E
SAT	MP	478	Jesus, our mighty Lord	G
		708	Savior, like a shepherd lead us	G
		645, 646	The King of love my shepherd is	G
		664	My Shepherd will supply my need	G
		663	The Lord my God my shepherd is	G
	EP	658	As longs the deer for cooling streams	Ps 42
		448, 449	O love, how deep, how broad, how high	E
		455, 456	O Love of God, how strong and true	E
		478	Jesus, our mighty Lord	E

Proper 18

SUN	MP	543	O Zion, tune thy voice	G
		628	Help us, O Lord, to learn	G
		626	Lord, be thy word my rule	G
		48	O day of radiant gladness	S
	EP	439	What wondrous love is this	E
		434	Nature with open volume stands	E
		253	Give us the wings of faith to rise	E
		286	Who are these like stars appearing	E
		181	Awake and sing the song	E
MON	MP	478	Jesus, our mighty Lord	G
		708	Savior, like a shepherd lead us	G
		645, 646	The King of love my shepherd is	G
		663	The Lord my God my shepherd is	G
		664	My Shepherd will supply my need	G
	EP	515	Holy Ghost, dispel our sadness	E
		499	Lord God, you now have set your servant free	E
		532, 533	How wondrous and great thy works, God of praise!	E
		529	In Christ there is no East or West	E
TUE	MP	121	Christ, when for us you were baptized	G
		139	When Jesus went to Jordan's stream	G
		116	"I come," the great Redeemer cries	G
	EP	423	Immortal, invisible, God only wise	E
		389	Let us, with a gladsome mind	E
		388	O worship the King, all glorious above!	E
		398	I sing the almighty power of God	E
WED	MP	457	Thou art the Way, to thee alone	G
		448, 449	O love, how deep, how broad, how high	G
		455, 456	O Love of God, how strong and true	G
	EP	531	O Spirit of the living God	E
		532, 533	How wondrous and great thy works, God of praise!	E
		529	In Christ there is no East or West	E
		537	Christ for the world we sing!	E
		539	O Zion, haste, thy mission high fulfilling	E
THU	MP	335	I am the bread of life (sts. 4-5)	G
		567	Thine arm, O Lord, in days of old	G
		457	Thou art the Way, to thee alone	G
		455, 456	O Love of God, how strong and true	G
	EP	603, 604	When Christ was lifted from the earth	E
		394, 395	Creating God, your fingers trace	E
		532, 533	How wondrous and great thy works, God of praise!	E
		529	In Christ there is no East or West	E

		537	Christ for the world we sing!	E
FRI	MP	455, 456	O Love of God, how strong and true	G
		457	Thou art the Way, to thee alone	G
		493	O for a thousand tongues to sing	G
		567	Thine arm, O Lord, in days of old	G
	EP	539	O Zion, haste, thy mission high fulfilling	E
		532, 533	How wondrous and great thy works, God of praise!	E
		529	In Christ there is no East or West	E
		531	O Spirit of the living God	E
SAT	MP	677	God moves in a mysterious way	L
		426	Songs of praise the angels sang	L
		379	God is love, let heaven adore him	L
		598	Lord Christ, when first thou cam'st to earth	G
		458	My song is love unknown	G
	EP	702	Lord, thou hast searched me and dost know	Ps 139
		511	Holy Spirit, ever living	E
		531	O Spirit of the living God	E
		532, 533	How wondrous and great thy works, God of praise!	E
		537	Christ for the world we sing!	E
		529	In Christ there is no East or West	E

Proper 19

SUN	MP	436	Lift up your heads, ye mighty gates	Ps 24
		677	God moves in a mysterious way	L
		385	Many and great, O God, are thy works	L
		398	I sing the almighty power of God	L
		674	"Forgive our sins as we forgive"	G
		593	Lord, make us servants of your peace	G
	EP	517	How lovely is thy dwelling-place	Ps 84
		47	On this day, the first of days	S
		52	This day at thy creating word	S
		50	This is the day the Lord hath made	S
MON	MP	643	My God, how wonderful thou art	G
		642	Jesus, the very thought of thee	G
		704	O thou who camest from above	G
	EP	394, 395	Creating God, your fingers trace	E
		532, 533	How wondrous and great thy works, God of praise!	E
		531	O Spirit of the living God	E
		539	O Zion, haste, thy mission high fulfilling	E
TUE	MP	458	My song is love unknown	G
		74	Blest be the King whose coming	G
		486	Hosanna to the living Lord!	G

		65	Prepare the way, O Zion	G
		156	Ride on! ride on in majesty!	G
	EP	531	O Spirit of the living God	E
		539	O Zion, haste, thy mission high fulfilling	E
		394, 395	Creating God, your fingers trace	E
		532, 533	How wondrous and great thy works, God of praise!	E
		537	Christ for the world we sing!	E
WED	MP	616	Hail to the Lord's Anointed	Ps 72
		544	Jesus shall reign where'er the sun	Ps 72
		655	O Jesus, I have promised	G
		473	Lift high the cross	G
		448, 449	O love, how deep, how broad, how high	G
	EP	33, 34, 35	Christ, mighty Savior, Light of all creation	S
		27, 28	O blest Creator, source of light	S
		24	The day thou gavest, Lord, is ended	S
THU	MP	584	God, you have given us power to sound	L
		473	Lift high the cross	G
		490	I want to walk as a child of the light	G
		603, 604	When Christ was lifted from the earth	G
		434	Nature with open volume stands	G
	EP	296	We know that Christ is raised and dies no more	E
		298	All who believe and are baptized	E
		294	Baptized in water	E
		176, 177	Over the chaos of the empty waters	E
		432	O praise ye the Lord! Praise him in the height (omit st. 3)	E
		295	Sing praise to our Creator	E
FRI	MP	458	My song is love unknown	G
		448, 449	O love, how deep, how broad, how high	G
	EP	506, 507	Praise the Spirit in creation	E
		492	Sing, ye faithful, sing with gladness	E
		455, 456	O Love of God, how strong and true	E
		448, 449	O love, how deep, how broad, how high	E
SAT	MP	6, 7	Christ, whose glory fills the skies	G
		490	I want to walk as a child of the light	G
		465, 466	Eternal light, shine in my heart	G
		496, 497	How bright appears the Morning Star	G
	EP	664	My Shepherd will supply my need	Ps 23
		645, 646	The King of love my shepherd is	Ps 23
		663	The Lord my God my shepherd is	Ps 23
		422	Not far beyond the sea, nor high	E
		408	Sing praise to God who reigns above	E
		148	Creator of the earth and skies	E
		455, 456	O Love of God, how strong and true	E

Proper 20

SUN	MP	49	Come, let us with our Lord arise	S
		48	O day of radiant gladness	S
		51	We the Lord's people, heart and voice uniting	S
	EP	610	Lord, whose love through humble service	E
		628	Help us, O Lord, to learn	E
MON	MP	76	On Jordan's bank the Baptist's cry	G
		70	Herald, sound the note of judgment	G
		75	There's a voice in the wilderness crying	G
		67	Comfort, comfort ye my people	G
		69	What is the crying at Jordan?	G
	EP	298	All who believe and are baptized	E
		176, 177	Over the chaos of the empty waters	E
		294	Baptized in water	E
		296	We know that Christ is raised and dies no more	E
		295	Sing praise to our Creator	E
TUE	MP	121	Christ, when for us you were baptized	G
		139	When Jesus went to Jordan's stream	G
		116	"I come," the great Redeemer cries	G
	EP	632	O Christ, the Word incarnate	E
		630	Thanks to God, whose Word was spoken	E
		633	Word of God, come down on earth	E
WED	MP	120	The sinless one to Jordan came	G
		559	Lead us, heavenly Father, lead us	G
		284	O ye immortal throng	G
		443	From God Christ's deity came forth	G
		448, 449	O love, how deep, how broad, how high	G
	EP	294	Baptized in water	E
		299	Spirit of God, unleashed on earth	E
		295	Sing praise to our Creator	E
		176, 177	Over the chaos of the empty waters	E
		298	All who believe and are baptized	E
THU	MP	71, 72	Hark! the glad sound! the Savior comes	G
		539	O Zion, haste, thy mission high fulfilling	G
		448, 449	O love, how deep, how broad, how high	G
	EP	532, 533	How wondrous and great thy works, God of praise!	E
		531	O Spirit of the living God	E
		539	O Zion, haste, thy mission high fulfilling	E
FRI	MP	567	Thine arm, O Lord, in days of old	G
		633	Word of God, come down on earth	G
		1, 2	Father, we praise thee, now the night is over	G
		371	Thou, whose almighty word	G
	EP	408	Sing praise to God who reigns above	E

		683, 684	O for a closer walk with God	E
SAT	MP	680	O God, our help in ages past	Ps 90
		567	Thine arm, O Lord, in days of old	G
		493	O for a thousand tongues to sing	G
		537	Christ for the world we sing!	G
	EP	389	Let us, with a gladsome mind	Ps 136
		360, 361	Only-begotten, Word of God eternal	E
		509	Spirit divine, attend our prayers	S

Proper 21

		538	God of mercy, God of grace	Ps 67
SUN	MP	536	God has spoken to his people	G
		615	"Thy kingdom come!" on bended knee	G
		573	Father eternal, Ruler of creation	G
		600, 601	O day of God, draw nigh	G
		462	The Lord will come and not be slow	G
	EP	409	The spacious firmament on high	Ps 19
		431	The stars declare his glory	Ps 19
		687, 688	A mighty fortress is our God	Ps 46
		574, 575	Before thy throne, O God, we kneel	E
		694	God be in my head	E
MON	MP	597	O day of peace that dimly shines	L
		600, 601	O day of God, draw nigh	L
		661	They cast their nets in Galilee	G
		530	Spread, O spread, thou mighty word	G
	EP	40, 41	O Christ, you are both light and day	E
		525	The Church's one foundation	E
		524	I love thy kingdom, Lord	E
		511	Holy Spirit, ever living	E
TUE	MP	1, 2	Father, we praise thee, now the night is over	G
		567	Thine arm, O Lord, in days of old	G
		493	O for a thousand tongues to sing	G
		566	From thee all skill and science flow	G
	EP	564, 565	He who would valiant be	E
		552, 553	Fight the good fight with all thy might	E
		563	Go forward, Christian soldier	E
		555	Lead on, O King eternal	E
WED	MP	281	He sat to watch o'er customs paid	G
		706	In your mercy, Lord, you called me	G
		469, 470	There's a wideness in God's mercy	G
		467	Sing, my soul, his wondrous love	G
	EP	529	In Christ there is no East or West	E
		603, 604	When Christ was lifted from the earth	E
		537	Christ for the world we sing!	E

THU	MP	458	My song is love unknown	G
		630	Thanks to God whose Word was spoken	
			(omit sts. 3, 4)	G
		1, 2	Father, we praise thee, now the night is over	G
		493	O for a thousand tongues to sing	G
		567	Thine arm, O Lord, in days of old	G
	EP	659, 660	O Master, let me walk with thee	E
		556, 557	Rejoice, ye pure in heart	E
		24	The day thou gavest, Lord, is ended	E
		647	I know not where the road will lead	E
FRI	MP	560	Remember your servants, Lord	G
		437, 438	Tell out, my soul, the greatness of the Lord!	G
		593	Lord, make us servants of your peace	G
	EP	256	A light from heaven shone around	E
		255	We sing the glorious conquest	E
SAT	MP	593	Lord, make us servants of your peace	G
		674	"Forgive our sins as we forgive"	G
		5	O Splendor of God's glory bright	G
		3, 4	Now that the daylight fills the sky	G
		603, 604	When Christ was lifted from the earth	G
		602	Jesu, Jesu, fill us with your love	G
	EP	33, 34, 35	Christ, mighty Savior, Light of all creation	S
		31, 32	Most Holy God, the Lord of heaven	S
		27, 28	O blest Creator, source of light	S

Proper 22

SUN	MP	188, 189	Love's redeeming work is done	L
		444	Blessed be the God of Israel	G
		271, 272	The great forerunner of the morn	G
		70	Herald, sound the note of judgment	G
		76	On Jordan's bank the Baptist's cry	G
	EP	414	God, my King, thy might confessing	Ps 145
		404	We will extol you, ever-blessèd Lord	Ps 145
		488	Be thou my vision, O Lord of my heart	E
		694	God be in my head	E
		629	We limit not the truth of God	E
MON	MP	636, 637	How firm a foundation, ye saints of the Lord	G
		392	Come, we that love the Lord	G
		344	Lord, dismiss us with thy blessing	G
		626	Lord, be thy word my rule	G
		628	Help us, O Lord, to learn	G
	EP	530	Spread, O spread, thou mighty word	E
		647	I know not where the road will lead	E
		532, 533	How wondrous and great thy works, God of praise!	E

TUE	MP	668	I to the hills will lift mine eyes	Ps 121
		567	Thine arm, O Lord, in days of old	G
		493	O for a thousand tongues to sing	G
		371	Thou, whose almighty word	G
		566	From thee all skill and science flow	G
	EP	647	I know not where the road will lead	E
		563	Go forward, Christian soldier	E
		559	Lead us, heavenly Father, lead us	E
		555	Lead on, O King eternal	E
WED	MP	271, 272	The great forerunner of the morn	G
		444	Blessed be the God of Israel	G
		70	Herald, sound the note of judgment	G
		458	My song is love unknown	G
	EP	666	Out of the depths I call	Ps 130
		151	From deepest woe I cry to thee	Ps 130
		559	Lead us, heavenly Father, lead us	E
		647	I know not where the road will lead	E
THU	MP	670	Lord, for ever at thy side	Ps 131
		643	My God, how wonderful thou art	G
		641	Lord Jesus, think on me	G
		382	King of glory, King of peace	G
		469, 470	There's a wideness in God's mercy	G
	EP	455, 456	O love of God, how strong and true	E
		468	It was poor little Jesus	E
		364	O God, we praise thee, and confess	E
		366	Holy God, we praise thy Name	E
FRI	MP	597	O day of peace that dimly shines	L
		542	Christ is the world's true Light	L
		588, 589	Almighty God, your word is cast	G
		536	God has spoken to his people	G
		626	Lord, be thy word my rule	G
		628	Help us, O Lord, to learn	G
	EP	647	I know not where the road will lead	E
		555	Lead on, O King eternal	E
		564, 565	He who would valiant be	E
		563	Go forward, Christian soldier	E
SAT	MP	603, 604	When Christ was lifted from the earth	G
		529	In Christ there is no East or West	G
		669	Commit thou all that grieves thee	G
	EP	388	O worship the King, all glorious above!	Ps 104
		647	I know not where the road will lead	E
		559	Lead us, heavenly Father, lead us	E
		468	It was poor little Jesus	E

Proper 23

SUN	MP	429	I'll praise my Maker while I've breath	Ps 146
		605	What does the Lord require	L
		544	Jesus shall reign where'er the sun	G
		537	Christ for the world we sing!	G
		469, 470	There's a wideness in God's mercy	G
	EP	593	Lord, make us servants of your peace	E
		52	This day at thy creating word	S
		47	On this day, the first of days	S
MON	MP	567	Thine arm, O Lord, in days of old	G
		493	O for a thousand tongues to sing	G
		429	I'll praise my Maker while I've breath	G
		371	Thou, whose almighty word	G
	EP	255	We sing the glorious conquest	E
		256	A light from heaven shone around	E
TUE	MP	493	O for a thousand tongues to sing	G
		590	O Jesus Christ, may grateful hymns be rising	G
		567	Thine arm, O Lord, in days of old	G
		411	O bless the Lord, my soul!	G
		566	From thee all skill and science flow	G
	EP	647	I know not where the road will lead	E
		555	Lead on, O King eternal	E
		564, 565	He who would valiant be	E
		563	Go forward, Christian soldier	E
WED	MP	528	Lord, you give the great commission	G
		320	Zion, praise thy Savior, singing (sts. 5-6)	G
		300	Glory, love, and praise, and honor	G
		708	Savior, like a shepherd lead us	G
		478	Jesus, our mighty Lord	G
	EP	635	If thou but trust in God to guide thee	E
		669	Commit thou all that grieves thee	E
		677	God moves in a mysterious way	E
THU	MP	469, 470	There's a wideness in God's mercy	L
		467	Sing, my soul, his wondrous love	L
		254	You are the Christ, O Lord	G
		675	Take up your cross, the Savior said	G
		484, 485	Praise the Lord through every nation	G
	EP	608	Eternal Father, strong to save	E
		641	Lord Jesus, think on me	E
		398	I sing the almighty power of God	E
FRI	MP	129, 130	Christ upon the mountain peak	G
		136, 137	O wondrous type! O vision fair	G
		133, 134	O Light of Light, Love given birth	G

	EP	566	From thee all skill and science flow	E
		429	I'll praise my Maker while I've breath	E
		411	O bless the Lord, my soul!	E
SAT	MP	567	Thine arm, O Lord, in days of old	G
		371	Thou, whose almighty word	G
		448, 449	O love, how deep, how broad, how high	G
		566	From thee all skill and science flow	G
	EP	380	From all that dwell below the skies	Ps 117 & E
		536	God has spoken to his people	E
		532, 533	How wondrous and great thy works, God of praise!	E
		531	O Spirit of the living God	E
		530	Spread, O spread, thou mighty word	E

Proper 24

SUN	MP	593	Lord, make us servants of your peace	L
		254	You are the Christ, O Lord	G
		443	From God Christ's deity came forth	G
		525	The Church's one foundation	G
		427	When morning gilds the skies	G
	EP	307	Lord, enthroned in heavenly splendor (omit sts. 2, 3)	E
		690	Guide me, O thou great Jehovah	E
		685	Rock of ages, cleft for me	E
MON	MP	458	My song is love unknown	G
		559	Lead us, heavenly Father, lead us	G
		564, 565	He who would valiant be	G
		655	O Jesus, I have promised	G
		478	Jesus, our mighty Lord	G
	EP	686	Come, thou fount of every blessing	E
		473	Lift high the cross	E
		697	My God, accept my heart this day	E
TUE	MP	540	Awake, thou Spirit of the watchmen (sts. 2-3)	G
		541	Come, labor on	G
		528	Lord, you give the great commission	G
		535	Ye servants of God, your Master proclaim	G
	EP	275	Hark! the sound of holy voices	E
		286	Who are these like stars appearing	E
		535	Ye servants of God, your Master proclaim	E
		253	Give us the wings of faith to rise	E
WED	MP	536	God has spoken to his people	G
		531	O Spirit of the living God	G
	EP	366	Holy God, we praise thy Name	E
		364	O God, we praise thee, and confess	E
THU	MP	551	Rise up, ye saints of God!	G
		581	Where charity and love prevail	G

		602	Jesu, Jesu, fill us with your love	G
		603, 604	When Christ was lifted from the earth	G
		610	Lord, whose love through humble service	G
	EP	697	My God, accept my heart this day	E
		686	Come, thou fount of every blessing	E
		294	Baptized in water	E
		297	Descend, O Spirit, purging flame	E
		514	To thee, O Comforter divine	E
FRI	MP	382	King of glory, King of peace	G
		701	Jesus, all my gladness	G
		642	Jesus, the very thought of thee	G
		488	Be thou my vision, O Lord of my heart	G
	EP	408	Sing praise to God who reigns above	E
		683, 684	O for a closer walk with God	E
		148	Creator of the earth and skies	E
SAT	MP	698	Eternal Spirit of the living Christ	G
		711	Seek ye first the kingdom of God	G
		518	Christ is made the sure foundation	G
		360, 361	Only-begotten, Word of God eternal (omit st. 4)	G
	EP	658	As longs the deer for cooling streams	Ps 42
		63, 64	O heavenly Word, eternal Light	E
		53	Once he came in blessing	E

Proper 25

SUN	MP	593	Lord, make us servants of your peace	G
		3, 4	Now that the daylight fills the sky	G
		581	Where charity and love prevail	G
		606	Where true charity and love dwell	G
		576, 577	God is love, and where true love is	G
	EP	411	O bless the Lord, my soul!	Ps 103
		410	Praise, my soul, the King of heaven	Ps 103
		390	Praise to the Lord, the Almighty	Ps 103
MON	MP	574, 575	Before thy throne, O God, we kneel	G
		500	Creator Spirit, by whose aid	G
		516	Come down, O Love divine	G
		656	Blest are the pure in heart	G
	EP	508	Breathe on me, Breath of God	E
		501, 502	O Holy Spirit, by whose breath	E
		38, 39	Jesus, Redeemer of the world	S
TUE	MP	258	Virgin-born, we bow before thee	G
		228	Holy Spirit, font of light	G
		5	O Splendor of God's glory bright	G
		6, 7	Christ, whose glory fills the skies	G

	EP	494	Crown him with many crowns	E
		481	Rejoice, the Lord is King	E
WED	MP	574, 575	Before thy throne, O God, we kneel	G
		148	Creator of the earth and skies	G
	EP	31, 32	Most Holy God, the Lord of heaven	S
		33, 34, 35	Christ, mighty Savior, Light of all creation	S
		29, 30	O Trinity of blessèd light	S
THU	MP	366	Holy God, we praise thy Name	G
		364	O God, we praise thee, and confess	G
		454	Jesus came, adored by angels	G
	EP	390	Praise to the Lord, the Almighty	Ps 103
		410	Praise, my soul, the King of heaven	Ps 103
		411	O bless the Lord, my soul!	Ps 103
		282, 283	Christ, the fair glory of the holy angels	E
FRI	MP	667	Sometimes a light surprises	G
		709	O God of Bethel, by whose hand	G
		711	Seek ye first the kingdom of God	G
		665	All my hope on God is founded	G
		574, 575	Before thy throne, O God, we kneel	G
		701	Jesus, all my gladness	G
	EP	536	God has spoken to his people	E
		686	Come, thou fount of every blessing	E
		697	My God, accept my heart this day	E
		294	Baptized in water	E
SAT	MP	705	As those of old their first fruits brought	L
		68	Rejoice! rejoice, believers	G
		61, 62	"Sleepers, wake!" A voice astounds us	G
		701	Jesus, all my gladness	G
	EP	702	Lord, thou hast searched me and dost know	Ps 139
		27, 28	O blest Creator, source of light	S
		31, 32	Most Holy God, the Lord of heaven	S

Proper 26

SUN	MP	436	Lift up your heads, ye mighty gates	Ps 24
		674	"Forgive our sins as we forgive"	G
		593	Lord, make us servants of your peace	G
		5	O Splendor of God's glory bright	G
		581	Where charity and love prevail	G
	EP	517	How lovely is thy dwelling-place	Ps 84
		612	Gracious Spirit, Holy Ghost	E
		576, 577	God is love, and where true love is	E
		581	Where charity and love prevail	E
		606	Where true charity and love dwell	E
MON	MP	592	Teach me, my God and King	L

		596	Judge eternal, throned in splendor	G
		574, 575	Before thy throne, O God, we kneel	G
		661	They cast their nets in Galilee	G
	EP	439	What wondrous love is this	E
		287	For all the saints, who from their labors rest (sts. 1-3)	E
		434	Nature with open volume stands	E
		181	Awake and sing the song	E
		253	Give us the wings of faith to rise	E
TUE	MP	409	The spacious firmament on high	L
		398	I sing the almighty power of God	L
		405	All things bright and beautiful	L
		392	Come, we that love the Lord	G
		344	Lord, dismiss us with thy blessing	G
		574, 575	Before thy throne, O God, we kneel	G
		148	Creator of the earth and skies	G
	EP	181	Awake and sing the song	E
		532, 533	How wondrous and great thy works, God of praise!	E
WED	MP	616	Hail to the Lord's Anointed	Ps 72
		544	Jesus shall reign, where'er the sun	Ps 72
		385	Many and great, O God, are thy works	L
		389	Let us, with a gladsome mind	L
		398	I sing the almighty power of God	L
		567	Thine arm, O Lord, in days of old	G
		493	O for a thousand tongues to sing	G
		566	From thee all skill and science flow	G
	EP	29, 30	O Trinity of blessèd light	S
		33, 34, 35	Christ, mighty Savior, Light of all creation	S
		27, 28	O blest Creator, source of light	S
THU	MP	279	For thy dear saints, O Lord	L
		287	For all the saints, who from their labors rest (st. 1-4)	L
		275	Hark! the sound of holy voices	L
		24	The day thou gavest, Lord, is ended (omit st. 1)	G
		380	From all that dwell below the skies	G
		339	Deck thyself, my soul, with gladness	G
		10	New every morning is the love	G
	EP	68	Rejoice! rejoice, believers	E
		61, 62	"Sleepers, wake!" A voice astounds us	E
		53	Once he came in blessing	E
FRI	MP	396, 397	Now thank we all our God	L
		590	O Jesus Christ, may grateful hymns be rising	G
		74	Blest be the King whose coming	G
		598	Lord Christ, when first thou cam'st to earth	G
	EP	596	Judge eternal, throned in splendor	E

		483	The head that once was crowned with thorns	E
		494	Crown him with many crowns	E
SAT	MP	635	If thou but trust in God to guide thee	L
		669	Commit thou all that grieves thee	L
		656	Blest are the pure in heart	G
		437, 438	Tell out, my soul, the greatness of the Lord!	G
		670	Lord, for ever at thy side	G
	EP	663	The Lord my God my shepherd is	Ps 23
		664	My Shepherd will supply my need	Ps 23
		645, 646	The King of love my shepherd is	Ps 23
		574, 575	Before thy throne, O God, we kneel	E

Proper 27

SUN	MP	9	Not here for high and holy things	G
		541	Come, labor on	G
		551	Rise up, ye saints of God!	G
	EP	513	Like the murmur of the dove's song	E
		531	O Spirit of the living God	E
		501, 502	O Holy Spirit, by whose breath	E
MON	MP	339	Deck thyself, my soul, with gladness	G
		202	The Lamb's high banquet called to share	G
	EP	596	Judge eternal, throned in splendor	E
		591	O God of earth and altar	E
		573	Father eternal, Ruler of creation	E
TUE	MP	675	Take up your cross, the Savior said	G
		484, 485	Praise the Lord through every nation	G
		10	New every morning is the love	G
		654	Day by day	G
	EP	202	The Lamb's high banquet called to share	E
		61, 62	"Sleepers, wake!" A voice astounds us	E
		213	Come away to the skies	E
WED	MP	140, 141	Wilt thou forgive that sin, where I begun	L
		148	Creator of the earth and skies	L
		645, 646	The King of love my shepherd is	G
		469, 470	There's a wideness in God's mercy	G
		664	My Shepherd will supply my need	G
	EP	494	Crown him with many crowns	E
		483	The head that once was crowned with thorns	E
		450, 451	All hail the power of Jesus' Name	E
THU	MP	467	Sing, my soul, his wondrous love	G
		469, 470	There's a wideness in God's mercy	G
		693	Just as I am, without one plea	G
		140, 141	Wilt thou forgive that sin, where I begun	G
		641	Lord Jesus, think on me	G

		EP	636, 637	How firm a foundation, ye saints of the Lord	E
			561	Stand up, stand up for Jesus	E
			584	God, you have given us power to sound	E
			655	O Jesus, I have promised	E
FRI	MP		488	Be thou my vision, O Lord of my heart	L
			6, 7	Christ, whose glory fills the skies	S
			8	Morning has broken	S
	EP		610	Lord, whose love through humble service	E
			628	Help us, O Lord, to learn	E
SAT	MP		680	O God, our help in ages past	Ps 90
			701	Jesus, all my gladness	G
			475	God himself is with us (sts. 1-2)	G
			707	Take my life, and let it be	G
	EP		389	Let us, with a gladsome mind	Ps 136
			568	Father all loving, who rulest in majesty	E
			603, 604	When Christ was lifted from the earth	E
			529	In Christ there is no East or West	E
			602	Jesu, Jesu, fill us with your love	E

Proper 28

SUN	MP		538	God of mercy, God of grace	Ps 67
			605	What does the Lord require	G
			610	Lord, whose love through humble service	G
			656	Blest are the pure in heart	G
	EP		546	Awake, my soul, stretch every nerve	E
			27, 28	O blest Creator, source of light	E
			422	Not far beyond the sea, nor high	E
			552, 553	Fight the good fight with all thy might (sts. 1-2)	E
			621, 622	Light's abode, celestial Salem	E
MON	MP		534	God is working his purpose out	L
			609	Where cross the crowded ways of life	G
			582, 583	O holy city, seen of John	G
			574, 575	Before thy throne, O God, we kneel	G
			437, 438	Tell out, my soul, the greatness of the Lord!	G
	EP		610	Lord, whose love through humble service	E
			628	Help us, O Lord, to learn	E
			704	O thou who camest from above	E
TUE	MP		667	Sometimes a light surprises	L
			674	"Forgive our sins as we forgive"	G
			541	Come, labor on	G
			11	Awake, my soul, and with the sun	G
			655	O Jesus, I have promised	G
	EP		574, 575	Before thy throne, O God, we kneel	E
			694	God be in my head	E

WED	MP	415	When all thy mercies, O my God	G
		396, 397	Now thank we all our God	G
		567	Thine arm, O Lord, in days of old	G
	EP	656	Blest are the pure in heart	E
		574, 575	Before thy throne, O God, we kneel	E
		670	Lord, for ever at thy side	E
		437, 438	Tell out, my soul, the greatness of the Lord!	E
THU	MP	61, 62	"Sleepers, wake!" A voice astounds us	G
		59	Hark! a thrilling voice is sounding	G
		53	Once he came in blessing	G
	EP	574, 575	Before thy throne, O God, we kneel	E
		582, 583	O holy city, seen of John	E
		605	What does the Lord require	E
FRI	MP	657	Love divine, all loves excelling	L
		709	O God of Bethel, by whose hand	G
		698	Eternal Spirit of the living Christ	G
		711	Seek ye first the kingdom of God	G
		695, 696	By gracious powers so wonderfully sheltered	G
	EP	462	The Lord will come and not be slow	E
		481	Rejoice, the Lord is King	E
		615	"Thy kingdom come!" on bended knee	E
SAT	MP	596	Judge eternal, throned in splendor	L
		6, 7	Christ, whose glory fills the skies	L
		672	O very God of very God	L
		670	Lord, for ever at thy side	G
		641	Lord Jesus, think on me	G
		140, 141	Wilt thou forgive that sin, where I begun	G
		437, 438	Tell out, my soul, the greatness of the Lord	G
	EP	566	From thee all skill and science flow	E
		567	Thine arm, O Lord, in days of old	E
		44, 45	To you before the close of day	E

Proper 29

SUN	MP	65	Prepare the way, O Zion	L & G
		71, 72	Hark! the glad sound! the Savior comes	G
		74	Blest be the King whose coming	G
		486	Hosanna to the living Lord!	G
	EP	414	God, my King, thy might confessing	Ps 145
		404	We will extol you, ever-blessèd Lord	Ps 145
		458	My song is love unknown	E
		455, 456	O love of God, how strong and true	E
		432	O praise ye the Lord! Praise him in the height (omit st. 3)	E
		296	We know that Christ is raised and dies no more	E

MON	MP	480	When Jesus left his Father's throne	G
		701	Jesus, all my gladness	G
		655	O Jesus, I have promised	G
	EP	610	Lord, whose love through humble service	E
		43	All praise to thee, my God, this night	S
		46	The duteous day now closeth	S
TUE	MP	668	I to the hills will lift mine eyes	Ps 121
		633	Word of God, come down on earth	G
		567	Thine arm, O Lord, in days of old	G
		371	Thou, whose almighty Word	G
		458	My song is love unknown	G
		495	Hail, thou once despisèd Jesus! (sts. 1-2)	G
		493	O for a thousand tongues to sing	G
	EP	636, 637	How firm a foundation, ye saints of the Lord	E
		518	Christ is made the sure foundation	E
		525	The Church's one foundation	E
		500	Creator Spirit, by whose aid	E
		516	Come down, O Love divine	E
		656	Blest are the pure in heart	E
WED	MP	489	The great Creator of the worlds	G
		448, 449	O love, how deep, how broad, how high	G
		469, 470	There's a wideness in God's mercy	G
		382	King of glory, King of peace	G
	EP	666	Out of the depths I call	Ps 130
		151	From deepest woe I cry to thee	Ps 130
		706	In your mercy, Lord, you called me	E
		686	Come, thou fount of every blessing	E
		495	Hail, thou once despisèd Jesus! (sts. 1-2)	E
		432	O praise ye the Lord! Praise him in the height (omit st. 3)	E
THU	MP	670	Lord, for ever at thy side	Ps 131
		686	Come, thou fount of every blessing	L
		699	Jesus, Lover of my soul	L
		11	Awake, my soul, and with the sun	G
	EP	421	All glory be to God on high	E
		366	Holy God, we praise thy Name	E
		364	O God, we praise thee, and confess	E
		492	Sing, ye faithful, sing with gladness	E
		495	Hail, thou once despisèd Jesus!	E
FRI	MP	71, 72	Hark! the glad sound! the Savior comes	G
		65	Prepare the way, O Zion	G
		74	Blest be the King whose coming	G
		486	Hosanna to the living Lord!	G
		436	Lift up your heads, ye mighty gates	G
	EP	603, 604	When Christ was lifted from the earth	E
		472	Hope of the world, thou Christ of great compassion	E

	532, 533	How wondrous and great thy works, God of praise!	E
	380	From all that dwell below the skies	E
	531	O Spirit of the living God	E
SAT	MP	590	O Jesus Christ, may grateful hymns be rising	G
		598	Lord Christ, when first thou cam'st to earth	G
		458	My song is love unknown	G
	EP	388	O worship the King, all glorious above!	Ps 104
		477	All praise to thee, for thou, O King divine	E
		435	At the Name of Jesus	E
		60	Creator of the stars of night	E
		450, 451	All hail the power of Jesus' Name!	E

The Daily Office—Holy Days

St. Andrew (November 30)

MP	532, 533	How wondrous and great thy works, God of praise!	L
	535	Ye servants of God, your Master proclaim	E
	549, 550	Jesus calls us; o'er the tumult	S
EP	678, 679	Surely it is God who saves me	L
	231, 232	By all your saints still striving	G
	549, 550	Jesus calls us; o'er the tumult	G

St. Thomas (December 21)

MP	209	We walk by faith, and not by sight	L & E
	242	How oft, O Lord, thy face hath shone	L & E
	206	O sons and daughters, let us sing *St. Thomas' Day*	L & E
	472	Hope of the world, thou Christ of great compassion	E
EP	457	Thou art the Way, to thee alone	G
	231, 232	By all your saints still striving	S

St. Stephen (December 26)

MP	240, 241	Hearken to the anthem glorious	L
	238, 239	Blessèd feasts of blessèd martyrs	L
	243	When Stephen, full of power and grace	E
	610	Lord, whose love through humble service	E
EP	243	When Stephen, full of power and grace	E
	240, 241	Hearken to the anthem glorious	E
	231, 232	By all your saints still striving	E

St. John (December 27)

MP	681	Our God, to whom we turn	L
	379	God is love, let heaven adore him	L
	386, 387	We sing of God, the mighty source	L
	245	Praise God for John, evangelist	S
	231, 232	By all your saints still striving	S
EP	489	The great Creator of the worlds	E
	661	They cast their nets in Galilee	S

Holy Innocents (December 28)

MP	480	When Jesus left his Father's throne (sts. 1-2)	G
	231, 232	By all your saints still striving	S
	98	Unto us a boy is born!	S
	113	Oh, sleep now, holy baby (Duérmete, Niño lindo)	S
EP	480	When Jesus left his Father's throne (sts. 1-2)	G
	246	In Bethlehem a newborn boy	S
	247	Lully, lullay, thou little tiny child	S

Confession of St. Peter (January 18)

MP	492	Sing, ye faithful, sing with gladness	E
	366	Holy God, we praise thy Name	E
	364	O God, we praise thee, and confess	E
	254	You are the Christ, O Lord	
EP	478	Jesus, our mighty Lord	L
	661	They cast their nets in Galilee	G
	231, 232	By all your saints still striving	G

Conversion of St. Paul (January 25)

MP	701	Jesus, all my gladness	E
	471	We sing the praise of him who died	E
	474	When I survey the wondrous cross	E
	255	We sing the glorious conquest	S
EP	256	A light from heaven shone around	E
	255	We sing the glorious conquest	E
	231, 232	By all your saints still striving	E

Eve of the Presentation

EP	259	Hail to the Lord who comes	S
	257	O Zion, open wide thy gates	S

| | 82 | Of the Father's love begotten | S |
| | 258 | Virgin-born, we bow before thee | S |

The Presentation (February 2)

MP	437, 438	Tell out, my soul, the greatness of the Lord!	L
	419	Lord of all being, throned afar	G
	656	Blest are the pure in heart	S
	259	Hail to the Lord who comes	S
	257	O Zion, open wide thy gates	S
EP	81	Lo, how a Rose e'er blooming	S
	499	Lord God, you now have set your servant free	S
	278	Sing we of the blessèd Mother	S
	258	Virgin-born, we bow before thee	S

St. Matthias (February 24)

MP	231, 232	By all your saints still striving	S
	233, 234	The eternal gifts of Christ the King	S
	238, 239	Blessèd feasts of blessèd martyrs	S
EP	525	The Church's one foundation	E
	40, 41	O Christ, you are both light and day	E
	231, 232	By all your saints still striving	S
	237	Let us now our voices raise	S
	240, 241	Hearken to the anthem glorious	S

St. Joseph (March 19)

MP	261, 262	By the Creator, Joseph was appointed	G
	260	Come now, and praise the humble saint	G
	231, 232	By all your saints still striving	G
	252	Jesus! Name of wondrous love!	G
	248, 249	To the Name of our salvation	G
EP	260	Come now, and praise the humble saint	S
	261, 262	By the Creator, Joseph was appointed	S
	231, 232	By all your saints still striving	S
	587	Our Father, by whose Name	S
	656	Blest are the pure in heart	S

Eve of the Annunciation

EP	270	Gabriel's message does away	L & E
	266	Nova, nova	L & E
	445, 446	Praise to the Holiest in the height	L & E
	60	Creator of the stars of night	L & E

Annunciation (March 25)

MP	267	Praise we the Lord this day	S
	443	From God Christ's deity came forth	E
	448, 449	O love, how deep, how broad, how high	E
EP	263, 264	The Word whom earth and sea and sky	G
	265	The angel Gabriel from heaven came	S
	258	Virgin-born, we bow before thee	S

St. Mark (April 25)

MP	231, 232	By all your saints still striving	E
	244	Come, pure hearts, in joyful measure	S
	235	Come sing, ye choirs exultant	S
	237	Let us now our voices raise	S
	238, 239	Blessèd feasts of blessèd martyrs	S
EP	231, 232	By all your saints still striving	E
	552, 553	Fight the good fight with all thy might (sts. 1-2)	E
	240, 241	Hearken to the anthem glorious	S
	236	King of the martyrs' noble band	S

SS. Philip & James (May 1)

MP	231, 232	By all your saints still striving	G
	233, 234	The eternal gifts of Christ the King	S
	238, 239	Blessèd feasts of blessèd martyrs	S
	240, 241	Hearken to the anthem glorious	S
EP	231, 232	By all your saints still striving	G
	237	Let us now our voices raise	S
	236	King of the martyrs' noble band	S
	655	O Jesus, I have promised	G

Eve of the Visitation

EP	81	Lo, how a Rose e'er blooming	L
	496, 497	How bright appears the Morning Star	L
	443	From God Christ's deity came forth	E
	476	Can we by searching find out God	E

The Visitation (May 31)

MP	616	Hail to the Lord's Anointed	Ps 72

	268, 269	Ye who claim the faith of Jesus	S
	437, 438	Tell out, my soul, the greatness of the Lord!	S
EP	268, 269	Ye who claim the faith of Jesus	S
	437, 438	Tell out, my soul, the greatness of the Lord!	S
	258	Virgin-born, we bow before thee	S
	266	Nova, nova	S

St. Barnabas (June 11)

MP	231, 232	By all your saints still striving	E
	701	Jesus, all my gladness	E
	238, 239	Blessèd feasts of blessèd martyrs	S
EP	237	Let us now our voices raise	S
	240, 241	Hearken to the anthem glorious	S
	236	King of the martyrs' noble band	S

Eve of St. John the Baptist

EP	271, 272	The great forerunner of the morn	G
	231, 232	By all your saints still striving	G
	444	Blessed be the God of Israel	S

Nativity of St. John the Baptist (June 24)

MP	67	Comfort, comfort ye my people	L
	75	There's a voice in the wilderness crying	L
	271, 272	The great forerunner of the morn	G
	231, 232	By all your saints still striving	G
EP	271, 272	The great forerunner of the morn	G
	444	Blessed be the God of Israel	G
	231, 232	By all your saints still striving	G
	70	Herald, sound the note of judgment	G
	76	On Jordan's bank the Baptist's cry	G

SS. Peter & Paul (June 29)

MP	273, 274	Two stalwart trees both rooted	E
	231, 232	By all your saints still striving	E
	532, 533	How wondrous and great thy works, God of praise!	E
	233, 234	The eternal gifts of Christ the King	S
EP	532, 533	How wondrous and great thy works, God of praise!	E
	273, 274	Two stalwart trees both rooted	E
	231, 232	By all your saints still striving	E

Independence Day (July 4)

MP	437, 438	Tell out, my soul, the greatness of the Lord!	L
	596	Judge eternal, throned in splendor	E
	594, 595	God of grace and God of glory	S
	591	O God of earth and altar	S
EP	597	O day of peace that dimly shines	L
	607	O God of every nation	L
	542	Christ is the world's true Light	L
	613	Thy kingdom come, O God	L
	578	O God of love, O King of peace	L
	582, 583	O holy city, seen of John	E

St. Mary Magdalene (July 22)

MP	190	Lift your voice rejoicing, Mary	G
	183	Christians, to the Paschal victim	G
	203	O sons and daughters, let us sing *Easter* (sts. 1-3)	G
	673	The first one ever, oh, ever to know (st. 3)	G
	231, 232	By all your saints still striving	G
EP	425	Sing now with joy unto the Lord	L
	190	Lift your voice rejoicing, Mary	S
	673	The first one ever, oh, ever to know (st. 3)	S

St. James (July 25)

MP	276	For thy blest saints, a noble throng	G
	238, 239	Blessèd feasts of blessèd martyrs	S
	240, 241	Hearken to the anthem glorious	S
EP	231, 232	By all your saints still striving	G
	276	For thy blest saints, a noble throng	G
	236	King of the martyrs' noble band	S
	237	Let us now our voices raise	S
	655	O Jesus, I have promised	G

Eve of the Transfiguration

EP	133, 134	O Light of Light, Love given birth	E
	136, 137	O wondrous type! O vision fair	E
	129, 130	Christ upon the mountain peak	S

The Transfiguration (August 6)

MP	136, 137	O wondrous type! O vision fair	L & E
	129, 130	Christ upon the mountain peak	L & E
	133, 134	O Light of Light, Love given birth	L & E
	6, 7	Christ, whose glory fills the skies	S
EP	133, 134	O Light of Light, Love given birth	G
	129, 130	Christ upon the mountain peak	G
	136, 137	O wondrous type! O vision fair	G

St. Mary the Virgin (August 15)

MP	437, 438	Tell out, my soul, the greatness of the Lord!	L
	231, 232	By all your saints still striving	S
	278	Sing we of the blessèd Mother	S
	620	Jerusalem, my happy home	S
EP	278	Sing we of the blessèd Mother	E & G
	277	Sing of Mary, pure and lowly	G
	268, 269	Ye who claim the faith of Jesus	S
	258	Virgin-born, we bow before thee	S
	618	Ye watchers and ye holy ones	S

St. Bartholomew (August 24)

MP	453	As Jacob with travel was weary one day	L & G
	•280	God of saints, to whom the number	S
	231, 232	By all your saints still striving	S
EP	280	God of saints, to whom the number	E
	231, 232	By all your saints still striving	E
	656	Blest are the pure in heart	E

Eve of Holy Cross

EP	603, 604	When Christ was lifted from the earth	E
	495	Hail, thou once despisèd Jesus!	E
	441, 442	In the cross of Christ I glory	S

Holy Cross Day (September 14)

MP	473	Lift high the cross	L & G
	471	We sing the praise of him who died	G
	165, 166	Sing, my tongue, the glorious battle	S
EP	445, 446	Praise to the Holiest in the height	L
	473	Lift high the cross	E
	434	Nature with open volume stands	S

| 161 | The flaming banners of our King | S |
| 162 | The royal banners forward go | S |

St. Matthew (September 21)

MP	530	Spread, O spread, thou mighty word	E
	531	O Spirit of the living God	E
	535	Ye servants of God, your Master proclaim	E
	281	He sat to watch o'er customs paid	S
	231, 232	By all your saints still striving	S
EP	281	He sat to watch o'er customs paid	S
	231, 232	By all your saints still striving	S
	244	Come, pure hearts, in joyful measure	S
	235	Come sing, ye choirs exultant	S

St. Michael & All Angels (September 29)

MP	373	Praise the Lord! ye heavens adore him	Ps 148
	426	Songs of praise the angels sang	L
	284	O ye immortal throng	E
	618	Ye watchers and ye holy ones	E
	625	Ye holy angels bright	S
EP	342	O praise ye the Lord! Praise him in the height	Ps 150
	282, 283	Christ, the fair glory of the holy angels	L(Dan)
	374	Come, let us join our cheerful songs	E
	535	Ye servants of God, your Master proclaim	E

St. Luke (October 18)

MP	285	What thanks and praise to thee we owe	G
	231, 232	By all your saints still striving	G
	235	Come sing, ye choirs exultant	G
	244	Come, pure hearts, in joyful measure	G
EP	285	What thanks and praise to thee we owe	E
	244	Come, pure hearts, in joyful measure	E
	235	Come sing, ye choirs exultant	E

St. James of Jerusalem (October 23)

MP	231, 232	By all your saints still striving	S
	326	From glory to glory advancing, we praise thee, O Lord	S
	238, 239	Blessèd feasts of blessèd martyrs	S
	240, 241	Hearken to the anthem glorious	S
	655	O Jesus, I have promised	G

EP	231, 232	By all your saints still striving	S
	326	From glory to glory advancing, we praise thee, O Lord	S
	236	King of the martyrs' noble band	S
	237	Let us now our voices raise	S
	623	O what their joy and their glory must be	E

SS. Simon & Jude (October 28)

MP	231, 232	By all your saints still striving	S
	233, 234	The eternal gifts of Christ the King	S
	238, 239	Blessèd feasts of blessèd martyrs	S
	518	Christ is made the sure foundation	L
	525	The Church's one foundation	L & E
	521	Put forth, O God, thy Spirit's might	E
EP	231, 232	By all your saints still striving	G
	240, 241	Hearken to the anthem glorious	S
	236	King of the martyrs' noble band	S
	237	Let us now our voices raise	S
	522, 523	Glorious things of thee are spoken	L

Eve of All Saints

EP	287	For all the saints, who from their labors rest (sts. 1-4)	S
	279	For thy dear saints, O Lord	S
	231, 232	By all your saints still striving	S
	526	Let saints on earth in concert sing	S

All Saints' Day (November 1)

MP	286	Who are these like stars appearing	L
	545	Lo! what a cloud of witnessess	E
	253	Give us the wings of faith to rise	E
	546	Awake, my soul, stretch every nerve	E
EP	275	Hark! the sound of holy voices	E
	623	O what their joy and their glory must be	E
	620	Jerusalem, my happy home	E
	624	Jerusalem the golden	E
	621, 622	Light's abode, celestial Salem	E

Thanksgiving Day

MP	705	As those of old their first fruits brought	L
	424	For the fruit of all creation	L
	291	We plow the fields, and scatter	L

	288	Praise to God, immortal praise	L
EP	396, 397	Now thank we all our God	E
	415	When all thy mercies, O my God	E
	290	Come, ye thankful people, come	E
	416	For the beauty of the earth	E

The Daily Office – Special Occasions

Eve of the Dedication

EP	518	Christ is made the sure foundation	E
	525	The Church's one foundation	E

Anniversary of the Dedication of a Church

MP	367	Round the Lord in glory seated	L
	517	How lovely is thy dwelling-place	S
	524	I love thy kingdom, Lord	S
EP	51	We the Lord's people, heart and voice uniting (except on Sunday, omit st. 3)	S
	360, 361	Only-begotten, Word of God eternal	S
	289	Our Father, by whose servants	S

Eve of the Patronal Feast

EP	521	Put forth, O God, thy Spirit's might	E (Eph)
	525	The Church's one foundation	E (Eph)
	275	Hark! the sound of holy voices	E (Rev)
	625	Ye holy angels bright	E (Rev)
	618	Ye watchers and ye holy ones	E (Rev)

The Patronal Feast

MP	525	The Church's one foundation	E
	518	Christ is made the sure foundation	E
	521	Put forth, O God, thy Spirit's might	S
EP	610	Lord, whose love through humble service	E
	347	Go forth for God; go to the world in peace	E
	576, 577	God is love, and where true love is	E
	581	Where charity and love prevail	E
	606	Where true charity and love dwell	E
	593	Lord, make us servants of your peace	E

EP	623	O what their joy and their glory must be	E
	620	Jerusalem, my happy home	E
	624	Jerusalem the golden	E
	540	Awake, thou Spirit of the watchmen (sts. 2-3)	G
	541	Come, labor on	G

Holy Baptism

See the day of the Church Year — The Holy Eucharist (below, pp. 176-289)

Also see:

Entrance:	370	I bind unto myself today
	697	My God, accept my heart this day
	297	Descend, O Spirit, purging flame
	299	Spirit of God, unleashed on earth
	678, 679	Surely it is God who saves me (Canticle 9)
Sequence:	298	All who believe and are baptized
	547	Awake, O sleeper, rise from death
Procession to the font:	658	As longs the deer for cooling streams (Psalm 42)
	298	All who believe and are baptized
	297	Descend, O Spirit, purging flame
	299	Spirit of God, unleashed on earth
	547	Awake, O sleeper, rise from death
	686	Come, thou fount of every blessing
	359	God of the prophets, bless the prophets' heirs
	370	I bind unto myself today
	697	My God, accept my heart this day
	678, 679	Surely it is God who saves me (Canticle 9)
Return from the font:	645, 646	The King of love my shepherd is (Psalm 23)
	663	The Lord my God my shepherd is (Psalm 23)
	664	My Shepherd will supply my need (Psalm 23)
	294	Baptized in water
	295	Sing praise to our Creator
	296	We know that Christ is raised and dies no more
	213	Come away to the skies
	473	Lift high the cross
	176, 177	Over the chaos of the empty waters
Offertory:	294	Baptized in water
	296	We know that Christ is raised and dies no more
	295	Sing praise to our Creator
	176, 177	Over the chaos of the empty waters
Communion:	295	Sing praise to our Creator
	645, 646	The King of love my shepherd is

	663	The Lord my God my shepherd is	
	664	My Shepherd will supply my need	
Postcommunion:	432	O praise ye the Lord! Praise him in the height	
	473	Lift high the cross	
	213	Come away to the skies	

The Holy Eucharist

The First Sunday of Advent - Year A

Entrance:	53	Once he came in blessing	S
	57, 58	Lo! he comes with clouds descending	G
Sequence:	59	Hark! a thrilling voice is sounding	C & E
	11	Awake, my soul, and with the sun	E
	600, 601	O day of God, draw nigh	L
	596	Judge eternal, throned in splendor	L
	613	Thy kingdom come, O God	L
	542	Christ is the world's true Light	L
Offertory:	61, 62	"Sleepers, wake!" A voice astounds us	E & G
	68	Rejoice! rejoice, believers	G
	454	Jesus came, adored by angels	E & G
Communion:	63, 64	O heavenly Word, eternal Light	S
	454	Jesus came, adored by angels	E & G
Postcommunion:	73	The King shall come when morning dawns	S
	68	Rejoice! rejoice, believers	G
	486	Hosanna to the living Lord!	S

The Second Sunday of Advent

Entrance:	70	Herald, sound the note of judgment	C & G
	59	Hark! a thrilling voice is sounding	G
Sequence:	75	There's a voice in the wilderness crying	G
	67	Comfort, comfort ye my people	G
	534	God is working his purpose out	L & E
	597	O day of peace that dimly shines	L
	542	Christ is the world's true Light	L & E
	616	Hail to the Lord's Anointed	P
Offertory:	76	On Jordan's bank the Baptist's cry	G
Communion:	67	Comfort, comfort ye my people	G
	69	What is the crying at Jordan?	G
Postcommunion:	65	Prepare the way, O Zion	G

The Third Sunday of Advent

Entrance:	640	Watchman, tell us of the night	S
	65	Prepare the way, O Zion	G
	70	Herald, sound the note of judgment	G
	76	On Jordan's bank the Baptist's cry	G
Sequence:	67	Comfort, comfort ye my people	L & G
	75	There's a voice in the wilderness crying	L & G
	462	The Lord will come and not be slow	E
	615	"Thy kingdom come!" on bended knee	E
Offertory:	271, 272	The great forerunner of the morn	G
	71, 72	Hark! the glad sound! the Savior comes	G
Communion:	71, 72	Hark! the glad sound! the Savior comes	G
	65	Prepare the way, O Zion	G
	69	What is the crying at Jordan?	G
Postcommunion:	444	Blessed be the God of Israel	G

The Fourth Sunday of Advent

Entrance:	56	O come, O come, Emmanuel	L & G
	436	Lift up your heads, ye mighty gates	C & P
	657	Love divine, all loves excelling	C
	486	Hosanna to the living Lord!	C
Sequence:	54	Savior of the nations, come	E & G
	55	Redeemer of the nations, come	E & G
	496, 497	How bright appears the Morning Star	L & G
Offertory:	265	The angel Gabriel from heaven came	G
	270	Gabriel's message does away	G
Communion:	263, 264	The Word whom earth and sea and sky	G
	252	Jesus! Name of wondrous love!	G
	248, 249	To the Name of our salvation	G
Postcommunion:	71, 72	Hark! the glad sound! the Savior comes	C & G
	66	Come, thou long-expected Jesus	S
	268, 269	Ye who claim the faith of Jesus	G

Christmas Day I (Night)

Entrance:	83	O come, all ye faithful	G
	103	A child is born in Bethlehem, Alleluia!	G
Sequence:	125, 126	The people who in darkness walked	L
	94, 95	While shepherds watched their flocks by night	G
	91	Break forth, O beauteous heavenly light	G
	88	Sing, O sing, this blessèd morn	L & G

Offertory:	115	What child is this, who, laid to rest	G
	104	A stable lamp is lighted	G
	89, 90	It came upon the midnight clear	G
	80	From heaven above to earth I come	G
	78, 79	O little town of Bethlehem	G
	114	'Twas in the moon of wintertime	G
	110	The snow lay on the ground	G
Communion:	96	Angels we have heard on high	G
	97	Dost thou in a manger lie	G
	77	From east to west, from shore to shore	G
	112	In the bleak midwinter	G
	108	Now yield we thanks and praise	G
	111	Silent night, holy night	G
	101	Away in a manger, no crib for his bed	G
	98	Unto us a boy is born!	G
	113	Oh, sleep now, holy baby (Duérmete, Niño lindo)	G
Postcommunion:	87	Hark! the herald angels sing	G
	107	Good Christian friends, rejoice	G
	100	Joy to the world! the Lord is come	G
	109	The first Nowell the angel did say	G

Christmas Day II (Dawn)

Entrance:	106	Christians, awake, salute the happy morn	E & G
	99	Go tell it on the mountain	G
Sequence:	107	Good Christian friends, rejoice	E & G
	91	Break forth, O beauteous heavenly light	G
Offertory:	115	What child is this, who, laid to rest	G
	104	A stable lamp is lighted	G
	80	From heaven above to earth I come	G
Communion:	98	Unto us a boy is born!	G
	108	Now yield we thanks and praise	G
	96	Angels we have heard on high	G
Postcommunion:	105	God rest you merry, gentlemen	G
	87	Hark! the herald angels sing	G
	100	Joy to the world! the Lord is come	G

Christmas Day III (Christmas Day)

Entrance:	92	On this day earth shall ring	G
	102	Once in royal David's city	G
	93	Angels, from the realms of glory	E
Sequence:	77	From east to west, from shore to shore	G
	85, 86	O Savior of our fallen race	G

Offertory:	88	Sing, O sing, this blessèd morn	G
	82	Of the Father's love begotten	G
	112	In the bleak midwinter	G
Communion:	97	Dost thou in a manger lie	E & G
	491	Where is this stupendous stranger?	G
	468	It was poor little Jesus	G
	81	Lo, how a Rose e'er blooming	G
	84	Love came down at Christmas	G
	108	Now yield we thanks and praise	E
Postcommunion:	87	Hark! the herald angels sing	G
	107	Good Christian friends, rejoice	G
	105	God rest you merry, gentlemen	G
	100	Joy to the world! the Lord is come	G

The First Sunday After Christmas Day

Entrance:	496, 497	How bright appears the Morning Star	C, E & G
	421	All glory be to God on high	G
Sequence:	77	From east to west, from shore to shore	G
	85, 86	O Savior of our fallen race	G
Offertory:	82	Of the Father's love begotten	G
	443	From God Christ's deity came forth	G
	633	Word of God, come down on earth	G
	476	Can we by searching find out God	G
	386, 387	We sing of God, the mighty source (omit st. 2)	G
	489	The great Creator of the worlds	G
	324	Let all mortal flesh keep silence	G
Communion:	439	What wondrous love is this	G
	491	Where is this stupendous stranger?	G
	97	Dost thou in a manger lie	G
	468	It was poor little Jesus	G
	319	You, Lord, we praise in songs of celebration	G
Postcommunion:	100	Joy to the world! the Lord is come	G
	87	Hark! the herald angels sing	G
	452	Glorious the day when Christ was born	G

The Holy Name of Our Lord Jesus Christ

Entrance:	450, 451	All hail the power of Jesus' Name!	G
	477	All praise to thee, for thou, O King divine	G
Sequence:	60	Creator of the stars of night (sts. 1-4)	G
	252	Jesus! Name of wondrous love!	G
Offertory:	252	Jesus! Name of wondrous love!	G
	435	At the Name of Jesus	G
	477	All praise to thee, for thou, O King divine	G

	493	O for a thousand tongues to sing	G
Communion:	250	Now greet the swiftly changing year	G
	251	O God, whom neither time nor space	New Year
	252	Jesus! Name of wondrous love!	G
Postcommunion:	248, 249	To the Name of our salvation	G
	644	How sweet the Name of Jesus sounds	G

The Second Sunday After Christmas Day

When the emphasis is on the Holy Family and family life (Matthew 2:13-15, 19-23 or Luke 2:41-52):

Entrance:	85, 86	O Savior of our fallen race	S
	102	Once in royal David's city	S
	277	Sing of Mary, pure and lowly	S
	416	For the beauty of the earth	S
Sequence:	277	Sing of Mary, pure and lowly	S
	85, 86	O Savior of our fallen race	S
	84	Love came down at Christmas	S
Offertory:	587	Our Father, by whose Name	G
	480	When Jesus left his Father's throne	G
	261, 262	By the Creator, Joseph was appointed	G
	611	Christ the worker (sts. 1-2)	G
Communion:	480	When Jesus left his Father's throne	G
	587	Our Father, by whose Name	G
	113	Oh, sleep now, holy baby (Duérmete, Niño lindo)	G
	260	Come now, and praise the humble saint	G
Postcommunion:	396, 397	Now thank we all our God	S
	416	For the beauty of the earth	S
	709	O God of Bethel, by whose hand	S

When the Gospel is the story of the Magi (Matthew 2:1-12):

Entrance:	117, 118	Brightest and best of the stars of the morning	G
	496, 497	How bright appears the Morning Star	S
	93	Angels, from the realms of glory	G
	109	The first Nowell the angel did say	G
Sequence:	131, 132	When Christ's appearing was made known (sts. 1-2)	G
	124	What star is this, with beams so bright	G
Offertory:	127	Earth has many a noble city	G
	491	Where is this stupendous stranger?	G
	128	We three kings of Orient are	G
Communion:	496, 497	How bright appears the Morning Star	S
	491	Where is this stupendous stranger?	G

	128	We three kings of Orient are	G
Postcommunion:	119	As with gladness men of old	G
	124	What star is this, with beams so bright	G

The Feast of the Epiphany

Entrance:	117, 118	Brightest and best of the stars of the morning	G
	124	What star is this, with beams so bright	G
	496, 497	How bright appears the Morning Star	L
Sequence:	131, 132	When Christ's appearing was made known (sts. 1, 2 & 5 or 2 & 5)	G
	124	What star is this, with beams so bright	G
	616	Hail to the Lord's Anointed	P
	543	O Zion, tune thy voice	L
Offertory:	127	Earth has many a noble city	G
	491	Where is this stupendous stranger?	G
	128	We three kings of Orient are	G
Communion:	496, 497	How bright appears the Morning Star	L
	491	Where is this stupendous stranger?	G
	128	We three kings of Orient are	G
	112	In the bleak midwinter	G
	333	Now the silence	S
Postcommunion:	119	As with gladness men of old	G
	135	Songs of thankfulness and praise	G

The First Sunday After the Epiphany: The Baptism of Our Lord Jesus Christ

Entrance:	121	Christ, when for us you were baptized	G
	139	When Jesus went to Jordan's stream	G
	76	On Jordan's bank the Baptist's cry	G
Sequence:	131, 132	When Christ's appearing was made known (sts. 3 & 5)	G
Baptism:	121	Christ, when for us you were baptized	G
	370	I bind unto myself today	G
	297	Descend, O Spirit, purging flame	G
	697	My God, accept my heart this day	G
	294	Baptized in water	G
	295	Sing praise to our Creator	G
Offertory:	120	The sinless one to Jordan came	G
	116	"I come," the great Redeemer cries	G
	443	From God Christ's deity came forth	G
Communion:	370	I bind unto myself today	G
	116	"I come," the great Redeemer cries	G

| Postcommunion: | 139 | When Jesus went to Jordan's stream | G |
| | 120 | The sinless one to Jordan came | G |

The Second Sunday After the Epiphany

Entrance:	496, 497	How bright appears the Morning Star	C & L
	6, 7	Christ, whose glory fills the skies	C & L
	532, 533	How wondrous and great thy works, God of praise!	C & L
	440	Blessed Jesus, at thy word	C
	543	O Zion, tune thy voice	C & L
Sequence:	444	Blessed be the God of Israel	L
	131, 132	When Christ's appearing was made known (sts. 3 & 5)	G
Offertory:	443	From God Christ's deity came forth	G
	439	What wondrous love is this	G
	139	When Jesus went to Jordan's stream	G
	121	Christ, when for us you were baptized	G
	59	Hark! a thrilling voice is sounding	G
	549, 550	Jesus calls us; o'er the tumult	G
Communion:	439	What wondrous love is this	G
	324	Let all mortal flesh keep silence	C
	307	Lord, enthroned in heavenly splendor	G
Postcommunion:	535	Ye servants of God, your Master proclaim	G
	538	God of mercy, God of grace	C
	421	All glory be to God on high	G

The Third Sunday After the Epiphany

Entrance:	532, 533	How wondrous and great thy works, God of praise!	C & G
	537	Christ for the world we sing!	C & G
	543	O Zion, tune thy voice	C & G
Sequence:	125, 126	The people who in darkness walked	G
	581	Where charity and love prevail	E
	576, 577	God is love, and where true love is	E
	606	Where true charity and love dwell	E
	702	Lord, thou hast searched me and dost know	P
Offertory:	549, 550	Jesus calls us; o'er the tumult	G
	661	They cast their nets in Galilee	G
	135	Songs of thankfulness and praise (sts. 1-3)	G
Communion:	321	My God, thy table now is spread	G
	304	I come with joy to meet my Lord	E
Postcommunion:	381	Thy strong word did cleave the darkness	C & G

| 530 | Spread, O spread, thou mighty word | C |
| 539 | O Zion, haste, thy mission high fulfilling | C |

The Fourth Sunday After the Epiphany

Entrance:	616	Hail to the Lord's Anointed	S
	477	All praise to thee, for thou, O King divine	E
	440	Blessèd Jesus, at thy word	S
Sequence:	605	What does the Lord require	L
	434	Nature with open volume stands	E
	471	We sing the praise of him who died	E
	441, 442	In the cross of Christ I glory	E
	160	Cross of Jesus, cross of sorrow	E
Offertory:	560	Remember your servants, Lord	G
	593	Lord, make us servants of your peace	G
	628	Help us, O Lord, to learn	G
	554	'Tis the gift to be simple	G
	656	Blest are the pure in heart	G
Communion:	593	Lord, make us servants of your peace	G
	656	Blest are the pure in heart	G
Postcommunion:	593	Lord, make us servants of your peace	G
	437, 438	Tell out, my soul, the greatness of the Lord!	G
	542	Christ is the world's true Light	G

The Fifth Sunday After the Epiphany

Entrance:	543	O Zion, tune thy voice	L, P & G
	125, 126	The people who in darkness walked	L, P & G
	6, 7	Christ, whose glory fills the skies	L, P & G
	496, 497	How bright appears the Morning Star	L, P & G
Sequence:	667	Sometimes a light surprises	L
	629	We limit not the truth of God	E
	488	Be thou my vision, O Lord of my heart	E
	694	God be in my head	E
Offertory:	419	Lord of all being, throned afar	G
	628	Help us, O Lord, to learn	G
	543	O Zion, tune thy voice	G
Communion:	339	Deck thyself, my soul, with gladness	S
	324	Let all mortal flesh keep silence	S
Postcommunion:	381	Thy strong word did cleave the darkness	C, L, P, E & G
	540	Awake, thou Spirit of the watchmen	S
	542	Christ is the world's true Light	S
	371	Thou, whose almighty Word	S

The Sixth Sunday After the Epiphany

Entrance:	440	Blessèd Jesus, at thy word	G
	6, 7	Christ, whose glory fills the skies	S
	496, 497	How bright appears the Morning Star	S
	125, 126	The people who in darkness walked	S
	419	Lord of all being, throned afar	S
Sequence:	500	Creator Spirit, by whose aid	E
	635	If thou but trust in God to guide thee	C
	3, 4	Now that the daylight fills the sky	G
Offertory:	674	"Forgive our sins as we forgive"	G
	593	Lord, make us servants of your peace	G
	641	Lord Jesus, think on me	G
Communion:	593	Lord, make us servants of your peace	G
	304	I come with joy to meet my Lord	G
Postcommunion:	347	Go forth for God; go to the world in peace	G
	312	Strengthen for service, Lord	G
	344	Lord, dismiss us with thy blessing	G

The Seventh Sunday After the Epiphany

Entrance:	518	Christ is made the sure foundation	E
	636, 637	How firm a foundation, ye saints of the Lord	E
	525	The Church's one foundation	E
Sequence:	500	Creator Spirit, by whose aid	E
	516	Come down, O Love divine	E
	656	Blest are the pure in heart	E
	605	What does the Lord require	L
Offertory:	593	Lord, make us servants of your peace	G
	674	"Forgive our sins as we forgive"	G
	3, 4	Now that the daylight fills the sky	G
	5	O splendor of God's glory bright	G
Communion:	603, 604	When Christ was lifted from the earth	G
	394, 395	Creating God, your fingers trace	G
	602	Jesu, Jesu, fill us with your love	G
Postcommunion:	610	Lord, whose love through humble service	G
	347	Go forth for God; go to the world in peace	G
	593	Lord, make us servants of your peace	G

The Eighth Sunday After the Epiphany

Entrance:	408	Sing praise to God who reigns above	C, L & G
	390	Praise to the Lord, the Almighty	C, L & G
	388	O worship the King, all glorious above!	C, L & G
	398	I sing the almighty power of God	C, L & G

	543	O Zion, tune thy voice	L
Sequence:	695, 696	By gracious powers so wonderfully sheltered	C, L & G
	678, 679	Surely it is God who saves me	L
	635	If thou but trust in God to guide thee	C, L & G
	668	I to the hills will lift mine eyes	L
Offertory:	635	If thou but trust in God to guide thee	C, L & G
	667	Sometimes a light surprises	G
	709	O God of Bethel, by whose hand	C, L & G
	711	Seek ye first the kingdom of God	G
	669	Commit thou all that grieves thee	G
Communion:	701	Jesus, all my gladness	G
	709	O God of Bethel, by whose hand	C, L & G
Postcommunion:	408	Sing praise to God who reigns above	C, L & G
	375	Give praise and glory unto God	C, L & G
	559	Lead us, heavenly Father, lead us	C, L & G

The Last Sunday After the Epiphany

Entrance:	135	Songs of thankfulness and praise	G
	427	When morning gilds the skies	S
	6, 7	Christ, whose glory fills the skies	S
Sequence:	133, 134	O Light of Light, Love given birth	C, L & G
	129, 130	Christ upon the mountain peak	C, L & G
	546	Awake, my soul, stretch every nerve	E
	545	Lo! what a cloud of witnesses	E
	422	Not far beyond the sea, nor high	E
Offertory:	129, 130	Christ upon the mountain peak	C, L & G
	136, 137	O wondrous type! O vision fair	C, L & G
Communion:	133, 134	O Light of Light, Love given birth	C, L & G
	460, 461	Alleluia! sing to Jesus (omit sts. 2, 5)	S
	619	Sing alleluia forth in duteous praise	S
Postcommunion:	136, 137	O wondrous type! O vision fair	C, L & G
	122, 123	Alleluia, song of gladness	S
	135	Songs of thankfulness and praise	G

Ash Wednesday

No Entrance Hymn [entrance in silence, see BCP, p. 264]

Sequence:	152	Kind Maker of the world, O hear	L (Joel)
	144	Lord Jesus, Sun of Righteousness	L (Joel)
	574, 575	Before thy throne, O God, we kneel	L (Joel)
	140, 141	Wilt thou forgive that sin, where I begun	S
	146, 147	Now let us all with one accord	S

	148	Creator of the earth and skies	S
	559	Lead us, heavenly Father, lead us	E
Offertory:	151	From deepest woe I cry to thee	S
	145	Now quit your care	L (Isaiah)
	149	Eternal Lord of love, behold your Church	S
	411	O bless the Lord, my soul!	P
Communion:	142	Lord, who throughout these forty days	S
	318	Here, O my Lord, I see thee face to face	S
	693	Just as I am, without one plea	S
Postcommunion:	143	The glory of these forty days	S
	142	Lord, who throughout these forty days	S

The First Sunday in Lent

Entrance:	143	The glory of these forty days	C & G
	150	Forty days and forty nights	C & G
Sequence:	445, 446	Praise to the Holiest in the height	E
Offertory:	150	Forty days and forty nights	C & G
	142	Lord, who throughout these forty days	C & G
	443	From God Christ's deity came forth	G
Communion:	142	Lord, who throughout these forty days	C & G
	146, 147	Now let us all with one accord	C & G
Postcommunion:	559	Lead us, heavenly Father, lead us	C & G
	687, 688	A mighty fortress is our God	C & G
	563	Go forward, Christian soldier	C & G
	448, 449	O love, how deep, how broad, how high	G

The Second Sunday in Lent

Entrance:	401	The God of Abraham praise	L & E
	440	Blessèd Jesus, at thy word	S
	636, 637	How firm a foundation, ye saints of the Lord	L & E
	393	Praise our great and gracious Lord	L
Sequence:	634	I call on thee, Lord Jesus Christ	L & E
	635	If thou but trust in God to guide thee	L & E
	146, 147	Now let us all with one accord	L, E & G
	151	From deepest woe I cry to thee	L & E
Offertory:	489	The great Creator of the worlds	G
	473	Lift high the cross	G
	448, 449	O love, how deep, how broad, how high	G
	691	My faith looks up to thee (sts. 1-2)	E & G
Communion:	337	And now, O Father, mindful of the love	L, E & G
	313	Let thy Blood in mercy poured	G

| _Postcommunion:_ | 448, 449 | O love, how deep, how broad, how high | G |
| | 473 | Lift high the cross | G |

The Third Sunday in Lent

Entrance:	148	Creator of the earth and skies	S
	678, 679	Surely it is God who saves me	L & G
	399	To God with gladness sing	P
Sequence:	686	Come, thou fount of every blessing	E
	167	There is a green hill far away (omit sts. 3, 4)	E
	458	My song is love unknown	E
	455, 456	O Love of God, how strong and true	E
	685	Rock of ages, cleft for me	L
	691	My faith looks up to thee (sts. 1-2)	E
Offertory:	692	I heard the voice of Jesus say (st. 2)	G
	649, 650	O Jesus, joy of loving hearts	G
	700	O love that casts out fear	G
	673	The first one ever, oh, ever to know (st. 2)	G
	658	As longs the deer for cooling streams	G
Communion:	327, 328	Draw nigh and take the Body of the Lord	G
	343	Shepherd of souls, refresh and bless	L
	685	Rock of ages, cleft for me	L
	319	You, Lord, we praise in songs of celebration	E
Postcommunion:	540	Awake, thou Spirit of the watchmen (sts. 2-3)	G
	690	Guide me, O thou great Jehovah	L
	522, 523	Glorious things of thee are spoken	L

The Fourth Sunday in Lent

Entrance:	440	Blessèd Jesus, at thy word	G
	6, 7	Christ, whose glory fills the skies	G
	143	The glory of these forty days	S
Sequence:	547	Awake, O sleeper, rise from death	E
	490	I want to walk as a child of the light	E & G
	144	Lord Jesus, Sun of Righteousness	E
	5	O splendor of God's glory bright	E
	663	The Lord my God my shepherd is	P
	664	My Shepherd will supply my need	P
	645, 646	The King of love my shepherd is	P
Offertory:	465, 466	Eternal light, shine in my heart	G
	6, 7	Christ, whose glory fills the skies	G
	633	Word of God, come down on earth	G
	490	I want to walk as a child of the light	E & G
	692	I heard the voice of Jesus say (st. 3)	G
	567	Thine arm, O Lord, in days of old	G
	493	O for a thousand tongues to sing	G

Communion:	490	I want to walk as a child of the light	E & G
	339	Deck thyself, my soul, with gladness	G
Postcommunion:	429	I'll praise my Maker while I've breath	G
	371	Thou, whose almighty word	G
	499	Lord God, you now have set your servant free	G
	532, 533	How wondrous and great thy works, God of praise!	G
	538	God of mercy, God of grace	G

The Fifth Sunday in Lent

Entrance:	666	Out of the depths I call	P
	151	From deepest woe I cry to thee	P
Sequence:	495	Hail, thou once despisèd Jesus!	E
	252	Jesus! Name of wondrous love	E
	60	Creator of the stars of night (sts. 1-4)	E
	270	Gabriel's message does away	E
Offertory:	455, 456	O Love of God, how strong and true	G
	335	I am the bread of life (sts. 4-5)	G
Communion:	308, 309	O Food to pilgrims given	G
	320	Zion, praise thy Savior, singing (sts. 5-6)	G
	314	Humbly I adore thee, Verity unseen	G
	300	Glory, love, and praise, and honor	G
	335	I am the bread of life (sts. 4-5)	G
Postcommunion:	455, 456	O Love of God, how strong and true	G
	346	Completed, Lord, the Holy Mysteries	G
	457	Thou art the Way, to thee alone	G

The Sunday of the Passion: Palm Sunday

Liturgy of the Palms (Entrance)	153	Palm Sunday Anthems	
	154, 155	All glory, laud, and honor	
	156	Ride on! ride on in majesty!	
	157	Psalm 118:19-29	
Sequence:	164	Alone thou goest forth, O Lord	C & G
	156	Ride on! ride on in majesty!	C & G
	458	My song is love unknown	C & G
Offertory:	158	Ah, holy Jesus, how hast thou offended	G
	170	To mock your reign, O dearest Lord	G
	162	The royal banners forward go	G
	161	The flaming banners of our King	G
Communion:	474	When I survey the wondrous cross	G
	337	And now, O Father, mindful of the love (sts. 1-2)	G

	313	Let thy Blood in mercy poured	G
Postcommunion:	168, 169	O sacred head, sore wounded	G

Monday in Holy Week

Entrance:	164	Alone thou goest forth, O Lord	S
	458	My song is love unknown	S
	445, 446	Praise to the Holiest in the height	S
Sequence:	545	Lo! what a cloud of witnesses	E
	495	Hail, thou once despisèd Jesus!	E
	483	The head that once was crowned with thorns	E
Offertory:	643	My God, how wonderful thou art	G
	642	Jesus, the very thought of thee	G
Communion:	313	Let thy Blood in mercy poured	S
	301	Bread of the world, in mercy broken	S
	498	Beneath the cross of Jesus	G
	693	Just as I am, without one plea	G
Postcommunion:	471	We sing the praise of him who died	S

Tuesday in Holy Week

Entrance:	160	Cross of Jesus, cross of sorrow	E
	458	My song is love unknown	S
Sequence:	434	Nature with open volume stands	E
	165, 166	Sing, my tongue, the glorious battle	E
	441, 442	In the cross of Christ I glory	E
Offertory:	474	When I survey the wondrous cross	E
	441, 442	In the cross of Christ I glory	E
	489	The great Creator of the worlds	G (John)
Communion:	337	And now, O Father, mindful of the love (sts. 1-2)	S
Postcommunion:	434	Nature with open volume stands	E
	471	We sing the praise of him who died	E
	167	Three is a green hill far away (omit sts. 3, 4)	E

Wednesday in Holy Week

Entrance:	489	The great Creator of the worlds	S
	160	Cross of Jesus, cross of sorrow	E
	471	We sing the praise of him who died	S
Sequence:	448, 449	O love, how deep, how broad, how high	G

Offertory:	158	Ah, holy Jesus, how hast thou offended	G
Communion:	338	Wherefore, O Father, we thy humble servants	E
	337	And now, O Father, mindful of the love (sts. 1-2)	E
	327, 328	Draw nigh and take the Body of the Lord	E
	498	Beneath the cross of Jesus	S
	479	Glory be to Jesus	S
Postcommunion:	164	Alone thou goest forth, O Lord	G
	168, 169	O sacred head, sore wounded	L
	163	Sunset to sunrise changes now	S

Maundy Thursday

Entrance:	320	Zion, praise thy Savior, singing	E
	445, 446	Praise to the Holiest in the height	S
	495	Hail, thou once despisèd Jesus!	S
Sequence:	322	When Jesus died to save us	E
	329, 330, 331	Now, my tongue, the mystery telling (sts. 1-4)	E
	320	Zion, praise thy Savior, singing	E
At the footwashing:	602	Jesu, Jesu, fill us with your love	G
Offertory:	606	Where true charity and love dwell	S
	576, 577	God is love, and where true love is	S
	581	Where charity and love prevail	S
	602	Jesu, Jesu, fill us with your love	G
Communion:	315	Thou, who at thy first Eucharist didst pray	S
	322	When Jesus died to save us	E
	313	Let thy Blood in mercy poured	S
Postcommunion:	329, 330, 331	Now, my tongue, the mystery telling	E
	171	Go to dark Gethsemane	S

Good Friday

No Entrance Hymn [entrance in silence, see BCP, p. 276]

Sequence:	164	Alone thou goest forth, O Lord	L, E & G
	160	Cross of Jesus, cross of sorrow	L, E & G
After the sermon:	158	Ah, holy Jesus, how hast thou offended	L & G
	168, 169	O sacred head, sore wounded	L & G
	159	At the cross her vigil keeping	G
	167	There is a green hill far away (omit sts. 3, 4)	G
	172	Were you there when they crucified my Lord?	G
Before the cross:	165, 166	Sing, my tongue, the glorious battle	G

	441, 442	In the cross of Christ I glory	G
	474	When I survey the wondrous cross	G
	163	Sunset to sunrise changes now	G

Holy Saturday

No Entrance Hymn [entrance in silence, see BCP, p. 283]

Sequence:	173	O sorrow deep!	G
	172	Were you there when they crucified my Lord?	G
	458	My song is love unknown	G

The Great Vigil of Easter

Sequence:	183	Christians, to the Paschal victim [traditional sequence]	E & G
	184	Christ the Lord is risen again! [may be sung with above]	G
	199, 200	Come, ye faithful, raise the strain	E
	187	Through the Red Sea brought at last	E
At the baptisms, if after the sermon:	298	All who believe and are baptized	E
	176, 177	Over the chaos of the empty waters	S
	213	Come away to the skies	S
	296	We know that Christ is raised and dies no more	E
	294	Baptized in water	E
Offertory:	187	Through the Red Sea brought at last, Alleluia!	E
	202	The Lamb's high banquet called to share	S
Communion:	174	At the Lamb's high feast we sing	S
	202	The Lamb's high banquet called to share	S
	713	Christ is arisen (Christ ist erstanden)	G
Postcommunion:	187	Through the Red Sea brought at last, Alleluia!	E
	210	The day of resurrection!	G

Easter Day — Early Service

Entrance:	175	Hail thee, festival day! *Easter*	S
	179	"Welcome, happy morning!" age to age shall say	S
Sequence:	183	Christians, to the Paschal victim [traditional sequence]	E & G
	184	Christ the Lord is risen again! [may be sung with above]	G
	187	Through the Red Sea brought at last, Alleluia!	E
	198	Thou hallowed chosen morn of praise	S
Offertory:	190	Lift your voice rejoicing, Mary	G

	203	O sons and daughters, let us sing *Easter Day*	G
	180	He is risen, he is risen!	G
	201	On earth has dawned this day of days	G
Communion:	174	At the Lamb's high feast we sing	S
	202	The Lamb's high banquet called to share	S
	713	Christ is arisen (Christ ist erstanden)	G
Postcommunion:	210	The day of resurrection!	G
	199-200	Come, ye faithful, raise the strain	G
	196, 197	Look there! the Christ, our Brother, comes	G
	180	He is risen, he is risen!	G
	205	Good Christians all, rejoice and sing!	G

Easter Day — Principal Service

	175	Hail thee, festival day! *Easter*	L (Acts)
Entrance:	179	"Welcome, happy morning!" age to age shall say	L (Acts)
	199, 200	Come, ye faithful, raise the strain	L (OT) & G
Sequence:	183	Christians, to the Paschal victim [traditional sequence]	G
	184	Christ the Lord is risen again! [may be sung with above]	G
	196, 197	Look there! the Christ, our Brother, comes	L (Acts) & G
	207	Jesus Christ is risen today, Alleluia!	L (Acts) & G
	208	The strife is o'er, the battle done	L (Acts) & G
Offertory:	190	Lift your voice rejoicing, Mary	G
	205	Good Christians all, rejoice and sing	L (Acts) & G
	203	O sons and daughters, let us sing *Easter Day*	G
Communion:	185, 186	Christ Jesus lay in death's strong bands	S
	174	At the Lamb's high feast we sing	L (OT)
	202	The Lamb's high banquet called to share	L (OT)
	713	Christ is arisen	G
Postcommunion:	210	The day of resurrection	L (OT) & G
	192	This joyful Eastertide	S
	187	Through the Red Sea brought at last	L (OT)
	205	Good Christians all, rejoice and sing	L (Acts) & G

Easter Day — Evening Service

Entrance	203	O sons and daughters, let us sing *Easter Day*	S
	185, 186	Christ Jesus lay in death's strong bands	E
Sequence:	196, 197	Look there! the Christ, our Brother, comes	L (Acts) & G

	207	Jesus Christ is risen today, Alleluia!	L (Acts) & G
	208	The strife is o'er, the battle done	L (Acts) & G
	202	The Lamb's high banquet called to share	E
	184	Christ the Lord is risen again!	L (Acts) & G
Offertory:	305, 306	Come, risen Lord, and deign to be our guest	G
	185, 186	Christ Jesus lay in death's strong bands	E & G
Communion	185, 186	Christ Jesus lay in death's strong bands	E & G
	305, 306	Come, risen Lord, and deign to be our guest	G
	174	At the Lamb's high feast we sing	E
	202	The Lamb's high banquet called to share	E
Postcommunion:	210	The day of resurrection!	G
	205	Good Christians all, rejoice and sing!	G
	180	He is risen, he is risen!	G

Monday in Easter Week

Entrance:	205	Good Christians all, rejoice and sing!	E & G
	196, 197	Look there! the Christ, our Brother, comes	E & G
	207	Jesus Christ is risen today!	E & G
Sequence:	208	The strife is o'er, the battle done	E & G
	184	Christ the Lord is risen again	E & G
	196, 197	Look there! the Christ, our Brother, comes	E & G
Offertory:	178	Jesus is Lord of all the earth	E & G
	207	Jesus Christ is risen today, Alleluia!	E & G
Communion:	185, 186	Christ Jesus lay in death's strong bands	E & G
	174	At the Lamb's high feast we sing	S
Postcommunion:	210	The day of resurrection!	G
	178	Jesus is Lord of all the earth	E & G

Tuesday in Easter Week

Entrance:	196, 197	Look there! the Christ, our Brother, comes	E & G
	208	The strife is o'er, the battle done	E & G
	205	Good Christians all, rejoice and sing!	E & G
Sequence:	298	All who believe and are baptized	E
	176, 177	Over the chaos of the empty waters	E
	296	We know that Christ is raised and dies no more	E
	294	Baptized in water	E
	184	Christ the Lord is risen again	E

Offertory:	190	Lift your voice rejoicing, Mary	G
	183	Christians, to the Paschal victim	G
	673	The first one ever, oh, ever to know (st. 3)	G
Communion:	183	Christians, to the Paschal Victim	G
	211	The whole bright world rejoices now	S
	190	Lift your voice rejoicing, Mary	G
Postcommunion:	296	We know that Christ is raised and dies no more	E
	190	Lift your voice rejoicing, Mary	G
	192	This joyful Eastertide	E
	210	The day of resurrection!	G

Wednesday in Easter Week

Entrance:	208	The strife is o'er, the battle done	G
	180	He is risen, he is risen!	G
Sequence:	178	Jesus is Lord of all the earth	G
	196, 197	Look there! the Christ, our Brother, comes	G
	207	Jesus Christ is risen today, Alleluia!	G
	184	Christ the Lord is risen again	G
Offertory:	305, 306	Come, risen Lord, and deign to be our guest	G
	185, 186	Christ Jesus lay in death's strong bands	G
Communion:	185, 186	Christ Jesus lay in death's strong bands	G
	305, 306	Come, risen Lord, and deign to be our guest	G
	174	At the Lamb's high feast we sing	S
	202	The Lamb's high banquet called to share	S
Postcommunion:	210	The day of resurrection!	S
	205	Good Christians all, rejoice and sing!	G

Thursday in Easter Week

Entrance:	184	Christ the Lord is risen again	E & G
	203	O sons and daughters, let us sing *Easter*	G
Sequence:	207	Jesus Christ is risen today, Alleluia!	E & G
	208	The strife is o'er, the battle done	E & G
	196, 197	Look there! the Christ, our Brother, comes	E & G
	492	Sing, ye faithful, sing with gladness	E
Offertory:	212	Awake, arise, lift up your voice	G
	193	That Easter day with joy was bright	G
	208	The strife is o'er, the battle done	E & G
Communion:	174	At the Lamb's high feast we sing	S
	185, 186	Christ Jesus lay in death's strong bands	E & G

Postcommunion:	205	Good Christians all, rejoice and sing!	E & G
	208	The strife is o'er, the battle done	E & G
	196, 197	Look there! the Christ, our Brother, comes	E & G
	207	Jesus Christ is risen today, Alleluia!	E & G
	180	He is risen, he is risen!	G

Friday in Easter Week

Entrance:	207	Jesus Christ is risen today, Alleluia!	E
	205	Good Christians all, rejoice and sing!	E
Sequence:	196, 197	Look there! the Christ, our Brother, comes	E
	178	Jesus is Lord of all the earth	E
	208	The strife is o'er, the battle done	E
Offertory:	305, 306	Come, risen Lord, and deign to be our guest	G
	185, 186	Christ Jesus lay in death's strong bands	G
Communion:	185, 186	Christ Jesus lay in death's strong bands	G
	305, 306	Come, risen Lord, and deign to be our guest	G
	202	The Lamb's high banquet called to share	S
Postcommunion:	208	The strife is o'er, the battle done	E
	205	Good Christians all, rejoice and sing!	E

Saturday in Easter Week

Entrance:	211	The whole bright world rejoices now	S
	203	O sons and daughters, let us sing *Easter*	G
	180	He is risen, he is risen!	G
Sequence:	183	Christians, to the Paschal Victim	G
	184	Christ the Lord is risen again!	G
Offertory:	190	Lift your voice rejoicing, Mary	G
	183	Christians, to the Paschal Victim	G
	673	The first one ever, oh, ever to know (st. 3)	G
Communion:	305, 306	Come, risen Lord, and deign to be our guest	G
	185, 186	Christ Jesus lay in death's strong bands	G
Postcommunion:	210	The day of resurrection!	G
	182	Christ is alive! Let Christians sing	S
	192	This joyful Eastertide	S

The Second Sunday of Easter

| Entrance: | 205 | Good Christians all, rejoice and sing! | L (Acts) |
| | 208 | The strife is o'er, the battle done | L (Acts) |

Sequence:	184	Christ the Lord is risen again!	L (Acts)
	192	This joyful Eastertide	L (Acts)
	178	Jesus is Lord of all the earth	L (Acts)
	212	Awake, arise, lift up your voice	L (Acts) & G
Offertory:	206	O sons and daughters, let us sing *Second Sunday of Easter*	G
	242	How oft, O Lord, thy face hath shone	G
	209	We walk by faith, and not by sight	G
Communion:	209	We walk by faith, and not by sight	G
	212	Awake, arise, lift up your voice	G
	206	O sons and daughters, let us sing *Second Sunday of Easter*	G
	242	How oft, O Lord, thy face hath shone	G
Postcommunion:	193	That Easter day with joy was bright	G
	209	We walk by faith, and not by sight	G

The Third Sunday of Easter

Entrance:	208	The strife is o'er, the battle done	L (Acts), E & G
	205	Good Christians all, rejoice and sing!	L (Acts), E & G
	492	Sing, ye faithful, sing with gladness	L (Acts), E & G
Sequence:	432	O praise ye the Lord! Praise him in the height (omit st. 3)	L (Acts) & E
	298	All who believe and are baptized	L (Acts) & E
	176, 177	Over the chaos of the empty waters	L (Acts) &E
	296	We know that Christ is raised and dies no more	L (Acts) & E
	294	Baptized in water	L (Acts) & E
	184	Christ the Lord is risen again!	G
	196, 197	Look there! the Christ, our Brother, comes	G
Offertory:	305, 306	Come, risen Lord, and deign to be our guest	G
	185, 186	Christ Jesus lay in death's strong bands	L (Acts), E & G
Communion:	185, 186	Christ Jesus lay in death's strong bands	L (Acts), E & G
	343	Shepherd of souls, refresh and bless	G
	305, 306	Come, risen Lord, and deign to be our guest	G
Postcommunion:	180	He is risen, he is risen!	G
	343	Shepherd of souls, refresh and bless	G
	296	We know that Christ is raised and dies no more	L (Acts) & E

The Fourth Sunday of Easter

Entrance:	205	Good Christians all, rejoice and sing!	E
	184	Christ the Lord is risen again!	E
	208	The strife is o'er, the battle done	E
	492	Sing, ye faithful, sing with gladness	E
	399	To God with gladness sing	G
	377, 378	All people that on earth do dwell	G
	391	Before the Lord's eternal throne	G
Sequence:	478	Jesus, our mighty Lord	E & G
	243	When Stephen, full of power and grace	L (Acts)
	663	The Lord my God my Shepherd is	P
	664	My Shepherd will supply my need	P
Offertory:	645, 646	The King of love my shepherd is	P & G
	478	Jesus, our mighty Lord	E & G
Communion:	343	Shepherd of souls, refresh and bless	G
	645, 646	The King of love my shepherd is	P & G
	320	Zion, praise thy Savior, singing (sts. 5-6)	G
Postcommunion:	478	Jesus, our mighty Lord	E & G
	708	Savior, like a shepherd lead us	E & G
	334	Praise the Lord, rise up rejoicing	G

The Fifth Sunday of Easter

Entrance:	492	Sing, ye faithful, sing with gladness	L (Acts)
	455, 456	O Love of God, how strong and true	L (Acts)
	518	Christ is made the sure foundation	E & G
	49	Come, let us with our Lord arise	L (Acts)
	52	This day at thy creating word	L (Acts)
	47	On this day, the first of days	L (Acts) & E
	1, 2	Father, we praise thee, now the night is over	G
Sequence:	51	We the Lord's people, heart and voice uniting (st. 1 or sts. 1 & 3)	E
	432	O praise ye the Lord! Praise him in the height	E
	294	Baptized in water	E
	506, 507	Praise the Spirit in creation	L (Acts)
Offertory:	457	Thou art the Way, to thee alone	C & G
	487	Come, my Way, my Truth, my Life	C & G
	463, 464	He is the Way	C & G
Communion:	487	Come, my Way, my Truth, my Life	C & G
	463, 464	He is the Way	C & G
Postcommunion:	194, 195	Jesus lives! thy terrors now	G
	484, 485	Praise the Lord through every nation	G
	703	Lead us, O Father, in the paths of peace	G
	457	Thou art the Way, to thee alone	G

The Sixth Sunday of Easter

Entrance:	409	The spacious firmament on high	L (Acts)
	386, 387	We sing of God, the mighty source	L (Acts)
	405	All things bright and beautiful	L (Acts)
	385	Many and great, O God, are thy works	L (Acts)
	398	I sing the almighty power of God	L (Acts)
	651	This is my Father's world	L (Acts)
	394, 395	Creating God, your fingers trace	P
	291	We plow the fields and scatter	L (Acts)
	292	O Jesus, crowned with all renown	S
Sequence:	455, 456	O Love of God, how strong and true	E
	593	Lord, make us servants of your peace	E
Offertory:	198	Thou hallowed chosen morn of praise	G
	513	Like the murmur of the dove's song	G
	694	God be in my head	G
	488	Be thou my vision, O Lord of my heart	G
	705	As those of old their first fruits brought	S
Communion:	323	Bread of heaven, on thee we feed	
Postcommunion:	344	Lord, dismiss us with thy blessing	G
	392	Come, we that love the lord	G
	347	Go forth for God; go to the world in peace	E
	292	O Jesus, crowned with all renown	S

Ascension Day

Entrance:	214	Hail the day that sees him rise, Alleluia!	L (Acts) & G
	216	Hail thee, festival day! *Ascension*	S
Sequence:	217, 218	A hymn of glory let us sing	L (Acts) & G
	220, 221	O Lord Most High, eternal King	L (Acts) & G
Offertory:	215	See the Conqueror mounts in triumph	L (Acts) & G
	222	Rejoice, the Lord of life ascends	L (Acts) & G
	217, 218	A hymn of glory let us sing	L (Acts) & G
Communion:	460, 461	Alleluia! sing to Jesus!	L (Acts) & G
	307	Lord, enthroned in heavenly splendor	E
	220, 221	O Lord Most High, eternal King	L (Acts) & G
Postcommunion:	219	The Lord ascendeth up on high	L (Acts) & G
	222	Rejoice, the Lord of life ascends	L (Acts) & G
	495	Hail, thou once despisèd Jesus!	E
	481	Rejoice, the Lord is King	L (Acts) & E
	494	Crown him with many crowns	E

The Seventh Sunday of Easter: The Sunday After Ascension Day

Entrance:	481	Rejoice, the Lord is King	L (Acts)
	492	Sing, ye faithful, sing with gladness	L (Acts)
	450, 451	All hail the power of Jesus' Name!	S
Sequence:	483	The head that once was crowned with thorns	L (Acts), E & G
	484, 485	Praise the Lord through every nation	L (Acts) & E
Offertory:	495	Hail, thou once despisèd Jesus!	L (Acts) & G
	483	The head that once was crowned with thorns	L (Acts), E & G
	484, 485	Praise the Lord through every nation	L (Acts) & E
Communion:	315	Thou, who at thy first Eucharist didst pray	G
	307	Lord, enthroned in heavenly splendor	L (Acts)
	460, 461	Alleluia! sing to Jesus!	L (Acts)
	459	And have the bright immensities	S
Postcommunion:	484, 485	Praise the Lord through every nation	L (Acts) & E
	481	Rejoice, the Lord is King	L (Acts)
	494	Crown him with many crowns	S

The Day of Pentecost — Early or Vigil Service

No Entrance Hymn at the Vigil [See BCP, p.175 or 227]

Entrance (Early Service):	225	Hail thee, festival day! *Pentecost*	L (Acts)
	223, 224	Hail this joyful day's return	L (Acts)
	230	A mighty sound from heaven	L (Gen & Acts)
	506, 507	Praise the Spirit in creation	L (Acts)
Sequence:	*Veni Sancte Spiritus* (traditional sequence for Pentecost)		
	228	Holy Spirit, font of light	L (Acts) & E
	226, 227	Come, thou Holy Spirit bright	L (Acts) & E
	Veni Creator Spiritus		
	501, 502	O Holy Spirit, by whose breath	L (Acts)
	500	Creator Spirit, by whose aid	L (Acts)
	503, 504	Come, Holy Ghost, our souls inspire	L (Acts)
Baptism:	513	Like the murmur of the dove's song	L (Acts)
	297	Descend, O Spirit, purging flame	L (Acts)
	299	Spirit of God, unleashed on earth	L (Acts)
Offertory:	230	A mighty sound from heaven	L (Gen & Acts)
	506, 507	Praise the Spirit in creation	L (Acts)
	514	To thee, O Comforter divine	S
Communion:	229	Spirit of mercy, truth, and love	L (Acts)

	505	O Spirit of Life, O Spirit of God	S
Postcommunion:	531	O Spirit of the living God	L (Acts)
	521	Put forth, O God, thy Spirit's might	S
	506, 507	Praise the Spirit in creation	L (Acts)

The Day of Pentecost — Principal Service

Entrance:	225	Hail thee, festival day! *Pentecost*	L (Acts)
	223, 224	Hail this joyful day's return	L (Acts)
	230	A mighty sound from heaven	L (Acts)
	506, 507	Praise the Spirit in creation	L (Acts)
Sequence:		*Veni Sancte Spiritus* (traditional sequence for Pentecost)	
	228	Holy Spirit, font of light	L (Acts), E & G (Jn 14)
	226, 227	Come, thou Holy Spirit bright	L (Acts) & G (Jn 14)
		Veni Creator Spiritus	
	501, 502	O Holy Spirit, by whose breath	L (Acts) & E
	500	Creator Spirit, by whose aid	L (Acts) & G (Jn 14)
	503, 504	Come, Holy Ghost, our souls inspire	L (Acts)
Offertory:	513	Like the murmur of the dove's song	L (Acts) & E
	514	To thee, O Comforter divine	G (Jn 14)
	516	Come down, O Love divine	G (Jn 14)
	511	Holy Spirit, ever living	G (Jn 20)
	509	Spirit divine, attend our prayers	L (Acts)
	512	Come, gracious Spirit, heavenly Dove	G (Jn 14)
Communion:	229	Spirit of mercy, truth, and love	L (Acts)
	505	O Spirit of Life, O Spirit of God	S
Postcommunion:	531	O Spirit of the living God	L (Acts)
	521	Put forth, O God, thy Spirit's might	S
	506, 507	Praise the Spirit in creation	L (Acts)

The First Sunday After Pentecost: Trinity Sunday

Entrance:	423	Immortal, invisible, God only wise	L
	409	The spacious firmament on high	L
	405	All things bright and beautiful	L
	428	O all ye works of God, now come	L
	385	Many and great, O God, are thy works	L
Sequence:	371	Thou, whose almighty word	L & G
	365	Come, thou almighty King	S
Offertory:	295	Sing praise to our Creator	L, E & G
	368	Holy Father, great Creator	S
	369	How wondrous great, how glorious bright	S
Communion:	421	All glory be to God on high	S

	295	Sing praise to our Creator	L, E & G
Postcommunion:	370	I bind unto myself today	S
	363	Ancient of Days, who sittest throned in glory	S

Propers 1, 2, & 3: *See 6, 7 & 8* Epiphany *for the same lections (If the Sunday between May 24 and 28 inclusive follows Trinity Sunday, use Proper 3 [Epiphany 8] on that day).*

Proper 4: *(Sunday between May 29 and June 4 inclusive, if after Trinity Sunday)*

Entrance:	440	Blessèd Jesus, at thy word	L & G
	48	O day of radiant gladness	L & G
	49	Come, let us with our Lord arise	L & G
	52	This day at thy creating word	L & G
Sequence:	495	Hail, thou once despisèd Jesus! (sts. 1-2)	E
	432	O praise ye the Lord! praise him in the height (omit st. 3)	E
	671	Amazing grace! how sweet the sound	E
	686	Come, thou fount of every blessing	E
Offertory:	636, 637	How firm a foundation, ye saints of the Lord	G
	634	I call on thee, Lord Jesus Christ	L & G
	628	Help us, O Lord, to learn	L & G
	626	Lord, be thy word my rule	L & G
Communion:	332	O God, unseen yet ever near (sts. 3-4)	L & G
	628	Help us, O Lord, to learn	L & G
Postcommunion:	344	Lord, dismiss us with thy blessing	L, E & G
	522, 523	Glorious things of thee are spoken	G

Proper 5 *(Sunday between June 5 & 11 inclusive, if after Trinity Sunday)*

Entrance:	401	The God of Abraham praise	E
	393	Praise our great and gracious Lord	E
	686	Come, thou fount of every blessing	G
Sequence:	401	The God of Abraham praise	E
	393	Praise our great and gracious Lord	E
Offertory:	281	He sat to watch o'er customs paid	G
	706	In your mercy, Lord, you called me	G
	641	Lord Jesus, think on me	G
Communion:	701	Jesus, all my gladness (sts. 1-2)	G
	706	In your mercy, Lord, you called me	G
Postcommunion:	472	Hope of the world, thou Christ of great compassion	G

Proper 6 *(Sunday between June 12 & 18 inclusive, if after Trinity Sunday)*

Entrance:	401	The God of Abraham praise	L
	51	We the Lord's people, heart and voice uniting	L
	425	Sing now with joy unto the Lord	L
	377, 378	All people that on earth do dwell	P
	391	Before the Lord's eternal throne	P
Sequence:	495	Hail, thou once despisèd Jesus! (sts. 1-2)	E
	167	There is a green hill far away (omit sts. 3, 4)	E
	458	My song is love unknown	E
	455, 456	O Love of God, how strong and true	E
	685	Rock of ages, cleft for me	E
Offertory:	540	Awake, thou Spirit of the watchmen (sts. 2-3)	G
	541	Come, labor on	G
	528	Lord, you give the great commission	G
	472	Hope of the world, thou Christ	G
Communion:	321	My God, thy table now is spread	G
	319	You, Lord, we praise in songs of celebration	G
	479	Glory be to Jesus	E
Postcommunion:	541	Come, labor on	G
	535	Ye servants of God, your Master proclaim	G
	539	O Zion, haste, thy mission high fulfilling	G
	528	Lord, you give the great commission	G

Proper 7 *(Sunday between June 19 & 25 inclusive, if after Trinity Sunday)*

Entrance:	432	O praise ye the Lord! praise him in the height	E
	450, 451	All hail the power of Jesus' Name!	C & E
	248, 249	To the Name of our salvation	C
Sequence:	445, 446	Praise to the Holiest in the height	E
	270	Gabriel's message does away	E
	60	Creator of the stars of night (omit st. 6)	E
	176, 177	Over the chaos of the empty waters	E
	295	Sing praise to our Creator	E
	686	Come, thou fount of every blessing	E
Offertory:	540	Awake, thou Spirit of the watchmen	G
	530	Spread, O spread, thou mighty word	E & G
Communion:	655	O Jesus, I have promised	G
	676	There is a balm in Gilead	G

	564, 565	He who would valiant be	G
	675	Take up your cross, the Savior said	G
Postcommunion:	530	Spread, O spread, thou mighty word	E & G
	535	Ye servants of God, your Master proclaim	G

Proper 8 *(Sunday between June 26 & July 2 inclusive)*

Entrance:	47	On this day, the first of days	E
	437, 438	Tell out, my soul, the greatness of the Lord	L
	518	Christ is made the sure foundation	C
	525	The Church's one foundation	C
	521	Put forth, O God, thy Spirit's might	C
Sequence:	298	All who believe and are baptized	E
	294	Baptized in water	E
	296	We know that Christ is raised and dies no more	E
	656	Blest are the pure in heart	L
Offertory:	675	Take up your cross, the Savior said	G
	484, 485	Praise the Lord through every nation	G
	609	Where cross the crowded ways of life	G
	661	They cast their nets in Galilee	G
Communion:	654	Day by day	G
	675	Take up your cross, the Savior said	G
Postcommunion:	609	Where cross the crowded ways of life	G
	484, 485	Praise the Lord through every nation	G
	655	O Jesus, I have promised	G
	564, 565	He who would valiant be	G
	572	Weary of all trumpeting	G

Proper 9 *(Sunday between July 3 & 9 inclusive)*

Entrance:	616	Hail to the Lord's Anointed	L
	404	We will extol you, ever-blessèd Lord	P
	414	God, my King, thy might confessing	P
Sequence:	516	Come down, O Love divine	E
	11	Awake, my soul, and with the sun	E
	251	O God, whom neither time nor space (omit st. 2)	E
	500	Creator Spirit, by whose aid	E
Offertory:	692	I heard the voice of Jesus say (st. 1)	G
	74	Blest be the King whose coming	G
	476	Can we by searching find out God	G
	457	Thou art the Way, to thee alone	G
	644	How sweet the name of Jesus sounds	G

Communion:	342	O Bread of life, for sinners broken	G
	302, 303	Father, we thank thee, who hast planted	G
Postcommunion:	544	Jesus shall reign, where'er the sun	L & G
	457	Thou art the Way, to thee alone	G

Proper 10 *(Sunday between July 10 and 16 inclusive)*

Entrance:	440	Blessèd Jesus, at thy word	L & G
	678, 679	Surely it is God who saves me	L
	52	This day at thy creating word	L & G
	49	Come, let us with our Lord arise	L & G
	48	O day of radiant gladness	L & G
	50	This is the day the Lord hath made	L & G
Sequence:	294	Baptized in water	E
	512	Come, gracious Spirit, heavenly Dove	E
	298	All who believe and are baptized	E
	432	O praise ye the Lord! praise him in the height (omit st. 3)	E
	296	We know that Christ is raised and dies no more	E
Offertory:	588, 589	Almighty God, your word is cast	G
	505	O Spirit of Life, O Spirit of God	G
	530	Spread, O spread, thou mighty word	G
Communion:	302, 303	Father, we thank thee, who hast planted (st. 1)	G
	536	God has spoken to his people	G
Postcommunion:	530	Spread, O spread, thou mighty word	G
	344	Lord, dismiss us with thy blessing	G
	392	Come, we that love the Lord	G

Proper 11 *(Sunday between July 17 and 23 inclusive)*

Entrance:	440	Blessèd Jesus, at thy word	G
	375	Give praise and glory unto God	L
	482	The Lord will come and not be slow	L
	596	Judge eternal, throned in splendor	L
	600, 601	O day of God, draw nigh	L
Sequence:	60	Creator of the stars of night (omit st. 6)	E
	621, 622	Light's abode, celestial Salem	E
	623	O what their joy and their glory must be	E
	666	Out of the depths I call	E
Offertory:	588, 589	Almighty God, your word is cast	G
	290	Come, ye thankful people, come (sts. 2-4)	G
	505	O Spirit of Life, O Spirit of God	G

Communion:	536	God has spoken to his people	G
	505	O Spirit of Life, O Spirit of God	G
Postcommunion:	344	Lord, dismiss us with thy blessing	G
	392	Come, we that love the Lord	G
	530	Spread, O spread, thou mighty word	G

Proper 12 *(Sunday between July 24 and 30 inclusive)*

Entrance:	419	Lord of all being, throned afar	L
	488	Be thou my vision, O Lord of my heart	L
	584	God, you have given us power to sound	L
	375	Give praise and glory unto God	E
	388	O worship the King, all glorious above!	E
Sequence:	677	God moves in a mysterious way	E
	530	Spread, O spread, thou mighty word	E
	635	If thou but trust in God to guide thee	C & E
	698	Eternal Spirit of the living Christ	E
	447	The Christ who died but rose again	E
Offertory:	24	The day thou gavest, Lord, is ended (In the morning, omit st. 1)	G
	462	The Lord will come and not be slow	G
	615	"Thy Kingdom come!" on bended knee	G
	613	Thy kingdom come, O God!	G
Communion:	302, 303	Father, we thank thee, who hast planted	G
	600, 601	O day of God, draw nigh	G
Postcommunion:	534	God is working his purpose out	G
	573	Father eternal, Ruler of creation	G

Proper 13 *(Sunday between July 31 and August 5 inclusive; August 6 is celebrated as the Feast of the Transfiguration [See below, p. 269])*

Entrance:	51	We the Lord's people, heart and voice uniting	G
	48	O day of radiant gladness	G
	49	Come, let us with our Lord arise	G
Sequence:	447	The Christ who died but rose again	E
	194, 195	Jesus lives! thy terrors now	E
Offertory:	472	Hope of the world, thou Christ of great compassion	G
	343	Shepherd of souls, refresh and bless	L & G
	302, 303	Father, we thank thee, who hast planted (st. 1)	G
	339	Deck thyself, my soul, with gladness	G

Communion:	308, 309	O Food to pilgrims given	G
	320	Zion, praise thy Savior, singing (sts. 5-6)	G
	327, 328	Draw nigh and take the Body of the Lord	G
	321	My God, thy table now is spread	G
	301	Bread of the world, in mercy broken	G
Postcommunion:	690	Guide me, O thou great Jehovah	L, P & G
	522, 523	Glorious things of thee are spoken	L

Proper 14 *(Sunday between August 7 and 13 inclusive)*

Entrance:	388	O worship the King, all glorious above!	G
	398	I sing the almighty power of God	G
	390	Praise to the Lord, the Almighty	G
	428	O all ye works of God, now come	G
Sequence:	410	Praise, my soul, the King of heaven	E
	709	O God of Bethel, by whose hand	E
	444	Blessed be the God of Israel	E
Offertory:	669	Commit thou all that grieves thee	G
	636, 637	How firm a foundation, ye saints of the Lord	G
	689	I sought the Lord, and afterward I knew	G
	699	Jesus, Lover of my soul	G
Communion:	689	I sought the Lord, and afterward I knew	G
	669	Commit thou all that grieves thee	G
Postcommunion:	375	Give praise and glory unto God	G
	414	God, my King, thy might confessing	G
	373	Praise the Lord! ye heavens adore him	G

Proper 15 *(Sunday between August 14 and 20 inclusive)*

Entrance:	51	We the Lord's people, heart and voice uniting	L
	380	From all that dwell below the skies	L, E & G
	371	Thou, whose almighty word	L, E & G
	532, 533	How wondrous and great thy works, God of praise!	L, E & G
Sequence:	706	In your mercy, Lord, you called me	E
	469, 470	There's a wideness in God's mercy	E
	538	God of mercy, God of grace	P
Offertory:	544	Jesus shall reign, where'er the sun	G
	537	Christ for the world we sing!	E & G
Communion:	321	My God, thy table now is spread	G
	537	Christ for the world we sing!	E & G
Postcommunion:	530	Spread, O spread, thou mighty word	E & G
	531	O Spirit of the living God	E & G

	542	Christ is the world's true Light	E & G
	539	O Zion, haste, thy mission high fulfilling	E & G

Proper 16 *(Sunday between August 21 and 27 inclusive)*

Entrance:	525	The Church's one foundation	C & G
	521	Put forth, O God, thy Spirit's might	C & G
	518	Christ is made the sure foundation	G
Sequence:	677	God moves in a mysterious way	E
	521	Put forth, O God, thy Spirit's might	C & G
Offertory:	254	You are the Christ, O Lord	G
	443	From God Christ's deity came forth	G
	525	The Church's one foundation	C & G
	476	Can we by searching find out God	G
Communion:	302, 303	Father, we thank thee, who hast planted	C & G
	304	I come with joy to meet my Lord	C
Postcommunion:	334	Praise the Lord, rise up rejoicing	C
	525	The Church's one foundation	C & G
	521	Put forth, O God, thy Spirit's might	C & G
	427	When morning gilds the skies	G
	522, 523	Glorious things of thee are spoken	G

Proper 17 *(Sunday between August 28 and September 3 inclusive)*

Entrance:	477	All praise to thee, for thou, O King divine	C
	435	At the Name of Jesus	C
	450, 451	All hail the power of Jesus' Name!	C
	248, 249	To the Name of our salvation	C
	644	How sweet the Name of Jesus sounds	C
Sequence:	610	Lord, whose love through humble service	E
	707	Take my life, and let it be	E
	513	Like the murmur of the dove's song	E
	581	Where charity and love prevail	E
	576, 577	God is love, and where true love is	E
	606	Where true charity and love dwell	E
Offertory:	675	Take up your cross, the Savior said	G
	484, 485	Praise the Lord through every nation	G
	10	New every morning is the love	G
Communion:	10	New every morning is the love	G
	654	Day by day	G
Postcommunion:	484, 485	Praise the Lord through every nation	G
	572	Weary of all trumpeting	G
	344	Lord, dismiss us with thy blessing	C

Proper 18 *(Sunday between September 4 and 10 inclusive)*

Entrance:	518	Christ is made the sure foundation	G
	400	All creatures of our God and King	G
	406, 407	Most High, omnipotent, good Lord	G
	376	Joyful, joyful, we adore thee	E & G
Sequence:	610	Lord, whose love through humble service	E
	593	Lord, make us servants of your peace	E & G
	5	O Splendor of God's glory bright	E & G
	3, 4	Now that the daylight fills the sky	E & G
Offertory:	674	"Forgive our sins as we forgive"	G
	593	Lord, make us servants of your peace	E & G
Communion:	576, 577	God is love, and where true love is	E & G
	581	Where charity and love prevail	E & G
	606	Where true charity and love dwell	E & G
Postcommunion:	347	Go forth for God; go to the world in peace	E
	336	Come with us, O blessèd Jesus	E

Proper 19 *(Sunday between September 11 and 17 inclusive)*

Entrance:	406, 407	Most High, omnipotent, good Lord	L, E & G
	400	All creatures of our God and King	L, E & G
	376	Joyful, joyful, we adore thee	L, E & G
Sequence:	5	O Splendor of God's glory bright	L, E & G
	3, 4	Now that the daylight fills the sky	L, E & G
Offertory:	674	"Forgive our sins as we forgive"	L, E & G
	593	Lord, make us servants of your peace	L, E & G
Communion:	581	Where charity and love prevail	L, E & G
	576, 577	God is love, and where true love is	L, E & G
	606	Where true charity and love dwell	L, E & G
	593	Lord, make us servants of your peace	L, E & G
	674	"Forgive our sins as we forgive"	L, E & G
Postcommunion:	593	Lord, make us servants of your peace	L, E & G
	5	O Splendor of God's glory bright	L, E & G
	336	Come with us, O blessèd Jesus	L, E & G
	347	Go forth for God; go to the world in peace	L, E & G

Proper 20 *(Sunday between September 18 and 24 inclusive)*

Entrance:	410	Praise, my soul, the King of heaven	L
	411	O bless the Lord, my soul	L
	414	God, my King, thy might confessing	P

	404	We will extol you, ever-blessèd Lord	P
Sequence:	527	Singing songs of expectation	E
	617	Eternal Ruler of the ceaseless round	E
	279	For thy dear saints, O Lord	E
	694	God be in my head	E
Offertory:	9	Not here for high and holy things	G
	541	Come, labor on	G
	551	Rise up, ye saints of God!	G
Communion:	307	Lord, enthroned in heavenly splendor	S
	337	And now, O Father, mindful of the love	S
Postcommunion:	312	Strengthen for service, Lord	G
	541	Come, labor on	G
	551	Rise up, ye saints of God!	G
	326	From glory to glory advancing, we praise thee, O Lord	G
	659, 660	O Master, let me walk with thee	G

Proper 21 *(Sunday between September 25 and October 1 inclusive)*

Entrance:	410	Praise, my soul, the King of heaven	L & G
	411	O bless the Lord, my soul!	L & G
	450, 451	All hail the power of Jesus' Name!	E
Sequence:	477	All praise to thee, for thou, O King divine	E
	435	At the Name of Jesus	E
	483	The head that once was crowned with thorns	E
	60	Creator of the stars of night (omit st. 6)	E
Offertory:	574, 575	Before thy throne, O God, we kneel	L & G
	641	Lord Jesus, think on me	L & G
Communion:	313	Let thy Blood in mercy poured	L & G
	301	Bread of the world, in mercy broken	L & G
	337	And now, O Father, mindful of the love	L & G
Postcommunion:	411	O bless the Lord, my soul!	L & G
	410	Praise, my soul, the King of heaven	L & G

Proper 22 *(Sunday between October 2 and 8 inclusive)*

Entrance:	518	Christ is made the sure foundation	C & G
	360, 361	Only-begotten, Word of God eternal	C
	698	Eternal Spirit of the living Christ	C
Sequence:	546	Awake, my soul, stretch every nerve	E
	545	Lo! what a cloud of witnesses	E
	552, 553	Fight the good fight with all thy might (sts. 1-2)	E

	422	Not far beyond the sea, nor high	E
Offertory:	598	Lord Christ, when first thou cam'st to earth	G
	458	My song is love unknown	G
	483	The head that once was crowned with thorns	G
	495	Hail, thou once despisèd Jesus!	G
	170	To mock your reign, O dearest Lord	G
Communion:	313	Let thy Blood in mercy poured	G
	337	And now, O Father, mindful of the love	G
Postcommunion:	448, 449	O love, how deep, how broad, how high	G
	621, 622	Light's abode, celestial Salem	E
	495	Hail, thou once despisèd Jesus!	G
	483	The head that once was crowned with thorns	G

Proper 23 *(Sunday between October 9 and 15 inclusive)*

Entrance:	481	Rejoice, the Lord is King	L & G
	6, 7	Christ, whose glory fills the skies	E
	515	Holy Ghost, dispel our sadness	E
Sequence:	701	Jesus, all my gladness	E
	663	The Lord my God my shepherd is	P
	664	My Shepherd will supply my need	P
	645, 646	The King of love my shepherd is	P
Offertory:	321	My God, thy table now is spread	L & G
	339	Deck thyself, my soul, with gladness	G
	202	The Lamb's high banquet called to share	G
Communion:	321	My God, thy table now is spread	L & G
	300	Glory, love, and praise, and honor	L & G
Postcommunion:	316, 317	This is the hour of banquet and of song	L & G
	556, 557	Rejoice, ye pure in heart	E
	481	Rejoice, the Lord is King	E
	345	Savior, again to thy dear Name we raise	E

Proper 24 *(Sunday between October 16 and 22 inclusive)*

Entrance:	408	Sing praise to God who reigns above	L & E
	377, 378	All people that on earth do dwell	L
	391	Before the Lord's eternal throne	L
	372	Praise to the living God!	L
Sequence:	478	Jesus, our mighty Lord	C & E
	706	In your mercy, Lord, you called me	E
	689	I sought the Lord, and afterward I knew	E
	683, 684	O for a closer walk with God	E

Offertory:	591	O God of earth and altar	G
	596	Judge eternal, throned in splendor	G
Communion:	573	Father eternal, Ruler of creation	G
	596	Judge eternal, throned in splendor	G
	591	O God of earth and altar	G
Postcommunion:	594, 595	God of grace and God of glory	G
	718	God of our fathers, whose almighty hand	G
	544	Jesus shall reign, where'er the sun	G
	665	All my hope on God is founded	G

Proper 25 *(Sunday between October 23 and 29 inclusive)*

Entrance:	517	How lovely is thy dwelling-place	G
	450, 451	All hail the power of Jesus' Name!	G
	431	The stars declare his glory	G
	5	O Splendor of God's glory bright	L & G
Sequence:	605	What does the Lord require	L
	574, 575	Before thy throne, O God, we kneel	L
	568	Father all loving, who rulest in majesty	L
Offertory:	551	Rise up, ye saints of God!	G
	581	Where charity and love prevail	G
	602	Jesu, Jesu, fill us with your love	L & G
	450, 451	All hail the power of Jesus' Name!	G
Communion:	505	O Spirit of Life, O Spirit of God	L, E & G
	602	Jesu, Jesu, fill us with your love	L & G
Postcommunion:	610	Lord, whose love through humble service	L & G
	609	Where cross the crowded ways of life	L & G
	336	Come with us, O blessèd Jesus	L & G

Proper 26 *(October 30 or 31 or Sunday between November 2 & 5 inclusive; November 1 is celebrated as All Saint's Day, and the Sunday between November 2 & 7 inclusive may be also [See below, p. 273])*

Entrance:	545	Lo! what a cloud of witnesses	C
	546	Awake, my soul, stretch every nerve	C
	552, 553	Fight the good fight with all thy might	C
Sequence:	614	Christ is the King! O friends upraise	E
	632	O Christ, the Word Incarnate	E
	627	Lamp of our feet, whereby we trace	E
Offertory:	656	Blest are the pure in heart	G
	670	Lord, for ever at thy side	E & G
Communion:	670	Lord, for ever at thy side	E & G
	656	Blest are the pure in heart	G

Postcommunion:	312	Strengthen for service, Lord	G
	437, 438	Tell out, my soul, the greatness of the Lord!	G
	665	All my hope on God is founded	G

Proper 27 *(Sundays between November 6 and 12 inclusive; an additional celebration of All Saints' Day may be held on Sunday November 6 or 7 [See below, p. 273])*

Entrance:	462	The Lord will come and not be slow	L
	596	Judge eternal, throned in splendor	L
	574, 575	Before thy throne, O God, we kneel	L
	53	Once he came in blessing	L & G
Sequence:	194, 195	Jesus lives! thy terrors now	E
	57, 58	Lo! he comes with clouds descending	E
	620	Jerusalem, my happy home	E
Offertory:	61, 62	"Sleepers, wake!" A voice astounds us	G
	68	Rejoice! rejoice, believers	G
Communion:	324	Let all mortal flesh keep silence	G
	63, 64	O heavenly Word, eternal Light	C
	454	Jesus came, adored by angels	E
Postcommunion:	68	Rejoice! rejoice, believers	G
	436	Lift up your heads, ye mighty gates	G
	53	Once he came in blessing	L & G
	454	Jesus came, adored by angels	E

Proper 28 *(Sunday between November 13 and 19 inclusive)*

Entrance:	53	Once he came in blessing	L & E
	462	The Lord will come and not be slow	L
	574, 575	Before thy throne, O God, we kneel	L
	680	O God, our help in ages past	P
Sequence:	548	Soldiers of Christ, arise	E
	547	Awake, O sleeper, rise from death	E
	617	Eternal Ruler of the ceaseless round	E
Offertory:	598	Lord Christ, when first thou cam'st to earth	G
	53	Once he came in blessing	G
	9	Not here for high and holy things	G
Communion:	326	From glory to glory advancing, we praise thee, O Lord	G
Postcommunion:	312	Strengthen for service, Lord	G
	541	Come, labor on	G
	551	Rise up, ye saints of God!	G
	561	Stand up, stand up for Jesus	E
	621, 622	Light's abode, celestial Salem	G

Proper 29 *(Sunday between November 20 and 26 inclusive)*

Entrance:	399	To God with gladness sing	L & P
	492	Sing, ye faithful, sing with gladness	E
	616	Hail to the Lord's Anointed	S
	450, 451	All hail the power of Jesus' Name!	S
Sequence:	478	Jesus, our mighty Lord	L, P & G
	544	Jesus shall reign where'er the sun	S
Offertory:	610	Lord, whose love through humble service	G
	609	Where cross the crowded ways of life	G
	573	Father eternal, Ruler of creation	G
Communion:	324	Let all mortal flesh keep silence	S
	460, 461	Alleluia! sing to Jesus! (omit sts. 2, 5)	S
Postcommunion:	481	Rejoice, the Lord is King	G
	494	Crown him with many crowns	E
	484, 485	Praise the Lord through every nation	G
	614	Christ is the King! O friends upraise	G
	435	At the Name of Jesus	S
	555	Lead on, O King eternal	S

The First Sunday of Advent — Year B

Entrance:	57, 58	Lo! he comes, with clouds descending	G
	53	Once he came in blessing	S
	596	Judge eternal, throned in splendor	S
Sequence:	59	Hark! a thrilling voice is sounding	C
Offertory:	61, 62	"Sleepers, wake!" A voice astounds us	G
	454	Jesus came, adored by angels	G
	616	Hail to the Lord's Anointed	G
Communion:	63, 64	O heavenly Word, eternal Light	S
	672	O very God of very God	S
Postcommunion:	68	Rejoice! rejoice, believers	G
	73	The King shall come when morning dawns	G
	462	The Lord will come and not be slow	S
	615	"Thy kingdom come!" on bended knee	S

The Second Sunday of Advent

Entrance:	70	Herald, sound the note of judgment	C, L & G
	59	Hark! a thrilling voice is sounding	L & G
Sequence:	75	There's a voice in the wilderness crying	L & G
	67	Comfort, comfort ye my people	L & G
	53	Once he came in blessing	E
	63, 64	O heavenly Word, eternal Light	E

Offertory:	76	On Jordan's bank the Baptist's cry	**L & G**
	69	What is the crying at Jordan?	**G**
Communion:	67	Comfort, comfort ye my people	**L & G**
Postcommunion:	65	Prepare the way, O Zion	**L & G**

The Third Sunday of Advent

Entrance:	640	Watchman, tell us of the night	**S**
	76	On Jordan's bank the Baptist's cry	**G**
Sequence:	63, 64	O heavenly Word, eternal Light	**E**
	59	Hark! a thrilling voice is sounding	**E**
	597	O day of peace that dimly shines	**L**
Offertory:	271, 272	The great forerunner of the morn	**G**
	75	There's a voice in the wilderness crying	**G**
	67	Comfort, comfort ye my people	**G**
Communion:	70	Herald, sound the note of judgment	**G**
	65	Prepare the way, O Zion	**G**
	69	What is the crying at Jordan?	**G**
Postcommunion:	444	Blessed be the God of Israel	**G**

The Fourth Sunday of Advent

Entrance:	74	Blest be the King whose coming	**L**
	486	Hosanna to the living Lord	**C**
	657	Love divine, all loves excelling	**C**
	436	Lift up your heads, ye mighty gates	**C**
	56	O come, O come, Emmanuel	**S**
Sequence:	66	Come, thou long-expected Jesus	**L & G**
	60	Creator of the stars of night	**G**
Offertory:	265	The angel Gabriel from heaven came	**G**
	270	Gabriel's message does away	**G**
	266	Nova, nova	**G**
Communion:	258	Virgin-born, we bow before thee	**G**
	263, 264	The Word whom earth and sea and sky	**G**
Postcommunion:	268, 269	Ye who claim the faith of Jesus	**G**
	54	Savior of the nations, come!	**G**
	55	Redeemer of the nations, come	**G**

Christmas Day Through the First Sunday After the Epiphany: *See Year A (above), pp 177–181*

The Second Sunday After the Epiphany

Entrance:	496, 497	How bright appears the Morning Star	C
	6, 7	Christ, whose glory fills the skies	C
	543	O Zion, tune thy voice	C
	440	Blessèd Jesus, at thy word	C
Sequence:	125, 126	The people who in darkness walked	C & G
	295	Sing praise to our Creator	E
	656	Blest are the pure in heart	E
	516	Come down, O Love divine	E
	500	Creator Spirit, by whose aid	E
Offertory:	443	From God Christ's deity came forth	G
	477	All praise to thee, for thou, O King divine	G
	439	What wondrous love is this	G
	489	The great Creator of the worlds	G
Communion:	439	What wondrous love is this	G
	324	Let all mortal flesh keep silence	G
	319	You, Lord, we praise in songs of celebration	G
Postcommunion:	535	Ye servants of God, your Master proclaim	G
	532, 533	How wondrous and great thy works, God of praise!	C
	538	God of mercy, God of grace	C
	371	Thou, whose almighty Word	C

The Third Sunday After the Epiphany

Entrance:	532, 533	How wondrous and great thy works, God of praise!	C
	537	Christ for the world we sing!	C
	543	O Zion, tune thy voice	C
Sequence:	666	Out of the depths I call	P
	151	From deepest woe I cry to thee	P
Offertory:	549, 550	Jesus calls us; o'er the tumult	G
	661	They cast their nets in Galilee	G
Communion:	321	My God, thy table now is spread	C
Postcommunion:	381	Thy strong word did cleave the darkness	C
	530	Spread, O spread, thou mighty word	C
	537	Christ for the world we sing!	C
	539	O Zion, haste, thy mission high fulfilling	C
	532, 533	How wondrous and great thy works, God of praise!	C

The Fourth Sunday After the Epiphany

| Entrance: | 616 | Hail to the Lord's Anointed | S |

	440	Blessèd Jesus, at thy word	S
Sequence:	536	God has spoken to his people	L
	448, 449	O love, how deep, how broad, how high	G
	544	Jesus shall reign where'er the sun	S
	532, 533	How wondrous and great thy works, God of praise!	S
Offertory:	567	Thine arm, O Lord, in days of old	G
	493	O for a thousand tongues to sing	G
	448, 449	O love, how deep, how broad, how high	G
	443	From God Christ's deity came forth	G
	457	Thou art the Way, to thee alone	G
Communion:	339	Deck thyself, my soul, with gladness	G
	448, 449	O love, how deep, how broad, how high	G
Postcommunion:	535	Ye servants of God, your Master proclaim	G
	437, 438	Tell out my soul, the greatness of the Lord!	G
	530	Spread, O spread, thou mighty word	G
	371	Thou, whose almighty word	G
	380	From all that dwell below the skies	L & G

The Fifth Sunday After the Epiphany

Entrance:	135	Songs of thankfulness and praise (sts. 1-3)	G
	1, 2	Father, we praise thee, now the night is over	L & G
	371	Thou, whose almighty word	G
Sequence:	538	God of mercy, God of grace	L & G
	635	If thou but trust in God to guide thee	L
	536	God has spoken to his people	E
Offertory:	567	Thine arm, O Lord, in days of old	G
	443	From God Christ's deity came forth	G
	493	O for a thousand tongues to sing	G
Communion:	493	O for a thousand tongues to sing	G
	566	From thee all skill and science flow	G
Postcommunion:	411	O bless the Lord, my soul!	L & G
	538	God of mercy, God of grace	L & G
	371	Thou, whose almighty word	G

The Sixth Sunday After the Epiphany

Entrance:	135	Songs of thankfulness and praise (sts. 1-3)	G
	1, 2	Father, we praise thee, now the night is over	L & G
	371	Thou, whose almighty word	G
	616	Hail to the Lord's Anointed	S

Sequence:	546	Awake, my soul, stretch every nerve	E
	552, 553	Fight the good fight with all thy might (sts. 1-2)	E
	422	Not far beyond the sea, nor high	E
	658	As longs the deer for cooling streams	P
	538	God of mercy, God of grace	L & G
Offertory:	567	Thine arm, O Lord, in days of old	G
	493	O for a thousand tongues to sing	G
Communion:	493	O for a thousand tongues to sing	G
	566	From thee all skill and science flow	G
Postcommunion:	411	O bless the Lord, my soul!	L & G
	538	God of mercy, God of grace	L & G
	371	Thou, whose almighty word	G

The Seventh Sunday After the Epiphany

Entrance:	410	Praise, my soul, the King of heaven	L & G
	469, 470	There's a wideness in God's mercy	L & G
	1, 2	Father, we praise thee, now the night is over	G
	135	Songs of thankfulness and praise (sts. 1-3)	G
Sequence:	686	Come, thou fount of every blessing	E
	697	My God, accept my heart this day	E
	411	O bless the Lord, my soul!	L & G
Offertory:	567	Thine arm, O Lord, in days of old	G
	493	O for a thousand tongues to sing	G
Communion:	469, 470	There's a wideness in God's mercy	L & G
	566	From thee all skill and science flow	G
Postcommunion:	538	God of mercy, God of grace	G
	411	O bless the Lord, my soul!	L & G

The Eighth Sunday After the Epiphany

Entrance:	410	Praise, my soul, the King of heaven	C, L & P
	411	O bless the Lord, my soul!	C, L & P
	390	Praise to the Lord, the Almighty	C, L & P
Sequence:	326	From glory to glory advancing, we praise thee, O Lord	E
	657	Love divine, all loves excelling	E
	597	O day of peace that dimly shines	L
	411	O bless the Lord, my soul!	C, L & P
Offertory:	324	Let all mortal flesh keep silence	S
	705	As those of old their first fruits brought	S
	649, 650	O Jesus, joy of loving hearts	S
	707	Take my life, and let it be	S

Communion:	319	You, Lord, we praise in songs of celebration	S
	300	Glory, love, and praise, and honor	S
	333	Now the silence	S
	302, 303	Father, we thank thee who hast planted	S
Postcommunion:	326	From glory to glory advancing, we praise thee, O Lord	E
	336	Come with us, O blessèd Jesus	S
	312	Strengthen for service, Lord	S
	527	Singing songs of expectation	S

The Last Sunday After the Epiphany

Entrance:	135	Songs of thankfulness and praise	G
	427	When morning gilds the skies	S
	6, 7	Christ, whose glory fills the skies	S
Sequence:	133, 134	O Light of Light, Love given birth	C, L, E & G
	129, 130	Christ upon the mountain peak	C, L, E & G
Offertory:	129, 130	Christ upon the mountain peak	C, L, E & G
	136, 137	O wondrous type! O vision fair	C, L, E & G
Communion:	133, 134	O Light of Light, Love given birth	C, L, E & G
	460, 461	Alleluia! sing to Jesus (omit sts. 2, 5)	S
	619	Sing alleluia forth in duteous praise	S
Postcommunion:	136, 137	O wondrous type! O vision fair	C, L, E & G
	122, 123	Alleluia, song of gladness	S
	135	Songs of thankfulness and praise	G

Ash Wednesday:

See Year A *(above), p. 185*

The First Sunday in Lent

Entrance:	150	Forty days and forty nights	C & G
	143	The glory of these forty days	C & G
Sequence:	432	O praise ye the Lord! Praise him in the height (omit st. 3)	E
	149	Eternal Lord of Love, behold your Church	E
	120	The sinless one to Jordan came (sts. 1-5)	C, E & G
	448, 449	O love, how deep, how broad, how high (sts. 1-2)	G
Offertory:	120	The sinless one to Jordan came (sts. 1-5)	C, E & G

	121	Christ, when for us you were baptized	G
	150	Forty days and forty nights	C & G
	443	From God Christ's deity came forth	G

Communion:	142	Lord, who throughout these forty days	C & G
	146, 147	Now let us all with one accord	L & G
	310, 311	O saving Victim, opening wide	C & G

Postcommunion:	143	The glory of these forty days	C & G
	559	Lead us, heavenly Father, lead us	C & G
	142	Lord, who throughout these forty days	C & G
	448, 449	O love, how deep, how broad, how high	G

The Second Sunday in Lent

| _Entrance:_ | 401 | The God of Abraham praise | L |
| | 495 | Hail, thou once despisèd Jesus! | L, E & G |

Sequence:	447	The Christ who died but rose again	E
	448, 449	O love, how deep, how broad, how high	E
	455, 456	O Love of God, how strong and true	E

Offertory:	675	Take up your cross, the Savior said	G
	10	New every morning is the love	G
	484, 485	Praise the Lord through every nation	G
	572	Weary of all trumpeting	G

Communion:	327, 328	Draw nigh and take the Body of the Lord	L & G
	337	And now, O Father, mindful of the love	L & G
	654	Day by day	G
	338	Wherefore, O Father, we thy humble servants	L, E & G

Postcommunion:	10	New every morning is the love	G
	484, 485	Praise the Lord through every nation	G
	448, 449	O love, how deep, how broad, how high	E & G
	572	Weary of all trumpeting	G

The Third Sunday in Lent

Entrance:	372	Praise to the living God!	L
	431	The stars declare his glory	L & P
	152	Kind Maker of the world, O hear	S

Sequence:	148	Creator of the earth and skies	E
	144	Lord Jesus, Sun of Righteousness	E
	140, 141	Wilt thou forgive that sin, where I begun	E
	641	Lord Jesus, think on me	E
	666	Out of the depths I call	E

Offertory:	151	From deepest woe I cry to thee	E
	148	Creator of the earth and skies	E
	685	Rock of ages, cleft for me	E

Communion:	313	Let thy Blood in mercy poured	E
	318	Here, O my Lord, I see thee face to face	E
Postcommunion:	703	Lead us, O Father, in the paths of peace	E
	559	Lead us, heavenly Father, lead us	E

The Fourth Sunday in Lent

Entrance:	143	The glory of these forty days	S
	686	Come, thou fount of every blessing	E
Sequence:	432	O praise ye the Lord! Praise him in the height (omit st. 3)	E
	685	Rock of ages, cleft for me	E
	467	Sing, my soul, his wondrous love	E
	671	Amazing grace! how sweet the sound	E
	691	My faith looks up to thee (sts. 1-2)	E
	706	In your mercy, Lord, you called me	E
Offertory:	320	Zion, praise thy Savior, singing (sts. 5-6)	G
	302, 303	Father, we thank thee who hast planted (st. 1)	G
	339	Deck thyself, my soul, with gladness	G
Communion:	308, 309	O Food to pilgrims given	G
	327, 328	Draw nigh and take the Body of the Lord	G
	321	My God, thy table now is spread	G
	301	Bread of the world, in mercy broken	G
Postcommunion:	690	Guide me, O thou great Jehovah	G
	623	O what their joy and their glory must be	L & P
	624	Jerusalem, the golden	L & P
	620	Jerusalem, my happy home	L & P

The Fifth Sunday in Lent

Entrance:	495	Hail, thou once despisèd Jesus!	E
	471	We sing the praise of him who died	E & G
Sequence:	443	From God Christ's deity came forth	E
	448, 449	O Love of God, how strong and true	E
	439	What wondrous love is this	G
Offertory:	170	To mock your reign, O dearest Lord	G
	161	The flaming banners of our King	G
	162	The royal banners forward go	G
	474	When I survey the wondrous cross	G
	165, 166	Sing, my tongue, the glorious battle	G
	473	Lift high the cross	G
Communion:	327, 328	Draw nigh and take the Body of the Lord	E
	337	And now, O Father, mindful of the love	E & G

Postcommunion:	448, 449	O love, how deep, how broad, how high	G
	473	Lift high the cross	G
	161	The flaming banners of our King	G
	162	The royal banners forward go	G

The Sunday of the Passion: Palm Sunday through the Second Sunday of Easter: *See Year A (above), pp. 188–196*

The Third Sunday of Easter

Entrance:	208	The strife is o'er, the battle done	L (Acts), E & G
	205	Good Christians all, rejoice and sing!	L (Acts), E & G
	492	Sing ye faithful, sing with gladness	L (Acts), E & G
Sequence:	205	Good Christians all, rejoice and sing!	L (Acts), E & G
	208	The strife is o'er, the battle done	L (Acts), E & G
	184	Christ the Lord is risen again!	G
	196, 197	Look there! the Christ, our Brother, comes	G
Offertory:	185, 186	Christ Jesus lay in death's strong bands	L (Acts), E & G
	305, 306	Come, risen Lord, and deign to be our guest	G
	212	Awake, arise, lift up your voice	G
Communion:	305, 306	Come, risen Lord, and deign to be our guest	G
	343	Shepherd of souls, refresh and bless	G
	185, 186	Christ Jesus lay in death's strong bands	L (Acts), E & G
	212	Awake, arise, lift up your voice	G
Postcommunion:	492	Sing, ye faithful, sing with gladness	L (Acts), E & G
	180	He is risen, he is risen!	G
	193	That Easter Day with joy was bright	G
	182	Christ is alive! Let Christians sing	S

The Fourth Sunday of Easter

Entrance:	205	Good Christians all, rejoice and sing!	L (Acts) & G
	184	Christ the Lord is risen again!	L (Acts)
	208	The strife is o'er, the battle done	L (Acts)
	492	Sing, ye faithful, sing with gladness	L (Acts)
	399	To God with gladness sing	G
	377, 378	All people that on earth do dwell	P 100 & G
	391	Before the Lord's eternal throne	P 100 & G

| Sequence: | 663 | The Lord my God my shepherd is | Ps 23 |
| | 664 | My Shepherd will supply my need | Ps 23 |

| Offertory: | 478 | Jesus, our mighty Lord | L (OT) & G |
| | 645, 646 | The King of love my shepherd is | P 23 & G |

Communion:	645, 646	The King of love my shepherd is	P 23 & G
	343	Shepherd of souls, refresh and bless	G
	320	Zion, praise thy Savior, singing (sts. 5-6)	G
	304	I come with joy to meet my Lord	G

Postcommunion:	708	Savior, like a shepherd lead us	G
	334	Praise the Lord, rise up rejoicing	G
	205	Good Christians all, rejoice and sing!	G

The Fifth Sunday of Easter

Entrance:	448, 449	O love, how deep, how broad, how high	L (Acts)
	49	Come, let us with our Lord arise	L (Acts)
	52	This day at thy creating word	L (Acts)
	47	On this day, the first of days	L (Acts)

Sequence:	610	Lord, whose love through humble service	E
	297	Descend, O Spirit, purging flame	L (Acts)
	298	All who believe and are baptized	L (Acts)
	296	We know that Christ is raised and dies no more	L (Acts)
	176, 177	Over the chaos of the empty waters	L (Acts)

Offertory:	704	O thou who camest from above	E & G
	512	Come, gracious Spirit, heavenly Dove	G
	516	Come down, O Love divine	G
	228	Holy Spirit, font of light	G
	514	To thee, O Comforter divine	G
	500	Creator Spirit, by whose aid	G
	226, 227	Come, thou Holy Spirit bright	G

Communion:	319	You, Lord, we praise in songs of celebration	E
	304	I come with joy to meet my Lord	E
	487	Come, my Way, my Truth, my Life	C
	463, 464	He is the Way	C

| Postcommunion: | 457 | Thou art the Way, to thee alone | C |
| | 205 | Good Christians all, rejoice and sing! | E |

The Sixth Sunday of Easter

Entrance:	455, 456	O Love of God, how stong and true	E
	448, 449	O love, how deep, how broad, how high	E
	489	The great Creator of the worlds	E
	492	Sing, ye faithful, sing with gladness	E

Sequence:	700	O love that casts out fear	E
	603, 604	When Christ was lifted from the earth	E
Offertory:	581	Where charity and love prevail	E & G
	576, 577	God is love, and where true love is	E & G
	606	Where true charity and love dwell	E & G
	706	In your mercy, Lord, you called me	E & G
Communion:	319	You, Lord, we praise in songs of celebration	E & G
	602	Jesu, Jesu, fill us with your love	E & G
Postcommunion:	610	Lord, whose love through humble service	E & G
	593	Lord, make us servants of your peace	E & G
	344	Lord, dismiss us with thy blessing	G
	392	Come, we that love the Lord	G
	292	O Jesus, crowned with all renown	S

Ascension Day: *See Year A (above), p. 198*

The Seventh Sunday of Easter: The Sunday after Ascension Day

Entrance:	492	Sing, ye faithful, sing with gladness	S
	481	Rejoice, the Lord is King	S
	450, 451	All hail the power of Jesus' Name!	S
Sequence:	477	All praise to thee, for thou, O King divine	S
	435	At the Name of Jesus	S
Offertory:	484, 485	Praise the Lord through every nation	G
	483	The head that once was crowned with thorns	S
	495	Hail, thou once depisèd Jesus!	S
Communion:	307	Lord, enthroned in heavenly splendor	S
	460, 461	Alleluia! sing to Jesus!	S
Postcommunion:	494	Crown him with many crowns	S
	495	Hail, thou once despisèd Jesus!	S
	481	Rejoice, the Lord is King	S

The Day of Pentecost — Early or Vigil Service: *See Year A (above), p. 199*

The Day of Pentecost — Principal Service: *See Year A (above), p. 200*

The First Sunday after Pentecost: Trinity Sunday

| Entrance: | 401 | The God of Abraham praise | L |
| | 366 | Holy God, we praise thy Name | S |

	364	O God, we praise thee, and confess	S
	365	Come, thou almighty King	S
Sequence:	295	Sing praise to our Creator	E & G
	368	Holy Father, great creator	S
Offertory:	421	All glory be to God on high	G
	295	Sing praise to our Creator	E & G
	370	I bind unto myself today	S
Communion:	370	I bind unto myself today	S
	421	All glory be to God on high	G
Postcommunion:	559	Lead us, heavenly Father, lead us	S
	363	Ancient of Days, who sittest throned in glory	S
	368	Holy Father, great Creator	S

Propers *1, 2 & 3: See 6, 7 & 8* Epiphany *for the same lections (If the Sunday between May 24 and 28 inclusive follows Trinity Sunday, use Proper 3 [Epiphany 8] on that day).*

Proper 4 *(Sunday between May 29 and June 4, inclusive, if after Trinity Sunday)*

Entrance:	440	Blessèd Jesus, at thy word	L, E & G
	431	The stars declare his glory	L
	48	O day of radiant gladness	G
	49	Come, let us with our Lord arise	G
	52	This day at thy creating word	G
	50	This is the day the Lord hath made	G
Sequence:	296	We know that Christ is raised and dies no more	E
	465, 466	Eternal light, shine in my heart	E
	125, 126	The people who in darkness walked	E
	6, 7	Christ, whose glory fills the skies	E
	419	Lord of all being, throned afar	E
	5	O splendor of God's glory bright	E
	496, 497	How bright appears the Morning star	E
Offertory:	381	Thy strong word did cleave the darkness	L, E & G
	630	Thanks to God whose Word was spoken (omit sts. 3, 4)	L, E & G
Communion:	332	O God, unseen yet ever near (sts. 3-4)	L & G
Postcommunion:	381	Thy strong word did cleave the darkness	L, E & G
	630	Thanks to God whose Word was spoken (omit sts. 3, 4)	L, E & G

Proper 5 *(Sunday between June 5 and 11 inclusive, if after Trinity Sunday)*

Entrance:	50	This is the day the Lord hath made	E & G
	47	On this day, the first of days	E
Sequence:	194, 195	Jesus lives! thy terrors now	E
	621, 622	Light's abode, celestial Salem	E
	623	O what their joy and their glory must be	E
	60	Creator of the stars of night (omit st. 6)	L
	270	Gabriel's message does away	L
	295	Sing praise to our Creator	L
Offertory:	445, 446	Praise to the Holiest in the height	L & G
	452	Glorious the day when Christ was born	G
Communion:	452	Glorious the day when Christ was born	G
	445, 446	Praise to the Holiest in the height	L & G
Postcommunion:	381	Thy strong word did cleave the darkness	E & G
	535	Ye servants of God, your Master proclaim	G

Proper 6 *(Sunday between June 12 and 18 inclusive, if after Trinity Sunday)*

Entrance:	538	God of mercy, God of grace	C
	525	The Church's one foundation	C
Sequence:	209	We walk by faith, and not by sight	E
	621, 622	Light's abode, celestial Salem	E
	623	O what their joy and their glory must be	E
	620	Jerusalem, my happy home	E
	63, 64	O heavenly Word, eternal Light	E
Offertory:	588, 589	Almighty God, your word is cast	G
	290	Come, ye thankful people, come (st. 2)	G
	615	"Thy kingdom come!" on bended knee	G
	24	The day thou gavest, Lord, is ended (In the morning omit st. 1)	G
	613	Thy kingdom come, O God!	G
Communion:	302, 303	Father, we thank thee, who hast planted	C & G
	600, 601	O day of God, draw nigh	G
Postcommunion:	534	God is working his purpose out	G
	462	The Lord will come, and not be slow	G

Proper 7 *(Sunday between June 19 and 25 inclusive, if after Trinity Sunday)*

Entrance:	492	Sing, ye faithful, sing with gladness	E
	426	Songs of praise the angels sang	L
	390	Praise to the Lord, the Almighty	G
	410	Praise, my soul, the King of heaven	G

Sequence:	298	All who believe and are baptized	E
	296	We know that Christ is raised and dies no more	E
	176, 177	Over the chaos of the empty waters	E
	213	Come away to the skies	E
	603, 604	When Christ was lifted from the earth	E
	677	God moves in a mysterious way	L
	379	God is love, let heaven adore him	L
Offertory:	411	O bless the Lord, my soul!	E & G
	493	O for a thousand tongues to sing	E & G (5:1-20)
Communion:	429	I'll praise my Maker while I've breath	G (5:1-20)
	567	Thine arm, O Lord, in days of old	G (5:1-20)
	432	O praise ye the Lord! praise him in the height	E
	289	The great Creator of the worlds	E
Postcommunion:	530	Spread, O spread, thou mighty word	E & G
	535	Ye servants of God, your Master proclaim	E & G
	380	From all that dwell below the skies	G

Proper 8 (Sunday between June 26 and July 2 inclusive)

Entrance:	9	Not here for high and holy things	L & E
	47	On this day, the first of days	E
	518	Christ is made the sure foundation	C
	525	The Church's one foundation	C
	521	Put forth, O God, thy Spirit's might	C
Sequence:	705	As those of old their first fruits brought	L & E
	292	O Jesus, crowned with all renown	L & E
	568	Father all loving, who rulest in majesty	L & E
	707	Take my life, and let it be	E
	610	Lord, whose love through humble service	L & E
Offertory:	493	O for a thousand tongues to sing	G
	567	Thine arm, O Lord, in days of old	G
Communion:	567	Thine arm, O Lord, in days of old	G
	566	From thee all skill and science flow	G
Postcommunion:	530	Spread, O spread, thou mighty word	G
	411	O bless the Lord, my soul!	G

Proper 9 (Sunday between July 3 and 9 inclusive)

Entrance:	440	Blessèd Jesus, at thy word	L & G
	372	Praise to the living God!	L
Sequence:	636, 637	How firm a foundation, ye saints of the Lord	E
	548	Soldiers of Christ, arise	E
	635	If thou but trust in God to guide thee	E
	677	God moves in a mysterious way	E
	669	Commit thou all that grieves thee	E

Offertory:	633	Word of God, come down on earth	L & G
	634	I call on thee, Lord Jesus Christ	G
	630	Thanks to God whose Word was spoken	
		(omit sts. 3, 4)	L & G
	628	Help us, O Lord, to learn	G
	448, 449	O love, how deep, how broad, how high	G
Communion:	634	I call on thee, Lord Jesus Christ	G
	628	Help us, O Lord to learn	G
	332	O God, unseen yet ever near (sts. 3-4)	G
Postcommunion:	530	Spread, O spread, thou mighty word	L & G
	630	Thanks to God whose Word was spoken	
		(omit sts. 3, 4)	L & G
	371	Thou, whose almighty Word	L & G
	536	God has spoken to his people	L & G

Proper 10 *(Sunday between July 10 and 16 inclusive)*

Entrance:	440	Blessèd Jesus, at thy word	L, E & G
	372	Praise to the living God!	L
	492	Sing, ye faithful, sing with gladness	E
Sequence:	495	Hail, thou once despisèd Jesus!	E
	686	Come, thou fount of every blessing	E
	706	In your mercy, Lord, you called me	E
	294	Baptized in water	E
	295	Sing praise to our Creator	E
	671	Amazing grace! how sweet the sound	E
Offertory:	540	Awake, thou Spirit of the watchmen	G
	528	Lord, you give the great commission	G
Communion:	321	My God, thy table now is spread	G
	531	O Spirit of the living God	G
Postcommunion:	540	Awake, thou Spirit of the watchmen	G
	528	Lord, you give the great commission	G
	531	O Spirit of the living God	G
	535	Ye servants of God, your Master proclaim	G

Proper 11 *(Sunday between July 17 and 23 inclusive)*

Entrance:	518	Christ is made the sure foundation	E
	525	The Church's one foundation	E
Sequence:	495	Hail, thou once despisèd Jesus!	E
	693	Just as I am, without one plea	E
	643	My God, how wonderful thou art	L
	656	Blest are the pure in heart	L
	603, 604	When Christ was lifted from the earth	E

Offertory:	472	Hope of the world, thou Christ of great compassion	G
	478	Jesus, our mighty Lord	E & G
	302, 303	Father, we thank thee who hast planted	E & G
Communion:	327, 328	Draw nigh and take the Body of the Lord	E & G
	308, 309	O Food to pilgrims given	E & G
	320	Zion, praise thy Savior, singing (sts. 5-6)	G
	319	You, Lord, we praise in songs of celebration	E
	343	Shepherd of souls, refresh and bless	G
Postcommunion:	478	Jesus, our mighty Lord	E & G
	708	Savior, like a shepherd lead us	G

Proper 12 *(Sunday between July 24 and 30 inclusive)*

Entrance:	388	O worship the King, all glorious above!	G
	398	I sing the almighty power of God	G
	390	Praise to the Lord, the Almighty	G
	428	O all ye works of God, now come	G
Sequence:	547	Awake, O sleeper, rise from death	E
	521	Put forth, O God, thy Spirit's might	E
	511	Holy Spirit, ever living	E
	359	God of the prophets, bless the prophets' heirs	L
Offertory:	669	Commit thou all that grieves thee	G
	636, 637	How firm a foundation, ye saints of the Lord	G
	699	Jesus, Lover of my soul	G
Communion:	636, 637	How firm a foundation, ye saints of the Lord	G
	669	Commit thou all that grieves thee	G
Postcommunion:	375	Give praise and glory unto God	G
	414	God, my King, thy might confessing	G
	373	Praise the Lord! ye heavens adore him	G

Proper 13 *(Sunday between July 31 and August 5 inclusive; August 6 is celebrated as the Feast of the Transfiguration [See below, p.269])*

Entrance:	51	We the Lord's people, heart and voice uniting	G
	48	O day of radiant gladness	G
	49	Come, let us with our Lord arise	G
Sequence:	576, 577	God is love, and where true love is	E
	581	Where charity and love prevail	E
	606	Where true charity and love dwell	E
	574, 575	Before thy throne, O God, we kneel	E
Offertory:	335	I am the bread of life	G
	343	Shepherd of souls, refresh and bless	L & G
	302, 303	Father, we thank thee who hast planted (st. 1)	G

	339	Deck thyself, my soul, with gladness	G
Communion:	307	Lord, enthroned in heavenly splendor	L & G
	308, 309	O Food to pilgrims given	G
	320	Zion, praise thy Savior, singing (sts. 5-6)	G
	327, 328	Draw nigh and take the Body of the Lord	G
	321	My God, thy table now is spread	G
	301	Bread of the world, in mercy broken	G
Postcommunion:	690	Guide me, O thou great Jehovah	L, P & G
	522, 523	Glorious things of thee are spoken	L

Proper 14 *(Sunday between August 7 and 13 inclusive)*

Entrance:	51	We the Lord's people, heart and voice uniting	L & G
	49	Come, let us with our Lord arise	L & G
	48	O day of radiant gladness	L & G
	410	Praise, my soul, the King of heaven	L
	393	Praise our great and gracious Lord	L
Sequence:	581	Where charity and love prevail	E
	576, 577	God is love, and where true love is	E
	606	Where true charity and love dwell	E
	674	"Forgive our sins as we forgive"	E
	593	Lord, make us servants of your peace	E
Offertory:	343	Shepherd of souls, refresh and bless	L & G
	335	I am the bread of life	G
	320	Zion, praise thy Savior, singing (sts. 5-6)	G
	302, 303	Father, we thank thee who hast planted (st. 1)	G
	339	Deck thyself, my soul, with gladness	G
Communion:	308, 309	O Food to pilgrims given	L & G
	327, 328	Draw nigh and take the Body of the Lord	G
	323	Bread of heaven, on thee we feed	G
	301	Bread of the world, in mercy broken	G
	321	My God, thy table now is spread	G
Postcommunion:	690	Guide me, O thou great Jehovah	L & G
	346	Completed, Lord, the Holy Mysteries	G
	340, 341	For the bread which you have broken	G
	522, 523	Glorious things of thee are spoken	L

Proper 15 *(Sunday between August 14 and 20 inclusive)*

Entrance:	402, 403	Let all the world in every corner sing	E
	426	Songs of praise the angels sang	E
	420	When in our music God is glorified	E
	430	Come, O come, our voices raise	E
	360, 361	Only-begotten, Word of God eternal	G
Sequence:	584	God, you have given us power to sound	L & E

	467	Sing, my soul, his wondrous love	E
	402, 403	Let all the world in every corner sing	E
Offertory:	313	Let thy Blood in mercy poured	G
	324	Let all mortal flesh keep silence	G
	335	I am the bread of life	G
Communion:	323	Bread of heaven, on thee we feed	G
	327, 328	Draw nigh and take the Body of the Lord	G
	329, 330, 331	Now, my tongue, the mystery telling	G
	332	O God, unseen yet ever near (sts. 3-4)	G
	308, 309	O Food to pilgrims given	G
Postcommunion:	346	Completed, Lord, the Holy Mysteries	G
	334	Praise the Lord, rise up, rejoicing	G
	340, 341	For the bread which you have broken	G

Proper 16 *(Sunday between August 21 and 27 inclusive)*

Entrance:	425	Sing now with joy unto the Lord	L
	393	Praise our great and gracious Lord	L
	519, 520	Blessèd city, heavenly Salem	E
	440	Blessèd Jesus, at thy word	G
Sequence:	524	I love thy kingdom, Lord	E
	525	The Church's one foundation	E
Offertory:	633	Word of God, come down on earth	G
	634	I call on thee, Lord Jesus Christ	G
	628	Help us, O Lord, to learn	G
	632	O Christ, the Word Incarnate	G
	630	Thanks to God, whose Word was spoken (omit sts. 3, 4)ʼ	G
	626	Lord, be thy word my rule	G
Communion:	301	Bread of the world, in mercy broken	G
	307	Lord, enthroned in heavenly splendor	G
	421	All glory be to God on high	G
	460, 461	Alleluia! sing to Jesus!	G
Postcommunion:	530	Spread, O spread, thou mighty word	G
	633	Word of God, come down on earth	G
	381	Thy strong word did cleave the darkness	G

Proper 17 *(Sunday between August 28 and September 3 inclusive)*

Entrance:	435	At the Name of Jesus (sts. 1-5)	C & G
	477	All praise to thee, for thou, O King divine	C
	450, 451	All hail the power of Jesus' Name!	C
	248, 249	To the Name of our salvation	C
	644	How sweet the Name of Jesus sounds	C

Sequence:	548	Soldiers of Christ arise	E
	617	Eternal Ruler of the ceaseless round	E
	561	Stand up, stand up for Jesus	E
Offertory:	435	At the Name of Jesus (sts. 1-5)	C & G
	436	Lift up your heads, ye mighty gates	G
	656	Blest are the pure in heart	G
	144	Lord Jesus, Sun of Righteousness	G
Communion:	656	Blest are the pure in heart	G
	436	Lift up your heads, ye mighty gates	G
Postcommunion:	556, 557	Rejoice, ye pure in heart!	G
	382	King of glory, King of peace	C & G
	344	Lord, dismiss us with thy blessing	C & G
	435	At the Name of Jesus (sts. 1-5)	C & G

Proper 18 *(Sunday between September 4 and 10 inclusive)*

Entrance:	429	I'll praise my Maker while I've breath	L & P
	1, 2	Father, we praise thee, now the night is over	L & G
	411	O bless the Lord, my soul!	L & G
	390	Praise to the Lord, the Almighty	L & G
	423	Immortal, invisible, God only wise	E
Sequence:	610	Lord, whose love through humble service	E
	628	Help us, O Lord, to learn	E
	11	Awake, my soul, and with the sun	E
Offertory:	633	Word of God, come down on earth	L & G
	493	O for a thousand tongues to sing	L & G
	567	Thine arm, O Lord, in days of old	L & G
Communion:	567	Thine arm, O Lord, in days of old	L & G
	566	From thee all skill and science flow	L & G
Postcommunion:	538	God of mercy, God of grace	L & G
	493	O for a thousand tongues to sing	L & G
	633	Word of God, come down on earth	L & G

Proper 19 *(Sunday between September 11 and 17 inclusive)*

Entrance:	477	All praise to thee, for thou, O King divine	L & G (Mk 8)
	427	When morning gilds the skies	G (Mk 8)
Sequence:	610	Lord, whose love through humble service	E
	603, 604	When Christ was lifted from the earth	E
	602	Jesu, Jesu, fill us with your love	E
	628	Help us, O Lord, to learn	E
	529	In Christ there is no East or West	E

Offertory:	254	You are the Christ, O Lord	G (Mk 8)
	455, 456	O Love of God, how strong and true	L & G (Mk 8)
	434	Nature with open volume stands	L & G (Mk 8)
	675	Take up your cross, the Savior said	G (Mk 8)
	484, 485	Praise the Lord through every nation	G (Mk 8)
	493	O for a thousand tongues to sing	G (Mk 9)
	567	Thine arm, O Lord, in days of old	G (Mk 9)
Communion:	654	Day by day	G (Mk 8)
	448, 449	O love, how deep, how broad, how high	G (Mk 8 or 9)
Postcommunion:	484, 485	Praise the Lord through every nation	G (Mk 8)
	448, 449	O love, how deep, how broad, how high	G (Mk 8 or 9)
	410	Praise, my soul, the King of heaven	G (Mk 9)

Proper 20 *(Sunday between September 18 and 24 inclusive)*

Entrance:	477	All praise to thee, for thou, O King divine	L & G
	366	Holy God, we praise thy Name	L & G
	364	O God, we praise thee, and confess	L & G
	492	Sing, ye faithful, sing with gladness	L & G
Sequence:	574, 575	Before thy throne, O God, we kneel	E
	656	Blest are the pure in heart	E
	670	Lord, for ever at thy side	E
	437, 438	Tell out, my soul, the greatness of the Lord!	E
Offertory:	455, 456	O Love of God, how strong and true	L & G
	448, 449	O love, how deep, how broad, how high	L & G
	434	Nature with open volume stands	L & G
	659, 660	O Master, let me walk with thee	G
Communion:	448, 449	O love, how deep, how broad, how high	L & G
	455, 456	O Love of God, how strong and true	L & G
	434	Nature with open volume stands	L & G
	313	Let thy Blood in mercy poured	L & G
Postcommunion:	492	Sing, ye faithful, sing with gladness	L & G
	455, 456	O Love of God, how strong and true	L & G
	448, 449	O love, how deep, how broad, how high	L & G

Proper 21 *(Sunday between September 25 and October 1 inclusive)*

Entrance:	359	God of the prophets, bless the prophets' heirs	L
	431	The stars declare his glory	P
	546	Awake, my soul, stretch every nerve	C
	545	Lo! what a cloud of witnesses	C
	552, 553	Fight the good fight with all thy might	C

Sequence:	656	Blest are the pure in heart	E
	582, 583	O holy city, seen of John	E (5:1-6)
	628	Help us, O Lord, to learn	L
	627	Lamp of our feet, whereby we trace	L
	626	Lord, be thy word my rule	L
Offertory:	574, 575	Before thy throne, O God, we kneel	E & G
	609	Where cross the crowded ways of life	G
Communion:	308, 309	O Food to pilgrims given	L
	574, 575	Before thy throne, O God, we kneel	E & G
Postcommunion:	609	Where cross the crowded ways of life	G
	347	Go forth for God; go to the world in peace	E & G
	344	Lord, dismiss us with thy blessing	G

Proper 22 (Sunday between October 2 and 8 inclusive)

Entrance:	416	For the beauty of the earth	L & G
	376	Joyful, joyful, we adore thee	L & G
	450, 451	All hail the power of Jesus' Name!	E
	518	Christ is made the sure foundation	C
	360, 361	Only-begotten, Word of God eternal	C
	698	Eternal Spirit of the living Christ	C
Sequence:	448, 449	O love, how deep, how broad, how high	E
	455, 456	O Love of God, how strong and true	E
	458	My song is love unknown	E
	483	The head that once was crowned with thorns	E
	443	From God Christ's deity came forth	E
Offertory:	587	Our Father, by whose Name	L & G
	350	O God of love, to thee we bow	L & G
	352	O God, to those who here profess	L & G
	353	Your love, O God, has called us here	L & G
Communion:	587	Our Father, by whose Name	L & G
	352	O God, to those who here profess	L & G
	353	Your love, O God, has called us here	L & G
Postcommunion:	376	Joyful, joyful, we adore thee	L & G
	396, 397	Now thank we all our God	L & G
	416	For the beauty of the earth	L & G
	559	Lead us, heavenly Father, lead us	E

Proper 23 (Sunday between October 9 and 15 inclusive)

Entrance:	408	Sing praise to God who reigns above	G
	680	O God, our help in ages past	P
Sequence:	443	From God Christ's deity came forth	E
	460, 461	Alleluia! sing to Jesus! (sts. 1 & 4)	E

Offertory:	701	Jesus, all my gladness (sts. 1-2)	G
	707	Take my life, and let it be	G
	655	O Jesus, I have promised	G
Communion:	475	God himself is with us (sts. 1-2)	G
	701	Jesus, all my gladness	G
Postcommunion:	472	Hope of the world, thou Christ of great compassion	G
	346	Completed, Lord, the Holy Mysteries	G
	683, 684	O for a closer walk with God	G

Proper 24 *(Sunday between October 16 and 22 inclusive)*

Entrance:	492	Sing, ye faithful, sing with gladness	L, E & G
	478	Jesus, our mighty Lord	C, L & G
Sequence:	495	Hail, thou once despisèd Jesus! (sts. 1-2)	L, E & G
	443	From God Christ's deity came forth	L, E & G
	219	The Lord ascendeth up on high	E
	447	The Christ who died but rose again	E
Offertory:	477	All praise to thee, for thou, O King divine	G
	458	My song is love unknown	G
	474	When I survey the wondrous cross	G
	659, 660	O Master, let me walk with thee	G
Communion:	327, 328	Draw nigh and take the Body of the Lord	E
	460, 461	Alleluia! sing to Jesus!	E
	319	You, Lord, we praise in songs of celebration	G
	338	Wherefore, O Father, we thy humble servants	E & G
Postcommunion:	483	The head that once was crowned with thorns	L & G
	530	Spread, O spread, thou mighty word	L & G
	448, 449	O love, how deep, how broad, how high	G

Proper 25 *(Sunday between October 23 and 29 inclusive)*

Entrance:	672	O very God of very God	L & G
	6, 7	Christ, whose glory fills the skies	L & G
	371	Thou, whose almighty Word	L & G
	411	O bless the Lord, my soul!	L & G
Sequence:	326	From glory to glory advancing, we praise thee, O Lord	E
	704	O thou who camest from above	E
	465, 466	Eternal light, shine in my heart	L & G
Offertory:	493	O for a thousand tongues to sing	G

	567	Thine arm, O Lord, in days of old	G
	633	Word of God, come down on earth	G
	429	I'll praise my Maker while I've breath	G
Communion:	567	Thine arm, O Lord, in days of old	G
	493	O for a thousand tongues to sing	G
	566	From thee all skill and science flow	G
Postcommunion:	538	God of mercy, God of grace	L & G
	371	Thou, whose almighty Word	L & G
	410	Praise, my soul, the King of heaven	G

Proper 26 *(October 30 or 31 or Sunday between November 2 and 5 inclusive; November 1 is celebrated as All Saints' Day, and the Sunday between November 2 and 7 inclusive may be also [See below, p. 273])*

Entrance:	517	How lovely is thy dwelling-place	L & G
	431	The stars declare his glory	L & G
	545	Lo! what a cloud of witnesses	C
	546	Awake, my soul, stretch every nerve	C
	552, 553	Fight the good fight with all thy might	C
Sequence:	495	Hail, thou once despisèd Jesus!	E
	443	From God Christ's deity came forth	E
	219	The Lord ascendeth up on high	E
	693	Just as I am, without one plea	L
	699	Jesus, Lover of my soul	L
Offertory:	551	Rise up, ye saints of God!	L & G
	581	Where charity and love prevail	L & G
Communion:	327, 328	Draw nigh and take the Body of the Lord	E
	460, 461	Alleluia! sing to Jesus! (omit sts. 2, 5)	E
Postcommunion:	610	Lord, whose love through humble service	G
	382	King of glory, King of peace	G

Proper 27 *(Sunday between November 6 and 12 inclusive; an additional celebration of All Saints' Day may be held on Sunday November 6 or 7 [See below, p. 273])*

Entrance:	429	I'll praise my Maker while I've breath	P & L
	574, 575	Before thy throne, O God, we kneel	C & G
	9	Not here for high and holy things	G
Sequence:	57, 58	Lo! he comes, with clouds descending	E
	73	The King shall come when morning dawns	E
	686	Come, thou fount of every blessing	E
	160	Cross of Jesus, cross of sorrow	E
	219	The Lord ascendeth up on high	E
Offertory:	707	Take my life, and let it be	L & G
	313	Let thy Blood in mercy poured	L & G

Communion:	327, 328	Draw nigh and take the Body of the Lord	E
	307	Lord, enthroned in heavenly splendor	E
	337	And now, O Father, mindful of the love (sts. 1-2)	E
	338	Wherefore, O Father, we thy humble servants	E
	460, 461	Alleluia! sing to Jesus! (omit sts. 2, 5)	E
Postcommunion:	475	God himself is with us	C, L & G
	53	Once he came in blessing	C

Proper 28 *(Sunday between November 13 and 19 inclusive)*

Entrance:	462	The Lord will come and not be slow	L, E & G
	574, 575	Before thy throne, O God, we kneel	L & E
	596	Judge eternal, throned in splendor	L
Sequence:	53	Once he came in blessing	L & E
	63, 64	O heavenly Word, eternal Light	L & E
	57, 58	Lo! he comes, with clouds descending	S
	73	The King shall come when morning dawns	S
Offertory:	672	O very God of very God	G
	615	"Thy Kingdom come!" on bended knee	G
Communion:	615	"Thy Kingdom come!" on bended knee	G
	672	O very God of very God	G
Postcommunion:	454	Jesus came, adored by angels	S
	452	Glorious the day when Christ was born	S

Proper 29 *(Sunday between November 20 and 26 inclusive)*

Entrance:	616	Hail to the Lord's Anointed	S
	450, 451	All hail the power of Jesus' Name!	S
	544	Jesus shall reign, where'er the sun	S
Sequence:	454	Jesus came, adored by angels	E
	57, 58	Lo! he comes, with clouds descending	E
Offertory:	170	To mock your reign, O dearest Lord	G (Jn)
	598	Lord Christ, when first thou cam'st to earth	G (Jn)
	483	The head that once was crowned with thorns (sts. 1-2)	G (Jn)
	495	Hail, thou once despisèd Jesus!	G (Jn)
	458	My song is love unknown	G (Jn or Mk)
	74	Blest be the King whose coming	G (Mk)
	71, 72	Hark! the glad sound! the Savior comes	G (Mk)
	65	Prepare the way, O Zion	G (Mk)
	486	Hosanna to the living Lord!	G (Mk)
	436	Lift up your heads, ye mighty gates	G (Mk)

Communion:	307	Lord, enthroned in heavenly splendor	E
	324	Let all mortal flesh keep silence	E
Postcommunion:	494	Crown him with many crowns	E & G
	477	All praise to thee, for thou, O King divine	G
	435	At the Name of Jesus	E
	481	Rejoice, the Lord is King	E
	484, 485	Praise the Lord through every nation	S
	614	Christ is the King! O friends upraise	S

The First Sunday of Advent — Year C

Entrance:	462	The Lord will come and not be slow	L
	59	Hark! a thrilling voice is sounding	C
	61, 62	"Sleepers, wake !" A voice astounds us	S
	53	Once he came in blessing	S
Sequence:	60	Creator of the stars of night	L
	672	O very God of very God	L
	613	Thy kingdom come, O God!	L
	63, 64	O heavenly Word, eternal Light	E
Offertory:	71, 72	Hark! the glad sound! the Savior comes	G
	616	Hail to the Lord's Anointed	G
Communion:	454	Jesus came, adored by angels	G
	615	"Thy Kingdom come!" on bended knee	G
Postcommunion:	73	The King shall come when morning dawns	G
	57, 58	Lo! he comes, with clouds descending	G

The Second Sunday of Advent

Entrance:	70	Herald, sound the note of judgment	C & G
	59	Hark! a thrilling voice is sounding	G
Sequence:	75	There's a voice in the wilderness crying	L & G
	543	O Zion, tune thy voice	L
	53	Once he came in blessing	E
	63, 64	O heavenly Word, eternal Light	E
Offertory:	76	On Jordan's bank the Baptist's cry	G
Communion:	67	Comfort, comfort ye my people	L & G
	69	What is the crying at Jordan?	G
Postcommunion:	65	Prepare the way, O Zion	L & G

The Third Sunday of Advent

| Entrance: | 640 | Watchman, tell us of the night | S |
| | 67 | Comfort, comfort ye my people | S |

	75	There's a voice in the wilderness crying	S
Sequence:	70	Herald, sound the note of judgment	G
	678, 679	Surely it is God who saves me	Canticle 9
Offertory:	76	On Jordan's bank the Baptist's cry	G
	59	Hark! a thrilling voice is sounding	G
Communion:	70	Herald, sound the note of judgment	G
	69	What is the crying at Jordan?	G
	63, 64	O heavenly Word, eternal Light	S
	61, 62	"Sleepers, wake!" A voice astounds us	S
Postcommunion:	444	Blessed be the God of Israel	G

The Fourth Sunday of Advent

Entrance:	56	O come, O come, Emmanuel	S
	74	Blest be the King whose coming	L
	657	Love divine, all loves excelling	C
	486	Hosanna to the living Lord!	C
	436	Lift up your heads, ye mighty gates	C
Sequence:	55	Redeemer of the nations, come	L
	54	Savior of the nations, come!	L
	66	Come, thou long-expected Jesus	S
Offertory:	258	Virgin-born, we bow before thee	G
	268, 269	Ye who claim the faith of Jesus	G
Communion:	270	Gabriel's message does away	G
	265	The angel Gabriel from heaven came	G
	263, 264	The Word whom earth and sea and sky	G
Postcommunion:	268, 269	Ye who claim the faith of Jesus	G
	437, 438	Tell out, my soul, the greatness of the Lord!	G

Christmas Day Through the First Sunday After the Epiphany: *See Year A (above), pp. 177–181*

The Second Sunday After the Epiphany

Entrance:	496, 497	How bright appears the Morning Star	C
	6, 7	Christ, whose glory fills the skies	C
	125, 126	The people who in darkness walked	C
	543	O Zion, tune thy voice	C
	440	Blessèd Jesus, at thy word	C
Sequence:	131, 132	When Christ's appearing was made known (sts. 4-5)	G
	135	Songs of thankfulness and praise (sts. 1-2)	G

Offertory:	138	All praise to you, O Lord	G
	443	From God Christ's deity came forth	G
Communion:	316, 317	This is the hour of banquet and of song	G
	339	Deck thyself, my soul, with gladness	G
	487	Come, my Way, my Truth, my Life	G
	333	Now the silence	G
	324	Let all mortal flesh keep silence	G
Postcommunion:	138	All praise to you, O Lord	G
	135	Songs of thankfulness and praise (sts. 1-2)	G
	538	God of mercy, God of grace	C
	532, 533	How wondrous and great thy works, God of praise!	C

The Third Sunday After the Epiphany

Entrance:	616	Hail to the Lord's Anointed	G
	437, 438	Tell out, my soul, the greatness of the Lord!	G
	543	O Zion, tune thy voice	C
Sequence:	630	Thanks to God, whose Word was spoken	L & G
	631	Book of books, our people's strength	L & G
	632	O Christ, the Word incarnate	L & G
	633	Word of God, come down on earth	G
	505	O Spirit of Life, O Spirit of God	L & G
Offertory:	71, 72	Hark! the glad sound! the Savior comes	G
	493	O for a thousand tongues to sing	G
	443	From God Christ's deity came forth	G
	536	God has spoken to his people	G
Communion:	321	My God, thy table now is spread	C
	332	O God, unseen yet ever near (sts. 3-4)	G
Postcommunion:	530	Spread, O spread, thou mighty word	C & G
	531	O Spirit of the living God	C
	437, 438	Tell out, my soul, the greatness of the Lord!	C & G
	539	O Zion, haste, thy mission high fulfilling	C & G

The Fourth Sunday After the Epiphany

Entrance:	440	Blessèd Jesus, at thy word	G
	437, 438	Tell out, my soul, the greatness of the Lord!	G
Sequence:	444	Blessed be the God of Israel	L & G
	359	God of the prophets, bless the prophets' heirs	L
	521	Put forth, O God, thy Spirit's might	E
	694	God be in my head	E
Offertory:	633	Word of God, come down on earth	G
	630	Thanks to God whose Word was spoken	G

	443	From God Christ's deity came forth	G
	457	Thou art the Way, to thee alone	G
	422	Not far beyond the sea, nor high	G
	448, 449	O love, how deep, how broad, how high	G
Communion:	332	O God, unseen yet ever near (sts. 3-4)	G
	302, 303	Father, we thank thee, who hast planted (st. 1)	G
	448, 449	O love, how deep, how broad, how high	G
Postcommunion:	530	Spread, O spread, thou mighty word	G
	380	From all that dwell below the skies	L & G
	437, 438	Tell out, my soul, the greatness of the Lord!	G

The Fifth Sunday After the Epiphany

	543	O Zion, tune thy voice	S
Entrance:	125, 126	The people who in darkness walked	S
	6, 7	Christ, whose glory fills the skies	S
	496, 497	How bright appears the Morning Star	S
Sequence:	452	Glorious the day when Christ was born	E
	448, 449	O love, how deep, how broad, how high	E
	671	Amazing grace! how sweet the sound	E
	686	Come, thou fount of every blessing	E
	455, 456	O Love of God, how strong and true	E
	706	In your mercy, Lord, you called me	E
	689	I sought the Lord, and afterward I knew	E
Offertory:	661	They cast their nets in Galilee	G
	643	My God, how wonderful thou art	G
Communion:	321	My God, thy table now is spread	G
	540	Awake, thou Spirit of the watchmen (sts. 2-3)	G
Postcommunion:	535	Ye servants of God, your Master proclaim	G
	530	Spread, O spread, thou mighty word	G
	539	O Zion, haste, thy mission high fulfilling	G
	537	Christ for the world we sing!	G

The Sixth Sunday After the Epiphany

	440	Blessèd Jesus, at thy word	G
Entrance:	6, 7	Christ, whose glory fills the skies	S
	496, 497	How bright appears the Morning Star	S
	125, 126	The people who in darkness walked	S
Sequence:	194, 195	Jesus lives! thy terrors now	E
	188, 189	Love's redeeming work is done	E
	635	If thou but trust in God to guide thee	L
	448, 449	O love, how deep, how broad, how high	E & G
Offertory:	437, 438	Tell out, my soul, the greatness of the Lord!	G
	560	Remember your servants, Lord	G

	74	Blest be the King whose coming	G
Communion:	448, 449	O love, how deep, how broad, how high	G
	339	Deck thyself, my soul, with gladness	S
	319	You, Lord, we praise in songs of celebration	S
Postcommunion:	437, 438	Tell out, my soul, the greatness of the Lord!	G
	448, 449	O love, how deep, how broad, how high	G

The Seventh Sunday After the Epiphany

Entrance:	3, 4	Now that the daylight fills the sky	C & G
	5	O Splendor of God's glory bright	C & G
Sequence:	621, 622	Light's abode, celestial Salem	E
	677	God moves in a mysterious way	L
	612	Gracious Spirit, Holy Ghost	G
Offertory:	593	Lord, make us servants of your peace	G
	674	"Forgive our sins as we forgive"	G
	568	Father all loving, who rulest in majesty	G
	603, 604	When Christ was lifted from the earth	G
	5	O Splendor of God's glory bright	G
Communion:	602	Jesu, Jesu, fill us with your love	G
	581	Where charity and love prevail	G
	576, 577	God is love, and where true love is	G
	606	Where true charity and love dwell	G
	304	I come with joy to meet my Lord	G
Postcommunion:	593	Lord, make us servants of your peace	G
	347	Go forth for God; go to the world in peace	G
	610	Lord, whose love through humble service	G

The Eighth Sunday After the Epiphany

Entrance:	440	Blessèd Jesus, at thy word	L & G
	125, 126	The people who in darkness walked	S
	496, 497	How bright appears the Morning Star	S
	6, 7	Christ, whose glory fills the skies	S
Sequence:	188, 189	Love's redeeming work is done	E
	621, 622	Light's abode, celestial Salem	E
	194, 195	Jesus lives! thy terrors now	E
Offertory:	636, 637	How firm a foundation, ye saints of the Lord	L & G
	634	I call on thee, Lord Jesus Christ	L & G
	628	Help us, O Lord, to learn	L & G
	626	Lord, be thy word my rule	L & G
Communion:	332	O God, unseen yet ever near (sts. 3-4)	L & G
	626	Lord, be thy word my rule	L & G

	634	I call on thee, Lord Jesus Christ	L & G
Postcommunion:	344	Lord, dismiss us with thy blessing	G
	392	Come, we that love the Lord	G
	628	Help us, O Lord, to learn	L & G

The Last Sunday After the Epiphany

Entrance:	135	Songs of thankfulness and praise	G
	427	When morning gilds the skies	S
	6, 7	Christ, whose glory fills the skies	S
Sequence:	133, 134	O Light of Light, Love given birth	C, L & G
	129, 130	Christ upon the mountain peak	C, L & G
	612	Gracious Spirit, Holy Ghost	E
Offertory:	129, 130	Christ upon the mountain peak	C, L & G
	136, 137	O wondrous type! O vision fair	C, L & G
Communion:	133, 134	O Light of Light, Love given birth	C, L & G
	460, 461	Alleluia! sing to Jesus! (omit sts. 2, 5)	S
	619	Sing alleluia forth in duteous praise	S
Postcommunion:	136, 137	O wondrous type! O vision fair	C, L & G
	122, 123	Alleluia, song of gladness	S
	135	Songs of thankfulness and praise	G

Ash Wednesday: *See Year A (above), p. 185*

The First Sunday in Lent

Entrance:	143	The glory of these forty days	C & G
	150	Forty days and forty nights	C & G
Sequence:	635	If thou but trust in God to guide thee	E
	393	Praise our great and gracious Lord	L
	146, 147	Now let us all with one accord	G
Offertory:	150	Forty days and forty nights	C & G
	142	Lord, who throughout these forty days	C & G
	443	From God Christ's deity came forth	G
Communion:	142	Lord, who throughout these forty days	C & G
	120	The sinless one to Jordan came (sts. 1-5)	C & G
Postcommunion:	142	Lord, who throughout these forty days	C & G
	559	Lead us, heavenly Father, lead us	C & G
	687, 688	A mighty fortress is our God	C & G
	563	Go forward, Christian soldier	C & G
	448, 449	O love, how deep, how broad, how high	G

The Second Sunday in Lent

Entrance:	401	The God of Abraham praise	L
	146, 147	Now let us all with one accord	L, E & G
	152	Kind Maker of the world, O hear	E & G
	709	O God of Bethel, by whose hand	L
Sequence:	146, 147	Now let us all with one accord	L, E & G
	152	Kind Maker of the world, O hear	E & G
Offertory:	590	O Jesus Christ, may grateful hymns be rising	G
	148	Creator of the earth and skies	E & G
	598	Lord Christ, when first thou cam'st to earth	G
	140, 141	Wilt thou forgive that sin, where I begun	G
Communion:	148	Creator of the earth and skies	E & G
	301	Bread of the world, in mercy broken	S
	715	When Jesus wept, the falling tear	G
Postcommunion:	598	Lord Christ, when first thou cam'st to earth	G
	590	O Jesus Christ, may grateful hymns be rising	G

The Third Sunday in Lent

Entrance:	401	The God of Abraham praise	L
	393	Praise our great and gracious Lord	L & E
	386, 387	We sing of God, the mighty source	L
	411	O bless the Lord, my soul!	P
Sequence:	152	Kind Maker of the world, O hear	E & G
	149	Eternal Lord of love, behold your Church	E
	685	Rock of ages, cleft for me	E
	142	Lord, who throughout these forty days	E
	150	Forty days and forty nights	E
	146, 147	Now let us all with one accord	E
	648	When Israel was in Egypt's land	L
Offertory:	148	Creator of the earth and skies	E & G
	574, 575	Before thy throne, O God, we kneel	E & G
Communion:	313	Let thy Blood in mercy poured	G
	308, 309	O Food to pilgrims given	E
	685	Rock of ages, cleft for me	E
	439	What wondrous love is this	L
Postcommunion:	344	Lord, dismiss us with thy blessing	G
	392	Come, we that love the Lord	G
	142	Lord, who throughout these forty days	E
	411	O bless the Lord, my soul	P

The Fourth Sunday in Lent

Entrance:	686	Come, thou fount of every blessing	G

	411	O bless the Lord, my soul!	G
	690	Guide me, O thou great Jehovah	L
	393	Praise our great and gracious Lord	L
Sequence:	489	The great Creator of the worlds	E
	471	We sing the praise of him who died	E
	298	All who believe and are baptized	E
	603, 604	When Christ was lifted from the earth	E
Offertory:	140, 141	Wilt thou forgive that sin, where I begun	E & G
	641	Lord Jesus, think on me	G
	144	Lord Jesus, Sun of Righteousness	E & G
	469, 470	There's a wideness in God's mercy	E & G
	467	Sing, my soul, his wondrous love	E & G
Communion:	313	Let thy Blood in mercy poured	G
	301	Bread of the world, in mercy broken	G
	693	Just as I am, without one plea	G
	318	Here, O my Lord, I see thee face to face	E & G
Postcommunion:	469, 470	There's a wideness in God's mercy	E & G
	411	O bless the Lord, my soul	G
	559	Lead us, heavenly Father, lead us	E & G

The Fifth Sunday in Lent

Entrance:	495	Hail, thou once despisèd Jesus!	G
	471	We sing the praise of him who died	E
	425	Sing now with joy unto the Lord	L
	678, 679	Surely it is God who saves me	L
Sequence:	474	When I survey the wondrous cross	E
	471	We sing the praise of him who died	E
Offertory:	598	Lord Christ, when first thou cam'st to earth	G
	495	Hail, thou once despisèd Jesus!	G
	170	To mock your reign, O dearest Lord	G
	160	Cross of Jesus, cross of sorrow	G
	165, 166	Sing, my tongue, the glorious battle	G
	161	The flaming banners of our King	G
	162	The royal banners forward go	G
	158	Ah, holy Jesus, how hast thou offended	G
Communion:	313	Let thy Blood in mercy poured	G
	337	And now, O Father, mindful of the love (sts. 1-2)	G
Postcommunion:	448, 449	O love, how deep, how broad, how high	E & G
	455, 456	O Love of God, how strong and true	E & G
	473	Lift high the cross	G

The Sunday of the Passion: Palm Sunday Through the Second Sunday of Easter: *See Year A (above), pp.188–196*

The Third Sunday of Easter

Entrance:	492	Sing, ye faithful, sing with gladness	G
	191	Alleluia, alleluia! Hearts and voices heavenward raise	S
	204	Now the green blade riseth from the buried grain	S
Sequence:	374	Come, let us join our cheerful songs	E
	417, 418	This is the feast of victory for our God	E
	439	What wondrous love is this	E
	213	Come away to the skies	E
	256	A light from heaven shone around	L (Acts)
	255	We sing the glorious conquest	L (Acts)
Offertory:	305, 306	Come, risen Lord, and deign to be our guest	G
	185, 186	Christ Jesus lay in death's strong bands	G
Communion:	185, 186	Christ Jesus lay in death's strong bands	G
	305, 306	Come, risen Lord, and deign to be our guest	G
	343	Shepherd of souls, refresh and bless	G
	460, 461	Alleluia! sing to Jesus! (omit sts. 2, 5)	E & G
Postcommunion:	188, 189	Love's redeeming work is done	S
	182	Christ is alive! Let Christians sing	S
	194, 195	Jesus lives! thy terrors now	S

The Fourth Sunday of Easter

Entrance:	205	Good Christians all, rejoice and sing!	L (Acts)
	184	Christ the Lord is risen again!	L (Acts)
	208	Alleluia, alleluia, alleluia! The strife is o'er	L (Acts)
	492	Sing, ye faithful, sing with gladness	L (Acts)
	399	To God with gladness sing	G
	377, 378	All people that on earth do dwell	P & G
	391	Before the Lord's eternal throne	P & G
Sequence:	181	Awake and sing the song	E
	439	What wondrous love is this	E
	275	Hark! the sound of holy voices	E
	455, 456	O love of God, how strong and true	L (Acts)
	448, 449	O love, how deep, how broad, how high	L (Acts)
Offertory:	478	Jesus, our mighty Lord	L (Acts) & G
	664	My Shepherd will supply my need	G
	663	The Lord my God my shepherd is	G
Communion:	645, 646	The King of love my shepherd is	G
	343	Shepherd of souls, refresh and bless	G
	320	Zion, praise thy Savior, singing (sts. 5-6)	G
Postcommunion:	708	Saviour, like a shepherd lead us	G

| | 478 | Jesus, our mighty Lord | L (Acts) & G |
| | 334 | Praise the Lord, rise up rejoicing | G |

The Fifth Sunday of Easter

Entrance:	48	O day of radiant gladness ͘ ᵒᵖ	E
	457	Thou art the Way, to thee alone	C
	492	Sing, ye faithful, sing with gladness	S
Sequence:	213	Come away to the skies	E
	439	What wondrous love is this ͘	E
	515	Holy Ghost, dispel our sadness	L (Acts)
Offertory:	603, 604	When Christ was lifted from the earth	G
	581	Where charity and love prevail	G
	576, 577	God is love, and where true love is	G
	606	Where true charity and love dwell	G
	529	In Christ there is no East or West ͘	G
	602	Jesu, Jesu, fill us with your love ͘	G
Communion:	202	The Lamb's high banquet called to share	E
	316, 317	This is the hour of banquet and of song	E
	487	Come, my Way, my Truth, my Life	C
	463, 464	He is the Way	C
Postcommunion:	582, 583	O holy city, seen of John	E & G
	300	Glory, love, and praise, and honor	E
	610	Lord, whose love through humble service	G

The Sixth Sunday of Easter

Entrance:	409	The spacious firmament on high	L (Acts)
	386, 387	We sing of God, the mighty source	L (Acts)
	405	All things bright and beautiful	L (Acts)
	385	Many and great, O God, are thy works	L (Acts)
	398	I sing the almighty power of God	L (Acts)
	651	This is my Father's world	L (Acts)
	291	We plow the fields and scatter	L (Acts)
	292	O Jesus, crowned with all renown	S
Sequence:	538	God of mercy, God of grace	P & E
	374	Come, let us join our cheerful songs	E
	181	Awake and sing the song	E
	452	Glorious the day when Christ was born	E
	417, 418	This is the feast of victory for our God	E
Offertory:	513	Like the murmur of the dove's song	G
	512	Come, gracious Spirit, heavenly Dove	G
	505	O Spirit of Life, O Spirit of God	G
Communion:	505	O Spirit of Life, O Spirit of God	G
	439	What wondrous love is this	E

	712	Dona nobis pacem	G
Postcommunion:	535	Ye servants of God, your Master proclaim	E
	181	Awake and sing the song	E
	345	Savior, again to thy dear Name we raise	G
	292	O Jesus, crowned with all renown	S

Ascension Day: *See Year A (above), p. 198*

The Seventh Sunday of Easter: The Sunday After Ascension Day

Entrance:	450, 451	All hail the power of Jesus' Name!	S
	492	Sing, ye faithful, sing with gladness	S
	495	Hail, thou once despisèd Jesus!	S
Sequence:	481	Rejoice, the Lord is King	S
	435	At the Name of Jesus	S
Offertory:	484, 485	Praise the Lord through every nation	S
	483	The head that once was crowned with thorns	S
	495	Hail, thou once despisèd Jesus!	S
Communion:	327, 328	Draw nigh and take the Body of the Lord	E
	315	Thou, who at thy first Eucharist didst pray	G
	307	Lord, enthroned in heavenly splendor	S
	460, 461	Alleluia! sing to Jesus!	S
Postcommunion:	495	Hail, thou once despisèd Jesus!	S
	494	Crown him with many crowns	S

The Day of Pentecost — Early or Vigil Service: *See Year A (above), p. 199*

The Day of Pentecost — Principal Service: *See Year A (above), p. 200*

The First Sunday after Pentecost: Trinity Sunday

Entrance:	367	Round the Lord in glory seated	L & E
	362	Holy, holy, holy! Lord God Almighty!	L & E
	366	Holy God, we praise thy Name	L & E
	364	O God, we praise thee, and confess	L & E
	401	The God of Abraham praise	L & E
Sequence:	366	Holy God, we praise thy Name	L & E
	364	O God, we praise thee, and confess	L & E
Offertory:	369	How wondrous great, how glorious bright	L & E
	401	The God of Abraham praise	L & E

Communion:	421	All glory be to God on high	S
	295	Sing praise to our Creator	S
Postcommunion:	370	I bind unto myself today	S
	363	Ancient of Days, who sittest throned in glory	S
	368	Holy Father, great Creator	S

Propers 1, 2 & 3: *See 6, 7 & 8* Epiphany *for these same lections (If the Sunday between May 24 and 28 inclusive follows Trinity Sunday, use Proper 3 [Epiphany 8] on that day).*

Proper 4 *(Sunday between May 29 & June 4 inclusive, if after Trinity Sunday)*

Entrance:	518	Christ is made the sure foundation	L & E
	440	Blessèd Jesus, at thy word	L & E
Sequence:	634	I call on thee, Lord Jesus Christ	E & G
	626	Lord, be thy word my rule	E
	530	Spread, O spread, thou mighty word	E
	381	Thy strong word did cleave the darkness	E
Offertory:	493	O for a thousand tongues to sing	E & G
	567	Thine arm, O Lord, in days of old	G
Communion:	567	Thine arm, O Lord, in days of old	G
	538	God of mercy, God of grace	E & G
Postcommunion:	371	Thou, whose almighty Word	E & G
	380	From all that dwell below the skies	L & G
	530	Spread, O spread, thou mighty word	E
	381	Thy strong word did cleave the darkness	E

Proper 5 *(Sunday between June 5 & 11 inclusive, if after Trinity Sunday)*

Entrance:	411	O bless the Lord, my soul!	L & C
	448, 449	O love, how deep, how broad, how high	G
	52	This day at thy creating word	S
	49	Come, let us with our Lord arise	S
	48	O day of radiant gladness	S
	50	This is the day the Lord hath made	S
	47	On this day, the first of days	S
Sequence:	256	A light from heaven shone around	E
	255	We sing the glorious conquest	E
Offertory:	493	O for a thousand tongues to sing	G
	567	Thine arm, O Lord, in days of old	G
Communion:	567	Thine arm, O Lord, in days of old	G
	566	From thee all skill and science flow	G
	302, 303	Father, we thank thee who hast planted (st. 1)	G
	327, 328	Draw nigh and take the Body of the Lord	G

Postcommunion:	346	Completed, Lord, the Holy Mysteries	G
	411	O bless the Lord, my soul!	L & G
	448, 449	O love, how deep, how broad, how high	G

Proper 6 *(Sunday between June 12 and 18 inclusive, if after Trinity Sunday)*

Entrance:	410	Praise, my soul, the King of heaven	G
	411	O bless the Lord, my soul!	G
Sequence:	495	Hail, thou once despisèd Jesus!	E
	697	My God, accept my heart this day	E
	432	O praise ye the Lord! praise him in the height (omit st. 3)	E
Offertory:	643	My God, how wonderful thou art	G
	641	Lord Jesus, think on me	G
	382	King of glory, King of peace	G
	691	My faith looks up to thee	E & G
Communion:	301	Bread of the world, in mercy broken	G
	313	Let thy Blood in mercy poured	G
	318	Here, O my Lord, I see thee face to face	E & G
	337	And now, O Father, mindful of the love (sts. 1-2)	E & G
Postcommunion:	411	O bless the Lord, my soul!	G
	410	Praise, my soul, the King of heaven	G
	469, 470	There's a wideness in God's mercy	G

Proper 7 *(Sunday between June 19 and 25 inclusive, if after Trinity Sunday)*

Entrance:	678, 679	Surely it is God who saves me	L
	686	Come, thou fount of every blessing	L
	450, 451	All hail the power of Jesus' Name!	C
	248, 249	To the Name of our salvation	C
Sequence:	295	Sing praise to our Creator	E
	294	Baptized in water	E
	432	O praise ye the Lord! praise him in the height (omit st. 3)	E
	298	All who believe and are baptized	E
	296	We know that Christ is raised and dies no more	E
Offertory:	254	You are the Christ, O Lord	G
	443	From God Christ's deity came forth	G
	675	Take up your cross, the Savior said	G
Communion:	254	You are the Christ, O Lord	G
	654	Day by day	G
	10	New every morning is the love	G

Postcommunion:	484, 485	Praise the Lord through every nation	G
	675	Take up your cross, the Savior said	G
	572	Weary of all trumpeting	G

Proper 8 *(Sunday between June 26 and July 2 inclusive)*

Entrance:	518	Christ is made the sure foundation	C
	525	The Church's one foundation	C
	521	Put forth, O God, thy Spirit's might	C
Sequence:	513	Like the murmur of the dove's song	E
	697	My God, accept my heart this day	E
	500	Creator Spirit, by whose aid	E
	359	God of the prophets, bless the prophets' heirs	L
Offertory:	458	My song is love unknown	G
	655	O Jesus, I have promised	G
	564, 565	He who would valiant be	G
	559	Lead us, heavenly Father, lead us	G
	478	Jesus, our mighty Lord	G
	549, 550	Jesus calls us; o'er the tumult	G
Communion:	308, 309	O Food to pilgrims given	G
	654	Day by day	G
Postcommunion:	478	Jesus, our mighty Lord	G
	564, 565	He who would valiant be	G
	655	O Jesus, I have promised	G

Proper 9 *(Sunday between July 3 and 9 inclusive)*

Entrance:	522, 523	Glorious things of thee are spoken	L
	543	O Zion, tune thy voice	L
Sequence:	483	The head that once was crowned with thorns	E
	441, 442	In the cross of Christ I glory	E
	474	When I survey the wondrous cross	E
	434	Nature with open volume stands	E
	471	We sing the praise of him who died	E
	176, 177	Over the chaos of the empty waters	E
	296	We know that Christ is raised and dies no more	E
Offertory:	540	Awake, thou Spirit of the watchmen (sts. 2-3)	G
	541	Come, labor on	G
	528	Lord, you give the great commission	G
Communion:	321	My God, thy table now is spread	G
	531	O Spirit of the living God	G
Postcommunion:	540	Awake, thou Spirit of the watchmen (sts. 2-3)	G
	541	Come, labor on	G
	528	Lord, you give the great commission	G

544	Jesus shall reign, where'er the sun	G
535	Ye servants of God, your Master proclaim	G
539	O Zion, haste, thy mission high fulfilling	G

Proper 10 *(Sunday between July 10 and 16 inclusive)*

Entrance:	431	The stars declare his glory	L
	372	Praise to the living God!	L
	392	Come, we that love the Lord	E
	376	Joyful, joyful, we adore thee	G
Sequence:	467	Sing, my soul, his wondrous love	E
	495	Hail, thou once despisèd Jesus!	E
	326	From glory to glory advancing, we praise thee, O Lord	E
	657	Love divine, all loves excelling	E
Offertory:	581	Where charity and love prevail	G
	551	Rise up, ye saints of God!	G
	602	Jesu, Jesu, fill us with your love	G
	603, 604	When Christ was lifted from the earth	G
	568	Father all loving, who rulest in majesty	G
Communion:	602	Jesu, Jesu, fill us with your love	G
	304	I come with joy to meet my Lord	G
Postcommunion:	610	Lord, whose love through humble service	G
	609	Where cross the crowded ways of life	G
	590	O Jesus Christ, may grateful hymns be rising	G
	344	Lord, dismiss us with thy blessing	E

Proper 11 *(Sunday between July 17 and 23 inclusive)*

Entrance:	401	The God of Abraham praise	L
	440	Blessèd Jesus, at thy word	E & G
	52	This day at thy creating word	S
	48	O day of radiant gladness	S
	49	Come, let us with our Lord arise	S
Sequence:	495	Hail, thou once despisèd Jesus! (sts. 1, 2 & 4)	E
	440	Blessèd Jesus, at thy word	E & G
Offertory:	642	Jesus, the very thought of thee	G
	701	Jesus, all my gladness	G
	488	Be thou my vision, O Lord of my heart	G
	626	Lord, be thy word my rule	E
Communion:	314	Humbly I adore thee, Verity unseen	G
	487	Come, my Way, my Truth, my Life	G
Postcommunion:	316, 317	This is the hour of banquet and of song	G
	336	Come with us, O blessèd Jesus	G
	382	King of glory, King of peace	G

Proper 12 *(Sunday between July 24 and 30 inclusive)*

Entrance:	432	O praise ye the Lord! praise him in the height	E
	47	On this day, the first of days	E
	518	Christ is made the sure foundation	G
	360, 361	Only-begotten, Word of God eternal	G
	411	O bless the Lord, my soul!	L
	410	Praise, my soul, the King of heaven	L
	52	This day at thy creating word	E & G
	49	Come, let us with our Lord arise	E & G
Sequence:	294	Baptized in water	E
	298	All who believe and are baptized	E
	296	We know that Christ is raised and dies no more	E
	432	O praise ye the Lord! Praise him in the height (omit st. 3)	E
Offertory:	709	O God of Bethel, by whose hand	G
	698	Eternal Spirit of the living Christ	G
Communion:	711	— Seek ye first the kingdom of God	G
	698	Eternal Spirit of the living Christ	G
	337	And now, O Father, mindful of the love	G
	338	Wherefore, O Father, we thy humble servants	G
Postcommunion:	709	O God of Bethel, by whose hand	G
	10	New every morning is the love	G

Proper 13 *(Sunday between July 31 and August 5 inclusive; August 6 is celebrated as the Feast of the Transfiguration [See below, p. 269])*

Entrance:	426	Songs of praise the angels sang	E
	420	When in our music God is glorified	E
	408	Sing praise to God who reigns above	E
	430	Come, O come, our voices raise	E
Sequence:	674	"Forgive our sins as we forgive"	E
	581	Where charity and love prevail	E
	576, 577	God is Love, and where true love is	E
	606	Where true charity and love dwell	E
Offertory:	574, 575	Before thy throne, O God, we kneel	L, E & G
	665	All my hope on God is founded (sts. 1-2)	L & G
	701	Jesus, all my gladness (sts. 1-2)	L & G
Communion:	701	Jesus, all my gladness (sts. 1-2)	L & G
	574, 575	Before thy throne, O God, we kneel	L, E & G
Postcommunion:	665	All my hope on God is founded (sts. 1-2)	L & G
	582, 583	O holy city, seen of John	L, E & G

Proper 14 *(Sunday between August 7 and 13 inclusive)*

Entrance:	401	The God of Abraham praise	L & E
	393	Praise our great and gracious Lord	E
	636, 637	How firm a foundation, ye saints of the Lord	E
Sequence:	369	How wondrous great, how glorious bright	E
	709	O God of Bethel, by whose hand	E
	635	If thou but trust in God to guide thee	E
	545	Lo! what a cloud of witnesses	E
	634	I call on thee, Lord Jesus Christ	E
Offertory:	68	Rejoice! rejoice, believers	G
	701	Jesus, all my gladness	G
Communion:	701	Jesus, all my gladness	G
	316, 317	This is the hour of banquet and of song	G
Postcommunion:	61, 62	"Sleepers, wake!" A voice astounds us	G
	68	Rejoice! rejoice, believers	G

Proper 15 *(Sunday between August 14 and 20 inclusive)*

Entrance:	366	Holy God, we praise thy Name	E
	364	O God, we praise thee, and confess	E
	421	All glory be to God on high	E
	495	Hail, thou once despisèd Jesus!	E
	636, 637	How firm a foundation, ye saints of the Lord	E
Sequence:	545	Lo! what a cloud of witnesses	E
	546	Awake, my soul, stretch every nerve	E
	253	Give us the wings of faith to rise	E
	552, 553	Fight the good fight with all thy might (sts. 1-2)	E
	483	The head that once was crowned with thorns	E
	635	If thou but trust in God to guide thee	E
Offertory:	596	Judge eternal, throned in splendor	L & G
	574, 575	Before thy throne, O God, we kneel	L, E & G
	661	They cast their nets in Galilee	G
Communion:	324	Let all mortal flesh keep silence	S
	314	Humbly I adore thee, Verity unseen	S
	319	You, Lord, we praise in songs of celebration	S
Postcommunion:	596	Judge eternal, throned in splendor	L & G
	574, 575	Before thy throne, O God, we kneel	L & G

Proper 16 *(Sunday between August 21 and 27 inclusive)*

Entrance:	518	Christ is made the sure foundation	L
	525	The Church's one foundation	C & L
	521	Put forth, O God, thy Spirit's might	C

	24	The day thou gavest, Lord, is ended (In the morning omit st. 1)	C
Sequence:	368	Holy Father, great Creator	E
	687, 688	A mighty fortress is our God	P
	623	O what their joy and their glory must be	E
	624	Jerusalem the golden	E
Offertory:	339	Deck thyself, my soul, with gladness	G
	11	Awake, my soul, and with the sun	G
	10	New every morning is the love	G
Communion:	321	My God, thy table now is spread	G
	316, 317	This is the hour of banquet and of song	G
	300	Glory, love, and praise, and honor	G
Postcommunion:	380	From all that dwell below the skies	G
	346	Completed, Lord, the Holy Mysteries	G
	344	Lord, dismiss us with thy blessing	G

Proper 17 *(Sunday between August 28 and September 3 inclusive)*

Entrance:	477	All praise to thee, for thou, O King divine	C, L & G
	435	At the Name of Jesus	C
	450, 451	All hail the power of Jesus' Name!	C
	248, 249	To the Name of our salvation	C
	644	How sweet the Name of Jesus sounds	C
Sequence:	614	Christ is the King! O friends upraise	E
	636, 637	How firm a foundation, ye saints of the Lord	E
	279	For thy dear saints, O Lord	E
	545	Lo! what a cloud of witnesses	E
	610	Lord, whose love through humble service	E
Offertory:	477	All praise to thee, for thou, O King divine	C, L & G
	656	Blest are the pure in heart	L & G
Communion:	656	Blest are the pure in heart	L & G
	321	My God, thy table now is spread	G
	320	Zion, praise thy Savior, singing	G
Postcommunion:	437, 438	Tell out, my soul, the greatness of the Lord!	L & G
	656	Blest are the pure in heart	L & G
	344	Lord, dismiss us with thy blessing	C

Proper 18 *(Sunday between September 4 and 10 inclusive)*

Entrance:	400	All creatures of our God and King	E
	406, 407	Most High, omnipotent, good Lord	E
	376	Joyful, joyful, we adore thee	E

	394, 395	Creating God, your fingers trace	E
Sequence:	603, 604	When Christ was lifted from the earth	E
	581	Where charity and love prevail	E
	576, 577	God is love, and where true love is	E
	606	Where true charity and love dwell	E
Offertory:	675	Take up your cross, the Savior said	G
	484, 485	Praise the Lord through every nation	G
Communion:	10	New every morning is the love	G
	484, 485	Praise the Lord through every nation	G
Postcommunion:	484, 485	Praise the Lord through every nation	G
	675	Take up your cross, the Savior said	G
	347	Go forth for God; go to the world in peace	E

Proper 19 *(Sunday between September 11 and 17 inclusive)*

Entrance:	363	Ancient of Days, who sittest throned in glory	L, E & G
	423	Immortal, invisible, God only wise	E
	401	The God of Abraham praise	L
	393	Praise our great and gracious Lord	L
	410	Praise, my soul, the King of heaven	L, E & G
	411	O bless the Lord, my soul!	L, E & G
Sequence:	489	The great Creator of the worlds	E
	439	What wondrous love is this	E
	458	My song is love unknown	E
Offertory:	645, 646	The King of love my shepherd is	G
	706	In your mercy, Lord, you called me	G
	689	I sought the Lord, and afterward I knew	G
	469, 470	There's a wideness in God's mercy	G
Communion:	645, 646	The King of love my shepherd is	G
	706	In your mercy, Lord, you called me	G
	469, 470	There's a wideness in God's mercy	G
Postcommunion:	448, 449	O love, how deep, how broad, how high	L, E & G
	411	O bless the Lord, my soul!	L, E & G
	410	Praise, my soul, the King of heaven	L, E & G

Proper 20 *(Sunday between September 18 and 24 inclusive)*

Entrance:	596	Judge, eternal, throned in splendor	L
	49	Come, let us with our Lord arise	S
	48	O day of radiant gladness	S
	47	On this day, the first of days	S
	52	This day at thy creating word	S

	50	This is the day the Lord hath made	S
	51	We the Lord's people, heart and voice uniting	S
Sequence:	368	Holy Father, great Creator	E
	628	Help us, O Lord, to learn	S
	626	Lord, be thy word my rule	S
Offertory:	488	Be thou my vision, O Lord of my heart	G
	707	Take my life, and let it be	G
Communion:	488	Be thou my vision, O Lord of my heart	G
	701	Jesus, all my gladness (sts. 1-2)	G
	475	God himself is with us (sts. 1-2)	G
Postcommunion:	701	Jesus, all my gladness (sts. 1-2)	G
	475	God himself is with us (sts. 1-2)	G

Proper 21 *(Sunday between September 25 and October 1 inclusive)*

Entrance:	429	I'll praise my Maker while I've breath	P
	437, 438	Tell out, my soul, the greatness of the Lord!	G
	423	Immortal, invisible, God only wise	E
	546	Awake, my soul, stretch every nerve	C
	545	Lo! what a cloud of witnesses	C
Sequence:	552, 553	Fight the good fight with all thy might (sts. 1-2)	C & E
	574, 575	Before thy throne, O God, we kneel	L, E & G
Offertory:	609	Where cross the crowded ways of life	G
	574, 575	Before thy throne, O God, we kneel	L, E & G
	582, 583	O holy city, seen of John	L, E & G
Communion:	574, 575	Before thy throne, O God, we kneel	L, E & G
	300	Glory, love, and praise, and honor	S
	320	Zion, praise thy Savior, singing	S
Postcommunion:	623	O what their joy and their glory must be	G
	437, 438	Tell out, my soul, the greatness of the Lord	G
	346	Completed, Lord, the Holy Mysteries	G
	494	Crown him with many crowns	G

Proper 22 *(Sunday between October 2 and 8 inclusive)*

Entrance:	518	Christ is made the sure foundation	C
	360, 361	Only-begotten, Word of God eternal	C
	698	Eternal Spirit of the living Christ	C
Sequence:	151	From deepest woe I cry to thee	E
	704	O thou who camest from above	E
	669	Commit thou all that grieves thee	P
Offertory:	541	Come, labor on	G

	551	Rise up, ye saints of God!	G
	11	Awake, my soul, and with the sun	G
Communion:	655	O Jesus, I have promised	G
	659, 660	O Master, let me walk with thee	G
Postcommunion:	610	Lord, whose love through humble service	G
	541	Come, labor on	G
	312	Strengthen for service, Lord	G

Proper 23 (Sunday between October 9 and 15 inclusive)

	390	Praise to the Lord, the Almighty	G
Entrance:	390	Praise to the Lord, the Almighty	G
	410	Praise, my soul, the King of heaven	G
	411	O bless the Lord, my soul!	G
	1, 2	Father, we praise thee, now the night is over	G
Sequence:	483	The head that once was crowned with thorns	E
	548	Soldiers of Christ, arise	E
	561	Stand up, stand up for Jesus	E
	552, 553	Fight the good fight with all thy might (sts. 1-2)	E
	563	Go forward, Christian soldier	E
Offertory:	415	When all thy mercies, O my God	G
	567	Thine arm, O Lord, in days of old	G
	493	O for a thousand tongues to sing	G
Communion:	415	When all thy mercies, O my God	G
	567	Thine arm, O Lord, in days of old	G
Postcommunion:	396, 397	Now thank we all our God	G
	538	God of mercy, God of grace	G
	411	O bless the Lord, my soul!	G

Proper 24 (Sunday between October 16 and 22 inclusive)

	668	I to the hills will lift mine eyes	P
Entrance:	668	I to the hills will lift mine eyes	P
	638, 639	Come, O thou Traveler unknown	L
	478	Jesus, our mighty Lord	C
	421	All glory be to God on high	E
	366	Holy God, we praise thy Name	E
	364	O God, we praise thee, and confess	E
Sequence:	638, 639	Come, O thou Traveler unknown	L
	628	Help us, O Lord, to learn	E
	627	Lamp of our feet, whereby we trace	E
	631	Book of books, our people's strength	E
	630	Thanks to God whose Word was spoken	E
Offertory:	709	O God of Bethel, by whose hand	G
	698	Eternal Spirit of the living Christ	G

	711	Seek ye first the kingdom of God	G

Communion:	711	Seek ye first the kingdom of God	G
	695, 696	By gracious powers so wonderfully sheltered	G
	337	And now, O Father, mindful of the love	G
	698	Eternal Spirit of the living Christ	G

Postcommunion:	530	Spread, O spread, thou mighty word	E
	709	O God of Bethel, by whose hand	G
	10	New every morning is the love	G

Proper 25 *(Sunday between October 23 and 29 inclusive)*

Entrance:	517	How lovely is thy dwelling-place	P
	665	All my hope on God is founded	L

Sequence:	552, 553	Fight the good fight with all thy might (sts. 1 & 2)	E
	555	Lead on, O King eternal	E
	561	Stand up, stand up for Jesus	E
	636, 637	How firm a foundation, ye saints of the Lord	E

Offertory:	670	Lord, for ever at thy side	G
	641	Lord Jesus, think on me	L & G
	140, 141	Wilt thou forgive that sin, where I begun	L & G
	656	Blest are the pure in heart	G

Communion:	301	Bread of the world, in mercy broken	L & G
	313	Let thy Blood in mercy poured	L & G

Postcommunion:	437, 438	Tell out, my soul, the greatness of the Lord!	G
	665	All my hope on God is founded	L
	636, 637	How firm a foundation, ye saints of the Lord	E

Proper 26 *(October 30 or 31 or Sunday between November 2 & 5 inclusive; November 1 is celebrated as All Saints' Day, and the Sunday between November 2 and 7 inclusive may be also [See below, p. 273])*

Entrance:	605	What does the Lord require	L
	545	Lo! what a cloud of witnesses	C
	546	Awake, my soul, stretch every nerve	C
	552, 553	Fight the good fight with all thy might	C

Sequence:	704	O thou who camest from above	E
	634	I call on thee, Lord Jesus Christ	E

Offertory:	489	The great Creator of the worlds	G
	448, 449	O love, how deep, how broad, how high	G
	643	My God, how wonderful thou art	G
	641	Lord Jesus, think on me	G

Communion:	301	Bread of the world, in mercy broken	L & G
	313	Let thy Blood in mercy poured	L & G

	318	Here, O my Lord, I see thee face to face	L
	337	And now, O Father, mindful of the love	L
Postcommunion:	469, 470	There's a wideness in God's mercy	L &
	410	Praise, my soul, the King of heaven	L & G
	411	O bless the Lord, my soul!	L & G
	382	King of glory, King of peace	L & G

Proper 27 (Sunday between November 6 and 12 inclusive; an additional celebration of All Saints' Day may be held on Sunday November 6 or 7 [See below, p. 273])

Entrance:	574, 575	Before thy throne, O God, we kneel	C
	526	Let saints on earth in concert sing	G
Sequence:	194, 195	Jesus lives! thy terrors now	L
	188, 189	Love's redeeming work is done	L
Offertory:	401	The God of Abraham praise	G
	526	Let saints on earth in concert sing	G
Communion:	526	Let saints on earth in concert sing	G
	340, 341	For the bread which you have broken	G
Postcommunion:	623	O what their joy and their glory must be	G
	620	Jerusalem, my happy home	G
	621, 622	Light's abode, celestial Salem	G
	624	Jerusalem the golden	G
	326	From glory to glory advancing, we praise thee, O Lord	G

Proper 28 (Sunday between November 13 and 19 inclusive)

Entrance:	596	Judge eternal, throned in splendor	L
	6, 7	Christ, whose glory fills the skies	L
	371	Thou, whose almighty Word	L
	462	The Lord will come and not be slow	L & G
Sequence:	63, 64	O heavenly Word, eternal Light	E
	11	Awake, my soul, and with the sun	E
	454	Jesus came, adored by angels	E
	413	New songs of celebration render	P
Offertory:	53	Once he came in blessing	G
	635	If thou but trust in God to guide thee	G
	600, 601	O day of God, draw nigh	G
Communion:	672	O very God of very God	L & G
	615	"Thy kingdom come!" on bended knee	G
	490	I want to walk as a child of the light	L
Postcommunion:	615	"Thy kingdom come!" on bended knee	G
	672	O very God of very God	L & G

Entrance:	399	To God with gladness sing	L
	478	Jesus, our mighty Lord	L
	616	Hail to the Lord's Anointed	S
	450, 451	All hail the power of Jesus' Name!	S
Sequence:	326	From glory to glory advancing, we praise thee, O Lord	E
	421	All glory be to God on high	E
Offertory:	170	To mock your reign, O dearest Lord	G (Lk 23)
	598	Lord Christ, when first thou cam'st to earth	G (Lk 23)
	483	The head that once was crowned with thorns (sts. 1-2)	G (Lk 23)
	495	Hail, thou once despisèd Jesus!	G (Lk 23)
	458	My song is love unknown	G (Lk 23 or 19)
	74	Blest be the King whose coming	G (Lk 19)
	71, 72	Hark! the glad sound! the Savior comes	G (Lk 19)
	65	Prepare the way, O Zion	G (Lk 19)
	486	Hosanna to the living Lord!	G (Lk 19)
	436	Lift up your heads, ye mighty gates	G (Lk 19)
Communion:	324	Let all mortal flesh keep silence	S
	460, 461	Alleluia! sing to Jesus! (omit sts. 2, 5)	S
Postcommunion:	481	Rejoice, the Lord is King	S
	494	Crown him with many crowns	S
	544	Jesus shall reign where'er the sun	S
	614	Christ is the King! O friends upraise	S

Holy Days

Saint Andrew the Apostle (November 30)

Entrance:	231, 232	By all your saints still striving	G
	233, 234	The eternal gifts of Christ the King	S
	366	Holy God, we praise thy Name	S
	364	O God, we praise thee, and confess	S
Sequence:	233, 234	The eternal gifts of Christ the King	S
	238, 239	Blessèd feasts of blessèd martyrs	S
Offertory:	549, 550	Jesus calls us; o'er the tumult	G
	240, 241	Hearken to the anthem glorious	S
	236	King of the martyrs' noble band	S
	237	Let us now our voices raise	S
Communion:	321	My God, thy table now is spread	G

	340, 341	For the bread which you have brokern	S
	326	From glory to glory advancing, we praise thee, O Lord	S
Postcommunion:	549, 550	Jesus calls us; o'er the tumult	G
	614	Christ is the King! O friends upraise	G
	530	Spread, O spread, thou mighty word	G

Saint Thomas the Apostle (December 21)

Entrance:	231, 232	By all your saints still striving	G
	57, 58	Lo! he comes, with clouds descending	G
	233, 234	The eternal gifts of Christ the King	S
Sequence:	233, 234	The eternal gifts of Christ the King	S
	238, 239	Blessèd feasts of blessèd martyrs	S
	237	Let us now our voices raise	S
	240, 241	Hearken to the anthem glorious	S
	236	King of the martyrs' noble band	S
Offertory:	242	How oft, O Lord, thy face hath shone	G
	209	We walk by faith, and not by sight	G
	206	O sons and daughters, let us sing *Second Sunday of Easter and St. Thomas' Day*	G
Communion:	314	Humbly I adore thee, Verity unseen	G
	242	How oft, O Lord, thy face hath shone	G
Postcommunion:	209	We walk by faith, and not by sight	G
	57, 58	Lo! he comes, with clouds descending	G
	193	That Easter day with joy was bright (sts. 1-3 & 5)	G

Saint Stephen, Deacon and Martyr (December 26)

Entrance:	231, 232	By all your saints still striving	E
	238, 239	Blessèd feasts of blessèd martyrs	E
Sequence:	243	When Stephen, full of power and grace	E
	240, 241	Hearken to the anthem glorious	E
Offertory:	240, 241	Hearken to the anthem glorious	E
	243	When Stephen, full of power and grace	E
Communion	545	Lo! what a cloud of witnesses	E
	340, 341	For the bread which you have broken	S
	326	From glory to glory advancing, we praise thee, O Lord	S
Postcommunion:	236	King of the martyrs' noble band	S
	240, 241	Hearken to the anthem glorious	E
	237	Let us now our voices raise	E
	545	Lo! what a cloud of witnesses	S

Saint John, Apostle and Evangelist (December 27)

Entrance:	231, 232	By all your saints still striving	G
	366	Holy God, we praise thy Name	S
	364	O God, we praise thee, and confess	S
Sequence:	233, 234	The eternal gifts of Christ the King	S
	244	Come, pure hearts, in joyful measure	S
	235	Come sing, ye choirs exultant	S
Offertory:	245	Praise God for John, evangelist	G
	661	They cast their nets in Galilee	S
	235	Come sing, ye choirs exultant	S
	631	Book of books, our people's strength	S
	630	Thanks to God whose Word was spoken	S
	632	O Christ, the Word incarnate	S
Communion:	661	They cast their nets in Galilee	S
	340, 341	For the bread which you have broken	S
	326	From glory to glory advancing, we praise thee, O Lord	S
Postcommunion:	245	Praise God for John, evangelist	G
	614	Christ is the King! O friends upraise	S
	235	Come sing, ye choirs exultant	S
	630	Thanks to God whose Word was spoken	S
	632	O Christ, the Word incarnate	S

The Holy Innocents (December 28)

Entrance:	231, 232	By all your saints still striving	G
	98	Unto us a boy is born!	G
Sequence:	582, 583	O holy city, seen of John	E
	247	Lully, lullay, thou little tiny child	G
Offertory	246	In Bethlehem a newborn boy	C & G
	247	Lully, lullay, thou little tiny child	G
	98	Unto us a boy is born!	G
Communion:	246	In Bethlehem a newborn boy	G
	113	Oh, sleep now, holy baby (Duérmete, Niño lindo)	G
	324	Let all mortal flesh keep silence	S
Postcommunion:	246	In Bethlehem a newborn boy	G
	98	Unto us a boy is born!	G
	618	Ye watchers and ye holy ones	S

The Confession of Saint Peter the Apostle (January 18)

Entrance:	231, 232	By all your saints still striving	S
	496, 497	How bright appears the Morning Star	S

	233, 234	The eternal gifts of Christ the King	S
	366	Holy God, we praise thy Name	S
	364	O God, we praise thee, and confess	S
Sequence:	518	Christ is made the sure foundation	L & G
	525	The Church's one foundation	L & G
	521	Put forth, O God, thy Spirit's might	L & G
Offertory:	254	You are the Christ, O Lord	G
	443	From God Christ's deity came forth	G
Communion:	254	You are the Christ, O Lord	G
	324	Let all mortal flesh keep silence	S
Postcommunion:	254	You are the Christ, O Lord	G
	521	Put forth, O God, thy Spirit's might	L & G
	614	Christ is the King! O friends upraise	S

Conversion of Saint Paul the Apostle (January 25)

Entrance:	231, 232	By all your saints still striving	L & E
	538	God of mercy, God of grace	P
Sequence:	255	We sing the glorious conquest	L & E
	256	A light from heaven shone around	L & E
Offertory:	256	A light from heaven shone around	L & E
	255	We sing the glorious conquest	L & E
Communion:	302, 303	Father, we thank thee, who hast planted (st. 1)	S
	318	Here, O my Lord, I see thee face to face	S
Postcommunion:	530	Spread, O spread, thou mighty word	G
	531	O Spirit of the living God	G
	671	Amazing grace ! how sweet the sound	S
	689	I sought the Lord, and afterward I knew	S
	706	In your mercy, Lord, you called me	S

The Presentation of Our Lord Jesus Christ in the Temple (February 2)

Entrance:	259	Hail to the Lord who comes	G
	257	O Zion, open wide thy gates	G
	93	Angels, from the realms of glory	G
Sequence:	496, 497	How bright appears the Morning Star	E
	277	Sing of Mary, pure and lowly	E
	489	The great Creator of the worlds (sts. 1-4)	E
Offertory:	257	O Zion, open wide thy gates	G
	259	Hail to the Lord who comes	G

	278	Sing we of the blessèd Mother	G
Communion:	324	Let all mortal flesh keep silence	G
	656	Blest are the pure in heart	G
Postcommunion:	499	Lord God, you now have set your servant free	G
	258	Virgin-born, we bow before thee	G
	6, 7	Christ, whose glory fills the skies	G

Saint Matthias The Apostle (February 24)

Entrance:	231, 232	By all your saints still striving	L
	233, 234	The eternal gifts of Christ the King	S
Sequence:	546	Awake, my soul, stretch every nerve	E
	545	Lo! what a cloud of witnesses	E
	359	God of the prophets, bless the prophets' heirs	L
Offertory;	359	God of the prophets, bless the prophets' heirs	L
	233, 234	The eternal gifts of Christ the King	S
	238, 239	Blessèd feasts of blessèd martyrs	S
Communion:	340, 341	For the bread which you have broken	S
	545	Lo! what a cloud of witnesses	E
	326	From glory to glory advancing, we praise thee, O Lord	S
	323	Bread of heaven, on thee we feed	G
Postcommunion	240, 241	Hearken to the anthem glorious	S
	237	Let us now our voices raise	S
	236	King of the martyrs' noble band	S
	625	Ye holy angels bright	S

Saint Joseph (March 19)

Entrance:	231, 232	By all your saints still striving	G
	260	Come now, and praise the humble saint	G
Sequence:	260	Come now, and praise the humble saint	G
	279	For thy dear saints, O Lord	S
Offertory:	261, 262	By the Creator, Joseph was appointed	G
	260	Come now, and praise the humble saint	G
	611	Christ the worker	G
Communion	611	Christ the worker	G
	340, 341	For the bread which you have broken	S
	326	From glory to glory advancing, we praise thee, O Lord	S
Postcommunion:	656	Blest are the pure in heart	S
	261, 262	By the Creator, Joseph was appointed	G
	587	Our Father, by whose Name	G

The Annunciation of Our Lord Jesus Christ to the Blessed Virgin Mary
(March 25)

Entrance:	267	Praise we the Lord this day	G
	437, 438	Tell out, my soul, the greatness of the Lord!	S
Sequence:	60	Creator of the stars of night (omit st. 6)	G
	270	Gabriel's message does away	G
	77	From east to west, from shore to shore (sts. 1-3)	G
	489	The great Creator of the worlds (sts. 1-4)	E
	496, 497	How bright appears the Morning Star	E
Offertory:	270	Gabriel's message does away	G
	265	The angel Gabriel from heaven came	G
	266	Nova, nova	G
	267	Praise we the Lord this day	G
Communion:	258	Virgin-born, we bow before thee	G
	263, 264	The Word whom earth and sea and sky	G
	265	The angel Gabriel from heaven came	G
	266	Nova, nova	G
Postcommunion:	268, 269	Ye who claim the faith of Jesus	G
	278	Sing we of the blessèd Mother	G
	277	Sing of Mary, pure and lowly	G
	656	Blest are the pure in heart	G
	475	God himself is with us	G

Saint Mark the Evangelist (April 25)

Entrance:	231, 232	By all your saints still striving	S
	244	Come, pure hearts, in joyful measure	L & E
	238, 239	Blessèd feasts of blessèd martyrs	S
Sequence:	235	Come sing, ye choirs exultant	L & E
	244	Come, pure hearts, in joyful measure	L & E
	632	O Christ, the Word incarnate	L & E
Offertory:	244	Come, pure hearts, in joyful measure	L & E
	235	Come sing, ye choirs exultant	L & E
	631	Book of books, our people's strength	L & E
	630	Thanks to God whose Word was spoken	L & E
Communion:	340, 341	For the bread which you have broken	S
	545	Lo! what a cloud of witnesses	S
	326	From glory to glory advancing, we praise thee, O Lord	S
Postcommunion:	240, 241	Hearken to the anthem glorious	S
	236	King of the martyrs' noble band	S
	237	Let us now our voices raise	S

| 530 | Spread, O spread, thou mighty word | G |
| 540 | Awake, thou Spirit of the watchmen (sts. 2-3) | G |

Saint Philip and Saint James, Apostles (May 1)

Entrance:	231, 232	By all your saints still striving	S
	233, 234	The eternal gifts of Christ the King	S
	364	O God, we praise thee, and confess	S
	366	Holy God, we praise thy Name	S
Sequence:	233, 234	The eternal gifts of Christ the King	S
	236	King of the martyrs' noble band	S
Offertory:	457	Thou art the Way, to thee alone	G
	463, 464	He is the Way	G
Communion:	487	Come, my Way, my Truth, my Life	G
	340, 341	For the bread which you have broken	S
	326	From glory to glory advancing, we praise thee, O Lord	S
Postcommunion:	238, 239	Blessèd feasts of blessèd martyrs	S
	240, 241	Hearken to the anthem glorious	S
	237	Let us now our voices raise	S
	545	Lo! what a cloud of witnesses	S

The Visitation of the Blessed Virgin Mary (May 31)

Entrance:	263, 264	The Word whom earth and sea and sky	G
	265	The angel Gabriel from heaven came	G
Sequence:	266	Nova, nova	G
	270	Gabriel's message does away	G
Offertory:	268, 269	Ye who claim the faith of Jesus	G
	258	Virgin-born, we bow before thee	G
Communion:	258	Virgin-born, we bow before thee	G
	270	Gabriel's message does away	G
	266	Nova, nova	G
Postcommunion:	437, 438	Tell out, my soul, the greatness of the Lord!	G
	268, 269	Ye who claim the faith of Jesus	G
	618	Ye watchers and ye holy ones	G
	277	Sing of Mary, pure and lowly	G
	278	Sing we of the blessèd Mother	G
	620	Jerusalem, my happy home	G

Saint Barnabas the Apostle (June 11)

| *Entrance:* | 231, 232 | By all your saints still striving | S |

	233, 234	The eternal gifts of Christ the King	S
	364	O God, we praise thee, and confess	S
	366	Holy God, we praise thy Name	S
	238, 239	Blessèd feasts of blessèd martyrs	S

Sequence:	233, 234	The eternal gifts of Christ the King	S
	236	King of the martyrs' noble band	S
	237	Let us now our voices raise	S

Offertory:	240, 241	Hearken to the anthem glorious	S
	236	King of the martyrs' noble band	S
	237	Let us now our voices raise	S

Communion:	340, 341	For the bread which you have broken	S
	545	Lo! what a cloud of witnesses	S
	326	From glory to glory advancing, we praise thee, O Lord	S

Postcommunion:	548	Awake, thou Spirit of the watchmen (sts. 2-3)	G
	530	Spread, O spread, thou mighty word	G
	531	O Spirit of the living God	G

The Nativity of Saint John the Baptist (June 24)

Entrance:	231, 232	By all your saints still striving	G
	75	There's a voice in the wilderness crying	L
	67	Comfort, comfort ye my people	L

Sequence:	76	On Jordan's bank the Baptist's cry	C, L & E
	70	Herald, sound the note of judgment	C, L & E
	59	Hark! a thrilling voice is sounding	L

Offertory:	271, 272	The great forerunner of the morn	G
	444	Blessed be the God of Israel	G

Communion:	67	Comfort, comfort ye my people	L
	75	There's a voice in the wilderness crying	L
	69	What is the crying at Jordan?	L & E

Postcommunion:	444	Blessed be the God of Israel	G
	271, 272	The great forerunner of the morn	G

Saint Peter and Saint Paul, Apostles (June 29)

Entrance:	231, 232	By all your saints still striving	E
	238, 239	Blessèd feasts of blessèd martyrs	S
	518	Christ is made the sure foundation	C
	525	The Church's one foundation	C

Sequence:	287	For all the saints, who from their labors rest (sts. 1-3)	E
	552, 553	Fight the good fight with all thy might (sts. 1-2)	E

	546	Awake, my soul, stretch every nerve	E
	236	King of the martyrs' noble band	S
Offertory	273, 274	Two stalwart trees both rooted	S
	233, 234	The eternal gifts of Christ the King	S
Communion:	340, 341	For the bread which you have broken	S
	545	Lo! what a cloud of witnesses	S
	326	From glory to glory advancing, we praise thee, O Lord	S
Postcommunion:	521	Put forth, O God, thy Spirit's might	C
	540	Awake, thou Spirit of the watchmen (sts. 2-3)	E & G
	531	O Spirit of the living God	E & G
	530	Spread, O spread, thou mighty word	E & G
	237	Let us now our voices raise	S

Independence Day (July 4)

Entrance:	718	God of our fathers, whose almighty hand	S
	599	Lift every voice and sing	S
Sequence:	596	Judge eternal, throned in splendor	S
	716	God bless our native land	S
Offertory:	594, 595	God of grace and God of glory	S
	591	O God of earth and altar	S
Communion:	591	O God of earth and altar	S
	568	Father all loving, who rulest in majesty	S
Postcommunion:	569	God the Omnipotent! King who ordainest	S
	594, 595	God of grace and God of glory	S
	600, 601	O day of God draw nigh	S
	572	Weary of all trumpeting	S
	607	O God of every nation	S
	573	Father eternal, Ruler of creation	S
	680	O God, our help in ages past	S
	597	O day of peace that dimly shines	S

Saint Mary Magdalene (July 22)

Entrance:	231, 232	By all your saints still striving	G
	489	The great Creator of the worlds	C & E
Sequence:	203	O sons and daughters, let us sing *Easter* (sts. 1-3)	G
	183	Christians, to the Paschal victim	G
Offertory:	190	Lift your voice rejoicing, Mary	G
	673	The first one ever, oh, ever to know	G

	203	O sons and daughters, let us sing *Easter* (sts. 1-3)	G
Communion:	673	The first one ever, oh, ever to know	G
	340, 341	For the bread which you have broken	S
	326	From glory to glory advancing, we praise thee, O Lord	S
Postcommunion:	190	Lift your voice rejoicing, Mary	G
	275	Hark! the sound of holy voices	S
	203	O sons and daughters, let us sing *Easter* (sts. 1-3)	G

Saint James the Apostle (July 25)

Entrance:	231, 232	By all your saints still striving	E & G
	233, 234	The eternal gifts of Christ the King	S
	366	Holy God, we praise thy Name	S
	364	O God, we praise thee, and confess	S
Sequence:	238, 239	Blessèd feasts of blessèd martyrs	E
	236	King of the martyrs' noble band	E
Offertory:	276	For thy blest saints, a noble throng	E & G
	240, 241	Hearken to the anthem glorious	E
Communion:	340, 341	For the bread which you have broken	S
	545	Lo! what a cloud of witnesses	S
	326	From glory to glory advancing, we praise thee, O Lord	S
Postcommunion:	276	For thy blest saints, a noble throng	E & G
	545	Lo! what a cloud of witnesses	S
	237	Let us now our voices raise	E

The Transfiguration of Our Lord Jesus Christ (August 6)

Entrance:	6, 7	Christ, whose glory fills the skies	E
	427	When morning gilds the skies	S
	366	Holy God, we praise thy Name	S
	364	O God, we praise thee, and confess	S
Sequence:	6, 7	Christ, whose glory fills the skies	E
	133, 134	O Light of Light, Love given birth	L, E & G
Offertory;	129, 130	Christ upon the mountain peak	L, E & G
	136, 137	O wondrous type! O vision fair	L, E & G
	443	From God Christ's deity came forth	E & G
Communion:	133, 134	O Light of Light, Love given birth	L, E & G
	129, 130	Christ upon the mountain peak	L, E & G
Postcommunion	136, 137	O wondrous type! O vision fair	L, E & G

	129, 130	Christ upon the mountain peak	L, E & G
	133, 134	O Light of Light, Love given birth	L, E & G

Saint Mary the Virgin, Mother of Our Lord Jesus Christ (August 15)

Entrance:	231, 232	By all your saints still striving	S
	277	Sing of Mary, pure and lowly	E
Sequence:	277	Sing of Mary, pure and lowly	E
	489	The great Creator of the worlds (sts. 1-4)	E
	496, 497	How bright appears the Morning Star	E
Offertory:	278	Sing we of the blessèd Mother	S
	268, 269	Ye who claim the faith of Jesus	G
Communion	258	Virgin-born, we bow before thee	S
	278	Sing we of the blessèd Mother	S
	656	Blest are the pure in heart	S
Postcommunion:	268, 269	Ye who claim the faith of Jesus	G
	437, 438	Tell out, my soul, the greatness of the Lord	G
	620	Jerusalem, my happy home	G
	618	Ye watchers and ye holy ones	G
	278	Sing we of the blessèd Mother	S

Saint Bartholomew the Apostle (August 24)

Entrance:	231, 232	By all your saints still striving	S
	233, 234	The eternal gifts of Christ the King	S
	366	Holy God, we praise thy Name	S
	364	O God, we praise thee, and confess	S
Sequence:	233, 234	The eternal gifts of Christ the King	S
	238, 239	Blessèd feasts of blessèd martyrs	S
Offertory:	280	God of saints, to whom the number	S
	236	King of the martyrs' noble band	S
Communion:	280	God of saints, to whom the number	S
	340, 341	For the bread which you have broken	S
	326	From glory to glory advancing, we praise thee, O Lord	S
	545	Lo! what a cloud of witnesses	S
Postcommunion:	240, 241	Hearken to the anthem glorious	S
	237	Let us now our voices raise	S
	545	Lo! what a cloud of witnesses	S

Holy Cross Day (September 14)

Entrance:	477	All praise to thee, for thou, O King	
		divine	L & E (Phil)
	165, 166	Sing, my tongue the glorious battle	E (Gal) & G
	161	The flaming banners of our King	G
	162	The royal banners forward go	G
Sequence:	483	The head that once was crowned with	
		thorns	E (Phil)
	160	Cross of Jesus, cross of sorrow	E (Phil)
	441, 442	In the cross of Christ I glory	E (Gal)
	474	When I survey the wondrous cross	E (Gal)
Offertory:	473	Lift high the cross	G
	165, 166	Sing, my tongue, the glorious battle	E (Gal) & G
	161	The flaming banners of our King	G
	162	The royal banners forward go	G
Communion:	474	When I survey the wondrous cross	E (Gal)
	434	Nature with open volume stands	E (Gal)
Postcommunion:	473	Lift high the cross	G
	471	We sing the praise of him who died	E (Gal)
	483	The head that once was crowned with	
		thorns	E (Phil)

Saint Matthew, Apostle and Evangelist (September 21)

Entrance:	231, 232	By all your saints still striving	G
	244	Come, pure hearts, in joyful measure	L & E
	233, 234	The eternal gifts of Christ the King	S
Sequence:	235	Come sing, ye choirs exultant	L & E
	244	Come, pure hearts, in joyful measure	L & E
	631	Book of books, our people's strength	E
	628	Help us, O Lord, to learn	E
	627	Lamp of our feet, whereby we trace	E
	630	Thanks to God whose Word was spoken	E
Offertory:	281	He sat to watch o'er customs paid	G
	706	In your mercy, Lord, you called me	G
	244	Come, pure hearts, in joyful measure	G
Communion:	706	In your mercy, Lord, you called me	G
	340, 341	For the bread which you have broken	S
	236	King of the martyrs' noble band	S
	326	From glory to glory advancing, we praise	
		thee, O Lord	S
Postcommunion:	240, 241	Hearken to the anthem glorious	S
	530	Spread, O spread, thou mighty word	S
	237	Let us now our voices raise	S

Saint Michael and All Angels (September 29)

Entrance:	284	O ye immortal throng	S
	618	Ye watchers and ye holy ones	S
	432	O praise ye the Lord! Praise him in the height	S
	367	Round the Lord in glory seated	S
Sequence:	282, 283	Christ, the fair glory of the holy angels	E
	453	As Jacob with travel was weary one day	L
	373	Praise the Lord! ye heavens adore him	S
Offertory:	342	O praise ye the Lord! Praise him in the height	S
	535	Ye servants of God, your Master proclaim	S
	373	Praise the Lord! ye heavens adore him	S
Communion:	324	Let all mortal flesh keep silence	S
	282, 283	Christ, the fair glory of the holy angels	E
Postcommunion:	625	Ye holy angels bright	S
	618	Ye watchers and ye holy ones	S
	284	O ye immortal throng	S
	535	Ye servants of God, your Master proclaim	S

St. Luke the Evangelist (October 18)

Entrance:	231, 232	By all your saints still striving	E
	244	Come, pure hearts, in joyful measure	S
	366	Holy God, we praise thy Name	S
	364	O God, we praise thee, and confess	S
Sequence:	235	Come sing, ye choirs exultant	S
	552, 553	Fight the good fight with all thy might (sts. 1-2)	E
	287	For all the saints, who from their labors rest (sts. 1-3)	E
Offertory:	285	What thanks and praise to thee we owe	E
	244	Come, pure hearts, in joyful measure	S
	493	O for a thousand tongues to sing	G
Communion:	566	From thee all skill and science flow	L
	340, 341	For the bread which you have broken	S
	326	From glory to glory advancing, we praise thee, O Lord	S
Postcommunion:	285	What thanks and praise to thee we owe	E
	371	Thou, whose almighty word	G
	537	Christ for the world we sing!	G
	240, 241	Hearken to the anthem glorious	S
	237	Let us now our voices raise	S

Saint James of Jerusalem, Brother of Our Lord Jesus Christ, and Martyr (October 23)

Entrance:	231, 232	By all your saints still striving	E
	238, 239	Blessèd feasts of blessèd martyrs	L
Sequence:	483	The head that once was crowned with thorns	E
	240, 241	Hearken to the anthem glorious	L
Offertory:	240, 241	Hearken to the anthem glorious	L
	236	King of the martyrs' noble band	L
Communion:	324	Let all mortal flesh keep silence	S
	321	My God, thy table now is spread	L
	340, 341	For the bread which you have broken	S
Postcommunion:	326	From glory to glory advancing, we praise thee, O Lord	S
	529	In Christ there is no East or West	L
	237	Let us now our voices raise	L
	545	Lo! what a cloud of witnesses	S

Saint Simon and Saint Jude, Apostles (October 28)

Entrance:	231, 232	By all your saints still striving	S
	233, 234	The eternal gifts of Christ the King	S
	238, 239	Blessèd feasts of blessèd martyrs	S
Sequence:	518	Christ is made the sure foundation	E
	525	The Church's one foundation	E
	521	Put forth, O God, thy Spirit's might	E
Offertory	233, 234	The eternal gifts of Christ the King	S
	279	For thy dear saints, O Lord	S
	240, 241	Hearken to the anthem glorious	S
	236	King of the martyrs' noble band	S
Communion:	340, 341	For the bread which you have broken	S
	302, 303	Father, we thank thee, who hast planted	E
	326	From glory to glory advancing, we praise thee, O Lord	E
Postcommunion:	233, 234	The eternal gifts of Christ the King	S
	525	The Church's one foundation	E
	237	Let us now our voices raise	S
	545	Lo! what a cloud of witnesses	S

All Saints' Day (November 1)

Entrance:	287	For all the saints, who from their labors rest	S
	231, 232	By all your saints still striving	E (Rev)
Sequence:	286	Who are these like stars appearing	E (Rev)

	253	Give us the wings of faith to rise	E (Rev)
	275	Hark! the sound of holy voices	E (Rev)
	279	For thy dear saints, O Lord	S
Baptism:	298	All who believe and are baptized	S
	697	My God, accept my heart this day	S
	213	Come away to the skies	S
Offertory:	560	Remember your servants, Lord	G (Matt)
	656	Blest are the pure in heart	G (Matt)
Communion:	526	Let saints on earth in concert sing	S
	355	Give rest, O Christ	S
	340, 341	For the bread which you have broken	S
	326	From glory to glory advancing, we praise thee, O Lord	S
Postcommunion:	618	Ye watchers and ye holy ones	E (Rev)
	625	Ye holy angels bright	E (Rev)
	545	Lo! what a cloud of witnesses	S
	623	O what their joy and their glory must be	S
	624	Jerusalem the golden	E (Rev)
	620	Jerusalem, my happy home	S

Thanksgiving Day

Entrance:	290	Come, ye thankful people, come	S
	396, 397	Now thank we all our God	S
Sequence:	415	When all thy mercies, O my God	S
	396, 397	Now thank we all our God	S
Offertory:	709	O God of Bethel, by whose hand	G
	424	For the fruit of all creation	S
	416	For the beauty of the earth	E
	291	We plow the fields and scatter	E
	705	As those of old their first fruits brought	S
Communion:	416	For the beauty of the earth	S
	415	When all thy mercies, O my God	S
Postcommunion:	396, 397	Now thank we all our God	S
	288	Praise to God, immortal praise	S
	424	For the fruit of all creation	S
	291	We plow the fields and scatter	S

The Common of Saints

Of a Martyr

Entrance:	238, 239	Blessèd feasts of blessèd martyrs	S
	366	Holy God, we praise thy Name	E (Rev)
	364	O God, we praise thee, and confess	E (Rev)
Sequence:	286	Who are these like stars appearing	L (2 Esdras) & E (Rev)
	253	Give us the wings of faith to rise	S
	275	Hark! the sound of holy voices	E (Rev)
Offertory:	240, 241	Hearken to the anthem glorious	E (Rev)
	236	King of the martyrs' noble band	S
	655	O Jesus, I have promised	G (Mt)
	675	Take up your cross, the Savior said	G (Mk)
	484, 485	Praise the Lord through every nation	G (Mk)
Communion:	545	Lo! what a cloud of witnesses	S
	340, 341	For the bread which you have broken	S
	326	From glory to glory advancing, we praise thee, O Lord	S
Postcommunion:	237	Let us now our voices raise	S
	545	Lo! what a cloud of witnesses	S

Of a Missionary

Entrance:	614	Christ is the King! O friends upraise	S
	543	O Zion, tune thy voice	S
Sequence:	521	Put forth, O God, thy Spirit's might	E (Acts 1)
	628	Help us, O Lord, to learn	S
	534	God is working his purpose out	S
Offertory:	540	Awake, thou Spirit of the watchmen (sts. 2-3)	G (Lk)
	541	Come, labor on	G (Lk)
	528	Lord, you give the great commission	G (Lk & Mt)
Communion:	532, 533	How wondrous and great thy works, God of praise	S
	321	My God, thy table now is spread	S
	340, 341	For the bread which you have broken	S
	326	From glory to glory advancing, we praise thee, O Lord	S
Postcommunion:	531	O Spirit of the living God	E (Acts 1) & G (Mt)
	539	O Zion, haste, thy mission high fulfilling	L (Isa 52), (E Acts 1) & G (Mt)

	530	Spread, O Spread, thou mighty word	S
	473	Lift high the cross	S
	537	Christ for the world we sing!	S
	535	Ye servants of God, your Master proclaim	S
	380	From all that dwell below the skies	S

Of a Pastor

Entrance:	517	How lovely is thy dwelling-place	P (84)
	525	The Church's one foundation	L (Acts)
Sequence:	645, 646	The King of love my shepherd is	P (23)
	663	The Lord my God my shepherd is	P (23)
	664	My Shepherd will supply my need	P (23)
Offertory:	528	Lord, you give the great commission	S
	511	Holy Spirit, ever living	S
	359	God of the prophets, bless the prophets' heirs	S
Communion	511	Holy Spirit, ever living	S
	340, 341	For the bread which you have broken	S
	326	From glory to glory advancing, we praise thee, O Lord	S
Postcommunion:	535	Ye servants of God, your Master proclaim	S
	511	Holy Spirit, ever living	S
	359	God of the prophets, bless the prophets' heirs	S

Of a Theologian and Teacher

Entrance:	457	Thou art the Way, to thee alone	S
	463, 464	He is the Way	S
	614	Christ is the King! O friends upraise (sts. 1-2)	S
Sequence:	636, 637	How firm a foundation, ye saints of the Lord	E (1 Cor 3)
	628	Help us, O Lord, to learn	S
	694	God be in my head	S
	632	O Christ, the Word Incarnate	S
	627	Lamp of our feet, whereby we trace	S
	634	I call on thee, Lord Jesus Christ	S
	512	Come, gracious Spirit, heavenly Dove	S
Offertory:	369	How wondrous great, how glorious bright	S
	629	We limit not the truth of God	S
	422	Not far beyond the sea, nor high	S
	505	O Spirit of Life, O Spirit of God	S
Communion:	302, 303	Father, we thank thee who hast planted	S
	526	Let saints on earth in concert sing	S
	340, 341	For the bread which you have broken	S
	326	From glory to glory advancing, we praise thee, O Lord	S

Postcommunion:	630	Thanks to God whose Word was spoken	S
	631	Book of books, our people's strength	S
	530	Spread, O spread, thou mighty word	S

Of a Monastic

Entrance:	488	Be thou my vision. O Lord of my heart	S
	665	All my hope on God is founded	S
Sequence:	701	Jesus, all my gladness (sts. 1-2)	E (Phil)
	704	O thou who camest from above	S
Offertory:	655	O Jesus, I have promised	G (Lk 9)
	564, 565	He who would valiant be	G (Lk 9)
	656	Blest are the pure in heart	S
	475	God himself is with us (sts. 1-2)	S
	707	Take my life, and let it be	S
Communion:	642	Jesus, the very thought of thee	S
	701	Jesus, all my gladness (sts. 1-2)	E (Phil)
Postcommunion:	704	O thou who camest from above	S
	656	Blest are the pure in heart	S

Of a Saint

Entrance:	614	Christ is the King! O friends upraise	S
	287	For all the saints, who from their labors rest	S
	275	Hark! the sound of holy voices	S
	366	Holy God, we praise thy Name	S
	364	O God, we praise thee, and confess	S
Sequence:	545	Lo! what a cloud of witnesses	E (Heb)
	253	Give us the wings of faith to rise	E (Heb)
	552, 553	Fight the good fight with all thy might (sts. 1-2)	E (Heb)
	605	What does the Lord require	L (Micah)
	279	For thy dear saints, O Lord	S
Offertory:	560	Remember your servants, Lord	G (Lk)
	286	Who are these like stars appearing	S
	293	I sing a song of the saints of God	S
Communion:	526	Let saints on earth in concert sing	S
	340, 341	For the bread which you have broken	S
	326	From glory to glory advancing, we praise thee, O Lord	S
Postcommunion:	545	Lo! what a cloud of witnesses	E (Heb)
	546	Awake, my soul, stretch every nerve	E (Heb)
	623	O what their joy and their glory must be	S
	620	Jerusalem, my happy home	S

624	Jerusalem the golden	S
625	Ye holy angels bright	S
618	Ye watchers and ye holy ones	S

Various Occasions

1. Of the Holy Trinity

Entrance:	401	The God of Abraham praise	L
	365	Come, thou almighty King	S
	362	Holy, holy, holy! Lord God Almighty!	S
	367	Round the Lord in glory seated	S
Sequence:	369	How wondrous great, how glorious bright	E
	371	Thou, whose almighty word	S
	364	O God, we praise thee, and confess	S
	366	Holy God, we praise thy Name	S
Offertory:	295	Sing praise to our Creator	G
	370	I bind unto myself today	G
Communion:	421	All glory be to God on high	S
	295	Sing praise to our Creator	G
Postcommunion:	370	I bind unto myself today	G
	368	Holy Father, great Creator	S
	363	Ancient of Days, who sittest throned in glory	S
	559	Lead us, heavenly Father, lead us	S

2. Of the Holy Spirit

Entrance:	506, 507	Praise the Spirit in creation	S
	509	Spirit divine, attend our prayers	S
	501, 502	O Holy Spirit, by whose breath	E
	500	Creator Spirit, by whose aid	S
	503, 504	Come, Holy Ghost, our souls inspire	S
Sequence:	228	Holy Spirit, font of light	E
	226, 227	Come, thou Holy Spirit bright	S
	513	Like the murmur of the dove's song	S
	505	O Spirit of Life, O Spirit of God	S
	510	Come, Holy Spirit, heavenly Dove	S
	508	Breathe on me, Breath of God	S
Offertory:	512	Come, gracious Spirit, heavenly Dove	S
	516	Come down, O Love divine	S
	515	Holy Ghost, dispel our sadness	S
Communion:	514	To thee, O Comforter divine	S
	511	Holy Spirit, ever living	S

| Postcommunion: | 531 | O Spirit of the living God | S |
| | 521 | Put forth, O God, thy Spirit's might | S |

3. Of the Holy Angels

Entrance:	284	O ye immortal throng	S
	618	Ye watchers and ye holy ones	S
	432	O praise ye the Lord! Praise him in the height	P (148)
	366	Holy god, we praise thy Name	S
	364	O God, we praise thee, and confess	S
Sequence:	374	Come, let us join our cheerful songs	E
	373	Praise the Lord! ye heavens adore him	P (148)
Offertory:	282, 283	Christ, the fair glory of the holy angels	S
	535	Ye servants of God, your Master proclaim	E & G
Communion:	324	Let all mortal flesh keep silence	S
	282, 283	Christ, the fair glory of the holy angels	S
Postcommunion:	535	Ye servants of God, your Master proclaim	E & G
	625	Ye holy angels bright	S
	618	Ye watchers and ye holy ones	S

4. Of the Incarnation

Entrance:	496, 497	How bright appears the Morning Star	L (Isa)
	364	O God, we praise thee, and confess	S
	366	Holy God, we praise thy Name	S
Sequence:	439	What wondrous love is this	E (1 Jn)
	476	Can we by searching find out God	S
	491	Where is this stupendous stranger?	S
Offertory:	489	The great Creator of the worlds (sts. 1-4)	S
	477	All praise to thee, for thou, O King divine	S
	443	From God Christ's deity came forth	S
Communion:	439	What wondrous love is this	E (1 Jn)
	324	Let all mortal flesh keep silence	S
	307	Lord, enthroned in heavenly splendor	S
	319	You, Lord, we praise in songs of celebration	S
Postcommunion:	452	Glorious the day when Christ was born	S
	448, 449	O love, how deep, how broad, how high	S
	492	Sing, ye faithful, sing with gladness	S
	455, 456	O Love of God, how strong and true	S
	530	Spread, O spread, thou mighty word	S

5. Of the Holy Eucharist

Entrance:	460, 461	Alleluia! sing to Jesus!	G
	202	The Lamb's high banquet called to share	E (Rev)
Sequence:	320	Zion, praise thy Savior, singing	E (1 Cor 11) & G
	322	When Jesus died to save us	E (1 Cor 11)
	329, 330,	Now, my tongue, the mystery telling (sts. 1-4)	E (1 Cor 11)
Offertory:	302, 303	Father, we thank thee, who hast planted	E (1 Cor 10) & G
	343	Shepherd of souls, refresh and bless	L & G
	339	Deck thyself, my soul, with gladness	E (1 Cor 11) & G
Communion:	308, 309	O Food to pilgrims given	L, E (1 Cor 10) & G
	314	Humbly I adore thee, Verity unseen	G
	329, 331	Now, my tongue, the mystery telling	E (1 Cor 11)
	322	When Jesus died to save us	E (1 Cor 11)
	319	You, Lord, we praise in songs of celebration	S
	321	My God, thy table now is spread	L & G
Postcommunion:	346	Completed, Lord, the Holy Mysteries	S
	316, 317	This is the hour of banquet and of song	E (Rev)
	336	Come with us, O blessèd Jesus	S
	312	Strengthen for service, Lord	S

6. Of the Holy Cross

Entrance:	477	All praise to thee, for thou, O King divine	S
	165, 166	Sing, my tongue, the glorious battle	E & G
	161	The flaming banners of our King	G
	162	The royal banners forward go	G
Sequence:	441, 442	In the cross of Christ I glory	S
	474	When I survey the wondrous cross	S
Offertory:	473	Lift high the cross	G
	165, 166	Sing, my tongue, the glorious battle	E & G
	161	The flaming banners of our King	G
	162	The royal banners forward go	G
Communion:	474	When I survey the wondrous cross	S
	434	Nature with open volume stands	E
Postcommunion:	473	Lift high the cross	G
	471	We sing the praise of him who died	E
	483	The head that once was crowned with thorns	S

7. For All Baptized Christians

Entrance:	176, 177	Over the chaos of the empty waters	S
	432	O praise ye the Lord! Praise him in the height	S
	51	We the Lord's people, heart and voice uniting (omit st. 3)	S
	678, 679	Surely it is God who saves me	L
Sequence:	298	All who believe and are baptized	E
	296	We know that Christ is raised and dies no more	E
	294	Baptized in water	E
Offertory:	296	We know that Christ is raised and dies no more	E
	299	Spirit of God, unleashed on earth	S
	370	I bind unto myself today	S
	697	My God, accept my heart this day	E
Communion:	295	Sing praise to our Creator	S
	645, 646	The King of love my shepherd is	S
	663	The Lord my God my shepherd is	S
	664	My Shepherd will supply my need	S
	319	You, Lord, we praise in songs of celebration	S
Postcommunion:	432	O praise ye the Lord! praise him in the height	S
	473	Lift high the cross	S
	295	Sing praise to our Creator	S

8. For the Departed

Entrance:	429	I'll praise my Maker while I've breath	S
	680	O God, our help in ages past	S
	526	Let saints on earth in concert sing	S
Sequence:	194, 195	Jesus lives! thy terrors now	S
	188, 189	Love's redeeming work is done	E
	447	The Christ who died but rose again	S
Offertory:	208	The strife is o'er, the battle done	E
	457	Thou art the Way, to thee alone	S
	379	God is Love, let heaven adore him	S
	358	Christ the Victorious, give to your servants	S
Communion:	526	Let saints on earth in concert sing	S
	357	Jesus, Son of Mary	S
	355	Give rest, O Christ	S
	356	May choirs of angels lead you	S
	354	Into paradise may the angels lead you	S
	335	I am the bread of life (sts. 4-5) G (Jn 6 & Jn 11)	
	338	Wherefore, O Father, we thy humble servants	S
Postcommunion:	623	O what their joy and their glory must be	S
	621, 622	Light's abode, celestial Salem	S

	624	Jerusalem the golden	S
	620	Jerusalem, my happy home	S
	625	Ye holy angels bright	S
	618	Ye watchers and ye holy ones	S

9. Of the Reign of Christ

Entrance:	616	Hail to the Lord's Anointed	S
	544	Jesus shall reign, where'er the sun	S
	450, 451	All hail the power of Jesus' Name!	S
Sequence:	477	All praise to thee, for thou, O King divine	S
	435	At the Name of Jesus	S
Offertory:	495	Hail, thou once despisèd Jesus!	G
	170	To mock your reign, O dearest Lord	G
	458	My song is love unknown	G
	483	The head that once was crowned with thorns (sts. 1-2)	G
	598	Lord Christ, when first thou cam'st to earth	G
Communion:	460, 461	Alleluia! sing to Jesus! (sts. 1 & 4 or 1, 4 & 5)	S
	324	Let all mortal flesh keep silence	S
	307	Lord, enthroned in heavenly splendor	S
Postcommunion:	614	Christ is the King! O friends upraise	S
	481	Rejoice, the Lord is King	S
	494	Crown him with many crowns	S
	535	Ye servants of God, your Master proclaim	S

10. At Baptism

Entrance:	370	I bind unto myself today	S
	697	My God, accept my heart this day	E (Rom 6)
	297	Descend, O Spirit, purging flame	G (Jn 3)
	299	Spirit of God, unleashed on earth	S
	678, 679	Surely it is God who saves me	Canticle 9
	658	As longs the deer for cooling streams	P (42)
Sequence:	298	All who believe and are baptized	E (Rom 6 & 2 Cor 5)
	547	Awake, O sleeper, rise from death	S
Offertory:	295	Sing praise to our Creator	G (Jn 3)
	296	We know that Christ is raised and dies no more	E (Rom 6 & 2 Cor 5) & G (Jn 3)
	294	Baptized in water	E (Rom 6)
	176, 177	Over the chaos of the empty waters	E (2 Cor 5)
Communion:	295	Sing praise to our Creator	G (Jn 3)
	645, 646	The King of love my shepherd is	P (23)
	663	The Lord my God my shepherd is	P (23)

	664	My Shepherd will supply my need	P (23)
Postcommunion:	432	O praise ye the Lord! Praise him in the height	S
	473	Lift high the cross	S
	213	Come away to the skies	E (2 Cor 5)

11. At Confirmation

Entrance:	370	I bind unto myself today	S
	349	Holy Spirit, Lord of love	S
	348	Lord, we have come at your own invitation	S
Sequence:	704	O thou who camest from above	S
	707	Take my life, and let it be	E (Rom 12)
	547	Awake, O sleeper, rise from death	S
Offertory:	610	Lord, whose love through humble service	E (Rom 12)
	659, 660	O Master, let me walk with thee	S
	655	O Jesus, I have promised	S
	675	Take up your cross, the Savior said	G (Mt 16)
	546	Awake, my soul, stretch every nerve	S
Communion:	321	My God, thy table now is spread	S
	304	I come with joy to meet my Lord	S
Postcommunion:	347	Go forth for God; go to the world in peace	S
	610	Lord, whose love through humble service	E (Rom 12)

12. On the Anniversary of the Dedication of a Church

Entrance:	51	We the Lord's people, heart and voice uniting (except on Sunday omit st. 3)	E & G
	360, 361	Only-begotten, Word of God eternal	S
	518	Christ is made the sure foundation	E
	519, 520	Blessèd city, heavenly Salem	S
Sequence:	522, 523	Glorious things of thee are spoken	E
	51	We the Lord's people, heart and voice uniting (except on Sunday omit st. 3)	E & G
	517	How lovely is thy dwelling-place	P
Offertory:	289	Our Father, by whose servants	S
	360, 361	Only-begotten, Word of God eternal	S
	524	I love thy kingdom, Lord	S
Communion:	360, 361	Only-begotten, Word of God eternal	S
	524	I love thy kingdom, Lord	S
Postcommunion:	289	Our Father, by whose servants	S
	522, 523	Glorious things of thee are spoken	E
	517	How lovely is thy dwelling-place	P

| | 525 | The Church's one foundation | E |
| | 486 | Hosanna to the living Lord! | G |

13. For a Church Convention

Entrance:	518	Christ is made the sure foundation	G
	522, 523	Glorious things of thee are spoken	S
	543	O Zion, tune thy voice	S
Sequence:	501, 502	O Holy Spirit, by whose breath	S
	500	Creator Spirit, by whose aid	S
	503, 504	Come, Holy Ghost, our souls inspire	S
	513	Like the murmur of the dove's song	G
Offertory:	513	Like the murmur of the dove's song	G
	511	Holy Spirit, ever living	S
	524	I love thy kingdom, Lord	S
Communion:	521	Put forth, O God, thy Spirit's might	S
	530	Spread, O spread, thou mighty word	S
Postcommunion:	540	Awake, thou Spirit of the watchmen	S
	535	Ye servants of God, your Master proclaim	S
	531	O Spirit of the living God	S
	473	Lift high the cross	S
	537	Christ for the world we sing!	S
	539	O Zion, haste, thy mission high fulfilling	S

14. For the Unity of the Church

Entrance:	614	Christ is the King! O friends upraise	S
	525	The Church's one foundation	E
Sequence:	547	Awake, O sleeper, rise from death	E
	521	Put forth, O God, thy Spirit's might	E
Offertory:	302, 303	Father, we thank thee who hast planted	S
	581	Where charity and love prevail	S
	576, 577	God is love, and where true love is	S
	606	Where true charity and love dwell	S
Communion:	315	Thou, who at thy first Eucharist didst pray	G
	302, 303	Father, we thank thee who hast planted	S
	319	You, Lord, we praise in songs of celebration	S
Postcommunion:	525	The Church's one foundation	E
	521	Put forth, O God, thy Spirit's might	E
	527	Singing songs of expectation	E
	617	Eternal Ruler of the ceaseless round	S

15. For the Ministry (Ember Days)

Entrance:	511	Holy Spirit, ever living	S
	359	God of the prophets, bless the prophets' heirs	S
	51	We the Lord's people, heart and voice uniting (omit st. 3)	L (Ex)
Sequence:	359	God of the prophets, bless the prophets' heirs	S
	521	Put forth, O God, thy Spirit's might	E (Eph)
Offertory:	540	Awake, thou Spirit of the watchmen	G (Jn & Mt 9)
	541	Come, labor on	G (Jn & Mt 9)
	675	Take up your cross, the Savior said	G (Mt 16)
	484, 485	Praise the Lord through every nation	G (Mt 16)
	592	Teach me, my God and King	III
Communion:	531	O Spirit of the living God	S
	511	Holy Spirit, ever living	S
	482	Lord of all hopefulness, Lord of all joy	III
Postcommunion:	528	Lord, you give the great commission	S
	535	Ye servants of God, your Master proclaim	S
	540	Awake, thou Spirit of the watchmen	G (Jn & Mt 16)
	541	Come, labor on	G (Jn & Mt 16)
	539	O Zion, haste, thy mission high fulfilling	S

16. For the Mission of the Church

Entrance:	518	Christ is made the sure foundation	E (Eph 2)
	525	The Church's one foundation	E (Eph 2)
	542	Christ is the world's true Light	L (Isa 2)
Sequence:	521	Put forth, O God, thy Spirit's might	S
	513	Like the murmur of the dove's song	S
Offertory:	540	Awake, thou Spirit of the watchmen (sts. 2-3)	G (Lk)
	541	Come, labor on	G (Lk)
	528	Lord, you give the great commission	G (Lk & Mt)
Communion:	321	My God, thy table now is spread	S
	530	Spread, O spread, thou mighty word	S
Postcommunion:	531	O Spirit of the living God	G (Mt)
	539	O Zion, haste, thy mission high fulfilling	G (Mt)
	535	Ye servants of God, your Master proclaim	S
	537	Christ for the world we sing!	S
	527	Singing songs of expectation	S
	614	Christ is the King! O friends upraise	S

17. For the Nation: *See Independence Day [above, page 268]*

18. For Peace

Entrance:	569	God the Omnipotent! King who ordainest	S
	573	Father eternal, Ruler of creation	S
Sequence:	593	Lord, make us servants of your peace	E
	607	O God of every nation	S
	600, 601	O day of God, draw nigh	S
	584	God, you have given us power to sound	S
	246	In Bethlehem a newborn boy	S
Offertory:	597	O day of peace that dimly shines	S
	572	Weary of all trumpeting	S
	607	O God of every nation	S
Communion:	600, 601	O day of God, draw nigh	S
	578	O God of love, O King of peace	S
	712	Dona nobis pacem	S
Postcommunion:	594, 595	God of grace and God of glory	S
	573	Father eternal, Ruler of creation	S
	613	Thy kingdom come, O God!	L
	542	Christ is the world's true Light	L

19. For Rogation Days

Entrance:	400	All creatures of our God and King (sts. 1-4 & 7)	S
	406, 407	Most High, omnipotent, good Lord (sts. 1-5 & 8)	S
	291	We plough the fields, and scatter	S
	405	All things bright and beautiful	S
	388	O worship the King, all glorious above!	S
Sequence:	389	Let us, with a gladsome mind	S
	428	O all ye works of God, now come	S
Offertory:	9	Not here for high and holy things	S
	705	As those of old their first fruits brought	S
	292	O Jesus, crowned with all renown	I & III
	582, 583	O holy city, seen of John	II & III
	574, 575	Before thy throne, O God, we kneel	II & III
Communion:	320	Zion, praise thy Savior, singing (sts. 5-6)	S
	709	O God of Bethel, by whose hand	S
Postcommunion:	709	O God of Bethel, by whose hand	S
	390	Praise to the Lord, the Almighty	S

20. For the Sick

Entrance:	1, 2	Father, we praise thee, now the night is over	S
	390	Praiqe to the Lord, the Almighty	S
	410	Praise, my soul, the King of heaven	S
Sequence:	411	O bless the Lord, my soul!	S
	633	Word of God, come down on earth (st. 3)	S
	514	To thee, O Comforter divine	
Offertory:	493	O for a thousand tongues to sing	S
	567	Thine arm, O Lord, in days of old	S
	23	The fleeting day is nearly gone (evening)	S
	44, 45	To you, before the close of day (evening)	S
Communion:	567	Thine arm, O Lord, in days of old	S
	493	O for a thousand tongues to sing	S
	566	From thee all skill and science flow	S
Postcommunion:	410	Praise, my soul, the King of heaven	S
	371	Thou whose almighty word	S
	537	Christ for the world we sing!	S
	538	God of mercy, God of grace	S

21. For Social Justice

Entrance:	616	Hail to the Lord's Anointed	P
	544	Jesus shall reign, where'er the sun	P
Sequence:	582, 583	O holy city, seen of John	E
	574, 575	Before thy throne, O God, we kneel	E
	568	Father all loving, who rulest in majesty	E
Offertory:	609	Where cross the crowded ways of life	G
	596	Judge eternal, throned in splendor	S
	246	In Bethlehem a newborn boy	S
Communion:	600, 601	O day of God, draw nigh	S
	591	O God of earth and altar	S
Postcommunion:	605	What does the Lord require	S
	573	Father eternal, Ruler of creation	S
	594, 595	God of grace and God of glory	S

22. For Social Service

Entrance:	544	Jesus shall reign, where'er the sun	S
	616	Hail to the Lord's Anointed	S
Sequence:	593	Lord, make us servants of your peace	S
	590	O Jesus Christ, may grateful hymns be rising	S
Offertory:	610	Lord, whose love through humble service	S

	568	Father all loving, who rulest in majesty	S
	582, 583	O holy city, seen of John	S
	609	Where cross the crowded ways of life	S
	659, 660	O Master, let me walk with thee	G
Communion:	602	Jesu, Jesu, fill us with your love	S
	593	Lord, make us servants of your peace	S
Postcommunion:	610	Lord, whose love through humble service	S
	568	Father all loving, who rulest in majesty	S
	424	For the fruit of all creation	S

23. For Education

Entrance:	431	The stars declare his glory	L
	630	Thanks to God, whose Word was spoken	E
Sequence:	631	Book of books, our people's strength	E
	628	Help us, O Lord, to learn	E
	634	I call on thee, Lord Jesus Christ	E
	632	O Christ, the Word Incarnate	E
	627	Lamp of our feet, whereby we trace	E
Offertory:	584	God, you have given us power to sound	S
	628	Help us, O Lord, to learn	S
	629	We limit not the truth of God	S
	422	Not far beyond the sea, nor high	S
	681	Our God, to whom we turn	S
Communion:	463, 464	He is the Way	S
	457	Thou art the Way, to thee alone	S
Postcommunion:	629	We limit not the truth of God	S
	584	God, you have given us power to sound	S
	551	Rise up, ye saints of God!	L
	422	Not far beyond the sea, nor high	S

24. For Vocation in Daily Work

Entrance:	11	Awake, my soul, and with the sun	S
	9	Not here for high and holy things	S
Sequence:	592	Teach me, my God and King	S
	611	Christ the worker	S
Offertory:	586	Jesus, thou divine companion	S
	10	New every morning is the love	S
Communion:	482	Lord of all hopefulness, Lord of all joy	S
	592	Teach me, my God and King	S
Postcommunion:	586	Jesus, thou divine companion	S
	592	Teach me, my God and King	S

| | 9 | Not here for high and holy things | S |
| | 10 | New every morning is the love | S |

25. For Labor Day: *See 24. For Vocation in Daily Work (above)*

Pastoral Offices

Confirmation

See the day of the Church Year — Holy Eucharist (above, pp. 176-289)

Also see Various Occasions   11. At Confirmation (above p. 283)

The Celebration and Blessing of a Marriage

Entrance:	518	Christ is made the sure foundation
	366	Holy God, we praise thy Name
	364	O God, we praise thee, and confess
	400	All creatures of our God and King
	421	All glory be to God on high
	377, 378	All people that on earth do dwell
	430	Come, O come, our voices raise
	416	For the beauty of the earth
	375	Give praise and glory unto God
	414	God, my King, thy might confessing
	398	I sing the almighty power of God
	423	Immortal, invisible, God only wise
	376	Joyful, joyful, we adore thee
	396, 397	Now thank we all our God
	413	New songs of celebration render
	428	O all ye works of God, now come
	432	O praise ye the Lord! Praise him in the height
	410	Praise, my soul, the King of heaven
	390	Praise to the Lord, the Almighty
	373	Praise the Lord! ye heavens adore him
	408	Sing praise to God who reigns above
	401	The God of Abraham praise
	409	The spacious firmament on high
	431	The stars declare his glory
	399	To God with gladness sing
	492	Sing, ye faithful, sing with gladness
Before the Collect:	353	Your love, O God, has called us here
	352	O God, to those who here profess (Gen 2, Eph 5, Mk 10)
	350	O God of love, to thee we bow (Gen 2, Eph 5, Mk 10)

	351	May the grace of Christ our Savior
	138	All praise to you, O Lord
Sequence:	612	Gracious Spirit, Holy Ghost (1 Cor 13)
	351	May the grace of Christ our Savior
	350	O God of love, to thee we bow (Gen 2, Eph 5, Mk 10)
	352	O God, to those who here profess (Gen 2, Eph 5, Mk 10)
	353	Your love, O God, has called us here
	138	All praise to you, O Lord
Offertory:	138	All praise to you, O Lord
	351	May the grace of Christ our Saviour
	709	O God of Bethel, by whose hand
	587	Our Father, by whose Name
	581	Where charity and love prevail (Eph 5, Col 3, 1 Jn 4)
	593	Lord, make us servants of your peace (Col 3)
	612	Gracious Spirit, Holy Ghost (1 Cor 13)
Communion:	664	My Shepherd will supply my need
	645, 646	The King of love my shepherd is (sts. 1-2 & 5-6)
	663	The Lord my God my shepherd is
	138	All praise to you, O Lord
	612	Gracious Spirit, Holy Ghost (1 Cor 13)
	709	O God of Bethel, by whose hand
	581	Where charity and love prevail (Eph 5, Col 3, 1 Jn 4)
	593	Lord, make us servants of your peace (Col 3)
Postcommunion:	351	May the grace of Christ our Savior
	312	Strengthen for service, Lord
Exit:	635	If thou but trust in God to guide thee
	421	All glory be to God on high
	416	For the beauty of the earth
	375	Give praise and glory unto God
	414	God, my King, thy might confessing
	376	Joyful, joyful, we adore thee
	396, 397	Now thank we all our God
	432	O praise ye the Lord! Praise him in the height
	410	Praise, my soul, the King of heaven
	373	Praise the Lord! ye heavens adore him
	390	Praise to the Lord, the Almighty
	408	Sing praise to God who reigns above

A Thanksgiving for the Birth or Adoption of a Child

	587	Our Father, by whose Name
	480	When Jesus left his Father's throne (Lk 18)
	416	For the beauty of the earth

Ministration to the Sick

See Various Occasions   20. *For the Sick (above p. 287)*

The Burial of the Dead

Entrance:	680	O God, our help in ages past (Ps 90)
(Rite II only):	429	I'll praise my Maker while I've breath (Ps 146)
	526	Let saints on earth in concert sing
	636, 637	How firm a foundation, ye saints of the Lord
	687, 688	A mighty fortress is our God (Ps 46)
	388	O worship the King, all glorious above! (Ps 104)
Sequence:	668	I to the hills will lift mine eyes (Ps 121)
	194, 195	Jesus lives! thy terrors now (Rom 8 & Jn 14)
	188, 189	Love's redeeming work is done (1 Cor 15)
	447	The Christ who died but rose again (Rom 8)
	14, 15	O God, creation's secret force
	695, 696	By gracious powers so wonderfully sheltered
	635	If thou but trust in God to guide thee
	191	Alleluia, alleluia! Hearts and voices heavenward raise (1 Cor 15)
Offertory:	457	Thou art the Way, to thee alone (Jn 14)
	208	Alleluia, alléluia, alleluia! The strife is o'er (1 Cor 15)
	379	God is Love, let heaven adore him
	455, 456	O love of God, how strong and true
	690	Guide me, O thou great Jehovah
Communion:	526	Let saints on earth in concert sing
	357	Jesus, Son of Mary
	338	Wherefore, O Father, we thy humble servants
	664	My Shepherd will supply my need (Ps 23)
	645, 646	The King of love my shepherd is (Ps 23 & Jn 10)
	663	The Lord my God my shepherd is (Ps 23)
	335	I am the bread of life (sts. 4-5) (Jn 6 & Jn 11)
The Commendation:	355	Give rest, O Christ (1 Cor 15)
	358	Christ the Victorious, give to your servants (1 Cor 15)
Exit:	356	May choirs of angels lead you (Rev 7 & Rev 21)
	354	Into paradise may the angels lead you (Rev 7 & Rev 21)
	373	Praise the Lord! ye heavens adore him (Ps 148)
	492	Sing, ye faithful, sing with gladness (1 Cor 15)
	623	O what their joy and their glory must be (Rom 8, 2 Cor 4-5, Rev 21)
	620	Jerusalem, my happy home (2 Cor 4-5)

621	Light's abode, celestial Salem (Rom 8, 1 Cor15, 2 Cor 4-5, Rev 21)
624	Jerusalem the golden (Rev 7 & Rev 21)
625	Ye holy angels bright (Rev 7)
618	Ye watchers and ye holy ones (Rev 7)

Episcopal Services

Ordination (Of a Bishop, Of a Priest, Of a Deacon)

Entrance:	511	Holy Spirit, ever living
	359	God of the prophets, bless the prophets' heirs (Of a priest)
	370	I bind unto myself today
	528	Lord, you give the great commission
	525	The Church's one foundation
	518	Christ is made the sure foundation
	524	I love thy kingdom, Lord
Sequence:	521	Put forth, O God, thy Spirit's might
	511	Holy Spirit, ever living
	359	God of the prophets, bless the prophets' heirs (Of a priest)
	513	Like the murmur of the dove's song
	505	O Spirit of Life, O Spirit of God
Veni Creator Spiritus:	503, 504	Come Holy Ghost, our souls inspire
	500	Creator Spirit, by whose aid
	501, 502	O Holy Spirit, by whose breath
Veni Sancte Spiritus:	226, 227	Come, thou Holy Spirit bright
	228	Holy Spirit, font of light
Offertory:	528	Lord, you give the great commission
	531	O Spirit of the living God
	540	Awake, thou Spirit of the watchmen
	541	Come, labor on
	505	O Spirit of Life, O Spirit of God
Communion:	321	My God, thy table now is spread
	531	O Spirit of the living God
	530	Spread, O spread, thou mighty word
	593	Lord, make us servants of your peace
Postcommunion:	535	Ye servants of God, your Master proclaim
	531	O Spirit of the living God
	539	O Zion, haste, thy mission high fulfilling
	556, 557	Rejoice, ye pure in heart!
	610	Lord, whose love through humble service
	617	Eternal Ruler of the ceaseless round

Celebration of a New Ministry

Entrance:	511	Holy Spirit, ever living	
	359	God of the prophets, bless the prophets' heirs	
	370	I bind unto myself today	
	525	The Church's one foundation	
	518	Christ is made the sure foundation	G (Jn 14)
	524	I love thy kingdom, Lord	
	517	How lovely is thy dwelling-place	
Sequence:	521	Put forth, O God, thy Spirit's might	E (Eph 4)
	511	Holy Spirit, ever living	
	359	God of the prophets, bless the prophets' heirs	
After the Sermon:	528	Lord, you give the great commission	
	531	O Spirit of the living God	
	511	Holy Spirit, ever living	
	359	God of the prophets, bless the prophets' heirs	
	535	Ye servants of God, your Master proclaim	
Offertory:	528	Lord, you give the great commission	
	531	O Spirit of the living God	
	540	Awake, thou Spirit of the watchmen	G (Lk 10)
	541	Come, labor on	G (Lk 10)
Communion:	321	My God, thy table now is spread	
	531	O Spirit of the living God	
	530	Spread, O spread, thou mighty word	
	593	Lord, make us servants of your peace	E (Rom 12)
Postcommunion:	535	Ye servants of God, your Master proclaim	
	531	O Spirit of the living God	
	610	Lord, whose love through humble service	E (Rom 12)
	617	Eternal Ruler of the ceaseless round	

The Dedication and Consecration of a Church

Entrance:	360, 361	Only-begotten, Word of God eternal	
	519, 520	Blessèd city, heavenly Salem	E (Rev)
	518	Christ is made the sure foundation	E (Rev, 1 Cor, 1 Pet)
	522, 523	Glorious things of thee are spoken	G (Mt 7)
	517	How lovely is thy dwelling-place	Ps (84)
	524	I love thy kingdom, Lord	
	509	Spirit divine, attend our prayers	
At the dedication of the Font:	298	All who believe and are baptized	
	299	Spirit of God, unleashed on earth	
	294	Baptized in water	
	295	Sing praise to our Creator	

	296	We know that Christ is raised and dies no more
	213	Come away to the skies
	176, 177	Over the chaos of the empty waters
At the dedication of the Lectern and/or Pulpit:	631	Book of books, our people's strength
	627	Lamp of our feet, whereby we trace
	632	O Christ, the Word Incarnate
	630	Thanks to God, whose Word was spoken
	633	Word of God, come down on earth
At the dedication of an Instrument of Music:	413	New songs of celebration render
	432	O praise ye the Lord! Praise him in the height
	390	Praise to the Lord, the Almighty
	492	Sing ye faithful, sing with gladness
	426	Songs of praise the angels sang
	402, 403	Let all the world in every corner sing
	420	When in our music God is glorified
Offertory:	360, 361	Only-begotten, Word of God eternal
	519, 520	Blessèd city, heavenly Salem E (Rev)
	518	Christ is made the sure foundation
		E (Rev, 1 Cor, 1 Pet)
	517	How lovely is thy dwelling-place Ps (84)
	524	I love thy kingdom, Lord
	51	We the Lord's people, heart and voice uniting (except on Sunday omit st. 3)
		E (1 Pet) & G (Mt 21)
Communion:	360, 361	Only-begotten, Word of God eternal
	51	We the Lord's people, heart and voice uniting (except on Sunday omit st. 3)
		E (1 Pet) & G (Mt 21)
	517	How lovely is thy dwelling-place Ps (84)
	524	I love thy kingdom, Lord
Postcommunion:	522, 523	Glorious things of thee are spoken G (Mt 7)
	524	I love thy kingdom, Lord
	517	How lovely is thy dwelling-place Ps (84)
	360, 361	Only-begotten, Word of God eternal

The Book
of Occasional
Services

The Church Year

Advent Festival of Lessons and Music

For the	60	Creator of the stars of night
Phos hilaron:	6-7	Christ, whose glory fills the skies
	496-497	How bright appears the Morning Star
	56	O come, O come, Emmanuel

Genesis 2:4b-9, 12-25   *(God creates man and woman to live in obedience to him in the Garden of Eden)*

423	Immortal, invisible, God only wise
385	Many and great, O God, are thy works
405	All things bright and beautiful
651	This is my Father's world

Genesis 3:1-23   *or*   3:1-15   *(Adam and Eve rebel against God and are cast out of the Garden of Eden)*

445-446	Praise to the Holiest in the height
270	Gabriel's message does away
60	Creator of the stars of night

Isaiah 40:1-11   *(God comforts his people and calls on them to prepare for redemption)*

67	Comfort, comfort ye my people
75	There's a voice in the wilderness crying
65	Prepare the way, O Zion
543	O Zion, tune thy voice
462	The Lord will come and not be slow
70	Herald, sound the note of judgment
59	Hark! a thrilling voice is sounding
76	On Jordan's bank the Baptist's cry

Jeremiah 31:31-34   *(A new covenant is promised which will be written in our hearts)*

666	Out of the depths I call
486	Hosanna to the living Lord!
598	Lord Christ, when first thou cam'st to earth

Isaiah 64:1-9a   *(God is called upon to act and to come among us)*

63-64	O heavenly Word, eternal Light
59	Hark! a thrilling voice is sounding
672	O very God of very God
666	Out of the depths I call

Isaiah 6:1-11   *(God reveals his glory to the prophet and calls him to be his messenger)*

63, 64	O heavenly Word, eternal Light
59	Hark! a thrilling voice is sounding
70	Herald, sound the note of judgment
61, 62	"Sleepers, wake!" A voice astounds us
596	Judge eternal, throned in splendor
640	Watchman, tell us of the night

Isaiah 35:1-10   *(The prophet proclaims that God will come and save us)*

75	There's a voice in the wilderness crying
67	Comfort, comfort ye my people
65	Prepare the way, O Zion
71, 72	Hark! the glad sound! the Savior comes
616	Hail to the Lord's Anointed
70	Herald, sound the note of judgment

Baruch 4:36-5:9   *(The Scribe Baruch urges the people to look East because salvation is at hand)*

543	O Zion, tune thy voice
75	There's a voice in the wilderness crying
67	Comfort, comfort ye my people
65	Prepare the way, O Zion

Isaiah 7:10-15   *(God promises that a child shall be conceived who will be known as "God with us")*

56	O come, O come, Emmanuel
496, 497	How bright appears the Morning Star
66	Come, thou long-expected Jesus
491	Where is this stupendous stranger?
476	Can we by searching find out God

Micah 5:2-4   *(The one who is to rule Israel will be born in the village of Bethlehem)*

55	Redeemer of the nations, come
54	Savior of the nations, come!
74	Blest be the King whose coming
56	O come, O come, Emmanuel

Isaiah 11:1-9   *(The Spirit of the Lord will rest upon the Holy One)*

71, 72	Hark! the glad sound! the Savior comes
542	Christ is the world's true Light
534	God is working his purpose out
597	O day of peace that dimly shines
462	The Lord will come and not be slow

600, 601	O day of God, draw nigh
573	Father eternal, Ruler of creation
496, 497	How bright appears the Morning Star
56	O come, O come, Emmanuel

Zephaniah 3:14-18 *(The Lord will be among us; we are summoned to rejoice and sing)*

74	Blest be the King whose coming
71, 72	Hark! the glad sound! the Saviour comes
436	Lift up your heads, ye mighty gates
6, 7	Christ, whose glory fills the skies

Isaiah 65:17-25 *(God promises a new heaven and a new earth)*

597	O day of peace that dimly shines
600, 601	O day of God, draw nigh
66	Come, thou long-expected Jesus
56	O come, O come, Emmanuel
573	Father, eternal, Ruler of creation

Luke 1:5-25 *(An angel announces to Zechariah that his wife Elizabeth will bear a son)*

271, 272	The great forerunner of the morn
444	Blessed be the God of Israel
76	On Jordan's bank the Baptist's cry
69	What is the crying at Jordan?

Luke 1:26-38 *or* 1:26-56 *(The Angel Gabriel announces to the Virgin Mary that she will bear the Son of the Most High)*

265	The angel Gabriel from heaven came
270	Gabriel's message does away
263, 264	The Word whom earth and sea and sky
268, 269	Ye who claim the faith of Jesus
266	Nova, nova
258	Virgin-born, we bow before thee
437, 438	Tell out, my soul, the greatness of the Lord!
277	Sing of Mary, pure and lowly
278	Sing we of the blessèd Mother
60	Creator of the stars of night
55	Redeemer of the nations, come
54	Savior of the nations, come!
673	The first one ever, oh, ever to know (st. 1)

Vigil for Christmas Eve or Christmas Festival of Lessons and Music

For the	82	Of the Father's love begotten
Phos hilaron:	103	A child is born in Bethlehem, Alleluia!
	91	Break forth, O beauteous heavenly light

Genesis 2:4b-9, 12-25 *(God creates man and woman to live in obedience to him in the Garden of Eden)*

386, 387	We sing of God, the mighty source

	491	Where is this stupendous stranger?
Genesis 3:1-23 *or* 3:1-15		*(Adam and Eve rebel against God and are cast out of the Garden of Eden)*
	270	Gabriel's message does away
	60	Creator of the stars of night
	445, 446	Praise to the Holiest in the height
	100	Joy to the world! the Lord is come
	88	Sing, O sing, this blessèd morn
Isaiah 40:1-11		*(God comforts his people and calls on them to prepare for redemption)*
	77	From east to west, from shore to shore
	67	Comfort, comfort ye my people
	75	There's a voice in the wilderness crying
	65	Prepare the way, O Zion
	543	O Zion, tune thy voice
	462	The Lord will come and not be slow
	99	Go tell it on the mountain
Isaiah 35:1-10		*(The prophet proclaims that God will come and save us)*
	616	Hail to the Lord's Anointed
	71, 72	Hark! the glad sound! the Savior comes
	75	There's a voice in the wilderness crying
	67	Comfort, comfort ye my people
	65	Prepare the way, O Zion
	70	Herald, sound the note of judgment
Isaiah 7:10-15		*(God promises that a child shall be conceived who will be known as "God with us")*
	496, 497	How bright appears the Morning Star
	81	Lo, how a Rose e'er blooming
	125, 126	The people who in darkness walked
	491	Where is this stupendous stranger?
	476	Can we by searching find out God
	56	O come, O come, Emmanuel
	88	Sing, O sing, this blessèd morn
	87	Hark! the herald angels sing
Luke 1:5-25		*(An angel announces to Zechariah that his wife Elizabeth will bear a son)*
	271, 272	The great forerunner of the morn
	444	Blessed be the God of Israel
	69	What is the crying at Jordan?
	76	On Jordan's bank the Baptist's cry
Luke 1:26-58		*(The Angel Gabriel announces to the Virgin Mary that she will bear the Son of the Most High)*
	54	Savior of the nations, come!
	55	Redeemer of the nations, come
	265	The angel Gabriel from heaven came

270	Gabriel's message does away
263, 264	The Word whom earth and sea and sky
258	Virgin-born, we bow before thee
266	Nova, nova
77	From east to west, from shore to shore
81	Lo, how a Rose e'er blooming
82	Of the Father's love begotten
60	Creator of the stars of night
673	The first one ever, oh, ever to know (st. 1)

Luke 1:39-46 or 1:39-56   *(The Virgin Mary is greeted by Elizabeth and proclaims her joy)*

437, 438	Tell out, my soul, the greatness of the Lord!
268, 269	Ye who claim the faith of Jesus
278	Sing we of the blessèd Mother
277	Sing of Mary, pure and lowly
258	Virgin-born, we bow before thee
263, 264	The Word whom earth and sea and sky
265	The angel Gabriel from heaven came

Luke 1:57-80   *(John the Baptist is born and his father rejoices that his son will prepare the way of the Lord)*

271, 272	The great forerunner of the morn
444	Blessed be the God of Israel
69	What is the crying at Jordan?
76	On Jordan's bank the Baptist's cry
70	Herald, sound the note of judgment

Luke 2:1-20   *(Jesus is born at Bethlehem and is worshiped by angels and shepherds)*

103	A child is born in Bethlehem, Alleluia!
96	Angels we have heard on high
101	Away in a manger, no crib for his bed
91	Break forth, O beauteous heavenly light
106	Christians, awake, salute the happy morn
99	Go tell it on the mountain
83	O come, all ye faithful
78, 79	O little town of Bethlehem
111	Silent night, holy night
110	The snow lay on the ground
114	'Twas in the moon of wintertime
94, 95	While shepherds watched their flocks by night
113	Oh, sleep now, holy baby (Duérmete, Niño lindo)
80	From heaven above to earth I come
105	God rest you merry, gentlemen
89, 90	It came upon the midnight clear
102	Once in royal David's city
98	Unto us a boy is born!
115	What child is this, who, laid to rest

Luke 2:21-36   *(Jesus receives his name and is presented to Simeon in the Temple)*

	259	Hail to the Lord who comes
	257	O Zion, open wide thy gates
	499	Lord God, you now have set your servant free
	60	Creator of the stars of night (sts. 1-4)
	252	Jesus! Name of wondrous love!
	248, 249	To the Name of our salvation

Hebrews 1:1-12 *(In the fullness of time, God sent his Son whose reign is for ever and ever)*

	85, 86	O Savior of our fallen race
	77	From east to west, from shore to shore
	468	It was poor little Jesus
	476	Can we by searching find out God
	489	The great Creator of the worlds
	448, 449	O love, how deep, how broad, how high
	492	Sing, ye faithful, sing with gladness
	421	All glory be to God on high
	82	Of the Father's love begotten
	88	Sing, O sing, this blessèd morn
	84	Love came down at Christmas
	97	Dost thou in a manger lie
	108	Now yield we thanks and praise
	491	Where is this stupendous stranger?

John 1:1-18 *(The Word was made flesh and we have seen his glory)*

	87	Hark! the herald angels sing
	100	Joy to the world! the Lord is come
	107	Good Christian friends, rejoice
	491	Where is this stupendous stranger?
	452	Glorious the day when Christ was born
	439	What wondrous love is this
	106	Christians, awake, salute the happy morn
	108	Now yield we thanks and praise
	92	On this day earth shall ring
	104	A stable lamp is lighted
	112	In the bleak midwinter
	109	The first Nowell the angel did say
	435	At the Name of Jesus
	477	All praise to thee, for thou, O King divine
	421	All glory be to God on high
	443	From God Christ's deity came forth
	85, 86	O Savior of our fallen race
	88	Sing, O sing, this blessèd morn
	633	Word of God, come down on earth
	82	Of the Father's love begotten

Service For New Year's Eve

The Hebrew		
Year:	396, 397	Now thank we all our God
	424	For the fruit of all creation

	705	As those of old their first fruits brought
	709	O God of Bethel, by whose hand
The Promised	393	Praise our great and gracious Lord
Land:	690	Guide me, O thou great Jehovah
A Season for all	680	O God, our help in ages past	(Ps 90)
Things:	251	O God, whom neither time nor space
	289	Our Father, by whose servants
Remember your	666	Out of the depths I call	(Ps 130)
Creator:	251	O God, whom neither time nor space
	665	All my hope on God is founded
	680	O God, our help in ages past
Marking the	431	The stars declare his glory	(Ps 19)
Times, and	373	Praise the Lord! ye heavens adore him	(Ps 148)
Winter:	251	O God, whom neither time nor space
	394, 395	Creating God, your fingers trace	(Ps 148)
The Acceptable	250	Now greet the swiftly changing year
Time:	499	Lord God, you now have set your servant free
	635	If thou but trust in God to guide thee
While it is		
Called	635	If thou but trust in God to guide thee
Today:	250	Now greet the swiftly changing year
	697	My God, accept my heart this day
New Heavens		
and	594, 595	God of grace and God of glory
New Earth:	250	Now greet the swiftly changing year
	665	All my hope on God is founded
	709	O God of Bethel, by whose hand
	532, 533	How wondrous and great thy works, God of praise

Vigil for the Eve of the Baptism of Our Lord

The Story of the	641	Lord Jesus, think on me
Flood:	709	O God of Bethel, by whose hand
	404	We will extol you, ever-blessèd Lord
	414	God, my King, thy might confessing
	411	O bless the Lord, my soul!
The Lord who	425	Sing now with joy unto the Lord
Makes a Way	187	Through the Red Sea brought at last, Alleluia!
in the Sea:	393	Praise our great and gracious Lord
	363	Ancient of Days, who sittest throned in glory
The Washing and	359	God of the prophets, bless the prophets' heirs
Anointing of		
Aaron:	697	My God, accept my heart this day
	294	Baptized in water

	664	My Shepherd will supply my need	(Ps 23)
	645, 646	The King of love my shepherd is	(Ps 23)
	663	The Lord my God my shepherd is	(Ps 23)
The Anointing of	697	My God, accept my heart this day	
David:	294	Baptized in water	
	359	God of the prophets, bless the prophets' heirs	
The Cleansing of	686	Come, thou fount of every blessing	
Naaman in the	299	Spirit of God, unleashed on earth	
Jordan:	658	As longs the deer for cooling streams	
	641	Lord Jesus, think on me	
Salvation Offered	678, 679	Surely it is God who saves me	(Canticle 9)
Freely to All:	692	I heard the voice of Jesus say	
	658	As longs the deer for cooling streams	
	299	Spirit of God, unleashed on earth	
A New Heart and	584	God, you have given us power to sound (sts. 1-3)	
a New Spirit:	574, 575	Before thy throne, O God, we kneel	
	658	As longs the deer for cooling streams	(Ps 42)
	656	Blest are the pure in heart	
	432	O praise ye the Lord! Praise him in the height (omit st. 3)	
The Spirit of the	370	I bind to myself today	
Lord is Upon	297	Descend, O Spirit, purging flame	
Me or Behold my	279	Spirit of God, unleashed on Earth	
Servant:	295	Sing praise to our Creator	
When God's	294	Baptized in water	
Patience Waited	296	We know that Christ is raised and dies no more	
in the Days of	298	All who believe and are baptized	
Noah:			
or *God Anointed*	121	Christ, when for us you were baptized	
Jesus with the	120	The sinless one to Jordan came	
Holy Spirit:	139	When Jesus went to Jordan's stream	
The Baptism of	139	When Jesus went to Jordan's stream	
Jesus:	121	Christ, when for us you were baptized	
	116	"I come," the great Redeemer cries	
	120	The sinless one to Jordan came	
or *The*	176, 177	Over the chaos of the empty water	
Resurrection and	296	We know that Christ is raised and dies no more	
the Great	294	Baptized in water	
Commission:	187	Through the Red Sea brought at last, Alleluia!	

Candlemas Procession

For the Procession:	496, 497	How bright appears the Morning Star
	6, 7	Christ, whose glory fills the skies

499	Lord God, you now have set your servant free
259	Hail to the Lord who comes
257	O Zion, open wide thy gates

The Way of the Cross

For the Procession:	158	Ah, holy Jesus, how hast thou offended
	164	Alone thou goest forth, O Lord
	160	Cross of Jesus, cross of sorrow
	168, 169	O sacred head, sore wounded
	161	The flaming banners of our King (Vexilla regis)
	162	The royal banners forward go (Vexilla regis)
	167	There is a green hill far away (omit sts. 3,4)
	170	To mock your reign, O dearest Lord
	172	Were you there when they crucified my Lord?
	165, 166	Sing, my tongue, the glorious battle
	471	We sing the praise of him who died
	474	When I survey the wondrous cross

Rogation Procession

For the Procession:	292	O Jesus, crowned with all renown
	400	All creatures of our God and King
	406, 407	Most High, omnipotent, good Lord
	291	We plow the fields and scatter
	405	All things bright and beautiful
	389	Let us, with a gladsome mind
	428	O all ye works of God, now come
	709	O God of Bethel, by whose hand
	390	Praise to the Lord, the Almighty
	388	O worship the King, all glorious above!

Vigil for the Eve of All Saints' Day

The Call of Abraham:	709	O God of Bethel, by whose hand
	401	The God of Abraham praise
	393	Praise our great and gracious Lord
Daniel Delivered from the Lions' Den:	678, 679	Surely it is God who saves me
	564, 565	He who would valiant be
	563	Go forward, Christian soldier
	664	My Shepherd will supply my need (Ps 23)
	645, 646	The King of love my shepherd is (Ps 23)
	663	The Lord my God my shepherd is (Ps 23)
The Testament and Death of Mattathias:	678, 679	Surely it is God who saves me
	279	For thy dear saints, O Lord
	548	Soldiers of Christ, arise
	563	Go forward, Christian soldier

The Martyrdom of	275	Hark! the sound of holy voices
the Seven	236	King of the martyrs' noble band
Brothers:	240, 241	Hearken to the anthem glorious
	237	Let us now our voices raise

The Eulogy of the	289	Our Father, by whose servants
Ancestors:	527	Singing songs of expectation
	617	Eternal Ruler of the ceaseless round
	526	Let saints on earth in concert sing

Surrounded by a	545	Lo! what a cloud of witnesses
Great Cloud of	546	Awake, my soul, stretch every nerve
Witnesses:	253	Give us the wings of faith to rise
	293	I sing a song of the saints of God

The Reward of the	286	Who are these like stars appearing
Saints:	374	Come, let us join our cheerful songs
	417, 418	This is the feast of victory for our God
	299	Spirit of God, unleashed on earth

The Beatitudes:	560	Remember your servants, Lord
	656	Blest are the pure in heart
	697	My God, accept my heart this day

or "I will give	692	I heard the voice of Jesus say
you rest":	299	Spirit of God, unleashed on earth
	74	Blest be the King whose coming

or The	176, 177	Over the chaos of the empty waters
Resurrection and	296	We know that Christ is raised and dies no more
the Great	294	Baptized in water
Commission:	187	Through the Red Sea brought at last, Alleluia!

Service for All Hallows' Eve

The Witch of	666	Out of the depths I call	(Ps 130)
Endor:	640	Watchman, tell us of the night	
	677	God moves in a mysterious way	
	667	Sometimes a light surprises	

The Vision of	44, 45	To you before the close of day	
Eliphaz the	43	All praise to thee, my God, this night	
Temanite:	702	Lord, thou hast searched me and dost know	
	596	Judge eternal, throned in splendor	

The Valley of	358	Christ the Victorious, give to your servants	
Dry Bones:	356	May choirs of angels lead you	
	354	Into Paradise may the angels lead you	
	623	O what their joy and their glory must be	
	620	Jerusalem, my happy home	

The War in			
Heaven:	253	Give us the wings of faith to rise	
	286	Who are these like stars appearing	

282, 283	Christ, the fair glory of the holy angels	
275	Hark! the sound of holy voices	
545	Lo! what a cloud of witnesses	
526	Let saints on earth in concert sing	
428	O all ye works of God, now come	

Pastoral Services

A Vigil on the Eve of Baptism

The Story of the	641	Lord Jesus, think on me
Flood:	709	O God of Bethel, by whose hand
	404	We will extol you, ever-blessèd Lord
	414	God, my King, thy might confessing
	411	O bless the Lord, my soul!
The Story of the	697	My God, accept my heart this day
Convenant:	709	O God of Bethel, by whose hand
	370	I bind unto myself today
	686	Come, thou fount of every blessing
Salvation Offered	678, 679	Surely it is God who saves me (Canticle 9)
Freely to All:	692	I heard the voice of Jesus say
	658	As longs the deer for cooling streams
	299	Spirit of God, unleashed on earth
	432	O praise ye the Lord! Praise him in the height (omit st. 3)
A New Heart and	584	God, you have given us power to sound (sts. 1-3)
a New Spirit:	574, 575	Before thy throne, O God, we kneel
	656	Blest are the pure in heart
	658	As longs the deer for cooling streams (Ps 42)
The Valley of	298	All who believe and are baptized
Dry Bones:	294	Baptized in water
	296	We know that Christ is raised and dies no more
Baptized into	298	All who believe and are baptized
his Death:	294	Baptized in water
	296	We know that Christ is raised and dies no more
or *We are*	295	Sing praise to our Creator
Children of God:	432	O praise ye the Lord! Praise him in the height (omit st. 3)
	294	Baptized in water
	297	Descend, O Spirit, purging flame
or *Now is the*	298	All who believe and are baptized
Day of	213	Come away to the skies
Salvation:	176, 177	Over the chaos of the empty waters
	296	We know that Christ is raised and dies no more

	547	Awake, O sleeper, rise from death
	697	My God, accept my heart this day
	370	I bind unto myself today
The Baptism of	139	When Jesus went to Jordan's stream
Jesus:	121	Christ, when for us you were baptized
	116	"I come," the great Redeemer cries
	120	The sinless one to Jordan came
or *You Must be*	432	O praise ye the Lord! Praise him in the height
Born Again:		(omit st. 3)
	294	Baptized in Water
	295	Sing praise to our Creator
	297	Descend, O Spirit, purging flame
	296	We know that Christ is raised and dies no more
or *The*	176, 177	Over the chaos of the empty waters
Resurrection and	296	We know that Christ is raised and dies no more
the Great	294	Baptized in water
Commission:	187	Through the Red Sea brought at last, Alleluia!

Celebration for a Home

Sequence:	396, 397	Now thank we all our God
	416	For the beauty of the earth
	612	Gracious Spirit, Holy Ghost
	251	O God, whom neither time nor space (omit st. 2)
At the procession:	587	Our Father, by whose Name
	396, 397	Now thank we all our God
	350	O God of love, to thee we bow
	352	O God, to those who here profess
	353	Your love, O God, has called us here
	612	Gracious Spirit, Holy Ghost
	581	Where charity and love prevail
Offertory:	587	Our Father, by whose Name
	138	All praise to you, O Lord
	581	Where charity and love prevail
	593	Lord, make us servants of your peace
	350	O God of love, to thee we bow
	352	O God, to those who here profess
	353	Your love, O God, has called us here
	709	O God of Bethel, by whose hand
Communion:	593	Lord, make us servants of your peace	
	581	Where charity and love prevail	
	138	All praise to you, O Lord	
	664	My Shepherd will supply my need	(Ps 23)
	645, 646	The King of love my shepherd is	(Ps 23)
	663	The Lord my God my shepherd is	(Ps 23)
	709	O God of Bethel, by whose hand	

Postcommunion:	351	May the grace of Christ our Savior
	635	If thou but trust in God to guide thee
	312	Strengthen for service, Lord
	709	O God of Bethel, by whose hand

Anniversary of a Marriage

See The Celebration and Blessing of a Marriage (above, p. 289)

A Public Service of Healing

See Various Occasions   20. For the Sick (above, p. 287)

Burial of One Who Does Not Profess the Christian Faith

664	My Shepherd will supply my need	(Ps 23)
645, 646	The King of love my shepherd is	
		(Ps 23 & Jn 10)
663	The Lord my God my shepherd is	(Ps 23)
680	O God, our help in ages past	(Ps 90)
668	I to the hills will lift mine eyes	(Ps 121)
665	All my hope on God is founded (sts. 1-2)	
669	Commit thou all that grieves thee	
635	If thou but trust in God to guide thee	
379	God is love, let heaven adore him	
423	Immortal, invisible, God only wise	
372	Praise to the living God!	

The Founding of a Church

Laying of a Cornerstone

Opening hymn and	519, 520	Blessèd city, heavenly Salem
concluding hymn:	518	Christ is made the sure foundation (sts. 1-2)
	522, 523	Glorious things of thee are spoken
	517	How lovely is thy dwelling-place
	524	I love thy kingdom, Lord
	525	The Church's one foundation
	509	Spirit divine, attend our prayers

Episcopal Services

Consecration of Chrism

See Various Occasions   10. At Baptism (above, p. 282)

Reaffirmation of Ordination Vows

See Ordination (above, p. 292)

Recognition and Investiture of a Diocesan Bishop *or* Welcoming and Seating of a Bishop in the Cathedral
See Celebration of a New Ministry (above, p. 293)

Setting Apart for a Special Vocation

Entrance:	370	I bind unto myself today	
	524	I love thy kingdom, Lord	
	704	O thou who camest from above	
Sequence:	664	My Shepherd will supply my need	(Ps 23)
	645, 646	The King of love my shepherd is	(Ps 23)
	663	The Lord my God my sheperd is	(Ps 23)
	377, 378	All people that on earth do dwell	(Ps 100)
	391	Before the Lord's eternal throne	(Ps 100)
Offertory:	655	O Jesus, I have promised	
	659, 660	O Master, let me walk with thee	
	563	Go forward, Christian soldier	
	564, 565	He who would valiant be	
	546	Awake, my soul, stretch every nerve	(Phil)
	593	Lord, make us servants of your peace	(Col)
	675	Take up your cross, the Savior said	(Mt 16)
	610	Lord, whose love through humble service	
Communion:	592	Teach me, my God and King	(Col)
	482	Lord of all hopefulness, Lord of all joy	
	593	Lord, make us servants of your peace	(Col)
Postcommunion:	312	Strengthen for service, Lord	
	535	Ye servants of God, your Master proclaim	
	610	Lord, whose love through humble service	
	617	Eternal Ruler of the ceaseless round	
	559	Lead us, heavenly Father, lead us	
	556, 557	Rejoice, ye pure in heart!	
	541	Come, labor on	
	540	Awake, thou Spirit of the watchmen	
	531	O Spirit of the living God	

Lesser
Feasts and
Fasts

The Weekdays of Lent

The following pages suggest hymns for use with the propers provided in Lesser Feasts and Fasts for The Weekdays of Lent, The Weekdays of Easter Season, and The Lesser Feasts.

Thursday After Ash Wednesday

675	Take up your cross, the Savior said	G
476	Can we by searching find out God	G
443	From God Christ's deity came forth	G
150	Forty day and forty nights	S

Friday After Ash Wednesday

145	Now quit your care	C & L
489	The great Creator of the worlds	G
706	In your mercy, Lord, you called me	G
146, 147	Now let us all with one accord	S

Saturday After Ash Wednesday

145	Now quit your care	L
281	He sat to watch o'er customs paid	G
706	In your mercy, Lord, you called me	G
467	Sing, my soul, his wondrous love	G
469, 470	There's a wideness in God's mercy	G

The First Week of Lent

MON:	152	Kind Maker of the world, O hear	L
	148	Creator of the earth and skies	L
	3, 4	Now that the daylight fills the sky	L & G
	610	Lord, whose love through humble service	G
	609	Where cross the crowded ways of life	G
TUE:	142	Lord, who throughout these forty days	C
	150	Forty days and forty nights	C
	698	Eternal Spirit of the living Christ	G
	709	O God of Bethel, by whose hand	G
	674	"Forgive our sins as we forgive"	G
	581	Where charity and love prevail	G

WED:	148	Creator of the earth and skies	L & G
	152	Kind Maker of the world, O hear	L & G
	151	From deepest woe I cry to thee	L & G
	144	Lord Jesus, Sun of Righteousness	L & G
	140, 141	Wilt thou forgive that sin, where I begun	L & G

Also see: Various Occasions   15. For the Ministry (Ember Days) (above, p. 285)

THU:	142	Lord, who throughout these forty days	C
	150	Forty days and forty nights	C
	711	Seek ye first the kingdom of God	G
	698	Eternal Spirit of the living Christ	G
FRI:	150	Forty days and forty nights	C
	411	O bless the Lord, my soul!	L
	666	Out of the depths I call	P
	151	From deepest woe I cry to thee	P
	674	"Forgive our sins as we forgive"	G

Also see: Various Occasions   15. For the Ministry (Ember Days) (above, p. 285)

SAT:	5	O splendor of God's glory bright	C & G
	3, 4	Now that the daylight fills the sky	C & G
	593	Lord, make us servants of your peace	C & G
	603, 604	When Christ was lifted from the earth	C & G

Also see: Various Occasions   15. For the Ministry (Ember Days) (above, p. 285)

The Second Week of Lent

MON:	143	The glory of these forty days	L
	3, 4	Now that the daylight fills the sky	G
	5	O splendor of God's glory bright	G
	593	Lord, make us servants of your peace	G
	603, 604	When Christ was lifted from the earth	G
TUE:	140, 141	Wilt thou forgive that sin, where I begun	C & L
	144	Lord Jesus, Sun of Righteousness	C & L
	693	Just as I am, without one plea	L
	699	Jesus, Lover of my soul	L
	670	Lord, for ever at thy side	G
	656	Blest are the pure in heart	G
WED:	458	My song is love unknown	G
	478	Jesus, our mighty Lord	G
	143	The glory of these forty days	S
	149	Eternal Lord of love, behold your Church	S

THU:	635	If thou but trust in God to guide thee	L
	574, 575	Before thy throne, O God, we kneel	G
	582, 583	O holy city, seen of John	G
	346	Completed, Lord, the Holy Mysteries	G
FRI:	598	Lord Christ, when first thou cam'st to earth	G
	495	Hail, thou once despisèd Jesus!	G
	483	The head that once was crowned with thorns	G
	149	Eternal Lord of love, behold your Church	S
SAT:	664	My Shepherd will supply my need	L
	645, 646	The King of love my shepherd is	L
	663	The Lord my God my shepherd is	L
	411	O bless the Lord, my soul!	P
	467	Sing, my soul, his wondrous love	G
	469, 470	There's a wideness in God's mercy	G
	641	Lord Jesus, think on me	G
	144	Lord Jesus, Sun of Righteousness	G
	140, 141	Wilt thou forgive that sin, where I begun	G

The Third Week of Lent

MON:	658	As longs the deer for cooling streams	P
	448, 449	O Love, how deep, how broad, how high	G
	443	From God Christ's deity came forth	G
	143	The glory of these forty days	S

Another Proper in the Third Week of Lent:

	685	Rock of ages, cleft for me	L
	343	Shepherd of souls, refresh and bless	L
	692	I heard the voice of Jesus say (st. 2)	G
	673	The first one ever, oh, ever to know (st. 2)	G
	649, 650	O Jesus, joy of loving hearts	G
	700	O love that casts out fear	G
	699	Jesus, Lover of my soul	G
TUE:	674	"Forgive our sins as we forgive"	G
	593	Lord, make us servants of your peace	G
	5	O splendor of God's glory bright	G
	581	Where charity and love prevail	G
	146, 147	Now let us all with one accord	S
WED:	628	Help us, O Lord, to learn	L & G
	627	Lamp of our feet, whereby we trace	L & G
	626	Lord, be thy word my rule	L & G
	142	Lord, who throughout these forty days	S
THU:	146, 147	Now let us all with one accord	G
	695, 696	By gracious powers so wonderfully sheltered	S
	634	I call on thee, Lord Jesus Christ	S

	143	The glory of these forty days	S
FRI:	704	O thou who camest from above	G
	682	I love thee, Lord, but not because	G
	700	O love that casts out fear	G
	643	My God, how wonderful thou art	G
	551	Rise up, ye saints of God!	G
	581	Where charity and love prevail	G
SAT:	670	Lord, for ever at thy side	G
	641	Lord Jesus, think on me	G
	140, 141	Wilt thou forgive that sin, where I begun	G
	301	Bread of the world, in mercy broken	G
	313	Let thy Blood in mercy poured	G

The Fourth Week of Lent

MON:	411	O bless the Lord, my soul!	G
	371	Thou, whose almighty word	G
	493	O for a thousand tongues to sing	G
	567	Thine arm, O Lord, in days of old	G
	689	I sought the Lord, and afterward I knew	S

Another Proper in the Fourth Week of Lent:

	465, 466	Eternal light, shine in my heart	G
	692	I heard the voice of Jesus say (st. 3)	G
	6, 7	Christ, whose glory fills the skies	G
	633	Word of God, come down on earth (st. 3)	G
	490	I want to walk as a child of the light	G
TUE:	465, 466	Eternal light, shine in my heart	C
	692	I heard the voice of Jesus say (st. 2)	C & L
	649, 650	O Jesus, joy of loving hearts	C & L
	700	O love that casts out fear	C & L
	411	O bless the Lord, my soul!	G
	633	Word of God, come down on earth	C, L & G
WED:	343	Shepherd of souls, refresh and bless	C
	635	If thou but trust in God to guide thee	L
	695, 696	By gracious powers so wonderfully sheltered	L
	455, 456	O Love of God, how strong and true	G
THU:	633	Word of God, come down on earth	G
	628	Help us, O Lord, to learn	G
	627	Lamp of our feet, whereby we trace	G
	146, 147	Now let us all with one accord	S
FRI:	598	Lord Christ, when first thou cam'st to earth	G
	443	From God Christ's deity came forth	G
	439	What wondrous love is this	G
	472	Hope of the world, thou Christ of great compassion	G

SAT:	140, 141	Wilt thou forgive that sin, where I begun	C
	146, 147	Now let us all with one accord	C
	692	I heard the voice of Jesus say (st. 2)	G
	443	From God Christ's deity came forth	G

The Fifth Week of Lent

MON:	489	The great Creator of the worlds	G-Jn 8:1-11
	144	Lord Jesus, Sun of Righteousness	G-Jn 8:1-11
	140, 141	Wilt thou forgive that sin, where I begun	G-Jn 8:1-11
	151	From deepest woe I cry to thee	G-Jn 8:1-11
	692	I heard the voice of Jesus say (st. 3)	G-Jn 8:12-20
	490	I want to walk as a child of the light	G-Jn 8:12-20
	672	O very God of very God	G-Jn 8:12-20
	6, 7	Christ, whose glory fills the skies	G-Jn 8:12-20

Another Proper in the Fifth Week of Lent:

	455, 456	O Love of God, how strong and true	G
	445, 446	Praise to the Holiest in the height	G
	335	I am the bread of life (sts. 4-5)	G
	346	Completed, Lord, the Holy Mysteries	G
	144	Lord Jesus, Sun of Righteousness	S

TUE:	473	Lift high the cross	L & G
	691	My faith looks up to thee	G
	434	Nature with open volume stands	G
	149	Eternal Lord of love, behold your Church	S

WED:	636, 637	How firm a foundation, ye saints of the Lord	L
	635	If thou but trust in God to guide thee	L
	419	Lord of all being, throned afar	G
	642	Jesus, the very thought of thee	G

THU:	401	The God of Abraham praise	L & G
	146, 147	Now let us all with one accord	L
	439	What wondrous love is this	G
	149	Eternal Lord of love, behold your Church	S
	144	Lord Jesus, Sun of Righteousness	S

FRI:	170	To mock your reign, O dearest Lord	L & G
	164	Alone thou goest forth, O Lord	L & G
	160	Cross of Jesus, cross of sorrow	L & G
	165, 166	Sing, my tongue, the glorious battle	L & G

SAT:	598	Lord Christ, when first thou cam'st to earth	G
	458	My song is love unknown	G
	161	The flaming banners of our King	G
	162	The royal banners forward go	G

The Weekdays of Easter Season

The Second Week of Easter

MON:	429	I'll praise my Maker while I've breath	P
	432	O praise ye the Lord! Praise him in the height	G
	294	Baptized in water	G
	295	Sing praise to our Creator	G
	176, 177	Over the chaos of the empty waters	G
	296	We know that Christ is raised and dies no more	G
	297	Descend, O Spirit, purging flame	G
TUE:	473	Lift high the cross	G
	188, 189	Love's redeeming work is done	G
	184	Christ the Lord is risen again!	G
	196, 197	Look there! the Christ, our Brother, comes	G
WED:	489	The great Creator of the worlds	G
	448, 449	O love, how deep, how broad, how high	G
	439	What wondrous love is this	G
	452	Glorious the day when Christ was born	G
	530	Spread, O spread, thou mighty word	G
THU:	208	The strife is o'er, the battle done	L
	205	Good Christians all, rejoice and sing!	L
	178	Alleluia, alleluia! Give thanks to the risen Lord	L & G
	184	Christ the Lord is risen again!	L
	483	The head that once was crowned with thorns	L
FRI:	305, 306	Come, risen Lord, and deign to be our guest	G
	185, 186	Christ Jesus lay in death's strong bands	G
	343	Shepherd of souls, refresh and bless	G
	308, 309	O Food to pilgrims given	G
	321	My God, thy table now is spread	G
	320	Zion, praise thy Savior, singing (sts. 5-6)	G
	690	Guide me, O thou great Jehovah	G
SAT:	636, 637	How firm a foundation, ye saints of the Lord	G
	669	Commit thou all that grieves thee	G
	209	We walk by faith and not by sight	G
	447	The Christ who died but rose again	G

The Third Week of Easter

MON:	243	When Stephen, full of power and grace	L
	343	Shepherd of souls, refresh and bless	G
	320	Zion, praise thy Savior, singing (sts. 5-6)	G
	308, 309	O Food to pilgrims given	G
TUE:	243	When Stephen, full of power and grace	L
	240, 241	Hearken to the anthem glorious	L
	335	I am the bread of life	G

	185, 186	Christ Jesus lay in death's strong bands	G
	343	Shepherd of souls, refresh and bless	G
	308, 309	O Food to pilgrims given	G
	649, 650	O Jesus, joy of loving hearts	G
	307	Lord, enthroned in heavenly splendor	G
WED:	335	I am the bread of life	G
	320	Zion, praise thy Savior, singing (sts. 5-6)	G
	346	Completed, Lord, the Holy Mysteries	G
	690	Guide me, O thou great Jehovah	G
THU:	297	Descend, O Spirit, purging flame	L
	296	We know that Christ is raised and dies no more	L
	176, 177	Over the chaos of the empty waters	L
	298	All who believe and are baptized	L
	294	Baptized in water	L
	343	Shepherd of souls, refresh and bless	G
	335	I am the bread of life	G
	323	Bread of heaven, on thee we feed	G
	308, 309	O Food to pilgrims given	G
	320	Zion, praise thy Savior, singing (sts. 5-6)	G
FRI:	256	A light from heaven shone around	L
	255	We sing the glorious conquest	L
	335	I am the bread of life	G
	320	Zion, praise thy Savior, singing	G
	185, 186	Christ Jesus lay in death's stong bands	G
SAT:	529	In Christ there is no East or West	L
	626	Lord, be thy word my rule	G
	634	I call on thee, Lord Jesus Christ	G
	633	Word of God, come down on earth	G
	630	Thanks to God whose Word was spoken	G
	323	Bread of heaven, on thee we feed	G

The Fourth Week of Easter

MON:	478	Jesus, our mighty Lord	G
	664	My Shepherd will supply my need	G
	645, 646	The King of love my shepherd is	G
	708	Savior, like a shepherd lead us	G
	334	Praise the Lord, rise up rejoicing	G
	320	Zion, praise thy Savior, singing sts. (sts. 5-6)	G
	205	Good Christians all, rejoice and sing!	G
	304	I come with joy to meet my Lord	G
TUE:	478	Jesus, our mighty Lord	G
	663	The Lord my God my shepherd is	G
	708	Savior, like a shepherd lead us	G
	334	Praise the Lord, rise up rejoicing	G
	320	Zion, praise thy Savior, singing sts.(sts. 5-6)	G
WED:	531	O Spirit of the living God	L

	538	God of mercy, God of grace	P
	465, 466	Eternal light, shine in my heart	G
	6, 7	Christ, whose glory fills the skies	G
	490	I want to walk as a child of the light	G
THU:	443	From God Christ's deity came forth	L
	690	Guide me, O thou great Jehovah	L
	393	Praise our great and gracious Lord	L
	187	Through the Red Sea brought at last, Alleluia!	L
	202	The Lamb's high banquet called to share	L
FRI:	455, 456	O Love of God, how strong and true	L
	448, 449	O love, how deep, how broad, how high	L
	194, 195	Jesus lives! thy terrors now	G
	1, 2	Father, we praise thee, now the night is over	G
	484, 485	Praise the Lord through every nation	G
	457	Thou art the Way, to thee alone	G
	487	Come, my Way, my Truth, my Life	G
	463, 464	He is the Way	G
SAT:	532, 533	How wondrous and great thy works, God of praise	L
	455, 456	O Love of God, how strong and true	L
	413	New songs of celebration render	P
	457	Thou art the Way, to thee alone	G
	487	Come, my Way, my Truth, my Life	G
	463, 464	He is the Way	G

The Fifth Week of Easter

	626	Lord, be thy word my rule	G
MON:	626	Lord, be thy word my rule	G
	228	Holy Spirit, font of light	G
	226, 227	Come, thou Holy Spirit bright	G
	500	Creator Spirit, by whose aid	G
	514	To thee, O Comforter divine	G
	512	Come, gracious Spirit, heavenly Dove	G
	505	O Spirit of Life, O Spirit of God	G
TUE:	404	We will extol you, ever-blessèd Lord	P
	414	God, my King, thy might confessing	P
	194, 195	Jesus lives! thy terrors now	S
	182	Christ is alive! Let Christians sing	S
	181	Awake and sing the song	S
WED:	513	Like the murmur of the dove's song	G
	198	Thou hallowed chosen morn of praise	G
	323	Bread of heaven, on thee we feed	G
	392	Come, we that love the Lord	G
	344	Lord, dismiss us with thy blessing	G
THU:	394, 395	Creating God, your fingers trace	L
	532, 533	How wondrous and great thy works, God of praise	L
	529	In Christ there is no East or West	L
	192	This joyful Eastertide	S

	193	That Easter day with joy was bright	S
FRI:	603, 604	When Christ was lifted from the earth	G
	458	My song is love unknown	G
	319	You, Lord, we praise in songs of celebration	G
	392	Come, we that love the Lord	G
	344	Lord, dismiss us with thy blessing	G
	706	In your mercy, Lord, you called me	G
SAT:	394, 395	Creating God, your fingers trace	L
	532, 533	How wondrous and great thy works, God of praise	L
	377, 378	All people that on earth do dwell	P
	391	Before the Lord's eternal throne	P
	191	Alleluia, alleluia! Hearts and voices heavenward raise	S
	211	The whole bright world rejoices now	S
	204	Now the green blade riseth from the buried grain	S

The Sixth Week of Easter

MON:	296	We know that Christ is raised and dies no more	L
	294	Baptized in water	L
	176, 177	Over the chaos of the empty waters	L
	298	All who believe and are baptized	L
	506, 507	Praise the Spirit in creation	G
	514	To thee, O Comforter divine	G

Also see: Various Occasions   19. For Rogation Days (above, p. 286)

TUE:	296	We know that Christ is raised and dies no more	L
	294	Baptized in water	L
	176, 177	Over the chaos of the empty waters	L
	298	All who believe and are baptized	L
	188, 189	Love's redeeming work is done	S
	181	Awake and sing the song	S

Also see: Various Occasions   19. For Rogation Days (above, p. 286)

WED:	423	Immortal, invisible, God only wise	L
	432	O praise ye the Lord! Praise him in the height	L
	373	Praise the Lord! ye heavens adore him	P
	394, 395	Creating God, your fingers trace	P
	512	Come, gracious Spirit, heavenly Dove	G

Also see: Various Occasions   19. For Rogation Days (above, p. 286)

THU:	**Ascension Day** *[See above p. 198]*		
FRI:	298	All who believe and are baptized	L

	176, 177	Over the chaos of the empty waters	L
	294	Baptized in water	L
	296	We know that Christ is raised and dies no more	L
	413	New songs of celebration render	P
	695, 696	By gracious powers so wonderfully sheltered	G
	435	At the Name of Jesus	S
SAT:	632	O Christ, the Word Incarnate	L
	630	Thanks to God whose Word was spoken	L
	633	Word of God, come down on earth	L
	492	Sing, ye faithful, sing with gladness	S

The Seventh Week of Easter

MON:	295	Sing praise to our Creator	L
	176, 177	Over the chaos of the empty waters	L
	298	All who believe and are baptized	L
	296	We know that Christ is raised and dies no more	L
	294	Baptized in water	L
TUE:	495	Hail, thou once despisèd Jesus!	G
	483	The head that once was crowned with thorns	G
	481	Rejoice, the Lord is King	S
	220, 221	O Lord Most High, eternal King	S
WED:	525	The Church's one foundation	L
	484, 485	Praise the Lord through every nation	G
	222	Rejoice, the Lord of life ascends	G
	217, 218	A hymn of glory let us sing	S
	494	Crown him with many crowns	S
THU:	305, 306	Come, risen Lord, and deign to be our guest	G
	219	The Lord ascendeth up on high	S
	215	See the Conqueror mounts in triumph	S
	460, 461	Alleluia! sing to Jesus!	S
	459	And have the bright immensities	S
FRI:	484, 485	Praise the Lord through every nation	G
	483	The head that once was crowned with thorns	G
	307	Lord, enthroned in heavenly splendor	S
	450, 451	All hail the power of Jesus' Name!	S
SAT:	245	Praise God for John, evangelist	G
	530	Spread, O spread, thou mighty word	G
	535	Ye servants of God, your Master proclaim	G
	435	At the Name of Jesus	S
	477	All praise to thee, for thou, O King divine	S

The Lesser Feasts

See The Common of Saints (above, pp. 275-277)

For The Lesser Feasts the reader is directed to the appropriate Common of Saints [above, pp. 275-277]. Appropriate hymns written or translated by or oftentimes attributed to the person being commemorated are listed. (Authorship is indicated by the letter A, translation by the letter T, after the first line.) Also listed are some hymns particularly related to the propers, which are not included in the more general suggestions in the appropriate Common of Saints, and some other hymns (indicated by S) particularly appropriate to the specific commemoration.

December

1	Nicholas Ferrar, Deacon, 1637	*Of A Monastic*	
2	Channing Moore Williams, Missionary Bishop in China and Japan, 1910	*Of A Missionary*	
4	John of Damascus, Priest, c. 760	*Of A Theologian and Teacher*	
5	Clement of Alexandria, Priest, c. 210	*Of A Theologian and Teacher*	

Also: 478	Jesus, our mighty Lord	A
163	Sunset to sunrise changes now	A
467	Sing, my soul, his wondrous love	E
633	Word of God, come down on earth	G
301	Bread of the world, in mercy broken	G

6	Nicholas, Bishop of Myra, c. 342	*Of A Saint*

Also: 610	Lord, whose love through humble service	E
480	When Jesus left his Father's throne	G

7	Ambrose, Bishop of Milan, 397	*Of A Theologian and Teacher*

Also: 55	Redeemer of the nations, come	A
54	Savior of the nations, come!	A
5	O splendor of God's glory bright	A
19, 20	Now, Holy Spirit, ever One (Morning)	A

21, 22	O God of truth, O Lord of might (Noon)	A
14, 15	O God, creation's secret force (Evening)	A
68	Rejoice! rejoice, believers	G
61, 62	"Sleepers, wake!" A voice astounds us	G

January

10 William Laud, Archbishop of *Of A Pastor and*
Canterbury, 1645 *Of A Theologian and Teacher*

Also: 636, 637	How firm a foundation, ye saints of the Lord	E
675	Take up your cross, the Savior said	G
488, 485	Praise the Lord through every nation	G

12 Aelred, Abbot of Ricvaulx, 1167 *Of A Theologian and Teacher*
and Of A Monastic

13 Hilary, Bishop of Poitiers, 367 *Of A Pastor and*
Of A Theologian and Teacher

17 Antony, Abbot in Egypt, 356 *Of A Monastic*

19 Wulfstan, Bishop of Worcester, 1095 *Of A Pastor*

Also: 706	In your mercy, Lord, you called me	G
458	My song is love unknown	G
319	You, Lord, we praise in songs of celebration	G
323	Bread of heaven, on thee we feed	G

20 Fabian, Bishop and Martyr of Rome, 250 *Of A Martyr*

| *Also:* 564, 565 | He who would valiant be | G |
| 655 | O Jesus, I have promised | G |

21 Agnes, Martyr at Rome, 304 *Of A Martyr*

| *Also:* 213 | Come away to the skies | L |
| 670 | Lord, for ever at thy side | G |

22 Vincent, Deacon of Saragossa, and *Of A Martyr*
Martyr, 304

23 Phillips Brooks, Bishop of Massachusetts, *Of A Pastor and*
1893 *Of A Theologian and Teacher*

Also: 422	Not far beyond the sea, nor high	E
448, 449	O love, how deep, how broad, how high	E
455, 456	O Love of God, how strong and true	E

26 Timothy and Titus, Companions of *Of A Martyr and*
Saint Paul *Of A Saint*

Also:	704	O thou who camest from above	E
	645, 646	The King of love my shepherd is	P & G
	478	Jesus, our mighty Lord	G

27 John Chrysostom, Bishop of   *Of A Pastor and*
Constantinople, 407   *Of A Theologian and Teacher*

28 Thomas Aquinas, Priest and Friar, 1274   *Of A Theologian and Teacher*

Also:	320	Zion, praise thy Savior, singing	A
	329, 330	Now, my tongue, the mystery telling	A
	314	Humbly I adore thee, Verity unseen	A
	310, 311	O saving Victim, opening wide	A

February

3 Anskar, Archbishop of Hamburg,   *Of A Missionary*
Missionary to Denmark and Sweden, 865

4 Cornelius the Centurion   *Of A Saint*

5 The Martyrs of Japan, 1597   *Of A Martyr*

Also:	675	Take up your cross, the Savior said	G
	484, 485	Praise the Lord through every nation	G
	572	Weary of all trumpeting	G

13 Absalom Jones, Priest, 1818   *Of A Pastor*

Also:	71, 72	Hark! the glad sound! the Savior comes	L
	529	In Christ there is no East or West	G
	603, 604	When Christ was lifted from the earth	G
	602	Jesu, Jesu, fill us with your love	G
	458	My song is love unknown	G
	319	You, Lord, we praise in songs of celebration	G

14 Cyril, Monk, and Methodius, Bishop,   *Of A Missionary*
Missionaries to the Slavs, 869, 885

15 Thomas Bray, Priest and Missionary, 1730   *Of A Missionary*

| Also: | 630 | Thanks to God whose Word was spoken | S |
| | 632 | O Christ, the Word incarnate | S |

23 Polycarp, Bishop and Martyr of Smyrna,   *Of A Martyr*
156

| Also: | 561 | Stand up, stand up for Jesus | E |

27 George Herbert, Priest, 1633   *Of A Pastor and*
    Of A Theologian and Teacher

Also:	487	Come, my Way, my Truth, my Life	A
	382	King of glory, King of peace	A
	402, 403	Let all the world in every corner sing	A
	592	Teach me, my God and King	A

March

1 David, Bishop of Menevia, Wales, c. 544 *Of A Pastor and*
Of A Monastic

| *Also:* | 588, 589 | Almighty God, your word is cast | G |
| | 290 | Come, ye thankful people, come (st. 2) | G |

2 Chad, Bishop of Lichfield, 672 *Of A Pastor and*
Of A Monastic

| *Also:* | 670 | Lord, for ever at thy side | G |

3 John and Charles Wesley, Priests, 1791, *Of A Pastor and*
1788 *Of A Missionary*

Also:	6, 7	Christ, whose glory fills the skies	A
	493	O for a thousand tongues to sing	A
	481	Rejoice, the Lord is King	A
	526	Let saints on earth in concert sing	A
	699	Jesus, Lover of my soul	A
	704	O thou who camest from above	A
	657	Love divine, all loves excelling	A
	548	Soldiers of Christ, arise	A
	638, 639	Come, O thou Traveler unknown	A
	300	Glory, love and praise, and honor	A

Also see index of authors for seasonal hymns by John and Charles Wesley

7 Perpetua and her Companions, Martyrs at *Of A Martyr*
Carthage, 202

| *Also:* | 53 | Once he came in blessing | E & G |

9 Gregory, Bishop of Nyssa, c. 394 *Of A Theologian and Teacher*

| *Also:* | 513 | Like the murmur of the dove's song | G |

12 Gregory the Great, Bishop of Rome, 604 *Of A Pastor and*
Of A Missionary

| *Also:* | 146, 147 | Now let us all with one accord | A |
| | 659, 660 | O Master, let me walk with thee | G |

17 Patrick, Bishop and Missionary of Ireland, *Of A Missionary*
461

| *Also:* | 370 | I bind unto myself today | S |
| | 342 | O Bread of life, for sinners broken | G |

18	Cyril, Bishop of Jerusalem, 386		*Of A Theologian and Teacher*

20	Cuthbert, Bishop of Lindisfarne, 687		*Of A Pastor and Of A Monastic*

	Also: 559	Lead us, heavenly Father, lead us	E
	709	O God of Bethel, by whose hand	G
	711	Seek ye first the kingdom of God	G
	667	Sometimes a light surprises	G

21	Thomas Ken, Bishop of Bath and Wells, 1711		*Of A Pastor*

	Also: 11	Awake, my soul, and with the sun (Morning)	A
	43	All praise to thee, my God, this night (Evening)	A
	556, 557	Rejoice, ye pure in heart!	E
	560	Remember your servants, Lord	G
	656	Blest are the pure in heart	G

22	James DeKoven, Priest, 1879		*Of A Theologian and Teacher*

	Also: 483	The head that once was crowned with thorns	E

23	Gregory the Illuminator, Bishop and Missionary of Armenia, c. 332		*Of A Missionary*

	Also: 560	Remember your servants, Lord	G

27	Charles Henry Brent, Bishop of the Philippines and of Western New York, 1929		*Of A Missionary*

	Also: 546	Awake, O sleeper, rise from death	E
	521	Put forth, O God, thy Spirit's might	E
	527	Singing songs of expectation	E
	617	Eternal Ruler of the ceaseless round	E
	472	Hope of the world, thou Christ	G

29	John Keble, Priest, 1866		*Of A Pastor and Of A Theologian and Teacher*

	Also: 10	New every morning is the love	A
	656	Blest are the pure in heart	A
	560	Remember your servants, Lord	G

31	John Donne, Priest, 1631		*Of A Pastor and Of A Theologian and Teacher*

	Also: 140, 141	Wilt thou forgive that sin, where I begun	A
	322	When Jesus died to save us	A?

April

1	Frederick Denison Maurice, Priest, 1872		*Of A Pastor and Of A Theologian and Teacher*

Also:	422	Not far beyond the sea, nor high	E
	448, 449	O love, how deep, how broad, how high	E
	455, 456	O Love of God, how strong and true	E
	458	My song is love unknown	G

2 James Lloyd Breck, Priest, 1876   *Of A Missionary and*
                                           Of A Theologian and Teacher

Also:	588, 589	Almighty God, your word is cast	G
	290	Come, ye thankful people, come (st. 2)	G

3 Richard, Bishop of Chichester, 1253   *Of A Pastor*

Also:	654	Day by day	A
	610	Lord, whose love through humble service	G
	609	Where cross the crowded ways of life	G

4 Martin Luther King   *Of A Martyr*

Also:	599	Lift every voice and sing	S
	648	When Israel was in Egypt's land	S
	582, 583	O holy city, seen of John	E

8 William Augustus Muhlenberg, Priest, 1877 *Of A Pastor*

Also:	521	Put forth, O God, thy Spirit's might	E
	486	Hosanna to the living Lord!	G

9 William Law, Priest, 1761   *Of A Theologian and Teacher*

Also:	546	Awake, my soul, stretch every nerve	E
	422	Not far beyond the sea, nor high	E
	701	Jesus, all my gladness	E
	474	When I survey the wondrous cross	E
	471	We sing the praise of him who died	E

11 George Augustus Selwyn, First Missionary   *Of A Missionary*
Bishop of New Zealand, 1878

Also:	495	Hail, thou once despisèd Jesus!	E

19 Alphege, Archbishop of Canterbury, and   *Of A Pastor and*
Martyr, 1012   *Of A Martyr*

21 Anselm, Archbishop of Canterbury, 1109   *Of A Theologian and Teacher*

Also:	686	Come thou fount of every blessing	E
	167	There is a green hill far away	E
	458	My song is love unknown	E
	692	I heard the voice of Jesus say (st. 1)	G
	74	Blest be the King whose coming	G
	342	O Bread of life, for sinners broken	G

29 Catherine of Siena, 1380 *Of A Monastic and*
Of A Theologian and Teacher

Also: 490   I want to walk as a child of the light   E
711   Seek ye first the kingdom of God   G
709   O God of Bethel, by whose hand   G
667   Sometimes a light surprises   G

May

2 Athanasius, Bishop of Alexandria, 373 *Of A Theologian and Teacher*

Also: 655   O Jesus, I have promised   G

4 Monnica, Mother of Augustine of Hippo, *Of A Saint*
387

Also: 711   Seek ye first the kingdom of God   G – Jn

8 Dame Julian of Norwich, c. 1417 *Of A Monastic and*
Of A Theologian and Teacher

Also: 443   From God Christ's deity came forth   E
219   The Lord ascendeth up on high   E
686   Come, thou fount of every blessing   E
673   The first one ever, oh, ever to know (st. 2)   G
337   And now, O Father, mindful of the love   E
338   Wherefore, O Father, we thy humble servants   E

9 Gregory of Nazianzus, Bishop of *Of A Theologian and Teacher*
Constantinople, 389

Also: 419   Lord of all being, throned afar   G

19 Dunstan, Archbishop of Canterbury, 988 *Of A Monastic and*
Of A Pastor

20 Alcuin, Deacon, and Abbot of Tours, 804 *Of A Theologian and Teacher*

Also: 465, 466   Eternal light, shine in my heart   A

24 Jackson Kemper, First Missionary Bishop in *Of A Missionary*
the United States, 1870

Also: 518   Christ is made the sure foundation   E
525   The Church's one foundation   E

25 Bede, the Venerable, Priest, and Monk of *Of A Monastic and*
Jarrow, 735 *Of A Theologian and Teacher*

Also: 217, 218   A hymn of glory let us sing   A
271, 272   The great forerunner of the morn   A

26 Augustine, First Archbishop of Canterbury, *Of A Missionary*
605

Also:	298	All who believe and are baptized	E
	213	Come away to the skies	E
	176, 177	Over the chaos of the empty waters	E
	296	We know that Christ is raised and dies no more	E
	603, 604	When Christ was lifted from the earth	E
	661	They cast their nets in Galilee	G

A weekday following the Day of Pentecost: The First Book of Common Prayer

	377, 378	All people that on earth do dwell	S
	51	We the Lord's people, heart and voice uniting (omit st. 3)	S
	426	Songs of praise the angels sang	S
	634	I call on thee, Lord Jesus Christ	S
	521	Put forth, O God, thy Spirit's might	S
	322	When Jesus died to save us	S
	298	All who believe and are baptized	E
	299	Spirit of God, unleashed on earth	E

June

1 Justin, Martyr at Rome, c. 167 *Of A Theologian and Teacher*

Also:	434	Nature with open volume stands	E
	471	We sing the praise of him who died	E
	165, 166	Sing, my tongue, the glorious battle	E
	6, 7	Christ, whose glory fills the skies	G
	692	I heard the voice of Jesus say (st. 3)	G

2 The Martyrs of Lyons, 177 *Of A Martyr*

Also:	472	Hope of the world, thou Christ	E
	675	Take up your cross, the Savior said	G
	484, 485	Praise the Lord through every nation	G

3 The Martyrs of Uganda, 1886 *Of A Martyr*

| *Also:* | 53 | Once he came in blessing | E & G |

5 Boniface, Archbishop of Mainz, Missionary *Of A Missionary and*
to Germany and Martyr, 754 *Of A Martyr*

| *Also:* | 525 | The Church's one foundation | E |
| | 214 | Hail the day that sees him rise, Alleluia! | G |

9 Columba, Abbot of Iona, 597 *Of A Monastic*

Also:	636, 637	How firm a foundation, ye saints of the Lord	E
	518	Christ is made the sure foundation	E
	525	The Church's one foundation	E

	656	Blest are the pure in heart	E
	516	Come down, O Love divine	E
	500	Creator Spirit, by whose aid	E

10 Ephrem of Edessa, Syria, Deacon, 373   *Of A Theologian and Teacher*

Also:	443	From God Christ's deity came forth	A
	312	Strengthen for service, Lord	A
	420	When in our music God is glorified	S
	426	Songs of praise the angels sang	S

14 Basil the Great, Bishop of Caesarea, 379   *Of A Theologian and Teacher*

Also:	346	Completed, Lord, the Holy Mysteries	S

16 Joseph Butler, Bishop of Durham, 1752   *Of A Theologian and Teacher*

Also:	551	Rise up, ye saints of God!	G
	581	Where charity and love prevail	G

**18 Bernard Mizeki, Catechist and Martyr in   *Of A Martyr*
Rhodesia, 1896**

22 Alban, First Martyr of Britain, c. 304   *Of A Martyr*

Also:	661	They cast their nets in Galilee	G
	675	Take up your cross, the Savior said	G
	484, 485	Praise the Lord through every nation	G
	319	You, Lord, we praise in songs of celebration	E

28 Irenaeus, Bishop of Lyons, c. 202   *Of A Theologian and Teacher*

Also:	656	Blest are the pure in heart	E

July

**11 Benedict of Nursia, Abbot of Monte   *Of A Monastic*
Cassino, c. 540**

Also:	675	Take up your cross, the Savior said	G
	484, 485	Praise the Lord through every nation	G

**17 William White, Bishop of Pennsylvania,   *Of A Pastor and*
1836**   *Of A Theologian and Teacher*

24 Thomas a Kempis, Priest, 1471   *Of A Theologian and Teacher*

Also:	448, 449	O love, how deep, how broad, how high	A?
	481	Rejoice, the Lord is King	E
	560	Remember your servants, Lord	G
	656	Blest are the pure in heart	G
	345	Savior, again to thy dear Name we raise	E

26	**The Parents of the Blessed Virgin Mary**	*Of A Saint*	

Also see: Annunciation (above, p. 265)

27	**William Reed Huntington, Priest, 1909**	*Of A Theologian and Teacher and Of A Pastor*	

Also see: Various Occasions 14. For The Unity of The Church [above, p. 284]

29	**Mary and Martha of Bethany**	*Of A Saint*	

Also:	382	King of glory, King of peace	G
	487	Come, my Way, my Truth, my Life	G
	701	Jesus, all my gladness	G
	642	Jesus, the very thought of thee	G

30	**William Wilberforce, 1833**	*Of A Theologian and Teacher*	

Also:	603, 604	When Christ was lifted from the earth	E
	529	In Christ there is no East or West	E
	581	Where charity and love prevail	E
	610	Lord, whose love through humble service	G

31	**Joseph of Arimathea**	*Of A Saint*	

Also:	458	My song is love unknown	G
	172	Were you there when they crucified my Lord?	G
	173	O sorrow deep!	G

August

7	**John Mason Neale, Priest, 1866**	*Of A Pastor and Of A Theologian and Teacher*	

Also:	518	Christ is made the sure foundation	T
	672	O very God of very God	A
	327, 328	Draw nigh and take the Body of the Lord	T
	621, 622	Light's abode, celestial Salem	T
	624	Jerusalem the golden	T
	623	O what their joy and their glory must be	T

Also see index of authors for office hymns and seasonal hymns by John Mason Neale

8	**Dominic, Priest and Friar, 1221**	*Of A Monastic, Of A Missionary, and Of A Theologian and Teacher*	

Also:	248, 249	To the Name of our salvation	E
	252	Jesus! Name of wondrous love	E

10	**Laurence, Deacon, and Martyr at Rome, 258**	*Of A Martyr*	

Also: 655   O Jesus, I have promised   G

11   Clare, Abbess at Assisi, 1253   *Of A Monastic*

     Also: 213   Come away to the skies   L
           68   Rejoice! rejoice, believers   G
           61, 62   "Sleepers, wake!" A voice astounds us   G

13   Jeremy Taylor, Bishop of Down, Connor   *Of A Theologian and Teacher*
     and Dromore, 1667   *and Of A Pastor*

     Also: 478   Jesus, our mighty Lord   E
           494   Crown him with many crowns   E
           252   Jesus! Name of wondrous love!   E

18   William Porcher DuBose, Priest, 1918   *Of A Theologian and Teacher*

     Also: 440   Blessèd Jesus, at thy word   G
           305, 306   Come, risen Lord, and deign to be our guest   G
           343   Shepherd of souls, refresh and bless   G

20   Bernard, Abbot of Clairvaux, 1153   *Of A Monastic*

     Also: 649, 650   O Jesus, joy of loving hearts   A
           642   Jesus, the very thought of thee   A?
           168, 169   O sacred head, sore wounded   A?
           518   Christ is made the sure foundation   G
           392   Come, we that love the Lord   G
           344   Lord, dismiss us with thy blessing   G

25   Louis, King of France, 1270   *Of A Saint*

     Also: 709   O God of Bethel, by whose hand   G
           667   Sometimes a light surprises   G
           711   Seek ye first the kingdom of God   G

28   Augustine, Bishop of Hippo, 430   *Of A Theologian and Teacher*

     Also: 368   Holy Father, great Creator   E
           457   Thou art the Way, to thee alone   E
           703   Lead us, O Father, in the paths of peace   G
           518   Christ is made the sure foundation   G
           248, 249   To the Name of our salvation   G

31   Aidan, Bishop of Lindisfarne, 651   *Of A Monastic*

     Also: 655   O Jesus, I have promised   G

September

 1   David Pendleton Oakerhater, Deacon and   *Of A Missionary*
     Missionary of the Cheyenne, 1931

 2   The Martyrs of New Guinea, 1942   *Of A Martyr*

9   Constance, Nun, and her Companions,   *Of A Martyr*
commonly called "The Martyrs of
Memphis", 1878

    Also: 655   O Jesus, I have promised   G

12   John Henry Hobart, Bishop of New York,   *Of A Pastor and*
1830   *Of A Theologian and Teacher*

13   Cyprian, Bishop and Martyr of Carthage,   *Of A Theologian and Teacher*
256   *and Of A Martyr*

    Also: 478   Jesus, our mighty Lord   E & G
          645, 646   The King of love my shepherd is   G
          708   Savior, like a shepherd lead us   G
          334   Praise the Lord, rise up rejoicing   G

16   Ninian, Bishop in Galloway, c. 430   *Of A Missionary and*
                                   Of A Monastic

18   Edward Bouverie Pusey, Priest, 1882   *Of A Theologian and Teacher*

19   Theodore of Tarsus, Archbishop of   *Of A Pastor*
Canterbury, 690

    Also: 548   Soldiers of Christ, arise   E
          552, 553   Fight the good fight with all thy might (sts. 1-2)   E
          561   Stand up, stand up for Jesus   E
          563   Go forward, Christian soldier   E

20   John Coleridge Patteson, Bishop of   *Of A Missionary and*
Melanesia, and his Companions, Martyrs,   *Of A Martyr*
1871

    Also: 675   Take up your cross, the Savior said   G
          484, 485   Praise the Lord through every nation   G

25   Sergius, Abbot of Holy Trinity, Moscow,   *Of A Monastic*
1392

26   Lancelot Andrewes, Bishop of Winchester,   *Of A Theologian and Teacher*
1626   *and Of A Pastor*

    Also: 368   Holy Father, great Creator   E
          698   Eternal Spirit of the living Christ   G
          709   O God of Bethel, by whose hand   G

30   Jerome, Priest, and Monk of Bethlehem,   *Of A Theologian and Teacher*
420   *and Of A Monastic*

    Also: 630   Thanks to God whose Word was spoken   E
          632   O Christ, the Word Incarnate   E
          440   Blessèd Jesus, at thy word   G

October

1   Remigius, Bishop of Rheims, c. 530   *Of A Missionary*

Also:	1, 2	Father, we praise thee, now the night is over	G
	194, 195	Jesus lives! thy terrors now	G
	484, 485	Praise the Lord through every nation	G
	457	Thou art the Way, to thee alone	G
	487	Come, my Way, my Truth, my Life	G
	463, 464	He is the Way	G

4   Francis of Assisi, Friar, 1226   *Of A Monastic*

Also:	400	All creatures of our God and King	A
	406, 407	Most High, omnipotent, good Lord	A
	593	Lord, make us servants of your peace	A?
	471	We sing the praise of him who died	E
	441, 442	In the cross of Christ I glory	E
	434	Nature with open volume stands	E
	74	Blest be the King whose coming	G
	692	I heard the voice of Jesus say (st. 1)	G
	342	O Bread of life, for sinners broken	G

6   William Tyndale, Priest, 1536   *Of A Theologian and Teacher and Of A Martyr*

Also:	630	Thanks to God whose Word was spoken	S
	632	O Christ, the Word Incarnate	S
	628	Help us, O Lord, to learn	E
	6, 7	Christ, whose glory fills the skies	G
	692	I heard the voice of Jesus say (st. 3)	G

9   Robert Grosseteste, Bishop of Lincoln, 1253   *Of A Theologian and Teacher and Of A Pastor*

| *Also:* | 525 | The Church's one foundation | E |

15   Teresa of Avila, Nun, 1582   *Of A Monastic and Of A Theologian and Teacher*

| *Also:* | 698 | Eternal Spirit of the living Christ | E |
| | 513 | Like the murmur of the dove's song | E |

15   Samuel Isaac Joseph Schereschewsky, Bishop of Shanghai, 1906   *Of A Missionary*

Also:	630	Thanks to God whose Word was spoken	S
	632	O Christ, the Word Incarnate	S
	623	O what their joy and their glory must be	E
	621, 622	Light's abode, celestial Salem	E
	440	Blessèd Jesus, at thy word	G

16	Hugh Latimer and Nicholas Ridley, Bishops, 1555, and Thomas Cranmer, Archbishop of Canterbury, 1556	*Of A Theologian and Teacher and Of A Martyr*	

Also:	525	The Church's one foundation	E
	518	Christ is made the sure foundation	E
	636, 637	How firm a foundation, ye saints of the Lord	E

17	Ignatius, Bishop of Antioch, and Martyr, c. 115	*Of A Theologian and Teacher and Of A Martyr*	

Also:	548	Soldiers of Christ, arise	E
	655	O Jesus, I have promised	G

19	Henry Martyn, Priest, and Missionary to India and Persia, 1812	*Of A Missionary*	

Also:	630	Thanks to God whose Word was spoken	S
	632	O Christ, the Word Incarnate	S

26	Alfred the Great, King of the West Saxons, 899	*Of A Saint*	

Also:	392	Come, we that love the Lord	G
	636, 637	How firm a foundation, ye saints of the Lord	G
	344	Lord, dismiss us with thy blessing	G

29	James Hannington, Bishop of Eastern Equatorial Africa, and his Companions, Martyrs, 1885	*Of A Missionary and Of A Martyr*	

Also:	655	O Jesus, I have promised	G

November

2	Commemoration of All Faithful Departed		

See Various Occasions 8. For The Departed [above, p. 281]

3	Richard Hooker, Priest, 1600	*Of A Theologian and Teacher*

7	Willibrord, Archbishop of Utrecht, Missionary to Frisia, 739	*Of A Missionary*

10	Leo the Great, Bishop of Rome, 461	*Of A Theologian and Teacher and Of A Pastor*

Also:	704	O thou who camest from above	E

11	Martin, Bishop of Tours, 397	*Of A Monastic*

Also:	145	Now quit your care (sts. 3-5)	L
	610	Lord, whose love through humble service	G

| 609 | Where cross the crowded ways of life | G |

12 Charles Simeon, Priest, 1836   *Of A Theologian and Teacher and Of A Pastor*

| Also: 252 | Jesus! Name of wondrous love! | E |
| 248, 249 | To the Name of our salvation | E |

14 Consecration of Samuel Seabury, First   *Of A Pastor*
American Bishop, 1784

Also see Various Occasions 15. For The Ministry [above, p. 285]

16 Margaret, Queen of Scotland, 1093   *Of A Saint*

17 Hugh, Bishop of Lincoln, 1200   *Of A Monastic and Of A Pastor*

18 Hilda, Abbess of Whitby, 680   *Of A Monastic*

Also: 521	Put forth, O God, thy Spirit's might	E
525	The Church's one foundation	E
527	Singing songs of expectation	E
655	O Jesus, I have promised	G

19 Elizabeth, Princess of Hungary, 1231   *Of A Saint*

| Also: 610 | Lord, whose love through humble service | G |
| 609 | Where cross the crowded ways of life | G |

20 Edmund, King of East Anglia, and Martyr,   *Of A Martyr*
870

| Also: 458 | My song is love unknown | E |
| 655 | O Jesus, I have promised | G |

23 Clement, Bishop of Rome, c. 100   *Of A Theologian and Teacher and Of A Pastor*

Also: 548	Soldiers of Christ, arise	E
561	Stand up, stand up for Jesus	E
392	Come, we that love the Lord	G
344	Lord, dismiss us with thy blessing	G

25 James Otis Sargent Huntington, Priest and   *Of A Monastic*
Monk, 1935

Also: 441, 442	In the cross of Christ I glory	E
473	Lift high the cross	E
165, 166	Sing, my tongue, the glorious battle	E
471	We sing the praise of him who died	E
474	When I survey the wondrous cross	E
483	The head that once was crowned with thorns	E

28 Kamehameha and Emma, King and Queen *Of A Saint*
     of Hawaii, 1863, 1885

   Also: **610**   Lord, whose love through humble service   **G**